Pr

Adobe
Premiere Pro CC
2017 release

CLASSROOM IN A BOOK®
The official training workbook from Adobe

Maxim Jago

Adobe Press books are published by Peachpit, a division of Pearson Education located in San Francisco, California. For the latest on Adobe Press books, go to www.adobepress.com. To report errors, please send a note to errata@peachpit.com. For information on getting permission for reprints and excerpts, contact www.pearsoned.com/permissions.

Writer: Maxim Jago
Executive Editor: Nancy Davis
Development Editor: Nikki Echler McDonald
Senior Production Editor: Tracey Croom
Technical Reviewers: Conrad Chavez, Victor Gavenda
Copyeditor: Kim Wimpsett
Proofreader: Patricia Pane
Compositor: Kim Scott, Bumpy Design
Indexer: James Minkin
Cover Designer: Eddie Yuen
Cover Illustration: Yuri Shwedoff, behance.net/yurishwedoff
Interior Designer: Mimi Heft

Printed and bound in the United States of America

ISBN-13:   9780134665313
ISBN-10:   0134665317

WHAT'S ON THE DISC

Here is an overview of the contents of the Classroom in a Book disc

The *Adobe Premiere Pro CC Classroom in a Book (2017 release)* disc includes the lesson files that you'll need to complete the exercises in this book. Each lesson has its own folder in the Lessons folder. In addition, there is an Assets folder containing files that are used for multiple lessons.

You will need to copy **the entire Lessons folder** to your hard drive before you can begin the lessons. This will require about 8 GB of storage, so make sure you have sufficient free space on your storage device before beginning.

See the "Getting Started" section in the beginning of this book for more detailed instructions.

Important!

The video clips and other media files provided with this book are practice files, provided for your personal use in these lessons. You are not authorized to use these files commercially or to publish, share, or distribute them in any form without written permission from Adobe Systems, Inc., and the individual copyright holders of the various items. This includes, but is not limited to, distribution via social media or online video services including YouTube and Vimeo. You will find a complete copyright statement on the copyright page at the very start of this book.

ACKNOWLEDGMENTS

Producing effective learning materials for such an advanced technology is a team effort. Friends, colleagues, fellow filmmakers, and technology experts have all contributed to this book. There are too many names to mention, but let's say this: I have often joked that in Britain we don't say "awesome." Instead, we say "perfectly acceptable." On this occasion, "perfectly acceptable" simply isn't enough. Instead, I will have to say our British equivalent of "super awesome": those people who make this world better by sharing, nurturing, caring, showing, telling, demonstrating, making, and helping are all "more than acceptable."

Everything on these pages was inspected by a team of experienced editors who checked and corrected typos, spelling errors, naming errors, false attributions, suspect grammar, unhelpful phrasing, and inconsistent descriptions. This wonderful team didn't just highlight text that needed correcting. They offered positive alternatives that I could simply agree to, so in a literal sense, this book is the product of many people's contributions. I'd like to thank the whole team at Peachpit and Adobe Press, who made it possible to produce such a beautifully finessed work.

As each draft chapter was completed, the most excellent Conrad Chavez checked all references to technology and highlighted errors, opportunities to clarify, and potential details to expand upon. Conrad's comments are beautifully clear and simple, with great accuracy. Having worked previously with Conrad, who is also a technical author, I knew his knowledge and awareness of the reader's journey would be incredibly helpful.

A substantial amount of the content of this book is derived from material written by Richard Harrington three versions back. The current table of contents was originally worked out by the two of us, and though I have updated his chapters, rephrased, and reworded them, a substantial amount remains unchanged or is significantly informed by his original work.

Finally, let's not forget Adobe. The passion and enthusiasm demonstrated by those wonderful individuals, who are so committed to creatives like you and me, qualifies as "the most acceptable of all." They are, indeed, extraordinarily awesome!

CONTENTS

10 MULTICAMERA EDITING   228

11 EDITING AND MIXING AUDIO

GETTING STARTED

Adobe Premiere Pro CC, the essential editing tool for video enthusiasts and professionals, is the most scalable, efficient, and precise video-editing tool available. It supports a broad range of video formats, including AVCHD, HDV, Sony XDCAM EX, HD and HD422, Sony RAW, Panasonic P2 DVCPRO HD, AVC-Intra, Canon XF and Canon RAW, RED R3D, ARRIRAW, Digital SLR, Blackmagic CinemaDNG, Avid DNxHD and DNxHR, QuickTime and AVI files, GoPro Cineform, and many more. Premiere Pro lets you work faster and more creatively without converting your media. The complete set of powerful and exclusive tools lets you overcome any editorial, production, and workflow challenges to deliver the high-quality work you demand.

Importantly, Adobe has created a user experience that is intuitive, flexible, and efficient, with unified design elements that match across multiple applications, making it easier to explore and discover new workflows.

About Classroom in a Book

Adobe Premiere Pro CC Classroom in a Book (2017 release) is part of the official training series for Adobe graphics and publishing and creative video software. The lessons are designed so that you can learn at your own pace. If you're new to Premiere Pro, you'll learn the fundamental concepts and features you'll need to use the program. This book also teaches many advanced features, including tips and techniques for using the latest version of this software.

The lessons in this edition include opportunities for hands-on practice using features such as chromakeying, dynamic trimming, color correction, tapeless media, audio and video effects, and advanced integration with Photoshop, After Effects, and Audition. You'll also learn how to create files for the web and mobile devices with Media Encoder. Premiere Pro CC is available for both Windows and Mac OS.

Prerequisites

Before beginning to use *Adobe Premiere Pro CC Classroom in a Book*, make sure your system is set up correctly and that you've installed the required software and hardware. You can view updated system requirements here:

helpx.adobe.com/premiere-pro/system-requirements.html

You should have a working knowledge of your computer and operating system. You should know how to use the mouse and standard menus and commands and also how to open, save, and close files. If you need to review these techniques, see the documentation included with your Windows or Mac OS system.

Installing Premiere Pro CC

You must purchase an Adobe Creative Cloud subscription or obtain a trial version, separately from this book. For system requirements and complete instructions on installing the software, visit www.adobe.com/support. You can purchase Adobe Creative Cloud by visiting www.adobe.com/products/creativecloud. Follow the onscreen instructions. You may also want to install Photoshop, After Effects, Audition, Prelude, and Media Encoder, which are included with the full Adobe Creative Cloud license.

Optimizing performance

Editing video places high demands on your computer processor and memory. A fast processor and a lot of memory will make your editing experience faster and more efficient. This translates to a more fluid and enjoyable creative experience.

Premiere Pro takes advantage of multicore processors (CPUs) and multiprocessor systems. The faster the processors, and the more there are, the better the performance you'll experience.

The minimum system memory is 8 GB, and 16 GB or more is recommended for ultra-high-definition (UHD) media.

The speed of the storage drives you use for video playback is also a factor. A dedicated fast storage drive is recommended for your media. A RAID disk array or fast solid-state disk is strongly recommended, particularly if you're working with 4K or higher-resolution media. Storing your media files and program files on the same hard drive can affect performance. Keep your media files on a separate disk if possible.

The Premiere Pro Mercury Playback Engine can utilize the power of your GPU, harnessing the power of your computer's graphics hardware to improve playback performance. GPU acceleration provides a significant performance improvement, and most video cards with at least 1 GB of dedicated memory will work. You will find information about hardware and software requirements on the Adobe website at http://helpx.adobe.com/premiere-pro/system-requirements.html.

Using the lesson files

The lessons in this book use supplied source files, including video clips, audio files, and image files created in Photoshop and Illustrator. To complete the lessons in this book, you must copy all the lesson files to your computer's storage drive. Some lessons use files from other lessons, so you'll need to keep the entire collection of lesson assets on your storage drive as you work through the book. You will need about 8 GB of storage space in addition to the space needed to install Premiere Pro.

If you have purchased an ebook edition of this book, you'll need to download the lesson files from peachpit.com. You'll find instructions for doing so on the first page of the ebook, in the section "How to get your lesson files."

If you've purchased the printed version, you can copy the lesson files from the *Adobe Premiere Pro CC Classroom in a Book* disc (inside the back cover of this book).

Here's how to copy those assets from the disc to your storage drive:

1 Open the *Adobe Premiere Pro CC Classroom in a Book* disc in My Computer or Windows Explorer (Windows) or in Finder (Mac OS).

2 Right-click the folder called Lessons and choose Copy.

3 Navigate to the location you have chosen to store your Premiere Pro projects, right-click, and choose Paste.

If you do not have a disc drive on your computer, see the "Online Content" section for more information about downloading the lesson files.

▶ **Tip:** If you don't have dedicated storage for your video files, placing the lesson files on your computer's desktop will make them easy to find and work with.

Relinking the lesson files

The Premiere Pro projects included with the lesson files have links to specific media files. Because you are copying the files to a new location, those links may need to update when you open projects for the first time.

If you open a project and Premiere Pro is unable to find a linked media file, the Link Media dialog may open, inviting you to relink offline files. If this happens, select an offline clip and click the Locate button and a browse panel will appear to locate it.

● **Note:** If media files were originally stored in multiple locations, you may need to search more than once to relink all the media for a project.

Locate the Lessons folder using the navigator on the left, and click Search. Premiere Pro will locate the media file inside the Lessons folder. To hide all other files, making it easy to select the right one, select the option to display only exact name matches.

The last known file path and file name and the currently selected file path and file name are displayed at the top of the panel for reference. Select the file and click OK.

The option to relink other files is enabled by default, so once you've located one file, the rest should reconnect automatically. For more information about relocating offline media files, see Chapter 17, "Managing Your Projects."

How to use these lessons

The lessons in this book provide step-by-step instructions. Each lesson stands alone, but most build on previous lessons. For this reason, the best way to learn from this book is to proceed through the lessons one after another.

The lessons teach you new skills in the order you might use them while performing post-production for a real project. Rather than being feature-oriented, this book uses a real-world approach. The lessons begin with acquiring media files such as video, audio, and graphics, and go on to creating a rough cut sequence, adding effects, sweetening the audio, and ultimately exporting the project.

By the end of these lessons, you'll have a good understanding of the complete end-to-end post-production workflow, with the specific skills you need to edit on your own.

Online content

Lesson files

To work through the projects in this book, you will need to copy them from the disc (see "Using the lesson files") or download the lesson files from peachpit.com. You can download the files for individual lessons or it may be possible to download them all in a single file.

This book comes with a free Web Edition that can be accessed from any device with a connection to the Internet. Its benefits include the following:

- The complete text of the book
- Hours of instructional video keyed to the text
- Interactive quizzes

In addition, the Web Edition may be updated when Adobe adds significant feature updates between major Creative Cloud releases. To accommodate the changes, sections of the online book will be updated or new sections will be added.

Accessing the Web Edition

Your purchase of this Classroom in a Book in any format includes access to the corresponding Web Edition.

If you purchased an ebook from peachpit.com or adobepress.com, your Web Edition will automatically appear under the Digital Purchases tab on your Account page. Click the Launch link to access the product. Continue reading to learn how to register your product to get access to the lesson files.

If you purchased an eBook from a different vendor or you bought a print book, you must register your purchase on peachpit.com in order to access the online content:

1 Go to www.peachpit.com/register.

2 Sign in or create a new account.

3 Enter ISBN: **9780134665313**.

4 Answer the questions as proof of purchase.

5 The Web Edition will appear on the Digital Purchases tab of your Account page. Click the Launch link to access the product.

The Lesson Files can be accessed through the Registered Products tab on your Account page. Click the Access Bonus Content link below the title of your product to proceed to the download page. Click the lesson file links to download them to your computer.

Additional resources

Adobe Premiere Pro CC Classroom in a Book (2017 release) is not meant to replace documentation that comes with the program or to be a comprehensive reference for every feature. Only the commands and options used in the lessons are explained in this book. For comprehensive information about program features and tutorials, refer to these resources:

Adobe Premiere Pro CC Learn and Support: helpx.adobe.com/premiere-pro is where you can find and browse Help and Support content on Adobe.com. Adobe Premiere Pro Help and Adobe Premiere Pro Support Center are accessible from the Help menu in Premiere Pro. Help is also available as a printable PDF document. Download the document at helpx.adobe.com/pdf/premiere_pro_reference.pdf.

Adobe Forums: forums.adobe.com lets you tap into peer-to-peer discussions, questions, and answers on Adobe products.

Adobe Premiere Pro CC product home page: adobe.com/products/premiere has more information about the product.

Adobe Add-ons: creative.adobe.com/addons is a central resource for finding tools, services, extensions, code samples, and more to supplement and extend your Adobe products.

Resources for educators: adobe.com/education and edex.adobe.com offer a treasure trove of information for instructors who teach classes on Adobe software. You'll find solutions for education at all levels, including free curricula that use an integrated approach to teaching Adobe software and can be used to prepare for the Adobe Certified Associate exams.

Adobe Authorized Training Centers

Adobe Authorized Training Centers offer instructor-led courses and training on Adobe products, employing only Adobe Certified Instructors. A directory of AATCs is available at training.adobe.com/trainingpartners.

1 TOURING ADOBE PREMIERE PRO CC

Lesson overview

In this lesson, you'll learn about the following:

- Performing nonlinear editing
- Exploring the standard digital video workflow
- Enhancing the workflow with high-level features
- Checking out the workspace
- Customizing your workspace
- Setting keyboard shortcuts

This lesson will take approximately 60 minutes. Before you begin, you'll walk through a brief overview of video editing and an explanation of how Adobe Premiere Pro CC functions as the hub of your post-production workflow.

Adobe Premiere Pro is a video-editing system that supports the latest technology and cameras with powerful tools that are easy to use and that integrate perfectly with almost every video acquisition source.

Getting started

There's enormous demand for high-quality video content, and today's video producers and editors work in an ever-changing landscape of old and new technologies. Despite all this rapid change, however, the goal of video editing is the same: You want to take your footage and shape it, guided by your original vision, so that you can effectively communicate with your audience.

In Adobe Premiere Pro CC, you'll find a video-editing system that supports the latest technology and cameras with powerful tools that are easy to use. These tools integrate perfectly with almost every type of media, as well as a wide range of third-party plug-ins and other post-production tools.

You'll begin by reviewing the essential post-production workflow that most editors follow, and then you'll learn about the main components of the Premiere Pro interface and how to create custom workspaces.

Performing nonlinear editing in Premiere Pro

Premiere Pro is a *nonlinear editing system* (NLE). Like a word processor, Premiere Pro lets you place, replace, and move footage anywhere you want in your final edited video. You can also adjust any parts of the video clips you use at any time. You don't need to perform edits in a particular order, and you can make changes to any part of your video project at any time.

You'll combine multiple clips to create a sequence that you can change simply by clicking and dragging with your mouse. You can edit any part of your sequence, in any order, and then change the contents, move clips so that they play earlier or later in the video, blend layers of video together, add special effects, and more.

You can combine multiple sequences and jump to any moment in a video clip without needing to fast-forward or rewind. It's as easy to organize the clips you're working with as it is to organize files on your computer.

Premiere Pro supports both tape and tapeless media formats, including XDCAM EX, XDCAMHD 422, DPX, DVCProHD, AVCHD (including AVCCAM and NXCAM), AVC-Intra, DSLR video, and Canon XF. It also has native support for the latest raw video formats, including media from RED, ARRI, Canon, and Blackmagic cameras.

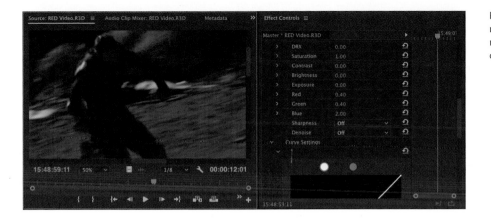

Premiere Pro features native support for raw media from RED cameras.

Looking at the standard digital video workflow

As you gain editing experience, you'll develop your own preference for the order in which to work on the different aspects of your project. Each stage requires a particular kind of attention and different tools. Also, some projects call for more time spent on one stage than another.

Whether you skip through some stages with a quick mental check or spend hours (even days!) dedicated to perfecting an aspect of your project, you'll work through the following steps:

1 Acquire your media. This can mean recording original footage or gathering assets for a project.

2 Ingest (or capture from tape) the video to your storage drive. With tape-based formats, Premiere Pro (with the appropriate hardware) can convert the video into digital files. With tapeless media, Premiere Pro can read the media files directly, usually with no need for conversion. If you're working with tapeless media, be sure to back up your files to a second location because storage drives sometimes fail unexpectedly.

3 Organize your clips. There can be a lot of video content to choose from in your project. Invest the time to organize clips into special folders (called *bins*) in your project. You can add color labels and other metadata (additional information about the clips) to help keep things organized.

4 Combine the parts of the video and audio clips you want as a sequence in the Timeline panel.

5 Place special transition effects between clips, add video effects, and create combined visual effects by placing clips on multiple layers (called *tracks* in the Timeline panel).

Note: The word *clip* comes from the days of film editing, where a section of film would be clipped to separate it from a reel.

6   Create or import titles and graphics, and add them to your sequence in the same way you would add video clips.

7   Mix your audio tracks to get the mix just right, and use transitions and effects on your audio clips to improve the sound.

8   Export your finished project to videotape, to a file for a computer or for Internet playback, or to a mobile device.

Premiere Pro supports each of these steps with industry-leading tools. A large community of creative and technical professionals is waiting to share their experience and support your development as an editor.

Enhancing the workflow with Premiere Pro

Premiere Pro has easy-to-use tools for video editing. It also has advanced tools for manipulating, adjusting, and fine-tuning your projects.

You may not incorporate all of the following features in your first few video projects. However, as your experience and understanding of nonlinear editing grow, you'll want to expand your capabilities.

The following topics will be covered in this book:

- **Advanced audio editing:** Premiere Pro provides audio effects and editing unequaled by any other nonlinear editor. Create and place 5.1 surround-sound audio channels, make sample-level edits, apply multiple audio effects to audio clips or tracks, and use state-of-the-art plug-ins as well as third-party Virtual Studio Technology (VST) plug-ins.

- **Color correction and grading:** Correct and enhance the look of your footage with advanced color-correction filters, including Lumetri, a dedicated color correction and grading panel. You can make secondary color-correction selections that allow you to adjust isolated colors and adjust parts of an image to improve the composition.

- **Keyframe controls:** Premiere Pro gives you the precise control you need to fine-tune the timing of visual and motion effects without using a compositing or motion graphics application. Keyframes use a standard interface design—learn to use them in Premiere Pro, and you'll know how to use them in all Adobe Creative Cloud products in which they're available.

- **Broad hardware support:** Choose from a wide range of dedicated capture cards and other hardware to assemble a system that best fits your needs and budget. Premiere Pro system specifications extend from low-cost computers for digital video editing up to high-performance workstations that can easily edit 3D stereoscopic video, high definition (HD), 4K, 360 VR video, and beyond.

- **GPU acceleration:** The Mercury Playback Engine operates in two modes: software-only and graphics processing unit (GPU) acceleration. GPU acceleration mode requires a graphics card that meets minimum specifications in your workstation. See http://helpx.adobe.com/premiere-pro/system-requirements.html for a list of tested graphics cards. Most cards with a minimum of 1GB of dedicated video memory will work.

- **Multicamera editing:** You can quickly and easily edit productions shot with multiple cameras. Premiere Pro displays multiple camera sources in a split-view display, and you can choose a camera view by clicking the appropriate screen or using shortcut keys. You can automatically sync multiple camera angles based on clip audio or timecode.

- **Project management:** Manage your media through a single dialog box. View, delete, move, search for, and reorganize clips and bins. Consolidate your projects by copying just the media used in sequences to a single location. Then reclaim storage space by deleting unused media files.

- **Metadata:** Premiere Pro supports Adobe XMP, which stores additional information about media as metadata that multiple applications can access. This information can be used to locate clips or communicate important information such as preferred takes or copyright notices.

- **Creative titles:** Create titles and graphics using the Premiere Pro Title Designer. You can also use graphics created in almost any suitable software, plus Adobe Photoshop documents can be imported as flattened images or as separate layers that you can incorporate, combine, and animate selectively.

- **Advanced trimming:** Use special trimming tools to adjust each clip and cut point in a sequence. Premiere Pro provides both quick, easy trimming shortcuts and advanced trimming tools, allowing you to make complex timing adjustments to multiple clips.

- **Media encoding:** Export your sequence to create a video and audio file that is perfect for your needs. Use the advanced features of Adobe Media Encoder to create copies of your finished sequence in several different formats, based on presets or your own detailed preferences. Media files can be uploaded to multiple social media platforms in a single step.

- **360-degree video for VR headsets:** Edit and post-produce stitched 360-degree video footage using a special VR Video display mode that allows you to see specific regions of the picture for a more natural and intuitive editing experience.

Expanding the workflow

Although it's possible to work with Premiere Pro as a stand-alone application, it is also a team player. Premiere Pro is part of Adobe Creative Cloud, which means you have access to a number of other specialized tools, including After Effects, Audition, and Prelude. Understanding the way these software components work together will improve your efficiency and give you more creative freedom.

Incorporating other components into the editing workflow

Premiere Pro is a versatile video and audio post-production tool, but it's just one component of Adobe Creative Cloud—Adobe's complete print, web, and video environment that includes video-focused software for the following:

* High-end 3D motion effects creation

* Complex text animation generation

* Layered graphics production

* Vector artwork creation

* Audio production

* Media management

To incorporate one or more of these features into a production, you can use other components of Adobe Creative Cloud. The software set has everything you need to produce advanced, professionally finished videos.

Here's a brief description of the other components:

* **Adobe After Effects:** The highly popular tool of choice for motion graphics and visual effects artists.

* **Adobe Photoshop:** The industry-standard image-editing and graphics creation product. You can work with photos, video, and 3D objects to prepare them for your project.

* **Adobe Audition:** A powerful tool for audio editing, audio cleanup and sweetening, music creation and adjustment, and multitrack mix creation.

* **Adobe Illustrator:** Professional vector graphics creation software for print, video, and the Web.

* **Adobe Dynamic Link:** A cross-product connection that allows you to work in real time with media, compositions, and sequences shared between After Effects, Audition, and Premiere Pro.

- **Adobe Prelude:** A tool that allows you to ingest, transcode, and add metadata, markers, and tags to file-based footage. Then create rough cuts you can share with Premiere Pro directly or with other NLEs.

- **Adobe Media Encoder:** A tool that allows you to process files to produce content for any screen directly from Premiere Pro and Adobe After Effects.

Looking at the Adobe Creative Cloud video workflow

Your Premiere Pro and Creative Cloud workflow will vary depending on your production needs. Here are a few scenarios:

- Use Photoshop CC to touch up and apply effects to still images and layered image compositions from a digital camera, a scanner, or a video clip. Then use them as media in Premiere Pro.

- Import and manage large numbers of media files with Prelude, adding valuable metadata, temporal comments, and tags. Create sequences from clips and sub-clips in Adobe Prelude and send them to Premiere Pro to continue editing them.

- Send clips directly from the Premiere Pro timeline to Adobe Audition for professional audio cleanup and sweetening.

- Send an entire Premiere Pro sequence to Adobe Audition to complete a professional audio mix. Premiere Pro can create an Adobe Audition session from your sequence; the session can contain video so you can compose and adjust levels based on the action.

- Using Dynamic Link, open Premiere Pro video clips in After Effects. Apply special effects, add animation, and add visual elements; then view the results in Premiere Pro. You can play After Effects compositions in Premiere Pro without waiting to render them and also benefit from After Effects Global Cache, which saves previews for later use.

- Use After Effects to create compositions containing advanced text animation, such as an opening or closing title sequence. Use those compositions in Premiere Pro with Dynamic Link. Adjustments made in After Effects appear in Premiere Pro immediately.

- Export video projects in multiple resolutions and codecs for display on websites, via social media, or for archiving, using built-in presets and integrated social media and FTP server support.

Most of this book will focus on standard workflows involving only Premiere Pro. However, several lessons and sidebars will explain ways you can use Adobe Creative Cloud components as part of your workflow for powerful effects work and finishing.

Touring the Premiere Pro workspace

It's helpful to begin by getting familiar with the editing interface so you can recognize the tools as you work with them in the following lessons. To make it easier to configure the user interface, Premiere Pro offers *workspaces*. Workspaces quickly configure the various panels and tools onscreen in ways that are helpful for particular activities, such as editing, special effects work, or audio mixing.

To begin with, you'll take a brief tour of the Editing workspace. In this exercise, you'll use a Premiere Pro project from this book's companion DVD (or downloaded lesson files if you are using the e-book):

1 Make sure you've copied all the lesson folders and contents from the DVD to your hard drive.

2 Launch Premiere Pro.

The Start screen gives clear instructions to get started.

The first time you launch Premiere Pro, you will see a Start screen. If you have opened projects previously, a list will appear in the middle of the welcome screen.

On the left there's the option to view recent projects stored locally or synchronized with the cloud in your CC Files folder. There's also an option to synchronize your user preferences if you're working on multiple computers.

You can create a new project, or you can open an existing project by browsing your storage drive for the project file or by clicking the name of the project in the recent items list.

● **Note:** If Premiere Pro fails when opening a project, try changing the Playback Renderer to a different default setting. To do this, click New Project in the Start screen, then choose an option in the Video Rendering and Playback – Renderer menu. If you have an AMD graphics card, you'll probably get better performance choosing OpenCL GPU acceleration, and if you have an NVIDIA graphics card, you'll probably choose CUDA. When you click OK to create the new project, Premiere Pro will remember the GPU acceleration setting for new and existing projects that you open.

If you have launched Premiere Pro before and created a project, you'll see a list of previously opened projects.

3 Click Open Project.

4 In the Open Project window, navigate to the Lesson 01 folder in the Lessons folder; then double-click the Lesson 01.prproj project file to open the first lesson.

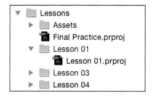

● **Note:** It's best to copy all the lesson assets from the DVD to your computer storage drive and leave them there until you complete this book; some lessons refer to assets from previous lessons.

● **Note:** All Premiere Pro project files have a .prproj extension.

● **Note:** You may be prompted with a dialog box asking where a particular file is. This will happen when the original files are saved on a storage drive (or drive letter) different from the one you're using. You'll need to tell Premiere Pro where the file is. In this case, navigate to the Lessons/Assets folder and select the file that the dialog box is prompting you to open. Premiere Pro will remember this location for the rest of the files.

Looking at the workspace layout

Before you begin, make sure you're using the default Editing workspace by choosing Window > Workspaces > Editing.

Then, to reset the Editing workspace, choose Window > Workspaces > Reset to Saved Layout. If the Workspaces panel is visible, use it to choose Editing to make sure it's selected. Then, to reset the Editing workspace, click the small panel menu next to the Editing option on the Workspaces panel and choose Reset to Saved Layout.

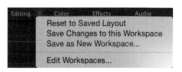

If you're new to nonlinear editing, the default workspace might look like a lot of buttons and menus. Don't worry. Things become much simpler when you know what the buttons are for. The interface is designed to make video editing easy, so commonly used controls are immediately accessible.

Each workspace item appears in its own panel, and multiple panels can be combined into a single frame. When many panels are combined, you may not be able to see all the tabs. If this is the case, a menu of additional panels is displayed. Click this menu to access a hidden panel in a frame.

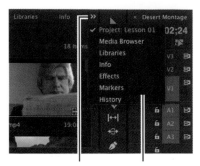

Additional panels menu   List of panels

You can display any panel by choosing it in the Window menu, so if you can't find a panel, just look there.

The principal elements are shown here.

The main user interface elements are as follows:

- **Timeline panel:** This is where you'll do most of your editing. You view and work on *sequences* (the term for video segments edited together) in the Timeline panel. One feature of sequences is that you can *nest* them (place a sequence inside another sequence). In this way, you can break up a production into manageable chunks or create unique special effects.

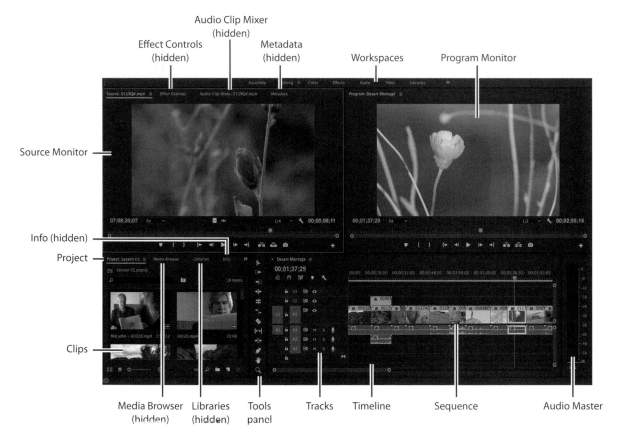

The main user-interface elements in Premiere Pro.

- **Tracks:** You can layer—or *composite*—video clips, images, graphics, and titles on an unlimited number of tracks. Video and graphic clips on upper video tracks cover whatever is directly below them on the Timeline. Therefore, you need to give clips on higher tracks some form of transparency or reduce their size if you want clips on lower tracks to show.

- **Monitor panels:** Use the Source Monitor (on the left) to view and select parts of clips (your original footage). To view a clip in the Source Monitor, double-click it in the Project panel. The Program Monitor (on the right) is for viewing your current sequence, displayed in the Timeline panel.

- **Project panel:** This is where you organize links to your project's media files: video clips, audio files, graphics, still images, and sequences. You can organize your media clips using bins. Bins are similar to folders—you can place one bin inside another for more advanced organization of your media assets.

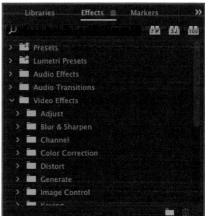

- **Media Browser:** This panel allows you to browse your storage to find media. It's especially useful for file-based camera media and RAW files.

- **Libraries:** This panel gives access to files you have added to your Creative Cloud Files folder on your storage drive, to custom Lumetri color Looks, and to shared libraries for collaboration, and this panel acts as a browser and store for Adobe Stock. For more information about the Libraries panel, go to https://helpx.adobe.com/premiere-pro/using/creative-cloud-libraries.html.

Effects panel

- **Effects panel:** This panel contains the effects you will use in your sequences, including video filters, audio effects, and transitions. Effects are grouped by type to make them easier to find, and there's a search box at the top of the panel to quickly locate an effect.

- **Audio Clip Mixer:** This panel is based on audio production studio hardware, with volume sliders and pan controls. There is one set of controls for each audio track on the Timeline. The adjustments you make are applied to audio clips. There's also an Audio Track Mixer for applying audio adjustments to tracks rather than clips.

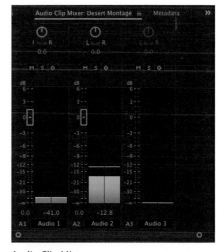

- **Effect Controls panel:** This panel displays the controls for any effects applied to a clip you select in a sequence or open in the Source Monitor. If you select a visual clip in the Timeline panel, Motion, Opacity, and Time Remapping controls are always available. Most effect parameters are adjustable over time.

Audio Clip Mixer

Effect Controls panel   Tools panel

- **Tools panel:** Each icon in this panel gives access to a tool that performs a specific function in the Timeline panel. The Selection tool is context-sensitive, which means it changes function depending on where you click. If your cursor doesn't work as you expect, it might be because you have the wrong tool selected.

- **Info panel:** The Info panel displays information about any asset you select in the Project panel or any clip or transition you select in a sequence.

- **History panel:** This panel tracks the steps you take and lets you back up easily. It's a kind of visual Undo list. When you select a previous step, all steps that came after it are also undone.

The name of each panel is displayed at the top. When a panel is displayed, a menu appears next to the name with options particular to that panel.

Customizing the workspace

In addition to choosing between the default workspaces, you can adjust the position and location of panels to create a workspace that works best for you. You can create multiple workspaces for different tasks.

- As you change the size of a frame, other frames change size to compensate.

- Every panel within a frame is accessible by clicking its name.

- All panels are dockable—you can drag a panel from one frame to another.

- You can drag a panel out of a frame to become a separate floating panel.

In this exercise, you'll try all these functions and save a customized workspace:

1 Click the Source Monitor panel (selecting its name if necessary), and then position your pointer on the vertical divider between the Source Monitor and the Program Monitor. The mouse cursor will change when it's in the right position. Drag left and right to change the sizes of those frames. You can choose to have different sizes for your video displays.

2 Now place the pointer on the horizontal divider between the Program Monitor and the Timeline. The mouse cursor will change when it's in the right position. Drag up and down to change the sizes of these frames.

3 Click the name of the Effects panel (to the left of the name) and drag it to the middle of the Source Monitor to dock the Effects panel in that frame. Remember, if you can't see the Effects panel, you can select it in the Window menu.

The drop zone is displayed as a center highlight.

Note: When you drag a panel by clicking its name, Premiere Pro displays a drop zone. If the panel is a rectangle, it will go into the selected frame as an additional tab. If it's a trapezoid, it will create a new frame.

You may need to resize a panel to see all of its controls.

4   Clicking the name at the top of the Effects panel, drag the panel to a point near the right of the Project panel to place it in its own frame.

Before you release the mouse button, the drop zone is a trapezoid that covers the right portion of the Project panel. Release the mouse button, and your workspace should have a new frame that contains just the Effects panel.

You can also pull panels out into their own floating panels.

5   Click the Source Monitor panel name, and hold down the Control (Windows) or Command (Mac OS) key while dragging it out of its frame.

6   Drop the Source Monitor anywhere, creating a floating panel. Resize it by dragging a corner or a side, as you would with any other panel.

7   As you gain experience, you might want to create and save the layout of your panels as a customized workspace. To do so, choose Window > Workspaces > Save as New Workspace. Type a name, and click OK.

Note: You can change the font size in the Project panel by clicking the panel menu and choosing Font Size > Small, Medium (default), Large, or Extra Large.

8   If you want to return a workspace to its default layout, choose Window > Workspaces > Reset to Saved Layout.

9   To return to a recognizable starting point, choose the preset Editing workspace, and reset it now.

Introducing preferences

The more you edit video, the more you'll want to customize Premiere Pro to match your specific needs. Premiere Pro has several types of settings. For example, panel menus, which are accessible by clicking the menu button next to a panel name, have options that relate to each panel, and individual clips in a sequence have settings you can access by right-clicking them.

It's worth noting that the panel name, displayed at the top of each panel, is usually referred to as the *panel tab*. It's the area of a panel you can click to move the panel, almost like a handle you can grab the panel by.

There are also application preferences, all grouped into one panel for easy access. Preferences will be covered in depth as they relate to the individual lessons in this book. Let's look at a simple one:

1   Choose Edit > Preferences > Appearance (Windows) or Premiere Pro > Preferences > Appearance (Mac OS).

2   Drag the Brightness slider to the left or right to suit your needs. When you're done, click OK, or click Cancel to return to the default setting.

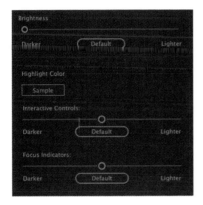

The default brightness is a dark gray to help you see colors correctly. There are additional options to control the brightness of interface highlights.

3   Experiment with the Interactive Controls and Focus Indicators brightness sliders. The difference in the onscreen Sample is subtle, but adjusting these sliders can make quite a big difference to your editing experience. Set all three settings to Default by clicking the Default buttons when you have finished.

4   Switch to the Auto Save preferences by clicking the preference name on the left.

Imagine if you had worked for hours and then there was a power outage. If you hadn't saved recently, you'd have lost a lot of work. With this dialog, you can decide how often you would like Premiere Pro to save an automated backup of your project and how many versions you would like to keep in total.

Project files are small relative to media files, so it's usually fine to increase the number of project versions without any impact on system performance.

You'll notice there's an option to save a backup project to Creative Cloud.

Save backup project to Creative Cloud

● **Note:** Premiere Pro automatically saves a backup copy of your project file while you work, in case of system failure. Premiere Pro is integrated with Adobe Creative Cloud, so an additional backup project file can be saved to your Creative Cloud shared files folder if you select the check box in this panel.

This option leads to an additional backup of your project file in your Creative Cloud Files folder. If you suffer a total system failure while working, you can log in to any Premiere Pro editing system with your Adobe ID to access the backup project file and quickly carry on working.

Click Cancel to close the Preferences dialog without saving the changes.

Keyboard shortcuts

Premiere Pro makes extensive use of keyboard shortcuts. These save time and are usually easier to use than mouse operations. Many keyboard shortcuts are shared universally by nonlinear editing systems. The spacebar, for example, starts and stops playback—this even works on some websites.

Some keyboard standard shortcuts come from celluloid film-editing traditions. The I and O keys, for example, are used to set In and Out marks on footage and sequences. These start and end markers were originally drawn on celluloid directly.

Other keyboard shortcuts are available but not configured. This allows flexibility when setting up your keyboard.

Choose Edit > Keyboard Shortcuts (Windows) or Premiere Pro CC > Keyboard Shortcuts (Mac OS).

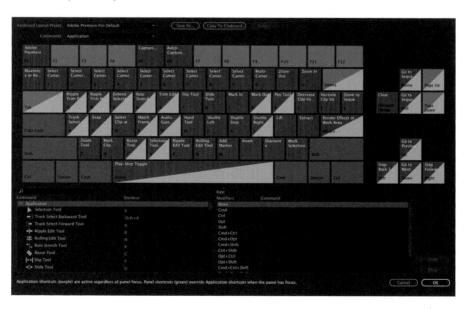

It can be a little daunting seeing the number of keyboard shortcuts available, but by the end of this book you will recognize most of the options displayed here.

Specialized keyboards are available with shortcuts printed on them and color-coded keys. These make it much easier to remember commonly used shortcuts.

Try holding the Control (Windows) or Command (Mac OS) key.

The keyboard shortcut display updates to show the results of combining the modifier key with the shortcuts. Notice there are many more keys without shortcuts assigned when you use a modifier key.

Try combinations of modifier keys including the Shift and Alt keys. You can set keyboard shortcuts with any combination of modifier keys.

If you press a shortcut key, or shortcut and modifier key combination, the shortcut information is displayed.

The list at the bottom left of this dialog includes every option you can assign to a key. Having found an option you would like to assign to a key, drag it from the list onto the key in the upper part of the dialog.

To remove a shortcut, click the key and choose Clear. For now, click Cancel.

Moving, backing up, and syncing user settings

User preferences include a number of important options. The defaults work well in most cases, but as you will discover, it's likely you'll want to make a few adjustments. For example, you might prefer the interface to be always brighter than the default.

Premiere Pro includes the option to share your user preferences between multiple machines: When installing Premiere Pro, you will have entered your Adobe ID to confirm your software license. You can use the same ID to store your user preferences in Creative Cloud, allowing you to sync and update them from any installation of Premiere Pro.

You can sync your preferences on the Start screen by choosing Sync Settings. You can also sync your preferences while working with Premiere Pro by choosing File > Sync Settings > Sync Settings Now (Windows) or Premiere Pro CC > Sync Settings > Sync Settings Now (Mac OS). Now close Premiere Pro by choosing File > Exit (Windows) or Premiere Pro CC > Quit Premiere Pro (Mac OS).

Review questions

1 Why is Premiere Pro considered a nonlinear editor?

2 Describe the basic video-editing workflow.

3 What is the Media Browser used for?

4 Can you save a customized workspace?

5 What is the purpose of the Source Monitor and the Program Monitor?

6 How can you drag a panel to its own floating panel?

Review answers

1 Premiere Pro lets you place video clips, audio clips, and graphics anywhere in a sequence; rearrange items already in a sequence; add transitions; apply effects; and do any number of other video-editing steps in any order that suits you.

2 Shoot your video; transfer it to your computer; create a sequence of video, audio, and still-image clips on the Timeline; add effects and transitions; add text and graphics; mix your audio; and export the finished product.

3 The Media Browser allows you to browse and import media files without having to open an external file browser. It's particularly useful when you're working with file-based camera footage.

4 Yes. You can save any customized workspace by choosing Window > Workspaces > Save as New Workspace.

5 You use the monitor panels to view your original clips and your sequence. You can view and trim your original footage in the Source Monitor and use the Program Monitor to view the Timeline sequence as you build it.

6 Drag the panel tab (the name of the panel) with your mouse while holding down Control (Windows) or Command (Mac OS).

2 SETTING UP A PROJECT

Lesson overview

In this lesson, you'll learn about the following:

- Choosing project settings
- Choosing video rendering and playback settings
- Choosing video and audio display settings
- Creating scratch disks
- Importing projects from Final Cut Pro and Avid Media Composer
- Using sequence presets
- Customizing sequence settings

 This lesson will take approximately 50 minutes.

Before you begin editing, you need to create a new project and choose some settings for your first sequence. If you're not familiar with video and audio technology, you might find all the options a little overwhelming. Luckily, Adobe Premiere Pro CC gives you easy shortcuts. Plus, the principles of video and sound reproduction are the same no matter what you're creating.

It's just a question of knowing what you want to do. To help you plan and manage your projects, this lesson contains information about formats and video technology. You may decide to revisit this lesson later, as your familiarity with Premiere Pro and nonlinear video-editing develops.

In practice, you're likely to make few changes to the default settings when creating a new project, but it's helpful to know what all the options mean.

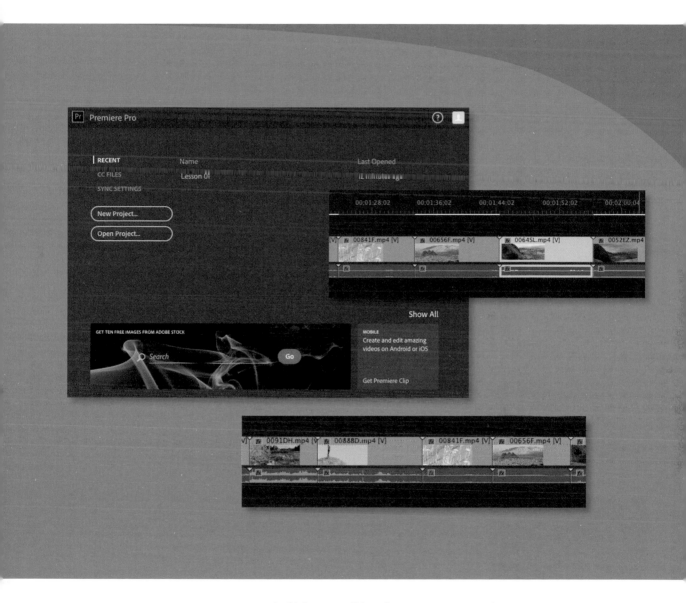

In this lesson, you'll learn how to create a new project and choose sequence settings that tell Premiere Pro how to play your video and audio clips.

Getting started

A Premiere Pro project file stores links to all the video, graphic, and sound files you have imported. Each item is called a clip. The name *clip* originally described sections of celluloid film (lengths of film were literally clipped to separate them from a roll), but these days the term refers to any item in the project, regardless of the type of media. You could have an audio clip or an image sequence clip, for example.

Clips displayed in the Project panel appear to be media files, but they are actually only links to those files. It's important to understand the relationship between the clips in the Project panel and the media files they link to. You can delete one without affecting the other (more on this later).

When working on a project, you will also create at least one *sequence*—that is, a series of clips that play, one after another, with special effects, titles, and sound, to form your completed creative work. You'll choose which parts of your clips to use and in which order they'll play.

The beauty of editing with Premiere Pro is that you can change your mind about almost anything, at any time.

Sequences contain a series of clips that play, one after another.

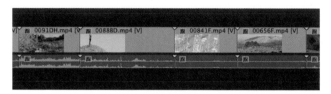

Premiere Pro project files have the file extension .prproj.

Starting a new project is simple. You create a new project file, import media, choose a sequence preset, and start editing.

When you create a sequence, you'll choose playback settings and place multiple clips in it. It's important to understand how the sequence settings change the way Premiere Pro plays your video and audio clips. To speed things up, you can use a sequence preset to choose the settings and then make adjustments if necessary.

You need to know the kind of video and audio your camera records because your sequence settings will usually be based on your original source footage. Most Premiere Pro sequence presets are named after cameras. If you know which camera was used to capture the footage and which particular video format was recorded, you'll know which sequence preset to choose.

In this lesson, you'll learn how to create a new project and choose sequence settings that tell Premiere Pro how to play your clips. You'll also learn about different kinds of audio tracks, what preview files are, and how to open projects created in Apple Final Cut Pro and Avid Media Composer.

Setting up a project

Let's begin by creating a new project.

1 Launch Premiere Pro. The Start screen appears.

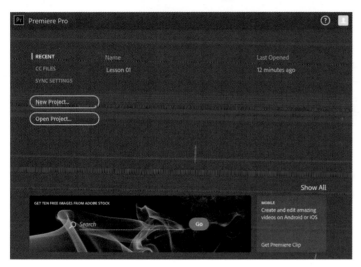

The Name heading lists previously opened projects. You should see Lesson 01 under this heading.

There are several other options in this window.

- **RECENT:** Displays recently opened project files stored locally (this is the default option).

- **CC Files:** Displays recently opened project files stored in your Creative Cloud Files folder. These are the same as any other project files but will automatically be stored in the cloud, in addition to your local storage.

- **New Project:** Click this link to open the New Project dialog box.

- **Open Project:** Click this link to browse to and open an existing Premiere Pro project file.

- **?:** The ? symbol at the top right of the Start screen opens the online Help system. You'll need to be connected to the Internet to access Adobe Premiere Pro Help.

- User icon: Next to the ? Help link is a thumbnail of your Adobe ID profile picture. If you have just signed up, this may be a generic thumbnail. Click the icon to manage your account online.

- **Show All:** Just below this option you'll see a link to a free tutorial. Click Show All to see more. Depending on your screen resolution and the size of the Start screen, you may see more links to information or less.

2 Click New Project to open the New Project dialog box.

This dialog box has three tabs: General, Scratch Disks, and Ingest Settings. All the settings in this dialog box can be changed later. In most cases, you'll want to leave them as they are. Let's take a look at what they mean.

Exploring video rendering and playback settings

While you're working creatively with video clips in your sequences, it's likely you will apply some visual effects. Some special effects can be played immediately, combining your original video with the effect and displaying the results as soon as you click Play. When this happens, it's called *real-time playback*.

Real-time playback is desirable because it means you can watch the results of your creative choices right away.

If you use lots of effects on a clip or if you use effects that are not designed for real-time playback, your computer may not be able to display the results at the full frame rate. That is, Premiere Pro will attempt to display your video clips, combined with the special effects, but it will not show every single frame each second. When this happens, it's described as *dropping* frames.

Premiere Pro displays colored lines along the top of the Timeline to tell you when extra work is required to play back your video. A red line means Premiere Pro may drop frames when playing that section of the sequence.

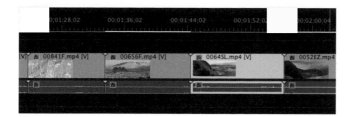

Note: A red line at the top of the Timeline panel doesn't necessarily mean frames will be dropped. It just means visual adjustments aren't accelerated, so on a less powerful machine dropped frames are more likely.

If you can't see every frame when you play your sequence, it's OK! It won't affect the final results. When you're done editing and you output your finished sequence, it'll be full quality, with all the frames (more on this in Lesson 18, "Exporting Frames, Clips, and Sequences").

What do *rendering* and *real time* mean?

Think of rendering as an artist's rendering, where something is visualized, taking up paper and taking time to draw. Imagine you have a piece of video that is too dark. You add a visual effect to make it brighter, but your video-editing system is unable to both play the original video and make it brighter. In this situation, you'd have your system render the effect, creating a new temporary video file that looks like the original video combined with the visual effect to make it brighter.

When your edited sequence plays, sections that are rendered display the newly rendered video file instead of the original clip (or clips). The process is invisible and seamless. In this example, the rendered file plays back like the original video file but brighter.

When the part of your sequence with the brightened clip is finished, your system invisibly and seamlessly switches back to playing your other original video files.

The downside of rendering is that it takes up extra space on your hard drive, and it takes time. Also, because you're viewing a new video file that is based on your original media, there might be some minor loss of quality. The upside with rendering is that you can be confident your system will be able to play the results of your effect at full quality, with all the frames per second. This might be important if you output to tape, though it's less critical if you output to a file.

Real-time playback, by contrast, is instant! When using a real-time special effect, your system plays the original video clip combined with the special effect right away, without waiting for it to render. The only downside with real-time performance is that the amount you can do without rendering depends on how powerful your system is. More effects are more work to play back, for example. In the case of Premiere Pro, you can dramatically improve real-time performance by using the right graphics card (see the sidebar "The Mercury Playback Engine"). Plus, you'll need to use effects that are designed for GPU acceleration, and not all effects are.

Real-time playback can make a difference to your editing experience and your ability to preview the effects you apply with confidence. There is a simple solution: preview rendering.

When you render, Premiere Pro plays back the results of your special effects at high quality and full frame rate, without your computer having to do any more work than playing a regular video file.

In the New Project dialog, if the Renderer menu is available, it means you have graphics hardware in your computer that meets the minimum requirements for GPU acceleration and it is installed correctly.

The menu has two main options.

- **Mercury Playback Engine GPU Acceleration:** If you choose this option, Premiere Pro will send many playback tasks to the graphics hardware on your computer, giving you lots of real-time effects and easy playback of mixed formats in your sequences. You may see an option to use OpenCL or to use CUDA for GPU acceleration, depending on your graphics hardware.

- **Mercury Playback Engine Software Only:** This is still a major advancement in playback performance, giving you excellent performance that uses all of the available power in your computer. If your system does not have graphics hardware that can be used for GPU Acceleration, only this option will be available, and you won't be able to click this menu.

You will almost certainly want to choose GPU Acceleration and benefit from the additional performance if you can. If you experience performance or stability issues using GPU acceleration, choose the Software Only option in this menu.

Do so now, if the option is available.

Setting the video and audio display formats

The next two options tell Premiere Pro how to measure time for your video and audio clips.

In most cases, you'll choose the default options: Timecode for video and Samples for audio. These settings don't change the way Premiere Pro plays video or audio clips, only the way time is measured.

The Mercury Playback Engine

The Mercury Playback Engine dramatically improves playback performance, making it faster and easier than ever to work with multiple video formats, multiple special effects, and multiple layers of video (for effects such as picture-in-picture).

The Mercury Playback Engine has three main features.

- **Playback performance:** Premiere Pro plays back video files with great efficiency, especially when working with the types of video that are difficult to play back, such as H.264 or AVCHD. If you're filming with a DSLR camera, for example, chances are your media is recorded using the H.264 codec. With the new Mercury Playback Engine, you'll find that these files play back with ease.

- **64-bit and multithreading:** Premiere Pro is a 64-bit application, which simply means it can use all the random access memory (RAM) on your computer. This is particularly useful when you're working with high-definition or ultra-high-definition video (or 4K and above). The Mercury Playback Engine is also multi-threaded, which means it uses all the CPU cores in your computer. The more powerful your computer is, the more performance you'll see in Premiere Pro.

- **CUDA, OpenCL, Apple Metal, and Intel graphics support:** If you have powerful enough graphics hardware, Premiere Pro can send some of the work for playing back video to the graphics card, rather than putting the entire processing burden on the CPU in your computer. The results are even better performance and responsiveness when working with sequences, and many special effects will play in real time.

For more information about supported graphics cards, see http://helpx.adobe.com/premiere-pro/system-requirements.html.

The Video Display Format option

There are four options for Video Display Format. The correct choice for a given project largely depends on whether you are working with video or celluloid film as your source material. It's rare to produce content using film, so if you are not sure, choose Timecode.

The choices are as follows:

- **Timecode:** This is the default option. Timecode is a universal standard for counting hours, minutes, seconds, and individual frames of video. The same system is used by cameras, professional video recorders, and nonlinear editing systems all around the world.

- **Feet + Frames 16 mm** or **Feet + Frames 35 mm:** If your source files are captured from film and you intend to give your editing decisions to a lab so they can cut the original negative to produce a finished film, you may want to use this standard method of measuring time. Rather than measuring time as seconds and frames, this system counts the number of feet plus the number of frames since the last foot. It's a bit like feet and inches but with frames rather than inches. Because 16mm film and 35mm film have different frame sizes (and so different numbers of frames per foot), there's an option for each.

● **Note:** Many of the terms used in Adobe Premiere Pro come from film editing, including the term *bin*. In traditional film editing, film editors hang film clips on hooks over large bins, with the long piece of celluloid trailing into the bin to keep it safe.

- **Frames:** This option simply counts the number of frames of video. This is sometimes used for animation projects and is another way that labs like to receive information about edits for film-based projects.

For this exercise, leave Video Display Format set to Timecode.

About seconds and frames

When a camera records video, it captures a series of still images of the action. If there are enough images captured each second, it looks like moving video when played back. Each picture is called a *frame*, and the number of frames each second is usually called *frames per second* (fps).

The fps will vary depending on your camera/video format and settings. It could be any number, including 23.976, 24, 25, 29.97, 50, or 59.94 fps. Most cameras allow you to choose between more than one frame rate and more than one frame size.

The Audio Display Format option

For audio files, time can be displayed as samples or milliseconds.

- **Audio Samples:** When digital audio is recorded, sound level samples are taken, as captured by the microphone, thousands of times a second. In the case of most professional video cameras, this happens 48,000 times per second. In Audio Samples mode, Premiere Pro can display time in your sequences as hours, minutes, seconds, and samples. The number of samples per second will depend on your sequence settings.

- **Milliseconds:** With this mode selected, Premiere Pro can display time in your sequences as hours, minutes, seconds, and thousandths of a second.

By default, Premiere Pro lets you zoom the Timeline enough to view individual clip segment frames. However, you can easily switch to displaying your audio display format instead. This powerful feature lets you make the tiniest adjustments to your audio.

For this project, leave the Audio Display Format option set to Audio Samples.

Setting the capture format

It's most common to record video as a file you can work with immediately. However, there may be times you need to capture from videotape.

The Capture Format settings menu tells Premiere Pro what videotape format you are using when capturing video to your storage drive.

Capturing from DV and HDV cameras

Premiere Pro can capture from DV and HDV cameras using the FireWire connection on your computer, if it has one. FireWire is also known as IEEE 1394 and i.LINK.

Capturing from third-party hardware

Not all video decks use a FireWire connection, so you may need additional third-party hardware installed to be able to connect your video deck for capture.

If you have additional hardware, you should follow the directions provided by the manufacturer to install it. Most likely you'll install software supplied with your hardware, and this will discover Premiere Pro on your computer, automatically adding extra options to this menu and to others.

Follow the directions provided with your third-party equipment to configure new Premiere Pro projects.

● **Note:** The Mercury Playback Engine can share performance with video-capture cards for playback, thanks to a feature called Adobe Mercury Transmit. This feature has been included since Adobe Premiere Pro CS6.

For more information about video capture hardware and video formats supported by Premiere Pro, visit http://helpx.adobe.com/premiere-pro/compatibility.html.

Ignore this setting for now because you will not be capturing from a tape deck in this exercise, and you can change the setting as needed later.

Displaying the project item names and label colors

A check box at the bottom of the New Project dialog box allows you to display the project item name and label color for all instances.

☐ Display the project item name and label color for all instances

With this option enabled, when you change the color of a clip or change the clip name, all copies of the clip used anywhere, in any sequence in the project, will update accordingly. If this option is not selected, only the copy you select will be changed.

Setting up the scratch disks

Whenever Premiere Pro *captures* (records) from tape or renders effects, new media files are created on your hard drive.

Scratch disks are the places these files are stored. They can be separate disks, as the name suggests, or any folder in your storage locations. Scratch disks can be created all in the same place or in separate locations, depending on your hardware and workflow requirements. If you're working with really large media files, you may get a performance boost by putting all your scratch disks on different hard drives.

There are generally two approaches to storage for video editing.

- **Project-based setup:** All associated media files are stored with the project file in the same folder (this is the default option for scratch disks).

- **System-based setup:** Media files associated with multiple projects are saved to one central location (perhaps high-speed network-based storage), and the project file is saved to another. This might include storing different kinds of media files in different locations.

Your scratch disks might be stored in local hard drives or on a network-based storage system; any storage location your computer has access to will work. However, the speed of your scratch disks can have a big impact on performance, so choose fast storage if possible.

Setting up Project Auto Save location

In addition to choosing where new media files are created, Premiere Pro allows you to choose the location for storing Auto Save files. These are additional backup copies of your project file that are created automatically while you work.

Storage drives occasionally fail, and you may lose files stored on them without notice. In fact, any computer engineer will tell you that if you have only one copy of a file, you can't count on having the file at all. For this reason, it's a great idea to set the Project Auto Save location to a physically separate drive, just in case.

In addition to storing Auto Save files in the location you choose here, Premiere Pro can store a backup of your project file in your Creative Cloud Files folder. This folder is created automatically when you install Adobe Creative Cloud. It allows you to access files in any location where Creative Cloud is installed and you are logged in.

This useful extra safety net is available by choosing Edit > Preferences > Auto Save (Windows) or Premiere Pro CC > Preferences > Auto Save (Mac OS).

CC Libraries downloads

The Premiere Pro Libraries panel allows you to download additional media files and access files shared with you. For example, you might download logos or graphic elements to incorporate into your sequence.

When you add items to your project in this way, Premiere Pro will create a copy of them in the location you choose here.

Using a project-based setup

By default, Premiere Pro keeps any newly created media together with the project file (this is the Same as Project option). Keeping everything together this way makes finding associated files simple.

It makes it easier to stay organized if you move media files into the same folder before you import them. When you're finished with your project, you can remove everything from your system by deleting the single folder your project file is stored in.

There's a downside, though: Storing your media files on the same drive as your project file means the drive has to work harder while you edit, and this can impact playback performance.

Using a system-based setup

Some editors prefer to have all their media stored in a single location. Others choose to store their capture folders and preview folders in a different location from their project. This is a common choice in editing facilities where multiple editors share several editing systems, all connected to the same storage. It's also common among editors who have fast hard drives for video media and slower hard drives for everything else.

There's a downside with this setup too: Once you finish editing, you'll likely want to gather everything together for archiving. This is slower and more complex when your media files are distributed across multiple storage locations.

Typical drive setup and network-based storage

Although all file types can coexist on a single hard drive, a typical editing system will have two hard drives: Drive 1, dedicated to the operating system and programs, and Drive 2 (often a faster drive), dedicated to footage items, including captured video and audio, video and audio previews, still images, and exported media.

Some storage systems use local computer networks to share storage between multiple systems. If this is the case for you, check with your system administrators to make sure you have the right settings.

For this project, we leave your scratch disks set to the default option: Same as Project.

Choosing ingest settings

Most editors describe adding media to a project as *importing*. However, the process is also described as *ingest*. The two words are often used interchangeably, but the word *ingest* has a broader meaning than *import*. Depending on the scenario, *ingest* might incorporate making changes to the media files as they are added to your project.

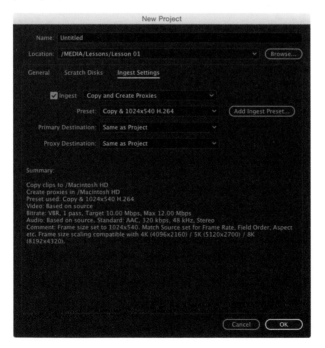

When you ingest media files, you might choose to do the following:

- Link them to clips in a project
- Copy or move them to a new storage location
- Convert them to a new codec and/or format (also called *transcoding*)
- Update them with new metadata and/or new filenames

It's common to combine these steps during ingest. These settings configure Premiere Pro to copy media files to a selected location, transcode them to a new format and codec, or produce low-resolution copies (proxy media files) that have smaller file sizes for collaborative workflows or to make playback easier on a less powerful editing system.

We'll be exploring these settings in Chapter 3, "Importing Media." They can be changed at any time, so for now leave them off, with no check in the box for Ingest.

Now you have checked the settings are correct for this project, so let's finish creating it.

1 Click in the Name box and name your new project Lesson 02.

2 Click the Browse button and browse to the Lessons folder. Create a folder called Lesson 02, and choose this new folder as the location for the new project.

3 If your project is set up correctly, the General and Scratch Disks tabs in your New Project window should look similar to the screens shown here. If the settings match, click OK to create the project file.

● **Note:** When choosing a location for your project file, you may want to choose a recently used location from the drop-down menu.

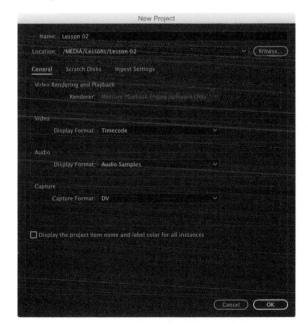

Importing projects from Final Cut Pro

Final Cut Pro is a nonlinear editing system produced by Apple. Adobe Premiere Pro CC can import and export Final Cut Pro sequences and links to media files using a file type called Final Cut Pro 7 XML.

Extensible Markup Language (XML) files store information about editing decisions in a way that can be understood by both Apple Final Cut Pro and Adobe Premiere Pro. This makes it ideal for sharing creative work between the applications.

Because of limitations in the way XML files are created and to improve compatibility, it's better to avoid nonalphanumeric characters (such as / \ ¢ ™ $ ® € . , [ ] { } ( ) ! ? | ; " ' * < >) in file and folder names when sharing creative work between different nonlinear editing systems.

Exporting an XML file from Final Cut Pro 7

You'll need to open the Final Cut Pro project file in Final Cut Pro to create an XML file. When you import the XML file into Premiere Pro, you'll need the media files used by Final Cut Pro. Premiere Pro can share the media files if both applications are installed on the same editing system.

1 Open the existing project in Final Cut Pro.

2 Either choose nothing in the project, in which case Final Cut Pro will export the entire project, or select some specific items, in which case Final Cut Pro will export only those items.

3 Choose File > Export > XML.

   In the XML dialog box you'll see a report of how many bins, clips, and sequences are selected.

4 Choose Apple XML Interchange Format version 5 and keep Save Project With Latest Clip Metadata (Recommended) selected.

5 Save the XML file in an easy-to-find location (such as in the same folder as your project).

Exporting an XML file from Final Cut Pro X

If you're working with Final Cut Pro X, a newer version of Apple Final Cut Pro, you can still export an XML file by choosing File > Export > XML. However, you'll need to convert the XML created to Final Cut Pro 7 XML using a third-party application such as XtoCC (http://intelligentassistance.com/xtocc.html).

Importing a Final Cut Pro 7 XML file

You can import a Final Cut Pro 7 XML file into Premiere Pro just like any other kind of file (for more details, see Lesson 3, "Importing Media"). When you import an XML file, Premiere Pro guides you through connecting the sequence and clip information to the original media files used by Final Cut Pro. There is a limit to the amount of information Final Cut Pro will include in an XML file, so you will find that some proprietary effects won't make it to Premiere Pro. Test this workflow before you depend upon it.

Media best practice

If you intend to work with both Final Cut Pro and Premiere Pro, you'll want to use a media format that both editing systems can play back easily. Premiere Pro has wide-ranging support for media formats and can easily work with Final Cut Pro ProRes media files.

For this reason, it's best for editors working with both applications to use Final Cut Pro to import media or capture video from tapes. You can set up your project using ProRes media in Final Cut Pro and then easily exchange projects with Premiere Pro.

Importing Avid Media Composer projects

Media Composer is a nonlinear editing system produced by Avid. Premiere Pro can import and export sequences and links to media files using AAF files exported from Avid Media Composer. AAF files store information about editing decisions in a way that can be understood by both Avid and Premiere Pro. This makes it ideal for sharing creative work between both applications.

Exporting an AAF file from Avid Media Composer

You'll need to open the Avid project file in Avid Media Composer to create an AAF file. When you import the AAF file into Premiere Pro, you'll need the media files used by Avid Media Composer.

1 Open a project in Media Composer.

2 Choose the sequence you'd like to transfer.

3 Choose File > Export. Click the Options button.

In the Export dialog, there's a menu at the bottom that contains templates. The Options button at the bottom allows customization.

4 In the Export Settings dialog, choose the following:

- Select the AAF Edit Protocol.

- You can choose to include marks and export only between In/Out marks.

- Use enabled tracks (optional).

- Include all video tracks in the sequence.

- Include all audio tracks in the sequence.

- Video Details: For Export Method, choose Link to (Don't Export) Media.

- Audio Details: For Export Method, choose Link to (Don't Export) Media.

- Audio Details (optional): Include Rendered Audio Effects.

5 Save the AAF file in an easy-to-find location.

Importing an Avid AAF file

You can import an Avid AAF file like any other kind of file (see Lesson 3). When you import an AAF file, Premiere Pro guides you through connecting the sequence and clip information to the original media files used by Avid. There is a limit to the amount of information Avid will include in an AAF file, so you will find that some proprietary effects will not make it to Premiere Pro. Test this workflow before you rely upon it.

Media best practice

Avid Media Composer uses a different media management system from the Premiere Pro system. However, since version 3.5 of Media Composer, a new system called AMA has permitted linking to media outside of Avid's own media organization system. Media files imported into Avid Media Composer using AMA tend to relink better when an AAF file is imported into Premiere Pro. Media in an Avid Media Composer AMA folder can be anything that Apple QuickTime can play, including P2, XDCAM, and even RED. You'll need to have the appropriate codec available on your Premiere Pro editing system. Consider using Avid DNxHD, which is a popular codec created by Avid that is supported natively in Premiere Pro.

You will usually achieve the best results if you use Avid Media Composer's AMA system to link to original media with P2 or XDCAM media.

Setting up a sequence

In your Premiere Pro project you will create a sequence (or several sequences), into which you'll place video clips, audio clips, and graphics. If necessary, Premiere Pro will automatically change video and audio clips that you add to a sequence so they match the settings for that sequence. Frame rates and frame sizes for clips, for example, can be converted during playback to match the settings you choose for your sequence. This is called *conforming*.

Each sequence in your project can have different settings, and you'll want to choose settings that match your original media as precisely as possible to minimize conforming during playback. Doing so reduces the work your system must do to play back your clips, improves real-time performance, and maximizes quality.

If you're editing a mixed-format project, you may have to make choices about which media to match with your sequence settings. You can mix formats easily, but playback performance improves when the sequence settings match.

If the first clip you add to a sequence does not match the playback settings of your sequence, Premiere Pro asks if you would like to change the sequence settings automatically to fit.

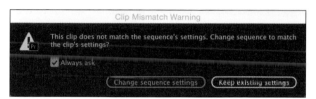

Premiere Pro will ask you what to do if your first clip does not match your sequence.

Creating a sequence that automatically matches your source

If you're not sure what sequence settings you should choose, don't worry. Premiere Pro can create a sequence based on your media.

At the bottom of the Project panel, there's a New Item menu (![icon]). You can use this menu to create new items, such as sequences, titles, and bins.

To automatically create a sequence that matches your media, drag and drop any clip (or multiple clips) in the Project panel onto the New Item menu. A new sequence will be created with the same name as the clip and a matching frame size and frame rate.

Now you're ready to start editing, and you can be confident your sequence settings will work with your media. If the Timeline panel is empty, you also can drag a clip (or multiple clips) into it to create a sequence automatically.

Choosing the correct preset

If you know the settings you need, you can configure a sequence. If you're not so sure, you can choose from a list of presets.

Click the New Item menu in the Project panel (![icon]) and choose Sequence.

The New Sequence dialog has three tabs: Sequence Presets, Settings, and Tracks.

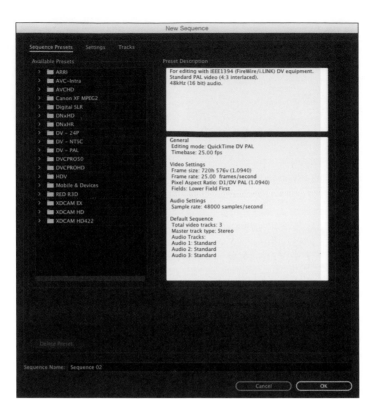

The Sequence Presets tab makes setting up a new sequence much easier. When you choose a preset, Premiere Pro applies settings for your sequence that closely match a particular video and audio format. After choosing a preset, you can adjust these settings on the Settings tab.

You'll find a wide range of preset configuration options for the most commonly used and supported media types. These settings are organized based on camera formats (with specific settings inside a folder named after the recording format).

You can click the disclosure triangle to see specific formats in a group. These are typically designed around frame rates and frame sizes. Let's look at an example:

1   Click the disclosure triangle next to the group AVCHD.

You can now see three subfolders, based on frame sizes and interlacing methods. Remember that video cameras can often shoot video using different frame sizes, as well as different frame rates and codecs.

2   Click the disclosure triangle next to the 720p subgroup.

3   Choose the AVCHD 720p25 preset by clicking its name.

Formats and codecs

Video file types like Apple QuickTime, Microsoft AVI, and MXF are containers that can carry many different video and audio codecs. The file is referred to as the *wrapper*, and the video and audio are referred to as the *essence*.

Codec is a shortening of the words *compressor* and *decompressor*. It's the way video and audio information is stored and replayed.

If you output your finished sequence to a file, you'll choose a format, a file type, and a codec.

When you're starting out in video editing, you may find the number of formats available a little overwhelming. Premiere Pro can work natively with a wide range of video and audio formats and codecs and will often play back mismatched formats smoothly.

However, when Premiere Pro has to adjust video for playback because of mismatched sequence settings, your editing system must work harder to play the video, and this will impact real-time performance. It's worth taking the time before you start editing to make sure you have sequence settings that closely match your original media files.

The essential factors are always the same: the number of frames per second, the frame size (the number of pixels in the picture), and the audio format. If you were to turn your sequence into a media file without applying a conversion, then the frame rate, audio format, frame size, and so on, would all match the settings you chose when configuring the sequence.

When you output to a file, you can convert your sequence to any format you like (for more on exporting, see Lesson 18, "Exporting Clips, Frames, and Sequences").

While the standard presets usually work, you may need to create a custom setting. To do so, first choose a sequence preset that matches your media closely, and then make custom selections in the Settings tab. You can save your custom preset by clicking the Save Preset button near the bottom of the Settings tab.

Give your customized project settings preset a name in the Save Settings dialog box, add notes if you want, and click OK. The preset will appear in a Custom folder under Sequence Presets.

● **Note:** The Preset Description area of the Sequence Presets tab often describes the kind of camera used to capture media in this format.

Customizing a sequence preset

Once you've selected the sequence preset that most closely matches your source video, you may want to adjust the settings to suit the specifics of your sequence.

To begin making adjustments, click the Settings tab and choose options that better suit the way you would like Premiere Pro to play back your video and audio files. Remember, Premiere Pro will automatically conform footage you add to your Timeline so that it matches your sequence settings, giving you a standard frame rate and frame size, regardless of the original clip format.

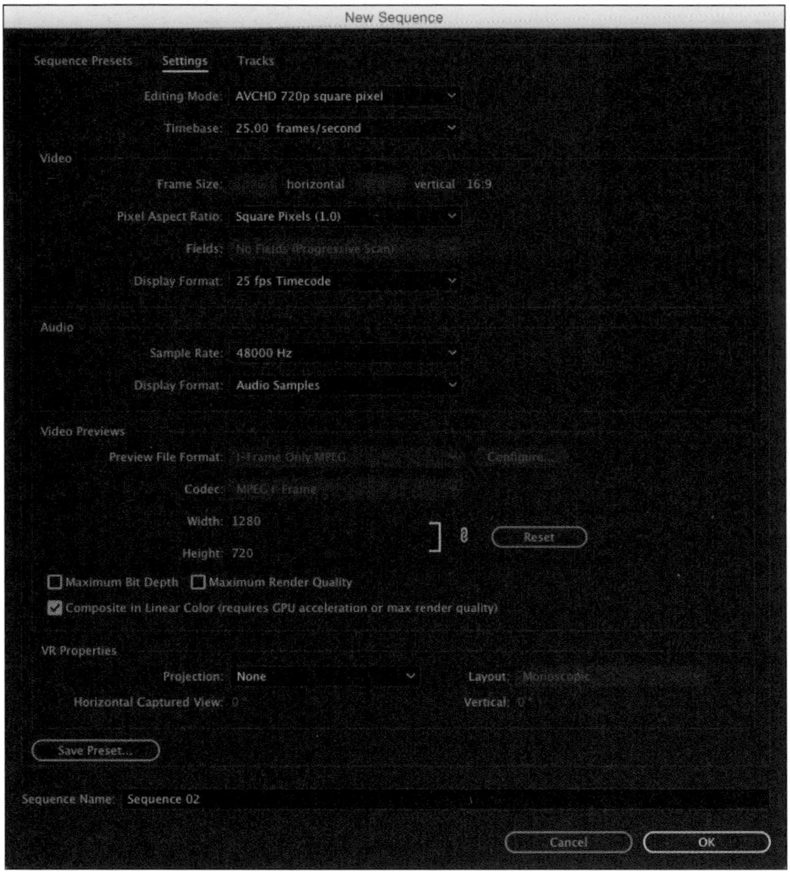

The Settings tab gives precise control over sequence configuration.

Tip: For now, leave the settings as they are, but examine the way the preset is going to configure the new sequence. Look at each setting from top to bottom to build familiar ity with the choices required to configure a sequence.

If your media matches one of the presets, it's not necessary to make changes on the Settings tab. In fact, it's recommended that you use the default settings.

You'll notice that some settings cannot be changed when you use a preset. This is because they're optimized for the media type you selected on the Preset tab. For complete flexibility, change the Editing Mode menu to Custom, and you will be able to change all the available options.

Maximum Bit Depth and Maximum Render Quality

If you enable Maximum Bit Depth, Premiere Pro can render special effects at the maximum quality possible. For many effects, this means 32-bit floating-point color, which allows for trillions of color combinations. This is the best-possible quality for your effects but is more work for your computer, so expect less real-time performance.

If you enable the Maximum Render Quality option or if you have GPU acceleration, Premiere Pro uses a more advanced system for scaling images. Without this option, you might see minor artifacts or noise in the picture when making images smaller. Without GPU acceleration, this option will impact playback performance and file export.

Both of these options can be turned off or on at any time, so you can edit without them to maximize performance, and then turn them on when you output your finished work. Even with both options on you can use real-time effects and expect good performance from Premiere Pro.

Understanding track types

When you add a video or audio clip to a sequence, you'll put it on a *track*. Tracks are horizontal areas in the Timeline panel that hold clips in a particular position in time. If you have more than one video track, any video clips placed on an upper track will appear in front of clips on a lower track. For example, if you have text or a graphic on your second video track and a video clip on your first video track, you'll see the graphic in front of the video.

The Tracks tab of the New Sequence dialog box allows you to preselect the track types for the new sequence.

All audio tracks are played at the same time, creating a complete audio mix. To create a mix, position your audio clips on different tracks, lined up in time. Narration, sound bites, sound effects, and music can be organized by putting them on different tracks. You can also rename tracks, making it easier to find your way around more complex sequences.

Premiere Pro lets you specify how many video and audio tracks will be included when the sequence is created. You can easily add and remove tracks later, but you can't change your Audio Master setting.

● **Note:** The Audio Master setting configures the sequence to output audio as stereo, 5.1, multichannel, or mono. Choose Stereo for now.

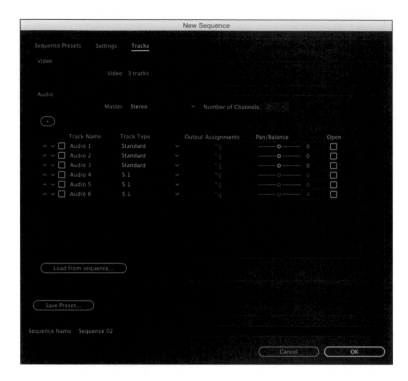

You can choose from several audio track types. Each track type is designed for specific types of audio. When you choose a particular track type, Premiere Pro gives you the right controls to make adjustments to the sound, based on the number of audio channels. For example, stereo clips need different controls than 5.1 surround-sound clips.

The types of audio tracks available in Premiere Pro are as follows:

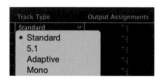

- **Standard:** These tracks are for both mono and stereo audio clips.

- **5.1:** These tracks are for audio clips with 5.1 audio (the kind used for surround sound).

- **Adaptive:** Adaptive tracks are for both mono and stereo audio and give you precise control over the output routing for each audio channel. For example, you could decide the track audio channel 3 should be output to your mix in channel 5. This workflow is used for multilingual broadcast TV, where precise control of audio channels is used at transmission.

- **Mono:** This track type will accept only mono audio clips.

When you add a clip to a sequence that has both video and audio, Premiere Pro makes sure the audio channels go to the right kind of track. You can't accidentally put an audio clip on the wrong kind of track; Premiere Pro will automatically create the right kind of track if one doesn't exist already.

You'll explore audio more in Lesson 11, "Editing and Mixing Audio."

Understanding submixes

Submixes are an advanced feature of the audio finishing tools in Premiere Pro. You can send the output from a track in your sequence to a submix track, rather than directly to the master output. You can then use the submix to apply audio effects and make changes to the volume. This may not seem useful for a single track, but you can send as many tracks as you like to a single submix. That means you could have, for example, ten audio tracks controlled by a single submix. Put simply, this means less clicking and faster editing.

You choose submixes based on the output options you want.

- **Stereo Submix:** For submixing to stereo tracks
- **5.1 Submix:** For submixing to 5.1 tracks
- **Adaptive Submix:** For submixing to mono or stereo tracks
- **Mono Submix:** For submixing to mono tracks

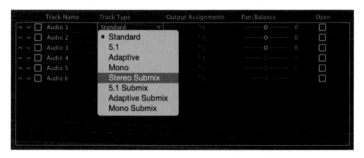

For this sequence, use the default settings. Take a moment to familiarize yourself with the options; then do the following:

1 Click in the Sequence Name box, and name your sequence **First Sequence**.

2 Click OK to create the sequence.

3 Choose File > Save. Congratulations! You have made a new project and sequence with Premiere Pro.

If you have not already copied the media and project files to your computer, please do so before continuing to Lesson 3, as you'll need them to follow along. You'll find instructions for copying the files in the "Getting started" section at the beginning of this book.

Review questions

1 What is the purpose of the Settings tab in the New Sequence dialog box?

2 How should you choose a sequence preset?

3 What is timecode?

4 How do you create a custom sequence preset?

5 What options are available in Premiere Pro to capture video from tape with no additional third-party hardware?

Review answers

1 The Settings tab is used to customize an existing preset or to create a new custom preset.

2 It's generally best to choose a preset that matches your original footage. Premiere Pro makes this easy by describing the presets in terms of camera systems.

3 Timecode is the universal system for measuring time in hours, minutes, seconds, and frames. The number of frames per second varies depending on the recording format.

4 When you've selected the settings you want for your custom preset, click the Save Preset button, give it a name and a description, and click OK.

5 Premiere Pro records DV and HDV files if you have a FireWire connection on your computer. If you have additional connections provided by installed third-party hardware, consult the documentation for that hardware for the best settings.

3

IMPORTING MEDIA

Lesson overview

In this lesson, you'll learn about the following:

- Using the Media Browser to load video files

- Using the Import command to load graphic files

- Working with proxy media

- Using Adobe Stock

- Choosing where to place cache files

- Recording a voice-over

 This lesson will take approximately 75 minutes to complete.

To create a sequence, you need to import media files into your project. This might include video footage, animation files, narration, music, atmospheric sound, graphics, or photos. Everything you include in a sequence must be imported before it can be used.

Any item included in a sequence must also be included in the Project panel. Importing a clip directly to a sequence automatically adds the clip to the Project panel, and deleting a clip in the Project panel removes it from sequences it appears in (you'll be given the option to cancel if you do this).

Whichever way you approach editing sequences, importing clips to the Project panel and organizing them is the first step.

Because Adobe Premiere Pro can work with so many types of assets, there are multiple methods for browsing and importing media.

Getting started

In this lesson, you'll learn to import media assets into Adobe Premiere Pro CC. For most files, you'll use the Media Browser, a robust asset browser that works with many media types you'll import into Premiere Pro. You'll also learn about special cases such as importing graphics or capturing from videotape.

For this lesson, you'll use the project file you created in Lesson 2, "Setting Up a Project." If you do not have the previous lesson file, you can open the file Lesson 03 Example.prproj from the Lesson 03 folder.

1 Continue to work with the project file from the previous lesson, or open it from your hard drive.

2 Choose File > Save As.

3 Rename the file **Lesson 03.prproj**.

4 Browse to Lessons/Lesson 03, and click Save to save the project with a new name.

Importing assets

When you import items into a Premiere Pro project, you are creating a link from the original media file to a pointer that lives inside your project. This means you are not making a copy or modifying the original files when editing; you're just manipulating the original media from its current location, in a nondestructive manner. For example, if you choose to edit only part of a clip into your sequence, you're not throwing away the unused media.

Media can be imported in two principal ways.

- Standard importing by choosing File > Import

- Using the Media Browser

Let's explore the benefits of each.

When to use the Import command

Using the Import command is straightforward (and may match your experience in other applications). To import any file, just choose File > Import.

You can also use the keyboard shortcut Control+I (Windows) or Command+I (Mac OS) to open the standard Import dialog box.

This method works best for self-contained assets such as graphics and audio, especially if you know exactly where those assets are on your drive and can quickly navigate to them. This importing method is not ideal for file-based camera footage, which often uses complex folder structures with separate files for audio, video, and important additional data, or for RAW media files. For camera-originated media, you'll want to use the Media Browser.

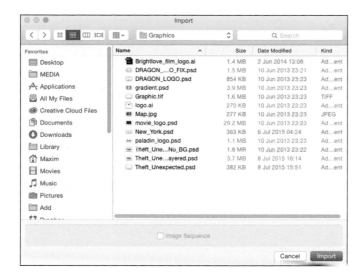

▶ **Tip:** Another way to open the Import dialog box is to double-click an empty area of the Project panel. You can even drag files directly from Explorer (Windows) or Finder (Mac OS) into Premiere Pro.

When to use the Media Browser

The Media Browser is a robust tool for reviewing your media assets and then importing them into Premiere Pro. The Media Browser shows the fragmented files you might capture with a digital video camera as whole clips; you'll see each recording as a single item, with the video and audio combined, regardless of the original recording format.

This means you can avoid dealing with complex camera folder structures and instead work with easy-to-browse icons and metadata. Being able to see this metadata (which contains important information, such as clip duration, recording date, and file type) makes it easier to select the correct clip in a long list.

By default, in the Editing workspace, you'll find the Media Browser in the lower-left corner of your Premiere Pro workspace. It's docked in the same frame as the Project panel. You can also quickly access the Media Browser by pressing Shift+8 (be sure to use the number key at the top of the keyboard).

Like any other panel, you can position the Media Browser in another frame by dragging it using the tab (where the name of the panel is displayed).

You can also undock it to make it a floating panel by clicking the menu on the panel tab ( ) and choosing Undock Panel.

Browsing for files in the Media Browser is similar to browsing with Explorer (Windows) or Finder (Mac OS). The contents of your storage are displayed as navigation folders on the left, with buttons to navigate forward and backward at the top.

You can use arrow keys to select items.

The major benefits of the Media Browser are as follows:

- Narrowing the display to a specific file type, such as JPEG, Photoshop, XML, or AAF.

- Autosensing camera data—AVCHD, Canon XF, P2, RED, ARRIRAW, Sony HDV, or XDCAM (EX and HD)—to correctly display the clips.

- Viewing and customizing the kinds of metadata to display.

- Correctly displaying media that has spanned clips across multiple camera media cards. Premiere Pro will import the files as a single clip even if a longer video file filled a storage card and continued onto a second.

> **Tip:** If you want to import assets used in another Premiere Pro project, you can browse inside that project in the Media Browser panel. Use the Media Browser to locate the project file and double-click it to view its contents. You can select and import clips and sequences to your current Project panel.

Working with ingest options and proxy media

Premiere Pro offers excellent performance when playing back, and adding effects to, a broad range of media formats and codecs. However, there may be occasions that your system hardware will struggle to play media, especially if it's high-resolution RAW footage.

You may decide it will be more efficient to work with low-resolution copies of your media while you edit and to switch to the full, original resolution media just before you check your effects and output your finished work. This is a *proxy workflow*—creating low-resolution "proxy" files to use instead of your original content.

Premiere Pro can automate creating proxy files during import, and this is part of a more advanced approach to media ingest. If you're happy with the performance on your system when working with original footage, you'll probably skip this feature. Still, it opens up significant advantages, both for system performance and for collaboration.

Importing from Adobe Prelude

Adobe Creative Cloud CC includes Adobe Prelude, which you can use to organize footage in a simple, streamlined interface.

Adobe Prelude is designed to allow producers or assistants to quickly and efficiently ingest (import), log, and transcode media (convert format and codec) for tapeless workflows.

Here's how to send a Prelude project to Premiere Pro:

1   Launch Adobe Prelude.

2   Open the project you want to transfer, and select one or more items in the Project panel.

Adobe Prelude has a similar appearance to Premiere Pro but with simplified controls.

3   Choose File > Export > Project.

4   Select the Project check box.

5   Enter a name in the Name field.

6   In the Type menu, choose Premiere Pro.

7   Click OK. The Choose Folder dialog box opens.

8   Navigate to a destination for the new project, and click Choose. A new Premiere Pro project is created.

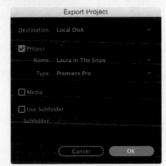

You can open the Premiere Pro project file directly, or you can import it into an existing project. Premiere Pro will relink the clip media files and maintain any bins you created in Prelude.

If both Premiere Pro and Prelude are running at the same time on the same computer, you can also send clips from Prelude to Premiere Pro by selecting them, right-clicking the selection, and choosing Send to Premiere Pro.

Let's check out the options:

1 Choose File > Project Settings > Ingest Settings.

This dialog contains the original project setup options you saw when creating the project. You can change any setting at any time.

By default, all the Ingest options are disabled.

2 Enable Ingest by clicking the check box, and click the first menu to see these options:

- **Copy:** When you import media files, Premiere Pro will copy the files to a location you choose in the Primary Destination menu. This is a valuable option if you are importing media files directly from your camera card media, since media must be available to Premiere Pro when your cards are not connected to the computer.

- **Transcode:** When you import media files, Premiere Pro will convert the files to a new format and codec based on the preset you choose and will place the new files in a destination location you choose.

- **Create Proxies:** When you import media files, Premiere Pro creates additional copies that are lower resolution, based on the preset you chose. These low-resolution media files are stored in the same location as your original media.

- **Copy and Create Proxies:** When you import media files, Premiere Pro will copy the files to a location you choose in the Primary Destination menu *and* create proxies (as discussed earlier) that are stored in the same new location.

3 Select the option Create Proxies, choose the Preset menu, and try selecting a few options. Look at the notes in the lower part of the dialog that explain each option.

```
• 1024x540 Apple ProRes 422 (Proxy)
  1024x540 GoPro CineForm
  1024x540 H.264
  1280x720 Apple ProRes 422 (Proxy)
  1280x720 GoPro CineForm
  1280x720 H.264
  1536x790 Apple ProRes 422 (Proxy)
  1536x790 GoPro CineForm
  1536x790 H.264
```

It's most important that the option you choose matches the aspect ratio of your original footage. This way, you'll see composition elements correctly while working with the proxy files.

If proxy media exists for clips in your project, it's easy to switch between displaying your original, full-quality media and your low-resolution proxy versions. Choose Edit > Preferences > Media (Windows) or Premiere Pro > Preferences > Media (Mac OS), and toggle the Enable Proxies option.

This was just an introduction to the proxy media workflow. For more information about managing proxy files, linking proxy media, and creating proxy file presets, see the Adobe Premiere Pro Help. When you have finished looking at the settings, click Cancel.

Working with the Media Browser

The Media Browser allows you to easily browse for files on your computer. It can stay open, it's fast and convenient, and it's well optimized for locating and importing footage.

Following a file-based camera workflow

Premiere Pro CC does not require footage from file-based cameras to be converted and can edit compressed media from camera systems such as P2, XDCAM; and AVCHD, RAW media from Canon, Sony, RED, and ARRI; and post-production-friendly codecs like Avid DNxHD, Apple ProRes, and GoPro Cineform natively.

For best results, follow these guidelines (no need to follow along now):

1 Create a new media folder for each project.

2 Copy camera media to your editing storage with the existing folder structure intact. Be sure to transfer the complete data folder directly from the root directory of the card. For best results, consider using the transfer application that is often included by the camera manufacturer to move your video files. Check that all media files have been copied and that the card and copied folder sizes match.

Note: Adobe Media Encoder does the work of transcoding files and creating proxies in the background, so you can use your original media right away, and as the new proxy files are created, they'll be used instead automatically.

Note: There's a Toggle Proxies button you can add to the Source or Program Monitor to quickly switch between viewing proxy or original media. Explore some of the more advanced ways you can modify the Premiere Pro interface to speed up your editing experience. See Chapter 4, "Organizing Media," to find out how to customize the monitor buttons.

Note: When you output a sequence that is set to display proxy media, the full-quality original media is automatically used rather than the low-resolution proxy media.

Note: To complete this lesson, you will import files from your computer. Be sure you have copied all the lesson files included with this book to your computer. For more details, see the "Getting started" section at the beginning of the book.

3 Clearly label the copied folder of the media with the camera information, including card number and date of shoot.

4 Create a second copy of the media on a physically separate, second drive in case of hardware failure.

5 Ideally, create a long-term archive copy using another backup method, such as LTO tape or an external storage drive.

● **Note:** Adobe Prelude makes managing the process of copying and importing tapeless media sources easier.

Understanding supported video file types

It's not unusual to work on a project with video clips from multiple cameras using different file formats. This is no problem for Premiere Pro because you can mix different clip formats in the same sequence. Also, the Media Browser can display almost any file format. It's particularly well suited to file-based camera formats.

If your system hardware struggles to play back high-resolution media, you may find it helpful to use proxy files while editing.

The following are the major file-based formats supported by Premiere Pro:

- Any DSLR camera that shoots H.264 media as a QuickTime MOV or MP4 file

- Panasonic P2, DV, DVCPRO, DVCPRO 50, DVCPRO HD, AVCI, AVC Ultra, AVC Ultra Long GOP

- RED ONE, RED EPIC, RED Mysterium X, the 6K RED Dragon, the 8K REDCODE RAW Weapon

- ARRI RAW, including ARRI AMIRA

- Sony XDCAM SD, XDCAM 50, XAVC, SStP, RAW, HDV (when shot on file-based media)

- AVCHD cameras

- Canon XF, Canon RAW

- Apple ProRes

- Avid DNxHD and DNxHR MXF files

- Blackmagic CinemaDNG

- Phantom Cine camera

Finding assets with the Media Browser

The good news is that the Media Browser is self-explanatory. In many ways, it's like a web browser (it has Forward and Back buttons to go through your recent navigation). It also has a list of shortcuts on the side. Finding materials is easy.

● **Note:** When importing media, be sure to copy the files to your local storage, or use the project ingest options to create copies before removing your memory cards or external drives.

Continue working with your Lesson 03.prproj project, or open Lesson 03 Example.prproj for this exercise.

Note: When you open a project created on another computer, you may see a message warning you about a missing renderer. It's fine to click OK on this message.

1 Begin by resetting the workspace to the default; in the Workspaces panel, click Editing. Then click the menu adjacent to the Editing option and choose Reset to Saved Layout.

Note: If you can't see the Workspaces panel, select it by choosing Window > Workspaces (at the bottom of the menu).

2 Click the Media Browser (it should be docked with the Project panel by default). Resize the panel to make it larger.

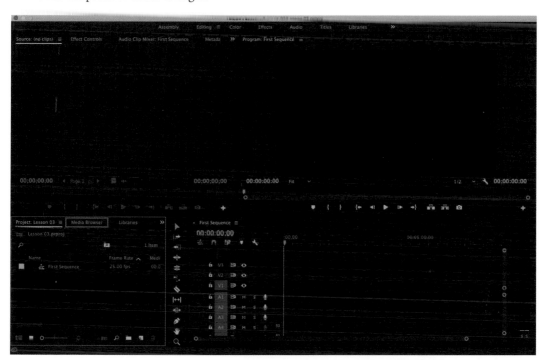

 3 To make the Media Browser easier to see, position your mouse pointer over the panel and then press the ` (accent grave) key (it is often in the upper-left corner of a keyboard).

The Media Browser panel should now fill the screen. You may need to adjust the width of columns to make it easier to see items.

▶ **Tip:** Some keyboard layouts make it difficult to find the right key. If so, you can click the panel menu and choose Panel Group Settings > Maximize Panel Group. The same menu will allow you to restore the panel size.

4 Using the Media Browser, navigate to the folder Lessons/Assets/Video and Audio Files/Theft Unexpected.

5 Drag the resize slider in the lower-left corner of the Media Browser to enlarge the thumbnails of the clips. You can use any size you like.

● **Note:** The Media Browser filters out nonmedia files, making it easier to browse for video or audio assets.

You can hover your mouse cursor over any unselected clip thumbnail to see a preview of the clip contents.

6 Click a clip once to select it.

You can now preview the clip using keyboard shortcuts.

7 Press the L key to play a clip.

8 To stop playback, press the K key.

9 To play backward, press the J key.

10 Experiment with playing back other clips. You should be able to hear the clip audio during playback.

You can press the J or L key multiple times to increase the playback rate for fast previews. Use the K key or the spacebar to pause.

11 Now you'll import all these clips into your project. Press Control+A (Windows) or Command+A (Mac OS) to select all the clips.

12 Right-click one of the selected clips and choose Import.

Alternatively, you can drag all the selected clips onto the Project panel's tab and then down into the empty area to import the clips.

13 Press the ` (accent grave) key or use the panel menu to restore the Media Browser to its original size. Then switch to the Project panel.

Clips in the Project panel can be viewed as icons or as a list, with information about each clip available. Switch between these two viewing modes by clicking the List View button ( ) or Icon View button ( ).

Making the most of the Media Browser

The Media Browser has a number of features that make it easy to navigate your storage.

- The Forward and Back ( ) buttons work like an Internet browser, allowing you to navigate to locations you have viewed previously.

- If you expect to import files from a location often, you can add the folder to a list of favorites at the top of the navigation panel. To create a favorite, right-click the folder and choose Add to Favorites.

- You can open multiple Media Browser panels and access the contents of several different folders at once. To open a new Media Browser panel, click the Panel menu (on the panel tab) and choose New Media Browser Panel.

Importing images

Graphics are an integral part of post-production. People expect graphics to both convey information and add to the visual style of a final edit. Premiere Pro can import just about any image and graphic file type. Support is especially excellent when you use the native file formats created by Adobe's leading graphic tools, Adobe Photoshop and Adobe Illustrator.

Importing flattened Adobe Photoshop files

Anyone who works with print graphics or performs photo retouching has probably used Adobe Photoshop. It's the workhorse of the graphic design industry. Adobe Photoshop is a powerful tool with great depth and versatility, and it's an increasingly important part of the video production world. Let's explore how to properly import files from Adobe Photoshop.

First, you'll import a basic graphic.

1 Click the Project panel to select it.

2 Choose File > Import, or press Control+I (Windows) or Command+I (Mac OS).

3 Navigate to Lessons/Assets/Graphics.

4 Select the file Theft_Unexpected.png, and click Import.

The PNG graphic is a simple logo file and imports into the Premiere Pro project.

An introduction to Dynamic Link

One way to work with Premiere Pro is with a suite of tools. You may be using a version of Adobe Creative Cloud that includes other components for related video-editing tasks. To make things easier, you'll find several options for speeding up your post-production workflow.

A good example is Dynamic Link. This allows you to import After Effects compositions into a Premiere Pro project in a way that creates a live connection between the two applications. Once added in this way, the After Effects compositions will look and behave like any other clip in your Premiere Pro project.

When you make changes in After Effects, they automatically update in Premiere Pro, which is a great time-saver.

Options for Dynamic Link exist between Premiere Pro and Adobe After Effects and between Premiere Pro and Audition.

You'll explore both Dynamic Link workflows later in this book.

Importing layered Adobe Photoshop files

Adobe Photoshop can create graphics with multiple layers. Layers are similar to tracks in your Timeline and allow for separation between visual elements. You can import Photoshop document layers into Premiere Pro individually to allow for isolation or animation. Let's look at the import options.

1 Double-click an empty area of the Project panel to open the Import dialog box.

2 Navigate to Lessons/Assets/Graphics.

3 Select the file Theft_Unexpected_Layered.psd, and click Import.

4 A new dialog box opens, giving you four Import As options that allow you to selectively import layers.

- **Merge All Layers:** This option merges all layers into one, importing the file into Premiere Pro as a single, flattened clip.

- **Merged Layers:** This option merges only specific the layers you select into a single, flattened clip.

- **Individual Layers:** This option imports only the specific layers you select, with each layer becoming a separate clip in a bin.

- **Sequence:** This option imports only the layers you select, each as a single clip. Premiere Pro then creates a new sequence (with its frame size based on the imported document) containing each clip on a separate track (matching the original stacking order).

If you choose the Sequence or Individual Layers options, you can select one of the following options from the Footage Dimensions menu:

- **Document Size:** This brings all the selected layers into Premiere Pro at the size of the original Photoshop document.

- **Layer Size:** This matches the frame size of the new Premiere Pro clips to the frame size of their individual layers in the original Photoshop file. Layers that do not fill the entire canvas will be cropped tightly, as transparent areas are removed. They'll also be centered in the frame, losing their original relative positioning.

5 For this exercise, choose Sequence, and use the Document Size option. Click OK.

6 Look in the Project panel for the newly created bin called Theft_Unexpected_Layered. Double-click it to open it.

7 Inside the bin, double-click the sequence Theft_Unexpected_Layered to load it. If you're unsure which item is which, hover the mouse cursor over an item name to find out whether it is a clip or a sequence.

8 Look at the sequence in the Timeline. Try turning off and on the Toggle Track Output option () for each track to see the way the two layers are isolated.

9 Close the Theft Unexpected bin.

● **Note:** There are several deselected layers in this PSD. These are layers the designer turned off in Photoshop because they were unwanted but not deleted. Premiere Pro honors the layer selection automatically on import.

▶ **Tip:** There are good reasons to import individual PSD layers with separate layer sizes. For example, some graphic designers create multiple images for editors to incorporate into video edits, with each image occupying a different layer in the PSD. The PSD itself is a kind of one-stop image store when used this way.

Importing Adobe Illustrator files

● **Note:** If you right-click Brightlove_film_logo.ai in the Project panel, you'll note that one option is Edit Original. If you have Illustrator installed on your computer, selecting Edit Original will open this graphic in Illustrator, ready to be edited. So even though the layers are merged in Premiere Pro, you can return to Adobe Illustrator, edit the original layered file, and save it, and the changes will immediately appear in Premiere Pro.

Another graphics component in Adobe Creative Cloud is Adobe Illustrator. Unlike Adobe Photoshop, which is primarily designed to work with pixel-based (or raster) graphics, Adobe Illustrator is a vector-based application. Vector graphics are mathematical descriptions of shapes rather than drawn pixels. This means you can scale them to any size and they always look sharp.

Vector graphics are typically used for technical illustrations, line art, or complex graphics.

Let's import a vector graphic.

1 Double-click an empty area of the Project panel to open the Import dialog box.

2 Navigate to Lessons/Assets/Graphics.

3 Select the file Brightlove_film_logo.ai, and click Import.

Here's the way Premiere Pro deals with Adobe Illustrator files:

- Like the Photoshop file you imported earlier, this is a layered graphic file. However, Premiere Pro doesn't give you the option to import Adobe Illustrator files in separate layers. It always merges them into a single layer clip.

- Premiere Pro uses a process called *rasterization* to convert the vector-based Adobe Illustrator art into the pixel-based image format used by Premiere Pro. This conversion happens during import automatically, so be sure your graphics are configured to be large enough in Illustrator before importing them into Premiere Pro.

- Premiere Pro automatically anti-aliases, or smooths the edges of, the Adobe Illustrator art.

- Premiere Pro sets all empty areas of Illustrator files as transparent so that clips below those areas in your sequence will show through.

Importing subfolders

When you import by choosing File > Import, you don't have to select individual files. You can also select a whole folder. In fact, if you have already organized your files into folders and subfolders on your storage drive, when you import them, the folders are re-created as bins in Premiere Pro.

Try this now:

1 Choose File > Import, or press Control+I (Windows) or Command+I (Mac OS).

2 Navigate to Lessons/Assets, and select the Stills folder. Don't browse inside the folder; just select it.

3 Click the Import Folder button (Windows) or Import button (Mac OS). Premiere Pro imports the whole folder, including two subfolders containing photos. In the Project panel, you'll find bins have been created to match the folders.

Using Adobe Stock

Adobe Stock offers millions of images and videos you can easily incorporate into your sequences via the Libraries panel.

The Libraries panel allows you to easily share design assets between projects and users. You can search Adobe Stock directly in the Libraries panel, choose video clips and graphics, and use a low-resolution preview in your project immediately.

If you're happy with a stock item and you'd like to purchase the full-resolution version, you can click the "License and Save to" shopping cart icon that appears on the item in the Libraries panel. The full-resolution item will be downloaded and automatically replaces the low-resolution version in your project and sequences.

For more information about Adobe Stock, check out stock.adobe.com.

Customizing the media cache

When you import certain video and audio formats, Premiere Pro may need to process and cache a version. This is particularly true for highly compressed formats. Imported audio files are automatically conformed to a new CFA file, for example. Most MPEG files are indexed, leading to an extra .mpgindex file that makes it easier to read the file. You'll know that the cache is being built if you see a small progress indicator in the lower-right corner of the screen when importing media.

The media cache improves preview playback performance by making it easier for your editing system to decode and play media. You can customize the cache to further improve performance. The media cache database helps Premiere Pro manage these cache files, which are shared between multiple Creative Cloud applications.

To access options for the cache, choose Edit > Preferences > Media (Windows) or Premiere Pro > Preferences > Media (Mac OS).

Here are some options to consider:

- To move the media cache files or the media cache database to a new location, click the appropriate Browse button, select the desired location, and click OK. In most cases, you should not move the media cache database during an editing project.

- You should clean the media cache database on a regular basis to remove old conformed and indexed files that are no longer required. To do so, click the Clean button. Any connected drives will have their cache files removed. It's a good idea to do this after you wrap up projects because it removes unnecessary preview render files too, saving space.

- Select "Save Media Cache files next to originals when possible" to keep cache files stored on the same drive as the media. If you want to keep everything in one central folder, leave this check box unselected. Remember, the faster the drive for the Media Cache, the better the playback performance you're likely to experience in Premiere Pro.

Tape vs. tapeless workflow

Tape is still sometimes used to acquire media, and it's fully supported by Premiere Pro. To bring footage from tape into a Premiere Pro project, you can capture it.

Capture digital video from tape to your storage disk before using it in a project. Premiere Pro captures video through a digital port, such as a FireWire or Serial Digital Interface (SDI) port (if you have third-party hardware). Premiere Pro saves captured footage to disk as files and imports the files into projects as clips, just as you would with file-based camera media. There are three basic approaches:

- You can capture your entire videotape as one long clip.

- You can log the beginning and end of each clip (each clip's In and Out marks) to batch capture them later.

- You can use the scene detection feature in Premiere Pro to automatically create separate clips based on every time you pressed Record on your camera (for some tapes).

By default, you can use DV and HDV sources with Premiere Pro if your computer has a FireWire port. If you'd like to capture other higher-end professional formats, you'll need to add a third-party capture device. These come in several form factors, including internal cards and breakout boxes that connect via FireWire, USB 3.0, and Thunderbolt.

Third-party hardware manufacturers can take advantage of Mercury Playback Engine features for previewing effects and video on a connected professional monitor. You can find a detailed list of supported hardware by visiting helpx.adobe.com/premiere-pro/compatibility.html.

Recording a voice-over

You may be working with a video project that includes a narration track. It's likely you will have the narration recorded by professionals (or at least recorded in a location quieter than your desks), but you can record temporary audio right into Premiere Pro too.

This can be helpful because it will give you a sense of timing for your edits.

Here's how to record a scratch audio track:

1 If you're not using a built-in microphone, make sure your external microphone is properly connected to your computer. You may need to see the documentation for your computer or sound card.

2 Choose Edit > Preferences > Audio Hardware (Windows) or Premiere Pro > Preferences > Audio Hardware (Mac OS) to configure your microphone so Premiere Pro can use it. Use one of the choices from the Default Input pop-up menu, such as Built-in Microphone, and click OK.

3 Turn down your computer speakers, or use headphones to prevent feedback or echo.

4 Open a sequence, and select an empty audio track in the Timeline.

5 Each track has a set of buttons and options on the far left. This area is called the *track header*. You may need to resize the audio track to be able to see the Voice-over Record button in the header. You can do this by hovering your mouse cursor over the track header and using the mouse scroll wheel.

6 Once the track is tall enough, you are likely to need to add the Voice-over Record button—it's hidden by default. Do this by right-clicking the track header and choosing Customize. The Button Editor opens.

▶ **Tip:** You can hover the mouse cursor over each button in the Button Editor to discover its name.

7 Drag the voice-over Record (🎤) button onto the track header, and click OK.

You'll have a voice-over Record button on every audio track header now.

8 Click the voice-over Record button to begin recording.

9 After a brief countdown, recording will begin. Press the spacebar to stop recording.

A new audio clip is created and added to the Project panel and the current sequence.

To access voice-over recording settings, right-click an audio track header, and choose Voice-Over Record Settings.

Review questions

1 Does Premiere Pro CC need to convert P2, XDCAM, R3D, or AVCHD footage when it is imported?

2 What is one advantage of using the Media Browser rather than the File > Import method to import file-based media?

3 When you're importing a layered Photoshop file, what are the four different ways to import the file?

4 Where can media cache files be stored?

5 How can you enable proxy media file creation when video is imported?

Review answers

1 No. Premiere Pro CC can edit P2, XDCAM, and AVCHD, as well as many other formats, natively.

2 The Media Browser understands the complex folder structures for P2, XDCAM, and many other formats, and it shows you the clips in a visually friendly way.

3 You can choose Merge All Layers into a single clip or select the specific layers you want by choosing Merged Layers. If you want layers as separate clips, choose Individual Layers and select the layers to import, or choose Sequence to import the selected layers and create a new sequence from them.

4 You can store media cache files in any specified location or automatically on the same drive as the original files (when possible). The faster the storage for your cache, the better the playback performance for previews.

5 You can enable proxy media file creation in the ingest settings. You'll find these in the Project settings dialog. You can also enable proxy creation by checking the box at the top of the Media Browser. There's a button to open the Ingest Settings there too.

4 ORGANIZING MEDIA

Lesson overview

In this lesson, you'll learn about the following:

- Using the Project panel
- Staying organized with bins
- Adding clip metadata
- Using essential playback controls
- Interpreting footage
- Making changes to your clips

 This lesson will take approximately 90 minutes.

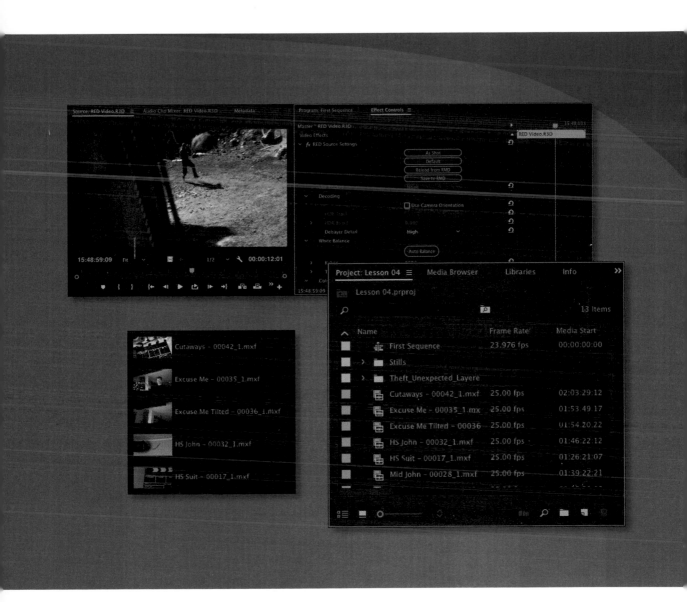

Once you have some video and sound assets in your project, you'll begin looking through your footage and adding clips to a sequence. Before you do, it's well worth spending a little time organizing the assets you have. Doing so can save you from spending hours hunting for things later.

Getting started

When you have lots of clips in your project, imported from several different media types, it can be a challenge to stay on top of everything and always find that magic shot when you need it.

In this lesson, you'll learn how to organize your clips using the Project panel, which is the heart of your project. You'll create special folders, called *bins*, to divide your clips into categories. You'll also learn about adding important metadata and labels to your clips.

You'll begin by getting to know the Project panel and organizing your clips.

1 To begin, reset the workspace to the default. In the Workspace panel, click Editing. Then click the menu adjacent to the Editing option and choose Reset to Saved Layout.

2 For this lesson, you'll use the project file you used in Lesson 3, "Importing Media." Continue to work with the project file from the previous lesson, or open it from your hard drive.

3 Choose File > Save As.

4 Rename the file **Lesson 04.prproj**.

5 Browse to the Lessons folder, and click Save to save the project.

If you do not have the previous lesson file, you can open the file Lesson 04.prproj from the Lessons/Lesson 04 folder.

Using the Project panel

Everything you import into your Adobe Premiere Pro CC project will appear in the Project panel. As well as giving you excellent tools for browsing your clips and working with their metadata, the Project panel has folder-like "*bins*" that you can use to stay organized.

Anything that appears in a sequence must also be in the Project panel. If you delete a clip in the Project panel that is already used in a sequence, the clip will automatically be removed from the sequence. Premiere Pro will warn you if deleting a clip will affect an existing sequence.

As well as acting as the repository for all your clips, the Project panel gives you important options for interpreting media. All your footage will have a frame rate (frames per second, or fps) and a pixel aspect ratio (pixel shape), for example. You may want to change these settings for creative reasons.

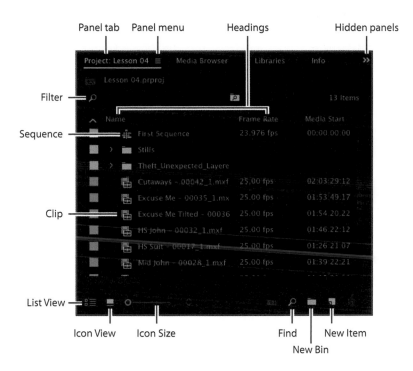

Panel tab — Panel menu — Headings — Hidden panels

Filter

Sequence

Clip

List View

Icon View — Icon Size — Find — New Item

New Bin

The Project panel in List View. To switch to this view, click the List View button at the bottom left of the panel.

You could, for example, interpret video recorded at 60fps video as 30fps to achieve a 50 percent slow-motion effect. You might occasionally receive a video file that has the wrong pixel aspect ratio setting and want to correct it.

Premiere Pro uses metadata associated with footage to know how to play it back. If you want to change the clip metadata, you can do so in the Project panel.

Customizing the Project panel

It's likely that you'll want to resize the Project panel from time to time. You'll alternate between looking at your clips as a list or as thumbnail icons. Sometimes it's quicker to resize the panel than to scroll to see more information.

The default Editing workspace is designed to keep the interface as clean as possible so you can focus on your creative work. Part of the Project panel that's hidden from view by default, called the Preview Area, gives additional information about your clips.

Let's take a look:

Tip: You can access lots of clip information by scrolling the List view or by hovering the mouse cursor over a clip name in Icon view.

1 Click the panel menu for the Project panel (on the panel tab).

2 Choose Preview Area.

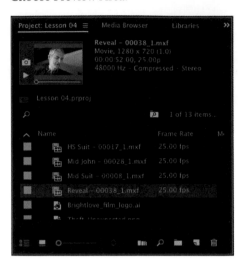

The Preview Area displays useful information for clips you select.

The Preview Area shows you several kinds of useful information about a selected clip in the Project panel, including the frame size, pixel aspect ratio, and duration.

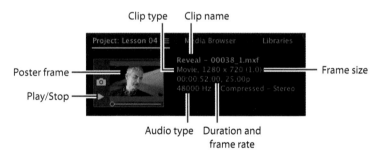

Clip type   Clip name

Poster frame

Play/Stop

Frame size

Audio type   Duration and frame rate

Tip: There's a quick way to toggle between seeing the Project panel in a frame and seeing it full-screen: Hover your mouse cursor over the panel and press the ` (accent grave) key. You can do this with any panel. If your keyboard does not have a ` (accent grave) key, you can click the panel menu and choose Panel Group Settings > Maximize Panel Group.

If it's not already selected, click the List View button ( ) at the bottom left of the Project panel. In this view, you'll find a lot of information about each clip in the Project panel, but you need to scroll horizontally to see it.

3 Click the panel menu for the Project panel (on the Panel tab).

4 Choose Preview Area to hide it.

Finding assets in the Project panel

Working with clips is a little like working with pieces of paper at your desk. If you have just one or two clips, it's easy. But when you have 100 to 200, you need a system.

One way you can help make things smoother during the edit is to invest a little time in organizing your clips at the beginning. If you rename your clips after importing them, it will make it easier for you to locate content later (see "Changing names" in this chapter).

1 Click the Name heading at the top of the Project panel. The items in the Project panel are displayed in alphabetical order or reverse alphabetical order each time you click the Name heading again.

If you're searching for several clips with particular features—such as a duration or a frame size—it can be helpful to change the order in which the headings are displayed.

2 Scroll to the right until you can see the Media Duration heading in the Project panel. This shows the total duration of each clip's media file.

3 Click the Media Duration heading. Premiere Pro now displays the clips in order of media duration. Notice the direction arrow on the Media Duration heading. Each time you click the heading, the direction arrow toggles between showing clips in duration order and in reverse duration order.

Media Duration ⌃   Media Duration ⌄

4 Drag the Media Duration heading to the left until you see a blue divider between the Frame Rate heading and the Name heading. When you release the mouse button, the Media Duration heading will be repositioned right next to the Name heading.

Name	Frame Rate	Media Start	Media End	Media Duration ⌃	Video In Point

The blue divider shows where you will drop the heading.

▶ **Tip:** You can scroll the Project panel view up and down using the scroll wheel on your mouse.

● **Note:** When you scroll to the right in the Project panel, Premiere Pro always maintains the clip names on the left so you know which clips you're seeing information about.

● **Note:** You may need to drag a divider to expand the width of a column before you can see its sorting order arrow.

Filtering bin content

Premiere Pro has built-in search tools to help you find your media. Even if you're using nondescriptive original clip names assigned in-camera, you can search for clips based on a number of factors, such as frame size or file type.

● **Note:** Graphic and photo files such as Photoshop PSD, JPEG, and Illustrator AI files import with a default frame duration you set after choosing Preferences > General > Still Image Default Duration.

At the top of the Project panel, you can type in the Filter Bin Content box to display only clips with names or metadata matching the text you enter. This is a quick way to locate a clip if you remember its name (or even part of its name). Clips that don't match the text you enter are hidden, and clips that do match are revealed, even if they are inside a closed bin.

Try this now:

1 Click in the Filter Bin Content box, and type **jo**.

Premiere Pro displays only the clips with the letters *jo* in the name or in the metadata. Notice that the name of the project is displayed above the text entry box, along with "(filtered)."

2 Click the X on the right of the Find box to clear your search.

3 Type **psd** in the box.

● **Note:** The name bin comes from film editing. The Project panel is also effectively a bin; it can contain clips and functions like any other bin.

Premiere Pro displays only clips that have the letters *psd* in their name or metadata. In this case, it's the Theft_Unexpected title you imported earlier as a layered image—this is a Photoshop PSD file. Using the Filter Bin Content box in this way, you can search for particular types of files.

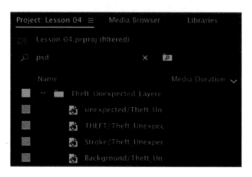

Be sure to click the X on the right of the Filter Bin Content box to clear your filter when you have found the clips you want.

Using advanced Find

Premiere Pro also has an advanced Find option. To learn about it, you can import a couple more clips.

Using any of the methods described in Lesson 3, import these items:

• Seattle_Skyline.mov from the Assets/Video and Audio Files/General Views folder

• Under Basket.MOV from the Assets/Video and Audio Files/Basketball folder

At the bottom of the Project panel, click the Find button (). Premiere Pro displays the Find panel, which has more advanced options for locating your clip.

You can perform two searches at once with the advanced Find panel. You can choose to display clips that match *all* search criteria or *any* search criteria. For example, depending on the setting you choose in the Match menu, you could do either of the following:

- Search for a clip with the words *dog* AND *boat* in its name.

- Search for a clip with the word *dog* OR *boat* in its name.

To do this, make selections from the following menus:

- **Column**: This option lets you select from the available headings in the Project panel. When you click Find, Premiere Pro will search using only the heading you select.

- **Operator**: This option gives you a set of standard search options. Use this menu to choose whether you want to find a clip that contains, matches exactly, begins with, or ends with whatever you search for.

- **Match**: Choose All to find a clip with both your first and your second search text. Choose Any to find a clip with either your first or your second search text.

- **Case Sensitive**: Selecting this option tells Premiere Pro whether you want your search to exactly match the uppercase and lowercase letters you enter.

- **Find What**: Type your search text here. You can add up to two sets of search text.

When you click Find, Premiere Pro highlights a clip that matches your search criteria. Click Find again, and Premiere Pro highlights the next clip that matches your search criteria. Click Done to exit the Find dialog box.

Working with bins

Bins allow you to organize clips by dividing them into groups.

Just like folders on your hard drive, you can have multiple bins inside other bins, creating a folder structure as complex as your project requires.

There's an important difference between bins and the folders on your storage drive: Bins exist only in your Premiere Pro project file to help organize clips. You won't find individual folders representing project bins on your storage drive.

Creating bins

Let's create a bin.

1   Click the New Bin button ( ) at the bottom of the Project panel.

Premiere Pro creates a new bin and automatically highlights the name, ready for you to rename it. It's a good habit to name bins as soon as you create them.

2   You have already imported some clips from a film, so let's give them a bin. Name the new bin **Theft Unexpected**.

3   You can also create a bin using the File menu. Let's do this now: Make sure the Project panel is active, and choose File > New > Bin.

4   Name the new bin **Graphics**.

● **Note:** It can be difficult to find a blank part of the Project panel to click when it is full of clips. Try clicking just to the left of the icons, inside the panel.

5   You can also make a new bin by right-clicking a blank area in the Project panel and choosing New Bin. Try this now.

6   Name the new bin **Illustrator Files**.

One of the quickest and easiest ways to create a new bin for clips you already have in your project is to drag and drop the clips onto the New Bin button at the bottom of the Project panel.

7   Drag and drop the clip Seattle_Skyline.mov onto the New Bin button.

8   Name the newly created bin **City Views**.

9   Make sure the Project panel is active but no existing bins are selected. Press the keyboard shortcut Control+B (Windows) or Command+B (Mac OS) to make another bin.

▶ **Tip:** If an existing bin is selected when you create a new bin, it will be created inside the selected bin. Deselect first to avoid this, or drag the new bin out of the selected bin once it appears.

10 Name the bin **Sequences**.

● **Note:** To rename a bin, select it and press Enter (not the carriage return), or click away from the text.

If your Project panel is set to List view, bins are displayed in alphabetical order among the clips.

Managing media in bins

Now that you have some bins, let's put them to use. As you move clips into bins, use the disclosure triangles to hide their contents and tidy up the view.

1   Drag the clip Brightlove_film_logo.ai into the Illustrator Files bin.

2   Drag Theft_Unexpected.png into the Graphics bin.

3   Drag the Theft_Unexpected_Layered bin (created automatically when you imported the layered PSD file as individual layers) into the Graphics bin.

4   Drag the clip Under Basket.MOV into the City Views bin. You may need to resize the panel or switch it to full-screen to see both the clip and the bin.

5   Drag the sequence called First Sequence into the Sequences bin.

6   Drag all the remaining clips into the Theft Unexpected bin.

   You should now have a nicely organized Project panel, with each kind of clip in its own bin.

   You can also copy and paste clips to make extra copies if this helps you stay organized. In the Graphics bin, you have a PNG file that might be useful for the Theft Unexpected content. Let's make an extra copy.

7   Click the disclosure triangle for the Graphics bin to display the contents.

8   Right-click the Theft_Unexpected.png clip and choose Copy.

9   Click the disclosure triangle for the Theft Unexpected bin to display the contents.

10 Right-click the Theft Unexpected bin, and choose Paste.

   Premiere Pro places a copy of the clip in the Theft Unexpected bin.

   ● **Note:** When you make copies of clips, you are not making copies of the media files they are linked to. You can make as many copies as you like of a clip in your Premiere Pro project. Those copies will all link to the same original media file.

● **Note:** When you import an Adobe Photoshop file with multiple layers and choose to import as a sequence, Premiere Pro automatically creates a bin for the layers and their sequence.

▶ **Tip:** You can make Shift-click and Control-click (Windows) or Command-click (Mac OS) selections in the Project panel, just as you can with files on your hard drive.

Finding your media files

If you're not sure where a media file is on your hard drive, right-click the clip in the Project panel and choose Reveal in Explorer (Windows) or Reveal in Finder (Mac OS).

Premiere Pro will open the folder in your storage drive that contains the media file and highlight it. This can be useful if you are working with media files stored on multiple hard drives or if you have renamed your clips in Premiere Pro.

Changing bin views

Although there is a distinction between the Project panel and bins, they have the same controls and viewing options. For all intents and purposes, you can treat the Project panel as a bin; many Premiere Pro editors use the terms *bin* and *Project panel* interchangeably.

Bins have two views. You choose between them by clicking the List View button () or Icon View button ( ) at the bottom left of the Project panel.

- **List view**: This view displays your clips and bins as a list, with a significant amount of metadata displayed. You can scroll through the metadata and use it to sort clips by clicking column headers.

- **Icon view**: This view displays your clips and bins as thumbnails you can rearrange and play back.

The Project panel has a zoom control, next to the List View and Icon View buttons, which changes the size of the clip icons or thumbnails.

1 Double-click the Theft Unexpected bin to open it in its own floating panel.

2 Click the Icon View button on the Theft Unexpected bin to display thumbnails for the clips.

3 Try adjusting the zoom control.

Premiere Pro can display large thumbnails to make browsing and selecting your clips easier.

You can also apply various kinds of sorting to clip thumbnails in Icon view by clicking the Sort Icons ( ) menu.

4 Switch to List view.

● **Note:** You can also change the font size in the Project panel by clicking the panel menu and choosing Font Size. This is particularly useful if you are working on a high-resolution screen.

5 Try adjusting the Zoom control for the bin.

When you're in List view, it doesn't help that much to zoom, unless you turn on the display of thumbnails in this view.

6 Click the panel menu (next to the name on the panel tab), and choose Thumbnails.

Premiere Pro now displays thumbnails in List view, as well as in Icon view.

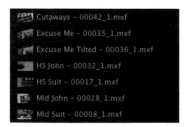

7 Try adjusting the Zoom control.

The clip thumbnails show the first frame of the media. In some clips, the first frame will not be particularly useful. Look at the clip HS Suit, for example. The thumbnail shows the clapperboard, but it would be useful to see the character.

8 Switch to Icon view.

In this view, you can hover the mouse cursor over clip thumbnails to preview clips.

9 Hover the mouse cursor over the HS Suit clip. Move the mouse until you find a frame that better represents the shot.

10 While the frame you have chosen is displayed, press the I key.

I is the keyboard shortcut for Mark In, a command that sets the beginning of a selection when choosing part of a clip that you intend to add to a sequence. The same selection also sets the poster frame for a clip in a bin.

11 Switch to List view.

Premiere Pro shows your newly selected frame as the thumbnail for this clip.

12 Use the panel menu (on the panel tab) to turn off thumbnails in List view.

13 Close the Theft Unexpected bin.

● **Note:** In addition to hovering the mouse cursor over a clip thumbnail, you can click to select the clip, which will reveal a small timeline control under the thumbnail. You can use this timeline to view the contents of the clip.

Creating Search bins

When using the Filter Bin Content box to display specific clips, you have the option to create a special kind of virtual bin, called a Search bin.

After typing in the Filter Bin Content box, click the Create New Search Bin button ( ).

You can rename search bins and place them in other bins.

Search bins appear in the Project panel automatically. They display the results of a search performed when using the Filter Bin Content box.

The contents of a Search bin will update dynamically, so if you add new clips to a project that meet the search criteria, they'll appear in the search bin automatically. This can be a fantastic time-saver when working with documentary material that changes over time as you obtain new footage.

▶ **Tip:** When you've finished using the Filter Bin Content box, be sure to click the X on the right side to clear the filter.

Assigning labels

Every item in the Project panel has a label color. In List view, the Label column shows the label color for every clip. When you add clips to a sequence, they are displayed in the Timeline panel with this label color.

Let's change the label color for a title.

1   Right-click Theft_Unexpected.png and choose Label > Forest.

You can change label colors for multiple clips in a single step by selecting them and then right-clicking the selected clips to choose another label color.

2   Press Control+Z (Windows) or Command+Z (Mac OS) to change the Theft_Unexpected.png label color back to Lavender.

When you add a clip to a sequence, Premiere Pro creates a new *instance*, or copy of that clip. You'll have one copy in the Project panel and one copy in the sequence.

By default, when you change the label color for a clip in the Project panel or rename a clip, it won't update copies of the clip in sequences.

You can change this by choosing File > Project Settings > General and enabling the option to display the project item name and label color for all instances.

Changing the available label colors

You can assign up to eight colors as labels to items in your project. There are also eight types of items that label colors can be assigned to, which means there aren't any spare label colors.

If you choose Edit > Preferences > Label Colors (Windows) or Premiere Pro > Preferences > Label Colors (Mac OS), you'll see the list of colors, each with a color swatch. You can click the color swatch to change the color.

If you select Label Defaults in the preferences, you can choose different default labels for each kind of item in your project

Changing names

Because clips in your project are separate from the media files they link to, you can rename items in Premiere Pro, and the names of your original media files on the hard drive are left untouched. This makes renaming clips safe to do—and it can be helpful when organizing a complex project.

1 Open the Graphics bin.

2 Right-click the clip Theft_Unexpected.png and choose Rename.

3 Change the name to **TU Title BW**.

4 Right-click the newly renamed clip, TU Title BW, and choose Reveal in Explorer (Windows) or Reveal in Finder (Mac OS).

The file is displayed. Notice that the original filename has not changed. It's helpful to be clear about the relationship between your original media files and the clips inside Premiere Pro because it explains much of the way the application works.

Customizing bins

When set to List view, the Project panel displays a number of clip information headings. You can easily add or remove headings. Depending on the clips you have and the types of metadata you are working with, you might want to display or hide some headings.

> **Tip:** To rename an item in the Project panel, you can also click the item name, wait a moment, and click again, or you can select the item and press Enter.

> **Note:** When you change the name of a clip in Premiere Pro, the new name is stored in the project file. Two project files could easily have different names representing the same clip. In fact, so could two copies of a clip in the same project.

1 Double-click to open the Theft Unexpected bin.

2 Click the panel menu, and choose Metadata Display.

The Metadata Display panel allows you to choose any kind of metadata to use as a heading in the List view of the Project panel (and any bins). All you have to do is select the check box for the kind of information you would like to be included.

3 Click the disclosure triangle for Premiere Pro Project Metadata to show those options.

4 Select the Media Type check box.

5 Click OK.

Media Type is now added as a heading for the Theft Unexpected bin only. You can apply the change to every bin in one step by using the panel menu in the Project panel, rather than in an individual bin.

Note: Several useful bin headings are displayed by default, including the Good check box. Select this box for clips you prefer, and then click the heading to sort selects from unwanted content.

Some headings are for information only, while others can be edited directly in the bin. The Scene heading, for example, allows you to add a scene number for each clip, while the Media Type heading gives information about the media and cannot be edited directly.

If you add information and press the Enter/Return key, Premiere Pro activates the same box for the next clip down. This way, you can use the keyboard to quickly enter information about several clips, jumping from one box to the next without using your mouse.

Having multiple bins open at once

Every bin panel behaves in the same way, with the same options, buttons, and settings. By default, when you double-click a bin, it opens in a floating panel.

You can change this in Preferences.

To change the options, choose Edit > Preferences > General (Windows) or Premiere Pro > Preferences > General (Mac OS).

The options allow you to choose what will happen when you double-click, double-click with the Control (Windows) or Command (Mac OS) key, or double-click with the Alt (Windows) or Option (Mac OS) key.

Monitoring footage

The greater part of video editing is spent watching clips and making creative choices about them. It's important to feel comfortable browsing media because you'll be doing a lot of it!

Premiere Pro has multiple ways to perform common tasks, such as playing video clips. You can use the keyboard, click buttons with your mouse, or use an external device like a jog/shuttle controller.

1 Double-click the Theft Unexpected bin to open it.

2 Click the Icon View button at the lower-left corner of the bin.

3 Hover your mouse (drag without clicking) across any of the images in the bin.

Premiere Pro displays the contents of the clip as you drag. The left edge of the thumbnail represents the beginning of the clip, and the right edge represents the end. In this way, the width of the thumbnail represents the whole clip.

4 Select a clip by clicking it once (be careful not to double-click, or the clip will open in the Source Monitor). Hover scrubbing is now turned off, and a mini playhead appears at the bottom of the thumbnail. Try dragging through the clip using the playhead.

▶ Tip: If you press the J or L key multiple times, Premiere Pro will play the video clips at multiple speeds.

When a clip is selected, you can use the J, K, and L keys on your keyboard to perform playback, just as you can in the Media Browser.

- **J**: Play backward

- **K**: Pause

- **L**: Play forward

5 Select a clip, and use the J, K, and L keys to play the video in the thumbnail.

When you double-click a clip, not only does Premiere Pro display the clip in the Source Monitor, but it adds it to a list of recent clips.

6 Double-click to open four or five clips from the Theft Unexpected bin in the Source Monitor.

▶ Tip: Notice that you have the option to close a single clip or close all clips, clearing the menu and the monitor. Some editors like to clear the menu and then open several clips that are part of a scene by selecting them in the bin and dragging them into the Source Monitor together. You can then use the Recent Items menu to browse only the clips from that selection.

7 Click the panel menu on the tab at the top of the Source Monitor to browse between your recent clips.

8 Click the Zoom menu at the bottom of the Source Monitor.

By default, this is set to Fit, which means Premiere Pro will display the whole frame, regardless of the original size. Change the setting to 100%.

These clips are high-resolution, and they are probably much bigger than your Source Monitor.

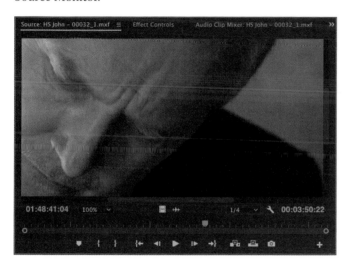

It's likely scroll bars have appeared at the bottom and on the right of your Source Monitor so you can view different parts of the image.

The benefit of viewing with Zoom set to 100% is that you see every pixel of the original video, which is useful for checking the quality.

9 Set the Zoom menu back to Fit.

Lowering the playback resolution

If you have an older or slower computer processor or are working with RAW media with large frame sizes, such as Ultra High-Definition (4K or above), your computer may struggle to play back all the frames of your video clips. Clips will play with the correct timing (so 10 seconds of video will still take 10 seconds), but some frames may not be displayed.

To work with a wide variety of computer hardware configurations, from powerful desktop workstations to lightweight portable laptops, Premiere Pro can lower the playback resolution to make playback smoother.

The default resolution is 1/2. You can switch the playback resolution as often as you like, using the Select Playback Resolution menu on the Source Monitor and Program Monitor panels.

Some lower resolutions are available only when working with particular media types.

Getting timecode information

At the bottom left of the Source Monitor, a timecode display shows the current position of the playhead in hours, minutes, seconds, and frames (00:00:00:00).

For example, 00:15:10:01 is 0 hours, 15 minutes, 10 seconds, and 1 frame.

Note that this is based on the original timecode for the clip, which probably does not begin at 00:00:00:00.

At the bottom right of the Source Monitor, a timecode display shows the duration of your clip. By default, this shows the whole clip duration, but later you'll add special marks to make a partial selection. When you do, that duration shown will change accordingly.

Displaying safe margins

Television monitors often crop the edges of the picture to achieve a clean edge. If you're producing video for a cathode ray tube (CRT) monitor, quite a lot of the image can be cropped. Click the Settings menu ( ) at the bottom of the Source Monitor and choose Safe Margins to display useful white outlines over the image.

The outer box is the action-safe zone. Aim to keep important action inside this box so that when the picture is displayed, edge cropping does not hide what's going on.

The inner box is the title-safe zone. Keep titles and graphics inside this box so that even on a badly adjusted display, your audience will be able to read the words.

Premiere Pro also has advanced overlay options that can be configured to display useful information in the Source Monitor and Program Monitor. To enable or disable overlays, go to the monitor Settings menu ( ) and choose Overlays.

You can access the specific settings for overlays and safe margins by clicking the monitor Settings menu and choosing Overlay Settings > Settings.

Click the Settings button at the bottom of the Source Monitor, and choose Safe Margins to hide them.

Using essential playback controls

Let's look at the playback controls.

1　Double-click the shot Excuse Me in the Theft Unexpected bin to open it in the Source Monitor.

2　At the bottom of the Source Monitor, you'll find a blue playhead marker. Drag it along the bottom of the panel to view different parts of the clip. You can also click wherever you want the playhead to go, and it will jump to that spot.

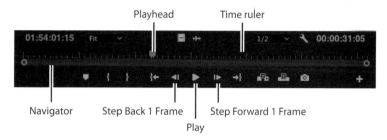

3　Below the time ruler and the playhead, there's a scroll bar that doubles as a Zoom control. Drag one end of the scroll bar to zoom in on the clip navigator.

4　Click the Play/Stop button to play the clip. Click it again to stop playback. You can also use the spacebar to play and stop playback.

▶ **Tip:** If you're not sure which button is which, hover the mouse cursor over each one to see the name and keyboard shortcut (in brackets).

5　Click the Step Back 1 Frame and Step Forward 1 Frame buttons to move through the clip one frame at a time. You can also use the Left Arrow and Right Arrow keys on your keyboard.

6　Try using the J, K, and L keys to play your clip.

● **Note:** Selection is important when using keyboard shortcuts. If you find the J, K, and L keys don't work, double-check the Source Monitor is selected, with a blue outline.

Customizing the monitors

To customize the way a monitor displays video, click the Settings menu (![icon]).

The Source Monitor and Program Monitor have similar options. You can view an audio waveform, which shows amplitude over time, and if your video has fields, you can choose which fields are shown.

Make sure Composite Video is selected in the Settings menu for now.

You can also switch between viewing the clip audio waveform and the video by clicking the Drag Video Only (![icon]) or Drag Audio Only (![icon]) icon. These icons are mainly used when editing clips into a sequence by dragging with the mouse but also provide this useful display shortcut.

You can change the buttons displayed at the bottom of the Source Monitor and Program Monitor.

1 Click the Button Editor (![icon]) at the bottom right of the Source Monitor.

A special set of buttons appears on a floating panel.

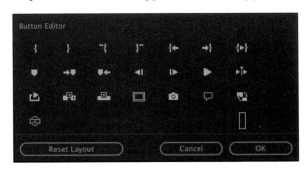

2 Drag the Loop button (![icon]) from the floating panel to a spot to the right of the Play button on the Source Monitor, and click OK.

3 Double-click the Excuse Me clip in the Theft Unexpected bin to open it in the Source Monitor if it isn't open already.

4 Click the new Loop button to enable it.

5 Click the Play button to play the clip. Play the video using the spacebar or the Play button on the Source Monitor. Stop the playback when you've seen the video start again.

With Loop turned on, Premiere Pro continuously repeats playback of a clip or sequence.

6 Click the Step Back 1 Frame and Step Forward 1 Frame buttons to move through the clip one frame at a time. You can also use the Left Arrow and Right Arrow keys on your keyboard.

Modifying clips

Premiere Pro uses metadata associated with clips to know how to play them back. This metadata is normally added correctly by the camera, but occasionally it might be wrong. You'll need to tell Premiere Pro how to interpret a clip.

You can change the interpretation of clips for one file or multiple files in a single step. All clips you have selected are affected by changes to interpretation.

Adjusting audio channels

Premiere Pro has advanced audio management features. You can create complex sound mixes and selectively target output audio channels with original clip audio. You can produce mono, stereo, 5.1, and even 32-channel sequences with precise control over the routing of audio channels.

If you're just starting out, you'll probably want to produce sequences mastered in stereo using mono or stereo source clips. In this case, the default settings are most likely what you need.

When recording audio with a professional camera, it's common to have one microphone record onto one audio channel and a different microphone record onto another audio channel. These are the same audio channels that would be used for regular stereo audio, but they now contain completely separate sound.

Your camera adds metadata to the audio to tell Premiere Pro whether the sound is meant to be mono (separate audio channels) or stereo (channel 1 audio and channel 2 audio combined to produce the complete stereo mix).

You can tell Premiere Pro how to interpret audio channels when new media files are imported by choosing Edit > Preferences > Audio > Default Audio Tracks (Windows) or Premiere Pro > Preferences > Audio > Default Audio Tracks (Mac OS).

If the setting was wrong when you imported your clips, it's easy to set a different way to interpret the audio channels in the Project panel.

1   Right-click the Reveal clip in the Theft Unexpected bin, and choose Modify >
    Audio Channels.

When the Preset menu is set to Use File, as it is here, Premiere Pro will use the file's metadata to set the channel format for the audio.

In this case, Clip Channel Format is set to stereo, and Number of Audio Clips is set to 1—that's the number of audio clips that will be added to a sequence if you edit this clip into it.

Now look at the channel matrix below those options:

The Left and Right audio channels of the source clip (described as Media Source Channel) are both assigned to a single clip (described as Clip 1).

When you add this clip to a sequence, it will appear as one video clip and one audio clip, with both audio channels in the same audio clip.

▶ **Tip:** Be sure to click the Preset menu and not the Clip Channel Format menu to correctly change this setting.

2 Click the Preset menu and change it to Mono.

Premiere Pro switches the Channel Format menu to Mono, so the Left and Right source channels are now linked to two separate clips.

This means that when you add the clip to a sequence, each audio channel will go on a separate track, as separate clips, allowing you to work on them independently.

3 Click OK.

Merging clips

It's common for video to be recorded on a camera with relatively low-quality audio, while high-quality sound is recorded on a separate device. When working this way, you'll want to combine the high-quality audio with the video by merging them in the Project panel.

The most important factor when merging video and audio files in this way is synchronization. You will either manually define a sync point—like a clapperboard mark—or allow Premiere Pro to sync your clips automatically based on their original timecode information or by matching up their audio.

A few tips on audio clip channel interpretation

Here are some things to keep in mind when working with audio clip channel interpretation:

- In the Modify Clip dialog box, every available audio channel will be listed. If your source audio has channels you don't need, you can deselect them.

- You can override the original file audio channel interpretation. This will mean a different type of audio track may be needed in a sequence.

- The list of clips on the left (which may be as short as one clip) shows how many audio clips will be added to a sequence when edited in.

- Use the check boxes to choose which source audio channels are included in each sequence audio clip. This means you can easily combine multiple source audio channels into a single sequence clip or separate them into different clips in any way that works for your project.

If you choose to sync clips using audio, Premiere Pro will analyze both the in-camera audio and the separately captured sound and match them up.

- If you don't have matching audio in the clips you are merging, you can manually add a marker. If you're adding a mark, place it on a clear sync point like a clapperboard.

- Select the camera clip and the separate audio clip, right-click either item, and choose Merge Clips.

- Under Synchronize Point, choose your sync point, and click OK.

A new clip is created that combines the video and the "good" audio in a single item.

Interpreting video footage

For Premiere Pro to play a clip correctly, it needs to know the frame rate for the video, the pixel aspect ratio (the shape of the pixels), and, if your clip is interlaced, the order in which to display the fields. Premiere Pro can find out this information from the file's metadata, but you can change the interpretation easily.

1 Import RED Video.R3D from the Lessons/Assets/Video and Audio Files/RED folder. Double-click the clip to open it in the Source Monitor. It's full anamorphic widescreen, which is too wide for this project.

2 Right-click the clip in the Project panel and choose Modify > Interpret Footage.

   The option to modify audio channels is unavailable because this clip has no audio.

3 Right now, the clip is set to use the pixel aspect ratio setting from the file: Anamorphic 2:1. This means the pixels are twice as wide as they are tall.

4 Use the Conform To menu to change the Pixel Aspect Ratio setting to DVCPRO HD (1.5). Then click OK.

From now on, Premiere Pro will interpret the clip as having pixels that are 1.5 times wider than they are tall. This reshapes the picture to make it standard 16:9 wide-screen. You can see the result in the Source Monitor.

This won't always work—in fact, it often introduces unwanted distortion—but it can provide a quick fix for mismatched media (a common problem for news editors), particularly if the image content is of natural environments without a frame of reference like a person in the shot.

Working with raw files

Premiere Pro has special settings for .R3D files created by RED cameras, .ari files created by ARRI cameras, and several others. These files are similar to the Camera RAW format used by professional digital single-lens reflex (DSLR) still cameras.

RAW files always have a layer of interpretation applied to them in order to view them. You can change the interpretation at any time without impacting playback performance. This means you can make changes, for example, to the colors in a shot without requiring any extra processing power. You could achieve a similar result using a special effect, but your computer would have to do more work to play the clip.

The Effect Controls panel gives access to controls for clips in sequences and in the Project panel. You also can use it to change the interpretation of RAW media files.

1 Double-click the RED Video.R3D clip to open it in the Source Monitor.

2 Using the panel tab, drag the Effect Controls panel over the Program Monitor so you can see both the Source Monitor and the Effect Controls panel at the same time.

Because the RED Video.R3D clip is displayed in the Source Monitor, the Effect Controls panel now shows the RED Source Settings options for that clip, which change the way the RAW media is interpreted.

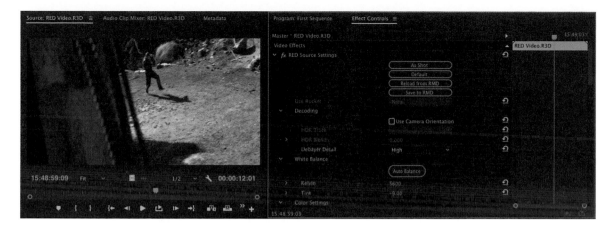

In many ways, this is a set of color adjustment controls, with automatic white balance and individual adjustments for the red, green, and blue values.

3   Scroll down to the end of the list, where you'll find Gain settings. Increase the Red gain to about 1.5. You can click the disclosure triangle to reveal a slider control, drag the blue number directly, or click and type over the number.

4   Take another look at the clip in the Source Monitor.

The picture has updated. If you had already edited this clip into a sequence, it would update in the sequence too.

For more information about working with RED media, go to http://helpx.adobe.com/premiere-pro/compatibility.html.

Different RAW media files will give different Source Settings options in the Effect Controls panel. There are many other ways to adjust the look of your video clips, and you'll be looking at some of the options in Lesson 14, "Improving Clips with Color Correction and Grading."

Review questions

1 How do you change the List view headings displayed in the Project panel?

2 How can you quickly filter the display of clips in the Project panel to make finding a clip easier?

3 How do you create a new bin?

4 If you change the name of a clip in the Project panel, does it change the name of the media file it links to on your hard drive?

5 What keyboard shortcuts can you use to play video and sound clips?

6 How can you change the way clip audio channels are interpreted?

Review answers

1 Click the panel menu for the Project panel, and choose Metadata Display. Select the check box for any heading you want to appear.

2 Click the Filter Bin Content box and start typing the name of the clip you are looking for. Premiere Pro hides clips that don't match what you typed and reveals those that do.

3 There are several ways to create a new bin: by clicking the New Bin button at the bottom of the Project panel, by choosing File > New > Bin, by right-clicking a blank area in the Project panel and choosing New Bin, or by pressing Control+B (Windows) or Command+B (Mac OS). You can also drag and drop clips onto the New Bin button on the Project panel.

4 No. You can duplicate, rename, or delete clips in your Project panel, and nothing will happen to your original media files.

5 The spacebar plays and stops. J, K, and L can be used like a shuttle controller to play backward and forward, and the arrow keys can be used to move one frame backward or one frame forward.

6 In the Project panel, right-click the clip you want to change and choose Modify > Audio Channels. Choose the correct option (usually by selecting a preset), and click OK.

5 MASTERING THE ESSENTIALS OF VIDEO EDITING

Lesson overview

In this lesson, you'll learn about the following:

- Working with clips in the Source Monitor

- Creating sequences

- Using essential editing commands

- Understanding tracks

This lesson will take approximately 60 minutes. This lesson will teach you the core editing skills you will use again and again when creating sequences with Adobe Premiere Pro CC.

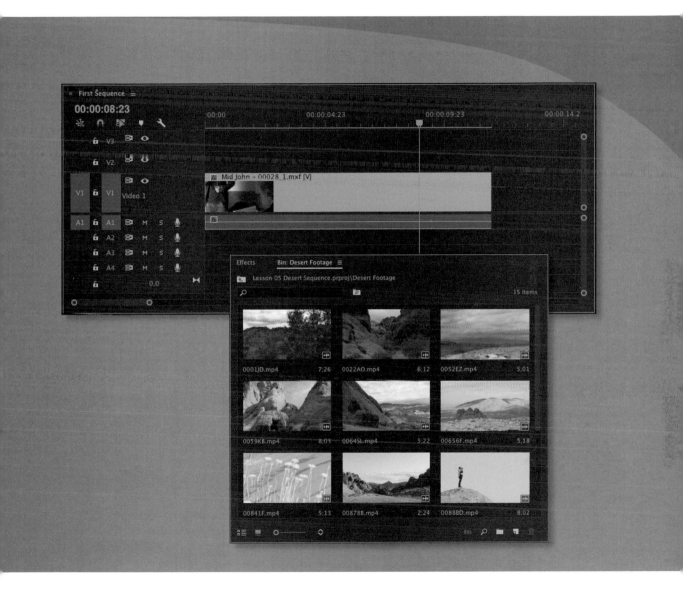

Editing is much more than choosing shots. You'll choose your cuts precisely, place clips in sequences at exactly the right point in time and on the tracks you want (to create layered visual effects), add new clips to existing sequences, and get rid of unwanted content.

Getting started

No matter how you approach video editing, you'll use a few simple techniques time and again. Most of the practice of video editing is making partial selections of your clips and placing them in your sequence. There are several ways of doing this in Premiere Pro.

Before you begin, make sure you're using the Editing workspace.

1 Open the Lesson 05.prproj project file from the Lesson 05 folder.

2 In the Workspaces panel, click Editing; then click the menu adjacent to the Editing option, and choose Reset to Saved Layout.

3 Choose File > Save As.

4 Rename the file **Lesson 05.prproj.**

5 Choose a preferred location on your hard drive, and click Save to save the project.

You'll begin by learning more about the Source Monitor and how to mark your clips to get them ready to be added to a sequence. Then you'll learn about the Timeline, where you'll work on your sequences.

Using the Source Monitor

The Source Monitor is the main place you'll go when you want to check your assets before including them in a sequence.

Note: Change clip interpretation by right-clicking it in the Project panel and choosing Modify > Interpret Footage.

When you view video clips in the Source Monitor, you watch them in their original format. They will play back with their frame rate, frame size, field order, audio sample rate, and audio bit depth exactly as they were recorded, unless you have changed the way the clip is interpreted.

However, when you add a clip to a sequence, Premiere Pro conforms it to the sequence settings. For example, if the clip and the sequence don't match, the clip frame rate and audio sample rate will be adjusted so that all the clips in the sequence play back the same way.

As well as being a viewer for multiple file types, the Source Monitor provides important additional functions. You can use two special kinds of markers, called *In marks* and *Out marks*, to select part of a clip for inclusion in a sequence. You can also add comments in the form of markers that you can refer to later or use to remind yourself about important facts relating to a clip. You might include a note about part of a shot you don't have permission to use, for example.

Loading a clip

To load a clip, do the following:

1   In the Project panel, browse to the Theft Unexpected bin. With the default preferences, double-click the bin in the Project panel while holding the Control (Windows) or Command (Mac OS) key to open the bin in the existing panel. To navigate back to the Project panel contents, click the Navigate Up button ( ).

2   Double-click a video clip, or drag a clip into the Source Monitor.

> **Tip:** When selecting clips, be sure to click the icon or thumbnail, rather than the name, to avoid accidentally renaming it.

Either way, the result is the same: Premiere Pro displays the clip in the Source Monitor, ready for you to watch it and add markers.

3   Position your mouse pointer so that it is over the Source Monitor and press the ` (grave) key. The panel fills the Premiere Pro application frame, giving you a larger view of your video clip. Press the ` (grave) key again to restore the Source Monitor to its original size. If your keyboard does not have a ` (grave) key, you can go to the panel menu and choose Panel Group Settings > Maximize Panel Group.

> **Tip:** Notice that active panels have a blue outline. It's important to know which panel is active because menus and keyboard shortcuts sometimes give different results depending on your current selection. For example, if you press Shift+` (grave), the currently selected frame will toggle to full-screen, regardless of the location of your mouse.

Viewing video on a second monitor

If you have a second monitor connected to your computer, Premiere Pro can use it to display full-screen video.

Choose Edit > Preferences > Playback (Windows) or Premiere Pro > Preferences > Playback (Mac OS), make sure Mercury Transmit is enabled, and select the check box for the monitor you want to use for full-screen playback.

You also have the option of playing video via a DV device, if you have one connected, or via third-party hardware

Loading multiple clips

Next, you'll create a selection of clips to work with in the Source Monitor.

1   Click the Source Monitor panel menu (on the panel tab), and choose Close All. This clears the monitor and also clears the list of recent items shown on the menu.

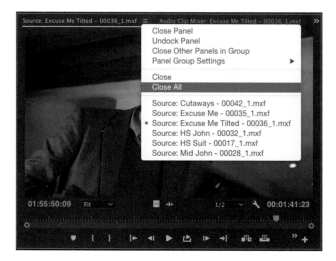

2   Click the List View button on the Theft Unexpected bin, and make sure the clips are displayed in alphabetical order by clicking the Name heading.

3   Select the first clip, Cutaways, and then hold down the Shift key and click the clip Mid John.

    This makes a selection of multiple clips in the bin.

4   Drag the clips from the bin to the Source Monitor.

    Now just the clips selected will be displayed in the Source Monitor panel menu. You can use the menu to choose which clip to view.

Using Source Monitor controls

As well as playback controls, there are some important additional buttons in the Source Monitor.

- **Add Marker**: This adds a marker to the clip at the location of the playhead. Markers can provide a simple visual reference or store comments.

- **Mark In**: This sets the beginning of the part of the clip you intend to use in a sequence. You can have only one In mark per clip or sequence. A new In mark will automatically replace an existing one.

- **Mark Out**: This sets the end of the part of the clip you intend to use in a sequence. You can have only one Out mark. A new Out mark will automatically replace an existing one.

- **Go to In**: This moves the playhead to the clip In mark.

- **Go to Out**: This moves the playhead to the clip Out mark.

- **Insert**: This adds the clip to the sequence currently displayed in the Timeline using the insert edit method (see "Using essential editing commands" later in this lesson).

- **Overwrite**: This adds the clip to the sequence currently displayed in the Timeline using the overwrite edit method (see "Using essential editing commands" later in this lesson).

- **Export Frame**: This allows you to create a still image from whatever is displayed in the monitor. See Lesson 18, "Exporting Frames, Clips, and Sequences," for more on this.

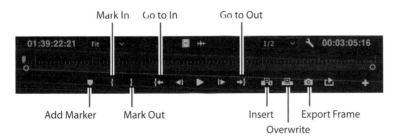

Selecting a range in a clip

You will usually want to include only a specific part of a clip in a sequence. Much of an editor's time is spent watching video clips and choosing not only which ones to use but also which parts to use. Making a selection is easy.

1 Use the Source Monitor panel menu to select the clip Excuse Me (not Excuse Me Tilted). It's a shot of John nervously asking whether he can sit down.

2 Play the clip to get an idea of the action.

John walks onscreen about halfway through the shot but takes a moment to speak.

3 Position the playhead just before John enters the shot or just before he speaks. Around 01:54:06:00, he pauses briefly and speaks. Note that the timecode reference is based on the original recording and does not start at 00:00:00:00.

4 Click the Mark In button. You can also press the I key on your keyboard.

Premiere Pro highlights the section of the clip that is selected. You have excluded the first part of the clip, but you'll be able to reclaim this part later if you need to do so—that's the wonderful freedom of nonlinear editing.

▶ **Tip:** If your keyboard has a separate numerical keypad, you can use it to enter timecode numbers directly. For example, if you type 700, Premiere Pro will position the playhead at 00:00:07:00. There's no need to enter the leading zeros or number separators. Be sure to use the numerical keypad, on the right on your keyboard, and not the numbers along the top of your keyboard (these have a different use).

5 Position the playhead just as John sits down. Around 01:54:14:00 is perfect.

6 Press the O key on your keyboard to add an Out point.

Now you'll add In and Out marks for the following two clips.

● **Note:** Some editors prefer to go through all available clips, adding In and Out marks as required, before building a sequence. Some editors prefer to add In and Out marks only as they use each clip. Your preference may depend on the kind of project you are working on.

● **Note:** In and Out marks added to clips are persistent. That is, they will still be present if you close and open the clip again.

7 For the HS Suit clip, add an In point just after John's line, about a quarter of the way into the shot (01:27:00:16).

8 Add an Out point just as the screen goes dark (01:27:02:14).

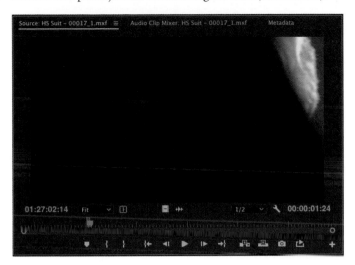

9 For the Mid John clip, add an In point just as John begins to sit down (01:39:52:00).

10 Add an Out point after he has a sip of tea (01:40:04:00).

▶ **Tip:** To help you find your way around your footage, Premiere Pro can display timecode numbers on the time ruler. Toggle this option on and off by clicking the Settings button (🔧) and choosing Time Ruler Numbers.

▶ **Tip:** The tool tip that pops up if you hover your mouse over a button tells you the keyboard shortcut key in brackets after the name of the button.

Creating subclips

If you have a long clip, you might want to use several parts in your sequence. It can be useful to separate the parts so they can be organized prior to building your sequence.

This is exactly why subclips were created. Subclips are partial copies of clips. They are commonly used when working with long clips, especially when there are several parts of the same original clip that might be used in a sequence.

Subclips have a few notable characteristics.

- They can be organized in bins, just like regular clips, though they have a different icon ( ) in the Project panel List view.

- They have a limited duration based on the In and Out marks used to create them, which makes it easier to view their contents when compared with viewing potentially much longer original clips.

- They share the same media files as the original clip they're based on.

- They can be edited to change their contents and even converted into a copy of the original full-length clip.

Let's make a subclip.

1 Double-click the Cutaways clip in the Theft Unexpected bin to view it in the Source Monitor.

2 While viewing the contents of the Theft Unexpected bin, click the New Bin button at the bottom of the panel to create a new bin. The new bin will appear in the existing Theft Unexpected bin.

3 Name the bin **Subclips** and open it to see the contents. Hold the Control (Windows) or Command (Mac OS) key while double-clicking the new Subclips bin to have it open in the same frame, rather than floating as an independent frame.

4 Choose a section of the clip to make into a subclip by marking the clip with an In point and an Out point. The moment roughly halfway through when the packet is removed and replaced might work well.

5 To create a subclip from the selection between your In and Out marks, do one of the following:

- Right-click in the picture display of the Source Monitor and choose Make Subclip. Name the subclip **Packet Moved** and click OK.

- With the Source Monitor active, click the Clip menu and choose Make Subclip. Name the subclip **Packet Moved** and click OK.

- With the Source Monitor active, press Control+U (Windows) or Command+U (Mac OS). Name the subclip **Packet Moved** and click OK.

- While holding the Control (Windows) or Command (Mac OS) key, drag the picture from the Source Monitor into the Project panel bin. Name the subclip **Packet Moved** and click OK.

● **Note:** If you select Restrict Trims To Subclip Boundaries, you won't be able to access the parts of your clip that are outside your selection when viewing the subclip. This might be exactly what you want (and you can change this setting by right-clicking the subclip in the bin and choosing Edit Subclip).

The new subclip is added to the Subclips bin, with the duration you specified with your In and Out marks.

Navigating the Timeline

The Timeline panel is your creative canvas. In this panel, you'll add clips to your sequences, make editorial changes to them, add visual and audio special effects, mix soundtracks, and add titles and graphics.

Here are a few facts about the Timeline:

- You view and edit sequences in the Timeline.

- You can open multiple sequences at the same time, with each displayed in its own Timeline panel.

- The terms *sequence* and *Timeline* are often used interchangeably, as in "in the sequence" or "on the Timeline."

- You can add any number of video tracks, limited only by your system's resources. Upper video tracks play "in front" of lower ones, so you would normally place graphics clips on tracks above background video clips.

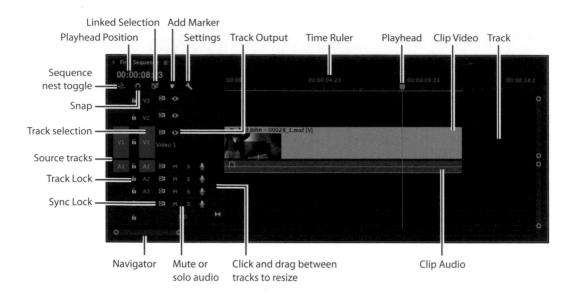

Playhead Position · Linked Selection · Add Marker · Settings · Track Output · Time Ruler · Playhead · Clip Video · Track

Sequence nest toggle

Snap

Track selection

Source tracks

Track Lock

Sync Lock

Navigator · Mute or solo audio · Click and drag between tracks to resize · Clip Audio

- You can also add any number of audio tracks that all play at the same time to create an audio mix. Audio tracks can be mono (1 channel), stereo (2 channels), 5.1 (6 channels), or adaptive—with up to 32 channels.

- You can change the height of Timeline tracks to gain access to additional controls and thumbnails on your video clips.

- Each track has a set of controls, shown on a track header on the far left, that change the way it functions.

- Time always moves from left to right on the Timeline, so when you play a sequence, the playhead will move in that direction.

- The Program Monitor shows you the contents of the currently displayed sequence at the position of the playhead.

- For most operations on the Timeline, you will use the standard Selection tool. There are several other tools that serve different purposes, and each tool has a keyboard shortcut. If in doubt, press the V key—this is the keyboard shortcut for the Selection tool.

- Zoom in and out of the Timeline using the (equals) = and (minus) – keys (at the top of your keyboard) to get a better view of your clips. Use the (backslash) \ key, if you have one, to toggle the zoom level between your current setting and show your whole sequence. You can also double-click the navigator at the bottom of the Timeline to view the whole timeline.

What is a sequence?

A *sequence* is a series of clips that play, one after another—sometimes with multiple blended layers and often with special effects, titles, and audio—making a complete film.

You can have as many sequences as you like in a project. Sequences are stored in the Project panel, just like clips, and have their own icon.

Let's make a new sequence for the Theft Unexpected drama.

1 In the Theft Unexpected bin, drag the clip Excuse Me (not Excuse Me Tilted) onto the New Item button at the bottom of the panel.

   This is a shortcut to make a sequence that perfectly matches your media.

   Premiere Pro creates a new sequence, which shares the name of the clip you selected.

● **Note:** You may need to click the Navigate Up button to see the Theft Unexpected bin.

2 The sequence is highlighted in the bin, and it would be a good idea to rename it right away. Right-click the sequence in the bin and choose Rename. Name the sequence **Theft Unexpected**.

The sequence is automatically open, and it contains the clip you used to create it. This works for our purposes, but if you had used a random clip to perform this shortcut, you might choose to select it in the sequence and delete it now (by pressing the Delete or Backspace key).

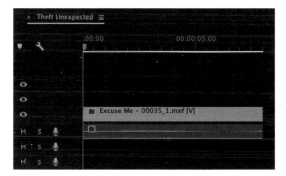

Close the sequence by clicking the X on its name tab in the Timeline.

Opening a sequence in the Timeline panel

To open a sequence in the Timeline, do one of the following:

*   Double-click the sequence in a bin.

*   Right-click the sequence in a bin and choose Open in Timeline.

Open the Theft Unexpected sequence you just created.

▶ **Tip:** You can also drag a sequence into the Source Monitor to use it as if it were a clip. Be careful not to drag a sequence into the Timeline to open it because this will add it to your current sequence.

Conforming

Sequences have a frame rate, a frame size, and an audio mastering format (mono or stereo, for example). They *conform*, or adjust, any clips you add to match these settings.

You can choose whether clips should be scaled visually to match your sequence frame size. For example, for a sequence with a frame size of 1920x1080 (regular high-definition) and a video clip that is 4096x2160 (Cinema 4K), you might decide to automatically scale the high-resolution clip down to match your sequence resolution or leave it as it is, viewing only part of the picture through the reduced "window" of the sequence.

When clips are scaled, the vertical and horizontal sizes are scaled equally to keep the original aspect ratio. If a clip has a different aspect ratio from your sequence, it may not completely fill the frame of your sequence when it is scaled. For example, if your clip had a 4:3 aspect ratio and you added it, scaled, to a 16:9 sequence, you'd see gaps at the sides.

Using Motion controls in the Effect Controls panel (see Lesson 9, "Putting Clips in Motion"), you can animate which part of the picture you see. You can even create a dynamic pan-and-scan effect inside the picture

Understanding tracks

Much as railway tracks keep trains in line, sequences have video and audio tracks that constrain the positions of clips you add to them. The simplest form of sequence would have just one video track and perhaps one audio track. You add clips to tracks, one after another, from left to right, and they play in the order you place them.

Sequences can have additional video and audio tracks. They become layers of video and additional audio channels. Since higher video tracks appear in front of lower ones, you can combine clips on different tracks to produce layered compositions.

For example, you might use an upper video track to add titles to a sequence or to blend multiple layers of video using visual effects.

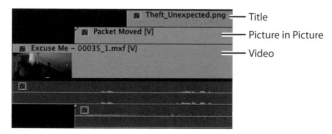

You might use multiple audio tracks to create a complete audio composition for your sequence, with original source dialogue, music, spot audio effects such as gunshots or fireworks, atmospheric sound, and voice-over.

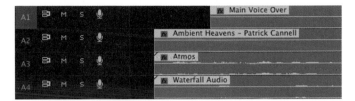

Premiere Pro has multiple scrolling options, giving you different results depending on the location of your cursor.

- If you hover your mouse pointer over the Source Monitor or Program Monitor, you can navigate earlier or later using the scroll wheel; trackpad gestures work too.

- You can navigate sequences in the Timeline panel this way if you enable Horizontal Timeline Mouse Scrolling in the General Premiere Pro preferences.

- If you hold the Alt key while scrolling with your mouse, the Timeline view will zoom in or out.

- If you hover your mouse over a track header and scroll, you'll increase or decrease the height of the track.

- If you hover your mouse over a video or audio track header and scroll while holding the Shift key, you'll increase or decrease the height of all tracks of that type.

▶ **Tip:** If you hold the Control (Windows) or Command (Mac OS) key while you scroll to adjust track height, you'll have finer control.

Targeting tracks

Track headers are more than nameplates. They also act as enable/disable buttons for the tracks when making selections to remove parts of a sequence or when rendering effects.

To the left of the track headers, you'll see a set of buttons that represent the available tracks for the clip currently displayed in the Source Monitor or selected in the Project panel. These are the source track indicators, and they are numbered, just like the Timeline tracks. This helps keep things clear when performing more complex edits.

If you drag and drop a clip into a sequence, the position of the source track indicators is ignored. However, when you use a keyboard shortcut or the buttons on the Source Monitor to add a clip to a sequence, source track indicators become important. The position of the source track indicators sets the track a new clip will be added to.

Source tracks

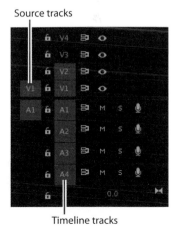

Timeline tracks

In the following example, the position of the source track indicators means a clip with one video track and one audio track would be added to the Video 1 and Audio 1 tracks on the Timeline when using buttons or a keyboard shortcut to add a clip to the current sequence.

In the following example, the source track indicators have been moved by dragging them to a new position relative to the timeline track indicators. In this example, the clip would be added to the Video 2 and Audio 2 tracks on the Timeline when using buttons or a keyboard shortcut to add a clip to the current sequence.

Click a source track indicator to enable it or disable it. A blue highlight indicates a track is enabled. You can make advanced edits by dragging the source track indicators to different tracks and selecting which tracks you have on or off.

● **Note:** Remember, Timeline track indicators matter when rendering effects or making Timeline selections, but they don't affect adding clips to a sequence; only the source track indicators do.

Using In and Out marks

The In and Out marks used in the Source Monitor define the part of a clip you will add to a sequence.

The In and Out marks you use on the Timeline have two primary purposes.

- To tell Premiere Pro where a new clip should be positioned when it is added to a sequence.

- To select parts of a sequence you would like to remove. You can make precise selections to remove whole clips, or parts of clips, from specific tracks by using In and Out marks in combination with the track header controls.

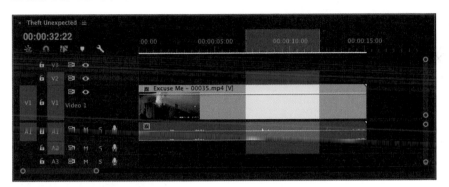

The light region indicates the selected part of the sequence, defined by an In mark and an Out mark.

Setting In and Out marks

Adding In and Out marks on the Timeline is almost the same as adding them in the Source Monitor.

One key difference is that unlike the controls in the Source Monitor, the controls on the Program Monitor also apply to the Timeline.

To add an In point to the Timeline at the current position of the playhead, make sure the Timeline panel or Program Monitor is active and then press the I key or click the Mark In button on the Program Monitor.

To add an Out point to the Timeline at the current position of the playhead, make sure the Timeline panel or Program Monitor is active and then press the O key or click the Mark Out button on the Program Monitor.

Clearing In and Out marks

If you open a clip that already has In and Out marks and you want to remove them (or there are In and Out marks on the Timeline that are cluttering up your view), it's easy to remove them. You'll use the same technique to remove In and Out marks on the Timeline, in the Program Monitor, and in the Source Monitor.

1 On the Timeline, select the Excuse Me clip by clicking it once.

2 Press the (forwardslash) / key. This adds an In mark to the Timeline at the start of the clip (on the left) and an Out mark at the end of the clip (on the right). Both are added to the time ruler at the top of the Timeline.

▶ **Tip:** If you have a (forwardslash) / key, you can use it to add In and Out marks to the Timeline based on clip segments you have selected.

3 Right-click the time ruler at the top of the Timeline, and take a look at the menu options.

Select the option you need in this menu, or use one of the following keyboard shortcuts:

- **Control+Shift+I (Windows) or Alt+I (Mac OS)**: Remove In Mark (Clear In)

- **Control+Shift+O (Windows) or Alt+O (Mac OS)**: Remove Out Mark (Clear Out)

 • **Control+Shift+X (Windows) or Alt+X (Mac OS)**: Remove In Mark and Out Mark (Clear In and Out)

4 That last option is particularly useful. It's easy to remember and quickly removes both marks. Try it now to remove the marks you added.

Using time rulers

The time rulers at the bottom of the Source Monitor and Program Monitor, and at the top of the Timeline, all serve the same purpose: They allow you to navigate through your clips or sequences in time.

Time goes from left to right in Premiere Pro, and the location of the playhead gives you a visual reference in relation to your clips.

Click the Timeline time ruler now (that's the time markings along the top of the panel), and drag left and right. The playhead moves to follow your mouse. As you drag across the Excuse Me clip, you see the contents of the clip in the Program Monitor. Dragging through your content in this way is called *scrubbing*.

Notice that the Source Monitor, Program Monitor, and Timeline all have navigation bars at the bottom of the panel. You can zoom the time ruler by hovering over the navigation bar and using your mouse wheel to scroll. Once you have zoomed in, you can move through the time ruler by clicking and dragging the navigator.

The Program Monitor navigator—drag the ends for precise zoom control on the time ruler.

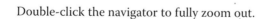

Double-click the navigator to fully zoom out.

Customizing track headers

Just as you can customize the Source Monitor and Program Monitor controls, you can change many of the options on the Timeline track headers.

To access the options, right-click a video or audio track header and choose Customize, or click the Timeline Settings menu ( ) and choose Customize Video Header or Customize Audio Header.

The video track Button Editor

The audio track Button Editor

To find out the name of an available button, hover your mouse over it to see the tool tip. Some of the buttons will be familiar to you already; others will be explained in later lessons.

To add a button to a track header, drag it from the Button Editor onto a track header. You can remove a button from a track header by dragging it away.

All track headers update to match the one you adjust.

Experiment with this feature, and when you have finished, click the Reset Layout button on the Button Editor to return the track header to the default options.

Finally, click Cancel to leave the Button Editor.

Using essential editing commands

Whether you use the mouse to drag a clip into a sequence, use a button on the Source Monitor, or use a keyboard shortcut, you'll apply one of two kinds of edits: an insert edit or an overwrite edit.

When a sequence has existing clips at the location where you want to add a new clip, these two choices—insert and overwrite—will produce markedly different results.

Overwrite edit

Continue working on the Theft Unexpected sequence. So far, you have just one clip, in which John asks if a seat is free.

First, you'll use an overwrite edit to add a reaction shot to John's request for a chair.

1   Open the shot HS Suit in the Source Monitor. You added In and Out marks to this clip earlier.

2   You'll need to set up the Timeline carefully for this edit. It may seem like a slow process when you first learn to use the Timeline, but after practice you'll find editing is fast and easy.

Position the Timeline playhead just after John makes his request. Around 00:00:04:00 is perfect.

Unless an In or Out mark has been added to the Timeline, the playhead is used to position new clips when editing with the keyboard or onscreen buttons. When you use the mouse to drag a clip into a sequence, the location of the playhead and existing In or Out marks are ignored.

● **Note:** The terms *shot* and *clip* are often used interchangeably.

3 Though the new clip has an audio track, you don't need it. You'll keep the audio that is already in the Timeline. Click the source track selection button A1 to turn it off. The button should be gray rather than blue.

4 Check that your track headers look like the following example (check the track enable/disable buttons carefully). Only the A1 and V1 timeline track selection buttons matter for this edit because the other tracks don't have any clips on them, so don't worry about their settings.

5 Click the Overwrite button ( ) on the Source Monitor.

● **Note:** The sequence will not get any longer when you perform an overwrite edit.

The clip is added to the Timeline, on the Video 1 track. The timing might not be perfect, but you're now editing dialogue!

By default, when you drag and drop a clip into a sequence using the mouse, you'll perform an overwrite edit. You can perform an insert edit by holding down the Control (Windows) or Command (Mac OS) key while you drag and drop.

Insert edit

To perform an insert edit in the Premiere Pro Timeline, do the following:

1 Drag the Timeline playhead so it is positioned over the Excuse Me clip just after John says, "Excuse me" (around 00:00:02:16).

2 Open the clip Mid Suit in the Source Monitor, add an In mark at 01:15:46:00, and add an Out mark at 01:15:48:00. This is actually from a different part of the action, but it will work well as a reaction shot.

3 Check that your Timeline has the source track indicators lined up as in the following example.

▶ **Tip:** It's important to be aware of what your audience will know or not know. You can often use footage from different times or spaces without your audience realizing.

4 Click the Insert button (⊞) on the Source Monitor.

Congratulations! You have completed an insert edit. The clip Excuse Me, already in the sequence, has been split, with the part after the playhead moved later to make space for the new clip.

5 Position the playhead at the beginning of the sequence and play through your edit. You can use the Home key on your keyboard to jump to the beginning; you can drag the playhead with the mouse; or you can press the Up Arrow key to jump the playhead to earlier edits (the Down Arrow key jumps to later edits).

6 Now open the Mid John clip in the Source Monitor. You added In and Out marks to this clip earlier.

7 Position the Timeline playhead at the end of the sequence—on the end of the Excuse Me clip. You can hold the Shift key to have the playhead snap to the ends of clips.

8 Click either the Insert or Overwrite button on the Source Monitor. Since the Timeline playhead is at the end of the sequence, there are no clips in the way, and it makes no difference which kind of edit you perform.

Now you'll insert one more clip.

9 Position the Timeline playhead just before John takes a sip of tea, around 00:00:14:00.

10 Open the clip Mid Suit in the Source Monitor and use In and Out marks to choose a part you think would go well between John sitting down and his first sip of tea. An In mark around 01:15:55:00 and an Out mark around 01:16:00:00 might work well.

● **Note:** When you apply an insert edit, it makes your sequence longer: The clips already on the selected track will move later in the sequence to make room for the new clip.

● **Note:** The words *sequence* and *edit* are often used interchangeably.

● **Note:** If you have an In mark or an Out mark on the Timeline, Premiere Pro will use it in preference to the location of the playhead when performing an edit.

Note: You can also edit clips into a sequence by dragging from the Project panel or Source Monitor into the Program Monitor. Hold the Control (Windows) or Command (Mac OS) key to perform an insert edit.

11 Edit the clip into the sequence using an insert edit.

The timing of the edit may not be perfect, but that's OK; you can change your mind about the timing later. The important thing, to begin with, is to get the order of the clips right.

Three-point editing

To perform an edit, Premiere Pro needs to know the clip duration you'll work with, in both the Source Monitor and the Timeline. If, for example, you choose 4 seconds of a clip in the Source Monitor, Premiere Pro automatically knows it will take 4 seconds of time in your sequence. This means the duration of one can be worked out from the other, so you need only three marks (often called *points*), not four.

When you made your last edit, Premiere Pro aligned the In mark from the clip (the start of the clip) with the In mark on the Timeline (the playhead).

Even though you didn't manually add an In mark to the Timeline, you're still performing a three-point edit, with the duration calculated from the Source Monitor clip.

If you do add an In mark to the Timeline, Premiere Pro uses that to place the new clip, ignoring the playhead.

You can achieve a similar result by adding an Out mark to the Timeline instead of an In mark. In this case, Premiere Pro will align the Out mark of the clip with the Out mark on the Timeline when you perform the edit. You might choose to do this if you have a piece of timed action, like a door closing at the end of a clip in the sequence, and your new clip needs to line up in time with it.

What happens if you use four marks?

You can use four marks to make an edit: both an In and Out mark in the Source Monitor and an In and Out mark on the Timeline. If the clip duration you select matches the sequence duration, the edit will take place as usual. If they're different, Premiere Pro will invite you to choose what you would like to happen.

You can stretch or compress the playback speed of the new clip to fit the selected duration on the Timeline or selectively ignore one of your In or Out marks.

Storyboard editing

The term *storyboard* usually describes a series of drawings that show the intended camera angles and action for a film. Storyboards are often quite similar to comic strips, though they usually include technical information, such as intended camera moves, lines of dialogue, and sound effects.

You can use clip thumbnails in a bin as storyboard images. Drag the thumbnails to arrange them in the order you would like the clips to appear in your sequence, from left to right and from top to bottom. Then drag and drop them into your sequence, or use a special automated edit feature to add them to your sequence with transition effects.

Using a storyboard to build a rough cut

An assembly edit is a sequence in which the order of the clips is correct but the timing has yet to be worked out. It's common to build sequences as an assembly first, just to make sure the structure works, and then adjust the timing later.

You can use storyboard editing to quickly get your clips in the right order.

1   Save the current project.

2   Open Lesson 05 Desert Sequence.prproj in the Lessons/Lesson 05 folder.

This project has a Desert Montage sequence that already has music. You'll add some beautiful shots.

The audio track A1 has been locked (click the padlock icon to lock and unlock a track). This means you can make adjustments to the sequence without risking making changes to the music track.

Arranging your storyboard

Double-click the Desert Footage bin to open it. There are beautiful shots in this bin.

1   If necessary, click the Icon View button (![icon]) on the bin to see thumbnails for the clips.

● **Note:** Premiere Pro has the option to sort clips in Icon view based on a number of criteria. Click the Sort Icons button (![icon]) for the options. Set the menu to User Order to be able to drag and drop the clips into a new order.

2   Drag the thumbnails in the bin to position them in the order in which you want them to appear in the sequence.

3   Make sure the Desert Footage bin is selected (with a blue outline). Select all the clips in the bin by pressing Control+A (Windows) or Command+A (Mac OS).

4   Drag the clips into the sequence, positioning them on the Video 1 track right at the beginning of the Timeline, above the music clip.

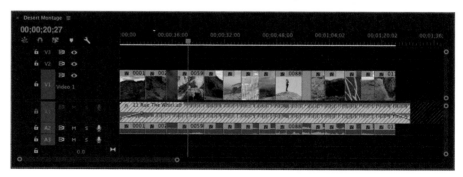

5   Play your sequence to see the result.

Setting the duration for still images

These video clips already have In and Out marks. These In and Out marks are used automatically when you're adding the clips to your sequence, even when adding them directly from the bin.

Graphics and photos can have any duration in a sequence. However, they have a default duration that is set as you import them. The default duration can be changed in Premiere Pro Preferences.

Choose Edit > Preferences > General (Windows) or Premiere Pro > Preferences > General (Mac OS) to change the duration in the Still Image Default Duration box. The change you make applies to clips only when you import them. It does not affect clips that are already in the project.

Still images also have no *timebase*, that is, the number of frames that should play each second. You can set the default timebase for still images by choosing Edit > Preferences > Media (Windows) or Premiere Pro > Preferences > Media (Mac OS) and setting an option for Indeterminate Media Timebase.

Automating your storyboard to a sequence

In addition to dragging and dropping your storyboard edit into the Timeline, you can use the Automate To Sequence option.

1   Undo your edit by pressing Control+Z (Windows) or Command+Z (Mac OS), and position your Timeline playhead at the beginning of the Timeline.

2   In the Desert Footage bin, with all the clips still selected, click the Automate To Sequence button ( ).

Automate To Sequence, as the name suggests, automatically adds your clips to the currently displayed sequence, starting at the position of the Timeline play-head. Here are the options:

- **Ordering**: This positions clips in your sequence in the order in which they appear in the bin or in the order in which you clicked to select them.

- **Placement**: By default, the clips will be added one after another. If you have markers on the Timeline (perhaps in time with the beat of your music), you can add clips wherever there is a marker.

- **Method**: Choose between Insert and Overwrite, which is significant only if there are other clips already on the timeline.

- **Clip Overlap**: This automatically overlaps the clips to allow for a transition effect, like a cross dissolve.

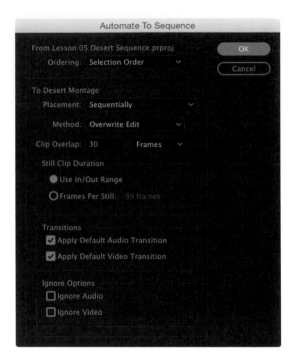

- **Still Clip Duration**: This allows you to choose a duration for all still images in this dialog box or to set individual durations using In and Out marks in the Source Monitor.

- **Transitions**: Choose to have a video or audio transition automatically added between each clip.

- **Ignore Options**: Choose to exclude the video or audio parts of your clips.

3 Set up the Automate To Sequence dialog box so that the settings match the previous example, and click OK.

This time, the clips overlap, and have a cross-dissolve transition effect between them. The overlap used to create the transition effect reduces the total duration of the sequence.

Review questions

1 What do In and Out marks do?

2 Is the Video 2 track in front of the Video 1 track or behind it?

3 How do subclips help you stay organized?

4 How would you select a sequence time range to work with?

5 What is the difference between an overwrite edit and an insert edit?

6 How much of your source clip will be added to a sequence if the source clip has no In or Out marks and there are no In or Out marks in the sequence?

Review answers

1 In the Source Monitor and in the Project panel, In and Out marks define the part of a clip you would like to use in a sequence. On the Timeline, In and Out marks are used to define parts of your sequence you would like to remove, edit, render, or export. They can also be used to define parts of your sequence you would like to render when working with effects and used to define parts of your Timeline you would like to export to create a video file.

2 Upper video tracks are always in front of lower ones.

3 Though subclips make little difference to the way Premiere Pro plays back video and sound, they make it easier for you to divide your footage into different bins. For larger projects with lots of longer clips, it can make a big difference to be able to divide content this way.

4 You'll use In and Out marks to define parts of your sequence you would like to work with. For example, you might render when working with effects or export parts of your sequence to export as a file. You also have the option to enable a Timeline Work Area Bar that you can position to make sequence time range selections. Enable the Work Area by going to the Timeline menu and choosing Work Area Bar. The bar appears at the top of the Timeline and replaces the In mark and Out mark when rendering or exporting.

5 Clips added to a sequence using an overwrite edit replace any content already in the sequence where they are placed. Clips added to a sequence using an insert edit displace existing clips, pushing them later (to the right) and making the sequence longer.

6 If you don't add In or Out marks to your source clip, the entire clip will be added the sequence. Setting an In mark, an Out mark, or both, will limit the portion of the source clip used in the edit.

6 WORKING WITH CLIPS AND MARKERS

Lesson overview

In this lesson, you'll learn about the following:

- Understanding the differences between the Program Monitor and the Source Monitor

- Playing 360 video for virtual reality (VR) headsets

- Using markers

- Applying sync locks and track locks

- Selecting items in a sequence

- Moving clips in a sequence

- Removing clips from a sequence

 This lesson will take approximately 60 minutes. Once you have some clips in a sequence, you're ready for the next stage of fine-tuning. You'll move clips around in your edit and remove the parts you don't want. You can also add comment markers to store information about clips and sequences, which can be useful during your edit or when you send your sequence to other Adobe Creative Cloud applications.

Adobe Premiere Pro CC makes it easy to fine-tune your edits with markers and advanced tools for syncing and locking tracks when you're editing clips in your video sequence.

Getting started

The art and craft of video editing is perhaps best demonstrated during the phase *after* your assembly edit. Once you've chosen your shots and put them in approximately the right order, the process of carefully adjusting the timing of your edits begins.

In this lesson, you'll learn about additional controls in the Program Monitor and discover how markers help you stay organized.

You'll also learn about working with clips that are already on the Timeline—the "nonlinear" part of nonlinear editing with Adobe Premiere Pro CC.

Open the file Lesson 06.prproj from the Lesson 06 folder.

Before you begin, make sure you are using the Editing workspace.

1   Choose File > Save As.

2   Rename the file **Lesson 06 Continued.prproj**.

3   Choose a location on your hard drive, and click Save to save the project.

4   Reset the workspace to the default; in the Workspace panel, click Editing. Then click the menu adjacent to the Editing option and choose Reset to Saved Layout.

Using Program Monitor controls

The Program Monitor is almost identical to the Source Monitor, but there are a small number of important differences.

Let's take a look…

What is the Program Monitor?

The Program Monitor displays the frame your sequence playhead is sitting on, or playing. The sequence in the Timeline shows the clip segments and tracks, while the Program Monitor shows the resulting video output. The Program Monitor time ruler is a miniature version of the Timeline.

In the early stages of editing, you're likely to spend a lot of time working with the Source Monitor. Once your sequence is roughly edited together, you will spend most of your time using the Program Monitor and the Timeline.

Current sequence frame

Settings

Navigator

Mark In   Mark Out   Playhead   Lift   Extract

The Program Monitor vs. the Source Monitor

The key differences between the Program Monitor and the Source Monitor are as follows:

- The Source Monitor shows the contents of a clip; the Program Monitor shows the contents of whichever sequence is currently displayed in the Timeline.

- The Source Monitor has Insert and Overwrite buttons for adding clips (or parts of clips) to sequences. The Program Monitor has equivalent Extract and Lift buttons for removing clips (or parts of clips) from sequences.

- Both monitors have a time ruler. The playhead on the Program Monitor matches the playhead in the sequence you're currently viewing in the Timeline panel (the name of the sequence is displayed in the top left of the Program Monitor). As one playhead moves, the other moves as well, so you can use either panel to change the currently displayed frame.

- When you work with special effects in Premiere Pro, you'll see the results in the Program Monitor. There's one exception to this rule: Master clip effects are viewed in both the Source Monitor and the Program Monitor (for more information about effects, see Lesson 13, "Adding Video Effects").

- The Mark In and Mark Out buttons on the Program Monitor work in the same way as the ones on the Source Monitor. In and Out marks are added to the currently displayed sequence when you add them to the Program Monitor.

Adding clips to the Timeline with the Program Monitor

You've already learned how to make a partial clip selection with the Source Monitor and then add the clip to a sequence by pressing a key, clicking a button, or dragging and dropping.

You can also drag and drop a clip from the Source Monitor into the Program Monitor to add it to the Timeline.

▶ Tip: You can use the Left Arrow and Right Arrow keys to expand and collapse bins in the Project panel when it's in the List view.

▶ Tip: You can press the End key (Windows) or fn+Right Arrow key (Mac OS) to move the playhead to the end of the sequence.

▶ Tip: Remember that you can click the timecode display, type the numbers without punctuation, and then press Enter to send the playhead to that time.

1 In the Sequences bin, open the Theft Unexpected sequence.

2 Position the Timeline playhead at the end of the sequence, just after the last frame of the clip Mid John. You can hold the Shift key to snap the playhead to edits, or you can press the Up Arrow and Down Arrow keys to navigate between edits.

3 Open the clip HS Suit from the Theft Unexpected bin in the Source Monitor. This is a clip that has already been used in the sequence, but you want a different part.

4 Set an In mark for the clip around 01:26:49:00. There's not much going on in the shot, so it works well as a cutaway. Add an Out point around 01:26:52:00 so you have a little time with the man in the suit.

5 Click in the middle of the picture in the Source Monitor and drag the clip into the Program Monitor, but don't release the mouse yet.

Several overlay images appear in the Program Monitor, each highlighting a drop zone that gives different options for the edit you're about to perform.

The overlays give maximum flexibility when editing by touch, with a computer screen that allows touch interaction. You can use the mouse to drag clips in, as well as dragging by touch.

As you move the cursor over each overlay, it's highlighted to indicate the type of edit you will apply if you release the mouse button.

Here's the list of options:

- **Insert:** Performs an insert edit, using the source track selection buttons to choose the track (or tracks) the clip will land on.

- **Overwrite:** Performs an overwrite edit, using the source track selection buttons to choose the track (or tracks) the clip will land on.

- **Overlay:** If you have a clip selected on the Timeline, the new clip will be added to the next available track above the selected clip. If there's already a clip on the next track, the one above that is used, and so on.

- **Replace:** The new clip will replace the clip currently under the Timeline playhead (more on replace edits in Lesson 8, "Performing Advanced Editing Techniques").

- **Insert After:** The new clip will be inserted immediately after the clip currently under the Timeline playhead.

- **Insert Before:** The new clip will be inserted immediately before the clip currently under the Timeline playhead.

  For this edit, no clip is selected on the Timeline, and there are no clips in the way to overwrite. Choose Insert—just because it's the largest drop zone and easier to aim for.

  When you release the mouse button, the clip is edited into the sequence at the playhead position, and your edit is complete.

Insert editing with the Program Monitor

Let's try an insert edit into the middle of the sequence using the same technique.

1   Position the Timeline playhead on the edit at 00:00:16:01, between the Mid Suit and Mid John shots. The continuity of movement isn't good on this cut, so let's add another part of that HS Suit clip.

2   Add a new In mark and Out mark to the HS Suit clip in the Source Monitor, selecting about 2 seconds in total. You can see the selected duration at the lower-right corner of the Source Monitor, displayed in white numbers.

3   Once again, drag the clip from the Source Monitor into the Program Monitor, making sure to drop the clip onto the insert overlay. When you release the mouse button, the clip is inserted into your sequence.

● **Note:** When you drag a clip into your sequence using the mouse, Premiere Pro still uses the Timeline Source Channel Selection buttons to control which parts of the clip (video and audio channels) are used.

`00:00:02:00`

If you prefer to drag clips into your sequence, rather than using keyboard shortcuts, clicking the Insert and Overwrite buttons on the Source Monitor, or dragging into the Program Monitor, there's still a way to bring in just the video or audio part of a clip.

Let's try a combination of techniques. You'll set up your Timeline track headers and then drag and drop into the Program Monitor.

1   Position the Timeline playhead at 00:00:25:20, just before John takes out his pen.

● **Note:** Remember, only the source track selection buttons matter when editing clips into a sequence, not the Timeline track selection buttons.

2   On the Timeline track headers, drag the Source V1 track selection button next to the Timeline Video 2 track. For the technique you're about to use, the track targeting is used to set the location of the clip you are adding.

Your Timeline track headers should look like this.

3   Open the Mid Suit clip in the Source Monitor. At about 01:15:54:00, John is wielding his pen. Add an In mark there.

4   Add an Out mark at about 01:15:56:00. You just need a quick alternative angle.

At the bottom of the Source Monitor, you'll see the Drag Video Only and Drag Audio Only icons ( ).

These icons serve two primary purposes.

- They tell you whether your clip has video, audio, or both. If there is no video, for example, the filmstrip icon is dimmed. If there is no audio, the waveform is dimmed.

- You can drag them with the mouse to selectively edit video or audio into your sequence.

5 Drag the filmstrip icon from the bottom of the Source Monitor into the Program Monitor, and release it on the Overwrite option. When you release the mouse button, just the video part of the clip is added to the Video 2 track on the Timeline.

This works even if both the Source Video and Source Audio selection buttons are enabled, so it's a quick, intuitive way to select the part of a clip you want.

6 Play your sequence from the beginning.

The timing may not be perfect, but the edit is off to a good start. The clip you just added plays in front of the end of the Mid John clip and the start of the HS Suit clip, changing the timing. Because Premiere Pro is a nonlinear editing system, you can adjust the timing later. You'll learn how to do this in Lesson 8, "Performing Advanced Editing Techniques."

Why are there so many ways to edit clips into a sequence?

This method may seem like yet another way to achieve the same thing, so what's the benefit? It's simple: As screen resolution increases and buttons get smaller, it's an increasingly delicate maneuver to aim and click in the right place.

If you prefer to use the mouse (or your finger with a touch screen) to edit (rather than the keyboard), the Program Monitor represents a conveniently large drop zone for you to add clips to the Timeline. It gives you accurate placement of clips—using the track header controls and the position of the playhead (or your In and Out marks)—while allowing you to work intuitively.

Setting the playback resolution

The Mercury Playback Engine enables Premiere Pro to play multiple media types, special effects, and more in real time. Mercury uses the power of your computer hardware to boost performance. This means that the speed of your CPU, the amount of RAM you have, the power of your GPU, and the speed of your hard drives are all factors that impact playback performance.

If your system has difficulty playing back every frame of video in your sequence (in the Program Monitor) or in your clip (in the Source Monitor), you can choose to lower the playback resolution to make it easier. If you see your video playback stuttering, stopping, and starting, it usually indicates that your system is unable to play the file because of CPU speed, hard drive speed, or GPU power.

Reducing the resolution means you won't see every pixel in your pictures, but it can dramatically improve performance, making creative work much easier. It's common for video to have a much higher resolution than can be displayed, simply because your Source Monitor and Program Monitor are usually smaller than the original media size. This means you may not see a difference in the display when you lower the playback resolution.

Changing playback resolution

Let's try adjusting playback resolution.

1   Open the clip Cutaways from the Theft Unexpected bin. By default, the clip should be displayed at half-resolution in the Source Monitor.

1/2

At the bottom right of the Source Monitor and Program Monitor, you'll see the Select Playback Resolution menu.

2   Play the clip to get a sense of the quality when it's set to half-resolution.

3   Change the resolution to Full, and play it again to compare. It probably looks similar.

Full resolution

4   Try reducing the resolution to 1/4. Now you might begin to see a difference during playback. Notice that the picture is sharp when you pause playback. This is because the pause resolution is independent of the playback resolution (see the next section).

You'll notice the biggest differences in picture elements like text. Compare the packet of sugar in the foreground of the shot, for example.

Quarter resolution—
notice the printed text
looks softer.

5 Try dropping the playback resolution to 1/8—you can't! Premiere Pro makes an assessment of each kind of media you work with, and if the benefits of reducing resolution are less than the effort it takes to drop the resolution, the option is unavailable.

● **Note:** The playback resolution controls are the same (but separate) on the Source Monitor and the Program Monitor.

If you're working on a powerful computer, you may want to maximize the playback quality when previewing. There's an extra option to do this: Choose High Quality Playback in the Settings menu (🔧) for the Source Monitor or Program Monitor.

Changing resolution when playback is paused

You can also change the playback resolution using the Settings menu on the Source and Program Monitors.

If you look in that Settings menu on either monitor, you'll find a second option related to display resolution: Paused Resolution.

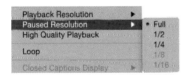

This menu works in the same way as the menu for playback resolution, but as you might have guessed, it changes the resolution only when the video is paused.

Most editors choose to leave Paused Resolution set to Full. That way, during playback you may see lower-resolution video, but when you pause, Premiere Pro reverts to showing you full resolution. This means when working with effects, you'll see the video at full resolution.

If you work with third-party special effects, it's possible you'll find they do not make use of your system hardware as efficiently as Premiere Pro does. As a consequence, it might take a long time to update the picture when you make changes to the effect settings. You can speed things up by lowering the paused resolution.

Playing back VR video

Virtual Reality headsets for the home are now commonplace, and demand for content suited to this new medium is high. Premiere Pro has built-in support for VR video, and there are industry-leading plug-ins designed to work with Creative Cloud that enable you to complete advanced post-production workflows.

Premiere Pro has a VR Video viewing mode that allows you to play 360 video and choose the angle of view live, during playback. This viewing mode is important because without it, following the action in 360 video can be difficult.

What's the difference between 360 video and VR?

360 video is captured a little like a panoramic photo. Video is recorded in multiple directions, and the different camera angles are "stitched" into a complete sphere. The sphere is flattened into 2D video footage that's described as "equi-rectangular." This is the term used to describe the way globes showing the earth are flattened into atlases you can view in a book.

Equi-rectangular video looks distorted, which makes it hard to view and follow the action. However, because it's a regular video file like any other, Premiere Po can easily work with it.

To view 360 video properly, it's usually necessary to wear a virtual reality headset. In the headset, 360 video is presented as all around you, and you can turn your head to see different parts of the image. Because a VR headset is required to see 360 video properly, it's often referred to as VR video.

True VR isn't actually video. It's a complete 3D environment you can move around in, viewing things from different directions, like 360 video, but also viewing things from different locations in the virtual reality space.

The key difference is this: In 360 video you can view in different angles, but in true VR you can view *from* different directions.

Let's try playing some 360 video.

1 Browse into the Further Media bin, and open the clip 360 Intro.mp4 in the Source Monitor. Play the clip.

   This is an introduction to a 360 film. The clip is in 4K resolution, which might be difficult for your system to play back—lower the playback resolution if you need to do so.

   The center of the image is quite easy to make out, but if you look toward the edges, it gets harder to follow what you're looking at.

That's because the clip is equi-rectangular video, where a spherical video intended for VR headsets has been flattened into a 3D image. To see this clearly, you're going to need to switch to the VR Video mode.

2   Click the Source Monitor's Settings menu, and choose VR Video > Enable.

Now the clip looks more like regular video, and additional controls appear in the Source Monitor.

● **Note:** The Source Monitor and Program Monitor have identical VR Video controls.

3   Play the clip again. This time, while it plays, click into the image and drag to change the angle of view.

The numbers under the image and to the right of the image allow you to precisely control the angle of view. They're helpful, but they take up a lot of space.

4   Go to the Source Monitor Settings menu, and choose VR Video > Hide Controls.

You can still click the image to change the angle of view, but now the image is much larger in the Source Monitor.

Also in the Settings menu, you'll find VR Video settings, where you can specify the height and width of the view in degrees to emulate different VR headsets.

5   For now, go to the Source Monitor's Settings menu and choose VR Video > Enable to deselect it.

Using markers

Sometimes it can be difficult to remember where you saw that useful part of a shot or what you intended to do with it. Wouldn't it be useful if you could mark clips with comments and flag areas of interest for later?

What you need are markers.

What are markers?

Markers allow you to identify specific times in clips and sequences and add comments to them. These temporal (time-based) markers are a fantastic aid to help you stay organized and communicate with co-editors.

You can use markers for personal reference or for collaboration. They can be connected to individual clips or a sequence.

When you add a marker to a clip, it's included in the metadata for the original media file. This means you can open the clip in another Premiere Pro project and see the same markers.

You can export markers associated with a clip or sequence as an HTML page, with thumbnails or a .csv (comma-separated value) file readable by spreadsheet-editing applications. This is useful for collaboration and as a reference.

Export markers by choosing File > Export > Markers.

Exploring the types of markers

More than one type of marker is available. You can change a marker type by double-clicking it.

- **Comment Marker:** This is a general marker you can assign a name, duration, and comments.

- **Chapter Marker:** This is a marker that Adobe Encore can convert into a regular chapter marker when making a DVD or Blu-ray Disc.

- **Segmentation Marker:** This marker makes it possible for certain video servers to divide content into parts.

- **Web Link:** Certain video formats such as QuickTime can use this marker to automatically open a web page while the video plays. When you export your sequence to create a supported format, web link markers are included in the file.

- **Flash Cue Point:** This is a marker used by Adobe Flash. By adding these cue points to the Timeline in Premiere Pro, you can begin to prepare your Flash project while still editing your sequence.

Sequence markers

Let's add some markers.

1 Open the City Views sequence.

   This is a simple assembly with a few shots from a travelogue program.

2 Set the Timeline playhead to around 00:01:12:00 and make sure no clips are selected (you can click the background of the Timeline to deselect clips).

Note: You can add markers on the time ruler for the Timeline, Source Monitor, or Program Monitor.

3 Add a marker in one of the following ways:

   - Click the Add Marker button (▯) at the top left of the Timeline.

   - Right-click the Timeline time ruler and choose Add Marker.

   - Press M.

Premiere Pro adds a green marker to the Timeline, just above the playhead.

The same marker appears at the bottom of the Program Monitor.

You can use this as a simple visual reminder or go into the settings and change it into a different kind of marker. You'll do that in a moment, but first let's look at this marker in the Markers panel.

4   Open the Markers panel. By default, the Markers panel is grouped with the Project panel. If you don't see it there, go to the Window menu and choose Markers.

The Markers panel shows you a list of markers, displayed in time order. The same panel shows you markers for a sequence or for a clip, depending on whether the Timeline or the Source Monitor is active. If neither is active, the panel will be blank.

5   Double-click the thumbnail for the marker in the Markers panel. This displays the Marker dialog box.

6   Click the Duration field and type **400**. Avoid the temptation to press Enter or Return, or the panel will close. Premiere Pro automatically adds punctuation, turning this into 00:00:04:00 (4 seconds) as soon as you click away or tab away from the field.

7   Click in the Name box and type a comment, such as **Replace this shot**.

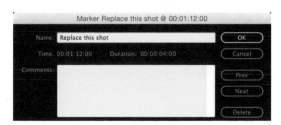

► **Tip:** You can open the Marker dialog box by double-clicking a marker in the Markers panel or by double-clicking the marker icon.

8 Click OK.

The marker now has a duration on the Timeline. Zoom in a little, and you'll see the comment you added. It's also displayed in the Markers panel.

9 Click the Marker menu, at the top of the Premiere Pro interface, to view the options.

At the bottom of the Marker menu, you have the option to ripple sequence markers. With this enabled, sequence markers will move in sync with clips when you use insert or extract edits, which change the sequence duration and timing. With this option disabled, markers stay where they are when your clips move.

Clip markers

Let's add markers to a clip.

1 Open the clip Seattle_Skyline.mov from the Further Media bin in the Source Monitor.

2 Play the clip, and while it plays, press the M key several times to add markers.

3 Look in the Markers panel. If the Source Monitor is active, every marker you added will be listed. When clips with markers are added to a sequence, they retain their markers.

4 Make sure the Source Monitor is active by clicking it. Go to the Marker menu, and choose Clear All Markers.

All the markers are removed from the clip.

> ▶ **Tip:** You can get to the same option to remove all markers—or a current marker—by right-clicking in the Source Monitor, in the Program Monitor, or on the Timeline Time Ruler and choosing Clear All Markers.

You can add a marker to a clip in a sequence by selecting it before you add the marker. Markers added to clips already edited into a sequence still appear in the Source Monitor when you view the clip.

Interactive markers

Interactive markers are used to trigger events during video playback. When you supply media, you may be asked to add such markers at key moments in a video. Adding an interactive marker is as easy as adding a regular marker.

1 Position the playhead anywhere you would like a marker on the Timeline and click the Add Marker button or press M. Premiere Pro adds a regular marker.

2 Double-click the marker you have added, either on the Timeline or in the Markers panel.

3 Change the marker type to Flash Cue Point and add the Name and Value details you need by clicking the (plus) + button at the bottom of the Marker dialog box.

4 Click OK.

Automating the editing to markers

In the previous lesson, you learned how to automate editing clips into a sequence from a bin. One of the options in that workflow is to automatically add clips to a sequence where you have added markers. Let's try it.

1 Open the sequence Desert Montage in the Sequences bin.

2 Set the Timeline playhead at the beginning of the sequence; then press the M key to add an initial marker.

3 Play the sequence for a while, and as it plays, press the M key to the beat of the music. You should be adding markers about 2 seconds apart.

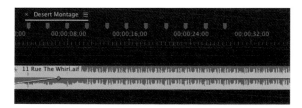

> ▶ **Tip:** You can quickly add a marker and display the Marker dialog by pressing M twice, in quick succession.

> ▶ **Tip:** You can use markers to quickly navigate your clips and sequences. If you double-click a marker in the Markers panel, you'll access the options for that marker. If you single-click it instead, Premiere Pro will take the playhead to the location of the marker—a fast way to find your way around.

4 Set your Timeline playhead to the start of the sequence. Then open the Desert Footage bin and select all of the clips by pressing Control+A (Windows) or Command+A (Mac OS).

5 Click the Automate To Sequence button ( ) at the bottom of the bin. Choose settings to match this example (be sure to check the option to Ignore Audio) and click OK.

The clips are added to the sequence, with the first frame of each clip lined up to a marker, starting with the position of the playhead.

This is a fast way of building a montage if you have music or sound effects you'd like to synchronize with your pictures.

Adding markers with Adobe Prelude

Adobe Prelude is a logging and ingest application included with Adobe Creative Cloud. Prelude provides excellent tools for managing large quantities of footage and can add markers to footage that are fully compatible with Premiere Pro.

Markers are added to clips in the form of metadata, and like the markers you add in Premiere Pro, they will travel with your media into other applications.

If you add markers to your footage using Adobe Prelude, those markers will automatically appear in Premiere Pro when you view the clips. In fact, you can even copy and paste a clip from Prelude into your Premiere Pro project, and the markers will be included.

Finding clips in the Timeline

As well as searching for clips in the Project panel, you can search for them in a sequence. Depending on whether you have the Project panel active or the Timeline active, choosing Edit > Find will display search options for that panel.

When clips in a sequence are found that match your search criteria, Premiere Pro highlights them. If you choose Find All, Premiere Pro will highlight all clips that meet the search criteria.

Using Sync Lock and Track Lock

Sync Lock

Track Lock

There are two distinct ways to lock tracks on the Timeline.

- You can lock clips in sync so when you use an insert edit to add a clip, other clips stay together in time.

- You can lock a track so that no changes can be made to it.

Using sync locks

Sync is not just for speech! It's helpful to think of sync as any two things that are meant to happen at the same time. You might have a musical event that happens at the same time as some climactic action or something as simple as a lower-third title that identifies a speaker. If it happens at the same time, it's synchronized.

Open the Theft Unexpected sequence in the Sequences bin.

When John arrives, at the beginning of the sequence, we don't know what he's looking at.

1 Open the Mid Suit shot, from the Theft Unexpected bin, in the Source Monitor. Add an In mark around 01:15:35:18 and add an Out mark around 01:15:39:00.

2 Position the Timeline playhead at the beginning of the sequence and make sure there are no In or Out marks on the Timeline.

> **Tip:** You can press the Home (Windows) or fn+Left Arrow (Mac OS) key to move the playhead to the end of the sequence.

3 Switch off the Sync Lock for the Video 2 track. Check that your Timeline is configured as in the following example, with the Source V1 track patched to the Timeline V1 track. The Timeline track header buttons are not important now, but having the right source track buttons enabled is.

> **Note:** You may need to zoom out to see the other clips in the sequence.

Before you do anything else, take a look at the position of the Mid Suit cutaway clip on the Video 2 track, toward the end of the sequence.

It's just over the cut between the clips Mid John and HS Suit on Video 1.

4 Insert-edit the source clip into the sequence.

Take another look at the location of the Mid Suit cutaway clip.

The Mid Suit cutaway clip has not moved, while the other clips have moved to the right to accommodate the new clip. This is a problem because the cutaway is now out of position with the clips to which it relates.

5 Undo by pressing Control+Z (Windows) or Command+Z (Mac OS) and try it again with the Video 2 track Sync Lock turned on.

6 Turn on Sync Lock for the Video 2 track, and perform the insert edit again.

This time, the cutaway clip moves with the other clips on the Timeline, even though nothing is being edited onto the Video 2 track. This is the power of sync locks—they keep things in sync!

● **Note:** Overwrite edits do not change the duration of your sequence, so they are not affected by sync locks.

Using track locks

Track locks prevent you from making changes to a track. They are an excellent way to avoid making accidental changes to your sequence and to fix clips on specific tracks in place while you work.

For example, you could lock your music track while you insert different video clips. By locking the music track, you can simply forget about it while editing because no changes can be made to it.

Lock and unlock tracks by clicking the Toggle Track Lock button. Clips on a locked track are highlighted with diagonal lines.

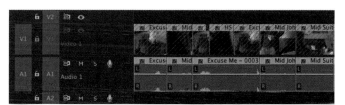

Finding gaps in the Timeline

Until now, you've been adding clips to a sequence. Part of the power of nonlinear editing is in having the freedom to move clips around in a sequence and remove the parts you don't want.

When removing clips or parts of clips, you'll either leave a gap by performing a lift edit or not leave a gap by performing an extract edit.

An extract edit is a little like an insert edit but in reverse. Rather than other clips in a sequence moving out of the way to make space for a new clip, the other clips move in to fill the gap left behind by a clip you are removing.

When you zoom out of a complex sequence, it can be difficult to see gaps left behind after performing an edit. To automatically locate the next gap, choose Sequence > Go to Gap > Next in Sequence.

Once you've found a gap, you can remove it by selecting it and pressing Delete.

Let's learn a little more about working with clips on the Timeline. Continue working with the Theft Unexpected sequence.

Selecting clips

Selection is an important part of working with Premiere Pro. Depending on the panel you have selected, different menu options will be available. You'll want to select clips in your sequences carefully before applying adjustments to them.

When working with clips that have video and audio, you'll have two or more segments for each clip: one video segment and at least one audio segment.

When the video and audio clip segments come from the same original media file, they are automatically treated as linked. If you select one, the other is automatically selected.

You can switch linked selections on and off on the Timeline globally by clicking the Linked Selection button ( ) at the top left of the Timeline. When Linked Selection is on, video and audio clips in a sequence are automatically selected together when you click them. When Linked Selection is off, clicking the video or audio part of a clip selects only that part. If there's more than one audio clip, you'll select just the one you click.

Selecting a clip or range of clips

When selecting clips in a sequence, there are two approaches:

*   Make time selections by using In and Out marks

    or

*   Make selections by choosing clip segments

The simplest way to select a clip in a sequence is to click it. Be careful not to double-click, which will open the clip in the Source Monitor, ready for you to adjust the In or Out marks (these will update, live, on the Timeline).

When making selections, you'll want to use the default Timeline tool—the Selection tool ( ). This tool has the keyboard shortcut V.

If you hold the Shift key while you click with the Selection tool, you can select or deselect additional clips.

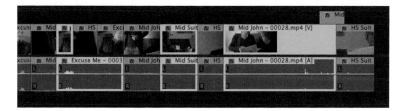

You can also drag the Selection tool over multiple clips to select them. Begin by clicking an empty part of the Timeline and then drag to create a selection box. Any clip you drag over with the selection box will be selected.

Premiere Pro gives you the option to automatically select whichever clip the Timeline playhead passes over. This is particularly useful for a keyboard-based editing workflow. You can enable the option by choosing Sequence > Selection Follows Playhead. You can also press the keyboard shortcut D to select the current clip under the Timeline playhead.

Selecting all the clips on a track

If you want to select every clip on a track, there are two handy tools to do just that: the Track Select Forward tool ( ), which has the keyboard shortcut A, and the Track Select Backward tool ( ), which has the keyboard shortcut Shift+A.

Try it now. Choose the Track Select Forward tool and click any clip on the Video 1 track.

Every clip, on every track, from the one you select until the end of the sequence is selected. This is useful if you want to add a gap to your sequence to make space for more clips. You can drag all the selected clips to the right to introduce a gap.

Try the Track Select Backward tool. When you click a clip with this tool, every clip up to the one you clicked is selected.

If you hold the Shift key while using either of the Track Select tools, you'll select clips on only one track.

When you have finished, switch to the Selection tool by clicking it on the Tools panel or by pressing the V key.

Selecting audio or video only

It's common to add a clip to a sequence and later realize you don't need the audio or video part of the clip. You may want to remove one or the other to keep your Timeline tidy, and there's an easy way to make the correct selection: If Linked Selection is on, you can temporarily override it.

► **Tip:** If you drag a sequence clip to another position on the Timeline while holding the Alt key (Windows) or Option key (Mac OS), you will create a copy of the clip.

Switch to the Selection tool and try clicking some clip segments on the Timeline while holding the Alt key (Windows) or Option key (Mac OS). Premiere Pro ignores the link between video and audio parts of your clips. You can even lasso in this way!

Splitting a clip

It's also common to add a clip to a sequence and then realize you need it in two parts. Perhaps you want to take just a section of a clip and use it as a cutaway, or maybe you want to separate the beginning and the end to make space for new clips.

You can split clips in several ways.

- Use the Razor tool (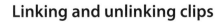) with the keyboard shortcut C. If you hold the Shift key while clicking with the Razor tool, you'll add an edit to clips on every track.

- Make sure the Timeline is selected, go to the Sequence menu, and choose Add Edit. Premiere Pro adds an edit, at the location of your playhead, to clips on any tracks that have their track header enabled. If you have selected clips in the sequence, Premiere Pro adds the edit only to the selected clips, ignoring the track selections.

- If you go to the Sequence menu and choose Add Edit to All Tracks, Premiere Pro adds an edit to clips on all tracks, regardless of whether they are turned on.

- Use the Add Edit keyboard shortcuts. Press Control+K (Windows) or Command+K (Mac OS) to add an edit to selected tracks or clips, or press Shift+Control+K (Windows) or Shift+Command+K (Mac OS) to add an edit to all tracks regardless of selection.

Clips that were originally continuous will still play back seamlessly unless you move them or make separate adjustments to different parts.

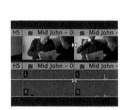

If you click the Settings button for the Timeline ( ), you can select Show Through Edits to see a special icon on edits of this kind.

You can rejoin clips that have the Through Edit icon by right-clicking the edit and choosing Join Through Edits.

Using the Selection tool, you can also click a Through Edit icon and press the Delete key to rejoin the two parts of a clip.

Try it with this sequence. Be sure to use Undo to remove the new cuts you add.

Linking and unlinking clips

You can switch off and on the link between a connected video and audio segment easily. Just select the clip or clips you want to change, right-click each of them, and choose Unlink. You can also use the Clip menu.

You can link a clip with its audio again by selecting both clip segments, right-clicking one of them, and choosing Link. There's no harm in linking or unlinking clips—it won't change the way Premiere Pro plays your sequence. It just gives you the flexibility to work with clips in the way you want.

Even if video and audio clip segments are linked, you'll need to make sure the Timeline Linked Selection option is enabled to select linked clips together.

Moving clips

Insert edits and overwrite edits add new clips to sequences in dramatically different ways. Insert edits push existing clips out of the way, whereas overwrite edits simply replace them. This theme of having two ways of working with clips extends to the techniques you'll employ to move clips around the Timeline and to remove clips from the Timeline.

When moving clips using the Insert mode, you may want to ensure you have the sync locks on for your tracks to avoid any possible loss of sync.

Let's try a few techniques.

Dragging clips

At the top left of the Timeline, you'll see the Snap button (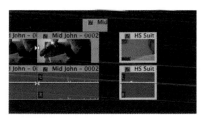). When snapping is enabled, clip segments snap automatically to each other's edges. This simple but useful feature will help you position clip segments frame-accurately.

1 Select the last clip on the Timeline, HS Suit, and drag it a little to the right.

Because there are no clips after this one, you simply introduce a gap before the clip. No other clips are affected.

2 Make sure the Snap option is enabled and drag the clip back to its original position. If you move the mouse slowly, you'll notice that the clip segment jumps into position at the last moment. When this happens, you can be confident it's perfectly positioned. Notice that the clip also snaps to the end of the cutaway shot on Video 2.

3 Drag the clip left until the end of the clip snaps to the end of the previous clip. When you release the mouse button, the clip replaces the end of that clip.

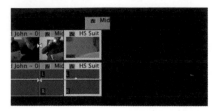

When you drag and drop clips, the default mode is Overwrite.

4 Undo repeatedly until the clip is in its original position.

Nudging clips

Many editors prefer to use the keyboard as much as possible, minimizing the use of the mouse because working with the keyboard is usually faster.

It's common to move clip segments inside a sequence by using the arrow keys in combination with a modifier key, nudging the selected items left and right in time or up and down between tracks.

You won't be able to nudge linked video and audio clips on V1 and A1 up and down until you separate them, or unlink them, because the separator between the video and audio tracks blocks the movement.

Default clip-nudging shortcuts

Premiere Pro includes many keyboard shortcut options, some of which are available but not yet assigned keys. You can set these up, prioritizing the use of available keys to suit your workflow.

Here are the shortcuts for nudging clips using the keyboard:

- **Nudge Clip Selection Left 1 Frame (add Shift for five frames)**: Alt+Left Arrow (Windows) or Command+Left Arrow (Mac OS)

- **Nudge Clip Selection Right 1 Frame (add Shift for five frames)**: Alt+Right Arrow (Windows) or Command+Right Arrow (Mac OS)

- **Nudge Clip Selection Up**: Alt+Up Arrow (Windows) or Option+Up Arrow (Mac OS)

- **Nudge Clip Selection Down**: Alt+Down Arrow (Windows) or Option+Down Arrow (Mac OS)

Rearranging clips in a sequence

If you hold the Control (Windows) or Command (Mac OS) key while you drag clips on the Timeline, Premiere Pro uses Insert mode instead of Overwrite mode to place the clip when you release the mouse button.

The HS Suit shot around 00:00:19:00 might work better if it appeared before the previous shot—and it might help you hide the poor continuity between the two shots of John.

1 Drag and drop that last HS Suit clip to the left of the clip before it. The left edge of the HS Suit clip should line up with the left edge of the Mid Suit clip. Once you have begun dragging, hold the Control (Windows) or Command (Mac OS) key. Release the key after you've dropped the clip.

► **Tip:** You may need to zoom in to the Timeline to see the clips clearly and move them easily.

2 Play the result. This creates the edit you want, but it introduces a gap where the clip HS Suit used to be.

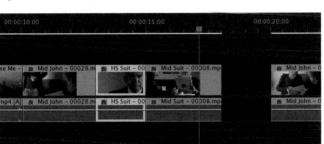

Let's try that again with an additional modifier key.

3 Undo to restore the clips to their original positions.

4 Holding Control+Alt (Windows) or Command+Option (Mac OS), drag and drop the HS Suit clip to the beginning of the previous clip again.

► **Tip:** Be careful when dropping the clip into position. The ends of clips snap to edges just as the beginnings do.

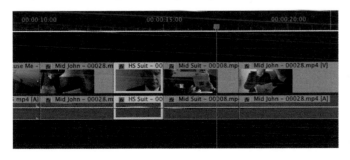

This time, no gap is left in the sequence. Play through the edit to see the result.

Using the clipboard

You can copy and paste clip segments on the Timeline just as you might copy and paste text in a word processor.

1   In a sequence, select any clip segment (or segments) you want to copy, and then press Control+C (Windows) or Command+C (Mac OS) to add them to the clipboard.

2   Position your playhead where you would like to paste the clips you copied and press Control+V (Windows) or Command+V (Mac OS).

Premiere Pro adds copies of the clips to your sequence based on the tracks you enable. The lowest enabled track receives the clip (or clips).

Extracting and deleting segments

Now that you know how to add clips to a sequence and how to move them around, all that remains is to learn how to remove them. Once again, you'll be operating in Insert or Overwrite mode.

There are two ways to select parts of a sequence you want to remove. You can use In and Out marks combined with track selections, or you can select clip segments. If you use In and Out marks, selecting clips overrides selecting tracks, so you can ignore track selection if you make careful clip selections.

You will still be working with a selected amount of time, but selecting clips can be quicker than selecting tracks.

Performing a lift edit

A lift edit will remove the selected part of a sequence, leaving blank space. It's similar to an overwrite edit but in reverse.

Open the sequence Theft Unexpected 02 in the Sequences bin. This sequence has some unwanted extra clips. They have different label colors to make them easier to identify.

You'll need to set In and Out marks on the Timeline to select the part that will be removed. You can do this by positioning the playhead and pressing I or O. You can also use a handy shortcut.

1   Position the playhead so that it's somewhere over the first unwanted clip, Excuse Me Tilted.

2   Make sure the Video 1 track header is turned on and press X.

    Premiere Pro automatically adds an In mark and an Out mark that match the beginning and end of the clip. You'll see a highlight that shows the selected part of the sequence.

The correct tracks are already selected, so there's no need to do anything else to prepare for the lift edit. In fact, because you have selected a clip, the track selection has no effect anyway. The edit you're about to perform will apply to the selected clip.

3 Click the Lift button (![icon]) at the bottom of the Program Monitor. If your keyboard has a (semicolon) ; key, you can press it instead.

Premiere Pro removes the part of the sequence you selected, leaving a gap. This might be fine on another occasion, but in this instance you don't want the gap. You could right-click in the gap and choose Ripple Delete, but for this exercise you'll use an extract edit.

Performing an extract edit

An extract edit removes the selected part of your sequence and does not leave a gap. It's similar to an insert edit but in reverse.

1 Undo the last edit.

2 Click the Extract button (![icon]) at the bottom of the Program Monitor. If your keyboard has an (apostrophe) ' key, you can press it.

This time, Premiere Pro removes the selected part of the sequence, and the other clips on the Timeline move to close the gap.

Performing a delete and ripple delete edit

There are also two ways of removing clips by selecting segments: Delete and Ripple Delete.

Click the second unwanted clip, Cutaways, and try these two options:

- Pressing the Backspace/Delete key removes the selected clip (or clips), leaving a gap behind. This is the same as a lift edit.

- Pressing Shift+Delete/Shift+Forward Delete removes the selected clip (or clips) without leaving a gap behind. This is the same as an extract edit. If you're using a Mac keyboard without a dedicated Forward Delete key, you can convert the Delete key into a Forward Delete key by pressing the Function (fn) and Delete keys together.

The result seems similar to that achieved by using In and Out marks because you used In and Out marks earlier to select a whole clip. You can use In and Out marks to choose any parts of clips, while selecting clip segments and pressing Delete will always remove whole clips.

Disabling a clip

Just as you can turn a track output off or on, you can also turn individual clips off or on. Clips that you disable are still in your sequence, but they cannot be seen or heard during playback or while scrubbing.

This is a useful feature for selectively hiding parts of a complex, multilayered sequence when you want to see background layers or compare different versions.

Try this on the cutaway shot on the Video 2 track, toward the end of the sequence.

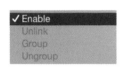

1 Right-click the Mid Suit clip on the Video 2 track and choose Enable to deselect it.

   Play through that part of the sequence, and you'll notice that the clip is present but you can no longer see it.

2 Right-click the clip again and choose Enable. This re-enables the clip.

Review questions

1 When dragging clips directly into the Timeline panel, what modifier key (Control/Command, Shift, or Alt) should you use to make an insert edit rather than an overwrite edit?

2 How do you drag and drop just the video or audio part of a clip into a sequence?

3 How do you reduce the playback resolution in the Source Monitor or Program Monitor?

4 How do you add a marker to a clip or sequence?

5 What is the difference between an extract edit and a lift edit?

6 What is the difference between Delete and Ripple Delete?

Review answers

1 Hold the Control (Windows) or Command (Mac OS) key when dragging a clip into the Timeline to make an insert edit rather than an overwrite edit.

2 Rather than grabbing the picture in the Source Monitor, drag and drop the filmstrip icon or the audio waveform icon to select only the video or audio part of the clip. You can also disable the Source Patching buttons for parts you want to exclude.

3 Use the Select Playback Resolution menu at the bottom of the monitor to change the playback resolution.

4 To add a marker, click the Add Marker button at the bottom of the monitor or on the Timeline, press the M key, or use the Marker menu.

5 When you extract a section of your sequence using In and Out marks, no gap is left behind. When you lift, a gap remains.

6 When you delete a clip, a gap is left behind. When you ripple delete a clip, no gap is left.

7 ADDING TRANSITIONS

Lesson overview

In this lesson, you'll learn about the following:

- Understanding transitions
- Understanding edit points and handles
- Adding video transitions
- Modifying transitions
- Fine-tuning transitions
- Applying transitions to multiple clips at once
- Using audio transitions

 This lesson will take approximately 75 minutes to complete.

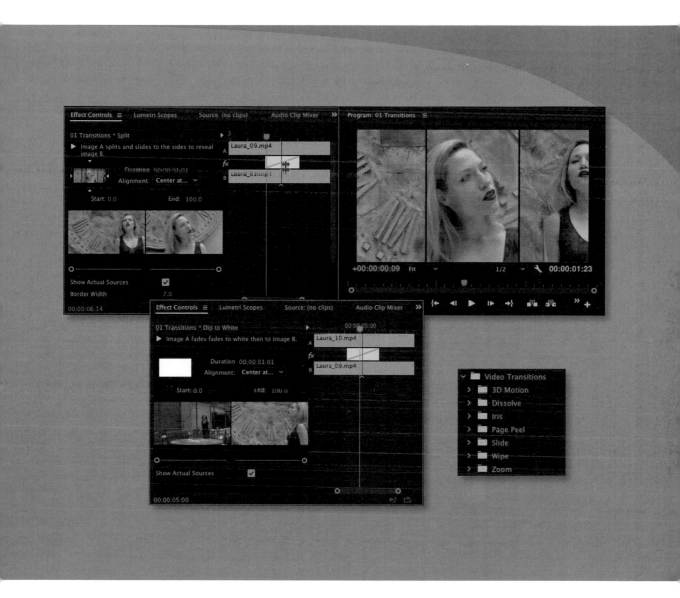

Transitions can help create a seamless flow between two video or audio clips. Video transitions are often used to signify a change in time or location. Audio transitions provide a useful way to avoid abrupt edits that jar the listener.

Getting started

In this lesson, you'll learn to use transitions between video and audio clips. Video editors often use transitions to help an edit flow more smoothly. You'll learn best practices for choosing transitions selectively.

For this lesson, you'll use a new project file.

1   Start Adobe Premiere Pro CC, and open the project Lesson 07.prproj.

   Open the sequence 01 Transitions.

2   Choose Effects in the Workspaces panel, or choose Window > Workspaces > Effects.

   This changes the workspace to the preset that was created to make it easier to work with transitions and effects. If you have been using Premiere Pro for a while, you may need to reset the workspace to the saved version by clicking the Effects menu in the Workspaces panel.

   This workspace uses stacked panels to maximize the number of panels that can be onscreen at a time.

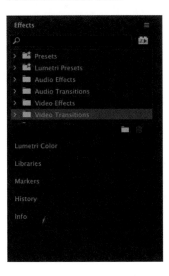

Stacked panels save space—enable or disable them in the panel menu.

You can enable stacked panels for any panel group by going to the panel menu and choosing Panel Group Settings > Stacked Panel Group. The same option will toggle off stacked panels.

Click the name for any panel in a stack to view it. Start with the Effects panel.

What are transitions?

Adobe Premiere Pro offers several special effects and preset animations to help you bridge neighboring clips in the Timeline. These transitions—such as dissolves, page wipes, dips to color, and so on—provide a way to ease viewers from one scene to the next. Occasionally, a transition can also be used to grab viewers' attention to signify a major jump in the story.

Adding transitions to your project is an art. Applying them starts simply enough; it's a mere drag-and-drop process. The skill comes in their placement, length, and parameters, such as direction, motion, and start/end locations.

You can adjust settings for transitions on the Timeline and in the Effect Controls panel. In addition to the various options unique to each transition, the Effect Controls panel displays an *A/B timeline*. This feature makes it easy to move transitions relative to the edit point, change the transition duration, and apply transitions to clips that don't have sufficient head or tail frames (additional content to provide an overlap). You can also apply a transition effect to a group of clips.

Knowing when to use transitions

Transitions are most effective when they help the viewer understand the story. For example, you may switch from indoors to outdoors in a video, or you may jump forward in time by several hours. An animated transition, a fade to black, or a dissolve helps the viewer understand that time has passed or that the location has changed.

Transitions are a standard storytelling tool in video editing. Most viewers understand the language of transitions and will correctly interpret their use. For example, a slow fade to black at the end of a scene is a clear indication that the scene has finished. The key with transitions is to use restraint—unless, of course, a total lack of restraint is the result you intend to show. Most importantly, the effects you use should look *intentional*.

Only you can know what is right for your creative work. As long as it looks like you meant to include a particular effect, your audience will tend to trust your decision (whether or not they agree with your creative choices). It takes practice and experience to develop sensitivity for the right time, and wrong time, to use effects such as transitions.

Implementing best practices with transitions

New editors sometimes overuse transitions, perhaps because it's easy to use them to add visual interest. You may be tempted to use them for every cut. Don't! Or at least, get them out of your system with your first edit.

Most TV shows and feature films use cuts-only edits. You'll rarely see any transitions. Why? Because an effect should be used if it gives a particular additional benefit, and most often, transition effects do not. In fact, they can be distracting.

If a news editor uses a transition effect, it's for a purpose. The most frequent use in newsroom editing is to take what would have been a jarring or abrupt edit—called a *jump cut*—and make it more acceptable.

Transitions do have their place in carefully planned stories. Consider the *Star Wars* movies with their highly stylized transition effects, such as obvious, slow wipes. Each of those transitions has a purpose. In this case, George Lucas purposely created a look reminiscent of old serialized movies and TV shows. The transition effects send a clear message: "Pay attention. We're transitioning across space and time."

● **Note:** Transitions are fun and interesting to add to your project. However, overuse can make a video seem amateurish. When choosing a transition, make sure it adds meaning to your project. Watch your favorite movies and TV shows to learn how to use transitions elegantly.

Using edit points and handles

To understand transition effects, you'll need to understand edit points and handles. An edit point is the point in your Timeline where one clip ends and the next begins. This is often called a *cut*. These are easy to see because Premiere Pro draws vertical lines to show where one clip ends and another begins (much like two bricks next to each other).

When you edit part of a clip into a sequence, the unused sections at the beginning and/or end are still available but hidden. Clip handles are those unused sections.

When you first edited a clip into a sequence, you set In and Out marks (also known as In and Out points) to select the part you wanted. There's a handle between the clip's original beginning and the In point you chose. There's also a handle between the clip's original end and the Out point you chose.

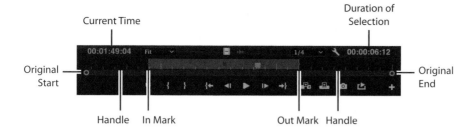

Current Time

Duration of Selection

Original Start

Original End

Handle   In Mark   Out Mark Handle

Of course, you may not have used In or Out points, or you may have set just one or other mark at the beginning or end of the clip. In this case, you would have no unused media or unused media at one end of the clip.

On the Timeline, if you see a little triangle in the upper-right or upper-left corner of a clip, it means you've reached the end of the original clip and there are no additional frames available (referred to as *handles*).

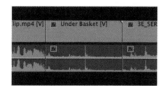

In this example, the middle clip has a handle available at the start (on the left) but no handle at the end (on the right).

For transitions to work, you need handles. When your clip has handles, there are no triangles displayed in the upper corners of the clip.

Portions of a clip that are not normally visible will be used when you apply a transition. Essentially, the outgoing clip is overlapped with the incoming clip to create an area for transitions to occur. For example, if you apply a 2-second Cross Dissolve transition centered between two video clips, you'd need a 1-second handle on both clips (1 additional second each that would normally be invisible in the Timeline).

Adding video transitions

Premiere Pro gives you multiple video transition effects to choose from. Most options are available in the Video Transitions group in the Effects panel.

The main transitions are organized into seven effect subcategories. You'll find additional transitions in the Video Effects > Transition group in the Effects panel. These effects are meant to be applied to an entire clip and can be used to reveal the footage (typically between its start and end frames). This second category works well for superimposing text or graphics.

● **Note:** If you need more transitions, check the Adobe website. Visit http://helpx.adobe.com/premiere-pro/compatibility.html and click the Plug-ins link. There, you'll find several third-party effects to explore.

Applying a single-sided transition

The easiest transition to understand is one that applies to just one end of a single clip. This could be a fade from black on the first clip in a sequence or a dissolve into an animated graphic that leaves the screen on its own.

Let's give it a try.

1 Use the sequence 01 Transitions.

This sequence has four video clips. The clips have handles long enough for transition effects to be applied between them.

● **Note:** You can use the Search field, at the top of the panel, to locate the effect by name or keyword, or you can manually open the folders of effects.

2 In the Effects panel, open the Video Transitions > Dissolve group. Find the Cross Dissolve effect.

3 Drag and drop the effect onto the start of the first video clip.

A highlight shows you where a transition effect will be added.

4 Drag the Cross Dissolve effect onto the end of the last video clip.

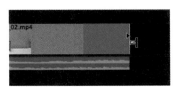

The Dissolve icon shows that the effect will start before the end of the clip and complete by the time it reaches the clip's end.

Because you're applying the Cross Dissolve transition effect at the ends of clips, where there is no connected clip, the picture dissolves into the background of the Timeline (which happens to be black).

Transitions of this kind don't extend the clip (using the handle) because the transition doesn't reach past the end of the clip.

5 Play the sequence to see the result.

You should see a fade from black at the start of the sequence and a fade to black at the end.

When you apply a Cross Dissolve effect in this way, the result looks similar to the Dip to Black effect, which transitions to black. However, in reality you are causing the clip to become gradually transparent in front of a black background. The difference is more obvious when you work with multiple layers of clips, with different-colored background layers.

Applying a transition between two clips

Let's apply transitions between several clips. For the purposes of exploration, you'll break some artistic rules and try a few different options.

1 Continue working with the previous sequence, 01 Transitions.

2 Move the playhead to the edit point between clip 1 and clip 2 on the Timeline and then press the equal sign (=) key two or three times to zoom in fairly close. If your keyboard does not have the = key, use the zoom slider control at the bottom of the Timeline.

▶ **Tip:** It's easy to remember that pressing the = key zooms in because it normally has a + symbol on the same key.

3 Drag the Dip to White transition from the Dissolve group in the Effects panel onto the edit point between clip 1 and clip 2.

4 Next, drag the Push transition from the Slide group onto the edit point between clip 2 and clip 3.

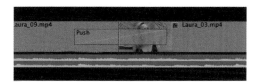

5 Click once on the Push transition effect on the Timeline to select it and go to the Effect Controls panel. Change the direction of the clip from West to East to East to West by clicking the direction control on the small thumbnail, at the top left of the controls.

6 Drag the Flip Over transition from the 3D Motion group onto the edit point between clip 3 and clip 4.

Note: When you drag a new video or audio transition effect from the Effects panel on top of an existing transition, it replaces the existing effect. It also preserves the alignment and duration of the previous transition. This is an easy way to swap transition effects and experiment.

7 Review the sequence by playing it from beginning to end.

Having watched this sequence, you can probably see why it's a good idea to use transitions with restraint.

Let's try replacing an existing effect.

8 Drag the Split transition from the Slide group onto the existing Push transition effect between clip 2 and clip 3. The new transition effect replaces the old one, taking the duration of the old effect.

9 Select the Split transition effect icon on the Timeline. In the Effect Controls panel, set Border Width to 7 and Anti-aliasing Quality to Medium to create a thin black border at the edge of the wipe.

Note: You may need to scroll down in the Effect Controls panel to access further controls.

The anti-aliasing method reduces potential flicker when the line animates.

10 Watch the sequence to see the new transition effect.

Transitions have a default duration, which can be set in seconds or frames (it's frames by default). The duration of a transition effect will change depending on the sequence frame rate, unless the default duration is set in seconds. The default transition duration can be changed in the General tab of the Preferences panel.

11 Choose Edit > Preferences > General (Windows) or Premiere Pro > Preferences > General (Mac OS).

12 This is a 24-frames-per-second sequence, but this doesn't matter if you change the Video Transition Default Duration option to 1 second. Do so now, and click OK.

The existing transition effects stay the same, but any future transitions you add will have the new duration.

Few transition effects employed by professional editors are as long as a full second in duration. You'll learn more about how to customize transitions later in this lesson.

Applying transitions to multiple clips at once

So far, you've been applying transitions to video clips. However, you can also apply transitions to still images, graphics, color mattes, and even audio, as you'll see in the next section of this lesson.

A common project type that editors encounter is the photo montage. Often these montages look good with transitions between photos. Applying transitions one at a time to 100 images would take a long time. Premiere Pro makes it easy to automate this process by allowing the default transition (that you define) to be added to any group of contiguous or noncontiguous clips.

1 In the Project panel, find and open the sequence 02 Slideshow.

This sequence has several images edited sequentially.

2 Play the Timeline by pressing the spacebar.

You'll notice that there's a cut between each pair of clips.

3 Press the backslash (\) key to zoom out the Timeline so the whole sequence is visible.

4 With the Selection tool, draw a marquee around all the clips to select them.

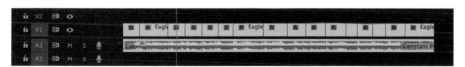

5 Go to the Sequence menu, and choose Apply Default Transitions to Selection.

This will apply the default transition between all the currently selected clips. The standard default transition effect is a 1-second Cross Dissolve. You can change the default transition by right-clicking an effect in the Effects panel and choosing Set Selected as Default Transition.

6 Play the Timeline to see the difference the Cross Dissolve transition makes to the montage.

You can also copy an existing transition effect to multiple edits using the keyboard. To do this, select the transition effect and press Control+C (Windows) or Command+C (Mac OS). Then hold the Control (Windows) or Command (Mac OS) key while you drag with the selection tool around multiple other edits to select them, rather than clips.

With the edits selected, you can press Control+V (Windows) or Command+V (Mac OS) to paste the transition effect onto all the selected edits.

This is a great way to apply matching transition effects between multiple clips.

Sequence display changes

When you add a transition to a sequence, a red or yellow horizontal line may appear above it in the Timeline panel. A yellow line indicates that Premiere Pro expects to be able to play the effect smoothly. A red line means that this section of the sequence must be rendered before you can record it to tape or view a preview without dropped frames.

Rendering happens automatically when you export your sequence as a file, but you can choose to render at any time to make these sections preview more smoothly on slower computers.

The easiest way to render is to press the Enter key (Windows) or Carriage Return key (Mac OS). You can also add In and Out points to select a part of your sequence and then render. Only the selected part will render. This is useful if you have many effects that need to render, but you're concerned with only one section for now.

Premiere Pro will create a video clip of that segment (tucked away in the Preview Files folder) and will change the line from red or yellow to green. As long as the line is green, playback should be smooth.

Using A/B mode to fine-tune a transition

The Effect Controls panel's A/B editing mode splits a single video track into two. What would normally be two consecutive and contiguous clips on a single track are now displayed as individual clips on separate tracks, giving you the option to apply a transition between them, to manipulate their head and tail frames (or handles), and to change other transition options.

Changing parameters in the Effect Controls panel

All transitions in Premiere Pro can be customized. Some effects have few customizable properties (such as duration or starting point). Other effects offer more options for direction, color, border size, and so on. The major benefit of the Effect Controls panel is that you can see the outgoing and incoming clip handles. This makes it easy to adjust the position of an effect.

Let's modify a transition.

1 Switch back to the sequence 01 Transitions.

2 Position the Timeline playhead at the Dip to White transition you added between clips 1 and 2, and click to select the transition.

3 In the Effect Controls panel, select the Show Actual Sources check box to view frames from the actual clips.

It's now easier to judge changes you make to the transition's source clips.

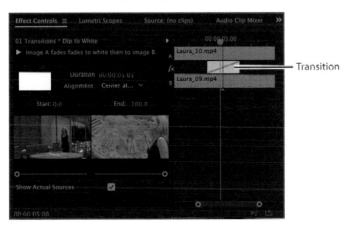

4 In the Effect Controls panel, click the Alignment menu and choose Start at Cut.

The transition icon switches to show the new position.

Note: You might need to resize the Effect Controls panel to make the Show/Hide Timeline View button (▶) visible. Also, the Effect Controls Timeline may already be visible. Clicking the Show/Hide Timeline View button in the Effect Controls panel toggles it on and off.

▶ **Tip:** You can position the start time of a dissolve asymmetrically by dragging it. This means you don't have to settle for the Centered, Start at Cut, and End at Cut options. You can drag the position of a transition effect directly on the Timeline too; there's no need to use the Effect Controls panel.

5 Click the small Play the Transition button at the top-left corner to play the transition in the Effect Controls panel.

6 Now you'll change the Duration field. Enter **1:12** for a 1.5-second duration effect.

The Alignment menu changes to Custom Start, because there isn't enough of the clip to play the transition at the new duration. To fit the new transition duration in, Premiere Pro sets the start a little earlier. Play the transition to see the changes.

▶ **Tip:** You may need to move the playhead earlier or later to see the edit point between two clips.

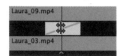

Let's customize the next effect.

7 Click the transition between clip 2 and clip 3 in the Timeline.

8 In the Effect Controls panel, hover the pointer over the edit line at the center of the transition rectangle.

That's the edit point between the two clips, and the pointer that appears is the Rolling Edit tool. This tool lets you reposition the edit point.

9 Drag the Rolling Edit tool left and right, and note that the changing Out point of the left clip and the changing In point of the right clip show up in the Program Monitor as soon as you release the mouse button. This is also called *trimming*. You'll explore trimming in more detail in Lesson 8, "Performing Advanced Editing Techniques."

● **Note:** When trimming, it's possible to shorten a transition to a duration of one frame. This can make it hard to grab and position the transition effect icon, so try using the Duration and Alignment controls. If you want to remove a transition, select it in the sequence and press Backspace (Windows) or Delete (Mac OS).

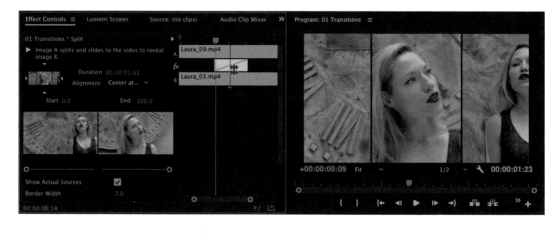

10 Move the pointer slightly to the left or right of the edit line, and notice that it changes to the Slide tool.

Using the Slide tool changes the start and end points of the transition without changing its overall length. The new start and end marks show up in the Program Monitor, but unlike using the Rolling Edit tool, moving the transition rectangle by using the Slide tool does not change the edit point between the two clips. Instead, it changes the timing of the transition effect.

11 Use the Slide tool to drag the transition rectangle left and right.

Using a Morph Cut effect

Morph Cut is a special transition effect that aims to be invisible. It's designed specifically to help with "talking head" video interviews, where a single speaker looks in the direction of the camera. If your subject pauses a lot or there is inappropriate content in the footage, you may want to remove a section of the interview.

This would normally produce a jump cut, but with the right media and a little experimentation, the Morph Cut effect might yield an invisible transition that seamlessly hides what you have removed. Let's try it.

1 Open the sequence 03 Morph Cut. Play the beginning of the sequence.

This sequence has one shot in it, with a jump cut near the start. It's a small jump cut but enough to jar the audience.

2 In the Effects panel, look in the Video Transitions > Dissolve group for the Morph Cut effect. Drag this effect to the join between the two parts of the clip.

The Morph Cut transition effect begins by analyzing the two clips in the background. You can continue to work on your sequence while this analysis takes place.

The Morph Cut transition effect works best when you experiment with different durations. Depending on your media, one duration may work better than another.

3 Double-click the Morph Cut transition effect to display Set Transition Duration dialog. Change the duration to 13 frames.

4 When the analysis is complete, press the Enter key (Windows) or Carriage Return key (Mac OS) to render the effect (if your system requires it) and preview the effect.

The result is not perfect, but it's close, and it's unlikely an audience will notice the join.

Dealing with inadequate (or nonexistent) head or tail handles

If you try to extend a transition for a clip that doesn't have enough frames as a handle, the transition appears but has diagonal warning bars through it. This means Premiere Pro is using a freeze frame to extend the duration of the clip.

You can adjust the duration and position of the transition to resolve the issue.

1 Open the sequence 04 Handles.

2 Locate the edit between the clips.

The two clips on the Timeline have no heads or tails. You can tell this because of the little triangles in the corners of the clips; a triangle indicates the last frame of an original clip.

3 Using the Ripple Edit tool on the Tools panel (), drag the right edge of the first clip to the left. Drag to shorten the duration of the first clip to about 1:10 and then release.

A tool tip appears while you trim to show the new clip duration.

The clip after the edit point ripples to close the gap. Notice that the little triangle at the end of the clip you have trimmed is no longer visible.

4 Drag the Cross Dissolve transition effect from the Effects panel onto the edit point between the two clips.

You can drag the transition only to the right side of the edit because there's no handle available to create a dissolve overlapping the end of the first clip without using freeze frames.

5 Press V to select the standard Selection tool, and click the transition effect once to select it. You may need to zoom in to make it easier to select a transition.

6 In the Effect Controls panel, set the duration of the effect to **1:12**.

There aren't enough frames of video to create this effect, and diagonal lines on the transition, both in the Effect Controls panel and on the Timeline, indicate still frames that have been automatically added fill the duration you set. The result is a freeze frame wherever you see the diagonal lines.

Play the transition to see the result.

7 Change the alignment of the transition to Center at Cut.

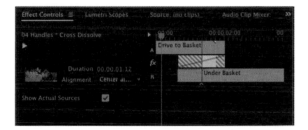

8 Drag the playhead slowly through the transition and watch the result.

- For the first half of the transition (up to the edit point), the B clip is a freeze frame, while the A clip continues to play.

- At the edit point, the A clip and the B clip start to play.

- After the edit, a short freeze frame is used.

There are several ways to fix this issue.

- You can change the duration or alignment of the effect.

- You can use the Rolling Edit tool (⊞) to reposition the transition.

- You can use the Ripple Edit (◄|►) tool to shorten a clip.

Rolling Edit tool

Ripple Edit tool

Note: Using the Rolling Edit tool lets you move the transition left or right but does not change the overall length of the sequence.

You'll learn more about the Rolling Edit and Ripple Edit tools in Lesson 8, "Performing Advanced Editing Techniques."

Adding audio transitions

Audio transitions can dramatically improve a sequence's soundtrack by removing unwanted audio pops or abrupt edits. The use of a crossfade transition at the end of (or between) audio clips is a fast way to add a fade-in, a fade-out, or a fade between your audio clips.

Creating a crossfade

You can choose from three styles of crossfade.

- **Constant Gain:**

  The Constant Gain crossfade (as its name implies) transitions audio by using a constant audio gain (volume) between the clips. Some find this transition type useful. It can, however, create a sudden transition in the audio as the sound of the outgoing clip fades out and the incoming clip then fades in at an equal gain. It's most useful in situations where you do not want much blending between two clips but rather more of a dip out and in between the clips.

- **Constant Power:**

  The default audio transition in Premiere Pro creates a smooth, gradual transition between two audio clips. The Constant Power crossfade works in a similar way to a video dissolve. The outgoing clip fades out slowly at first and then faster toward the end of the clip. For the incoming clip, the opposite occurs— the audio level increases quickly at the start of the incoming clip and more slowly toward the end of the transition. This crossfade is useful in situations where you want to blend the audio between two clips, without a noticeable drop in level in the middle.

- **Exponential Fade:**

  This effect is similar to the Constant Power crossfade. The Exponential Fade transition creates a fairly smooth fade between clips. It uses a logarithmic curve to fade out and fade up audio. Some editors prefer the Exponential Fade transition when performing a single-sided transition (such as fading in a clip from silence at the start or end of a program).

Applying audio transitions

There are several ways to apply an audio crossfade to a sequence. You can, of course, drag and drop an audio transition just as you would a video transition, but there are also useful shortcuts to speed up the process.

Audio transitions have a default duration, measured in seconds or frames. You can change the default duration by choosing Edit > Preferences > General (Windows) or Premiere Pro > Preferences > General (Mac OS).

Let's take a look at the three methods for applying audio transitions.

1 Open the sequence 05 Audio.

The sequence has several audio clips.

2 Open the Audio Transitions > Crossfade group in the Effects panel.

3 Drag the Exponential Fade transition to the start of the first audio clip.

4 Move to the end of the sequence.

5 Right-click the final edit point in the Timeline and choose Apply Default Transitions.

New video and audio transitions are added. To add only an audio transition, hold down Alt (Windows) or Option (Mac OS) when right-clicking to select only the audio clip.

The Constant Power transition is added to the end audio clip as a transition to create a smooth blend as the audio ends.

6 You can change the length of a transition by dragging its edge in the Timeline. Drag to extend the audio transition you just created and listen to the result.

7 To polish the project, add a Video Dissolve transition to the beginning of the sequence. Move the playhead near the beginning, select the first clip, and press Control+D (Windows) or Command+D (Mac OS) to add the default video transition.

You now have a fade from black at the beginning and a fade to black at the end. Now let's add a series of short audio dissolves to smooth out the background sound.

8 With the Selection tool, hold down Alt (Windows) or Option (Mac OS) and lasso all the audio clips on track Audio 1, being careful not to select any video clips.

● **Note:** The selection of clips does not have to be contiguous. You can Shift-click clips to select individual clips in a sequence.

▶ **Tip:** Shift+Ctrl+D (Windows) or Shift+Command+D (Mac OS) is the keyboard shortcut for adding the default audio transition to an edit point near the playhead. Track selection (or clip selection) is used to work out where the effect should be applied.

The Alt (Windows) or Option (Mac OS) key lets you temporarily unlink the audio clips from the video clips to isolate the transitions. Drag from below the audio clips to avoid accidentally selecting items on the video track.

9 Choose Sequence > Apply Default Transitions to Selection.

10 Play the sequence to see and hear the changes you made.

It's common for audio editors to add one- or two-frame audio transitions to every cut in a sequence to avoid jarring pops when an audio clip begins or ends. If you set your default duration for audio transitions to two frames, you can use the Apply Default Transitions option to quickly smooth your audio mix.

Review questions

1 How can you apply the default transition to multiple clips?

2 In the Effects panel, how can you locate a transition effect by name?

3 How do you replace a transition with another one?

4 Explain three ways to change the duration of a transition.

5 What is an easy way to fade audio at the beginning or end of a clip?

Review answers

1 Select clips already on the Timeline, and choose Sequence > Apply Default Transitions to Selection.

2 Start typing the transition name in the Contains Text box in the Effects panel. As you type, Premiere Pro displays all effects and transitions (audio and video) that have that letter combination anywhere in their names. Type more letters to narrow your search.

3 Drag the replacement transition on top of the transition you're rejecting. The new one automatically replaces the old one while adopting its timing.

4 Drag the edge of the transition rectangle in the Timeline, do the same thing in the Effect Controls panel's A/B timeline display, or change the Duration value in the Effect Controls panel. You can also double-click the transition icon in the Timeline panel.

5 An easy way to fade audio in or out is to apply an audio-crossfade transition to the beginning or end of the clip.

8 PERFORMING ADVANCED EDITING TECHNIQUES

Lesson overview

In this lesson, you'll learn about the following:

- Performing a four-point edit
- Changing the speed or duration of clips in your Timeline
- Replacing a clip in a sequence
- Replacing footage in a project
- Creating a nested sequence
- Performing basic trimming on media to refine edits
- Applying slip and slide edits to refine your edit
- Dynamically trimming clips

 This lesson will take approximately 90 minutes.

The main editing commands in Adobe Premiere Pro CC are easy to master. Some advanced techniques take time to learn, but they're worth it! These techniques accelerate editing and provide the understanding you'll need to produce the highest-level professional results. It's time to take your skills to the next level.

Getting started

In this lesson, you'll use several short sequences to explore advanced editing concepts in Adobe Premiere Pro CC. The goal is to get hands-on with the techniques you'll need for advanced editing.

1 Open the project Lesson 08.prproj.

2 Choose Editing in the Workspaces panel, or choose Window > Workspaces > Editing.

Reset the workspace to the saved version by clicking the Editing menu in the Workspaces panel or by choosing Window > Workspaces > Reset to Saved Layout.

Performing four-point editing

In and Out marks are also referred to as *points*. In previous lessons, you used the standard technique of three-point editing. You used three In and Out points (split between the Source Monitor as well as the Program Monitor or Timeline) to describe the source, duration, and location of an edit.

But what happens if you have four marks defined?

The short answer is that you have to make a choice. It's likely that the duration you've marked in the Source Monitor differs from the duration you've marked in the Program Monitor or on the Timeline.

In this case, when you attempt to perform the edit using a keyboard shortcut or onscreen button, a dialog box warns you about the discrepancy and asks you to make a decision, most commonly to discard one of the marks.

► **Tip:** Professional editors often use different language to describe the same thing. This book uses the most common names used by editors so you'll recognize tools, techniques, and other items more easily.

Editing options for four-point edits

If you perform a four-point edit, Premiere Pro opens the Fit Clip dialog to alert you to the problem. You'll need to choose from five options to resolve the conflict. You can ignore one of the four points or change the speed of the clip.

- **Change Clip Speed (Fit to Fill):** The first choice assumes that you set four points with different durations deliberately. Premiere Pro preserves the source clip's In and Out points but adjusts its playback speed to match the duration you have set with In and Out points on the Timeline or in the Program Monitor. This is an excellent choice if you want to adjust clip playback speed to fill a gap.

- **Ignore Source In Point:** If you choose this option, Premiere Pro ignores the source clip's In point, converting your edit back to a three-point edit. When you have an Out point and no In point in the Source Monitor, the In point is worked out based on the duration set in the Timeline or Program Monitor (or the end of the clip). This option is available only if the source clip is longer than the range set in the sequence.

- **Ignore Source Out Point:** When you select this option, Premiere Pro ignores the source clip's Out point, converting your edit back to a three-point edit. When you have an In point and no Out point in the Source Monitor, the In point is worked out based on the duration set in the Timeline or Program Monitor (or the end of the clip). This option is available only if the source clip is longer than the targeted duration.

- **Ignore Sequence In Point:** This choice tells Premiere Pro to ignore the In point you've set in the sequence and perform a three-point edit using only the sequence Out point. The duration is taken from the Source Monitor.

- **Ignore Sequence Out Point:** This option is similar to the previous one. It tells Premiere Pro to ignore the Out point in the sequence you set and perform a three-point edit. Again, the duration is taken from the Source Monitor.

Making a four-point edit

Let's make a four-point edit. You'll change the playback speed of a clip to fit a duration set in the sequence.

1   Open the sequence 01 Four Point.

2   Scroll through the sequence and locate the section with In and Out points already set. You should see a highlighted range in the Timeline.

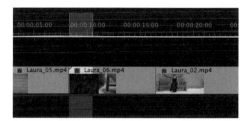

3   Locate the bin called Clips to Load, and open the clip called Laura_04 in the Source Monitor.

Clip In and Out points should already be set on this clip.

4 In the Timeline, check that the Source Track Selection buttons are patched with Source V1 linked to Timeline Video 1.

5 In the Source Monitor, click the Overwrite button to make the edit.

● **Note:** Changing the playback speed of a clip counts as a visual effect. Notice the small "fx" badge on the clip changes color to indicate an effect has been applied.

6 In the Fit Clip dialog box, choose the Change Clip Speed (Fit to Fill) option, and click OK.

The edit is applied. On the Laura_04 clip in the sequence, you'll see numbers that show the new playback speed. The speed has been adjusted perfectly to fit the new duration.

7 Watch the sequence now to see the effects of your edit and the speed change.

▶ **Tip:** You can choose to set a default behavior when a four-point edit occurs by making a selection and selecting Always Use This Choice. If you change your mind, open Premiere Pro General Preferences, and select Fit Clip. The Fit Clip dialog box opens for edit range mismatches.

Changing playback speed

Slow motion is one of the most commonly used effects in video production. You might change the speed of a clip for technical reasons or for artistic impact. It can be an effective way to add drama or to give the audience more time to experience a moment.

A Fit to Fill edit is just one way to change clip playback speed. The best way to achieve high-quality slow motion is usually to record at a higher frame rate than your sequence playback frame rate. If you play the video at a slower frame rate than it was recorded at, you'll see slow motion.

For example, imagine a 10-second video clip was recorded at 48 frames per second but your sequence is set to 24 frames per second. You can set your footage to play at 24 frames per second, matching the sequence. Playback will be smooth, with no frame-rate conversion when the clip is added to the sequence. However, the clip will be playing at half its original frame rate, resulting in 50% slow motion. It will also take twice as long to play back, so the clip will now have a 20-second duration.

Over-cranking

This technique is often called *over-cranking* because early film cameras were driven by turning a crank handle.

The faster the handle was turned, the more frames per second were captured. Slower turning would capture fewer frames per second. This way, when the film was played back at a regular speed, filmmakers would achieve fast motion or slow motion.

Modern cameras often allow recording at faster frame rates to provide excellent-quality slow motion in post-production. The camera will assign a frame rate to the clip that might differ from the actual recorded rate (the system frame rate is used).

This means clips may play in slow motion automatically when you import them into Premiere Pro. Use the Interpret Footage dialog box to tell Premiere Pro how to play clips.

Let's try this.

1 Open the sequence 02 Laura In The Snow. Play the clip in the sequence.

   The clip plays in slow motion for the following reasons:

   • The clip was recorded at 96 frames per second.

   • The clip is set to play back at 24 frames per second (this was set by the camera).

   • The sequence is configured for 24 frames per second playback.

2 In the Project panel, look in the Clips to Load bin for the Laura_01.mp4 clip. Right-click this clip and choose Modify > Interpret Footage.

Use the Interpret Footage dialog box to tell Premiere Pro how to play back clips.

3 Select the "Assume this frame rate" option, and enter **96** in the box. This tells Premiere Pro to play the clip at 96 frames per second. Click OK.

   Look back at the Timeline. The clip has changed appearance.

Diagonal lines on a clip indicate absent media.

You have given the clip a faster frame rate, so the original clip duration is no longer used. Diagonal lines indicate a portion of a clip that has no media.

Premiere Pro does not change the duration of the Timeline clip because doing so might change the timing of your edit. Instead, the part of the sequence clip that has no media is now empty.

● **Note:** If you're using a system with slow storage, you may need to lower the playback resolution in the Program Monitor to see the playback at the full frame rate.

4   Play the sequence again.

The clip plays at regular speed because it was originally recorded at 96 frames per second. It's much less smooth.

5   Drag the Laura_01.mp4 clip onto the Timeline next to the first instance.

The new clip instance is shorter and matches the total playback time at the new frame rate. If you slow down the playback speed of the clip now, it will retain all the original frames, giving better-quality slow motion.

Changing the speed/duration of a clip

Although it's more common to slow clips down, speeding up clips is a useful effect as well. The Speed/Duration command can change the playback speed for a clip in two different ways. You can set the duration of a clip to match a certain time, or you can set the playback speed as a percentage.

For example, if you set a clip to play at 50% speed, it will play back at half-speed; 25% would be one-quarter speed. Premiere Pro allows you to set playback speeds up to two decimal places, so you could have 27.13% if you wanted.

Let's explore this technique.

1   Open the sequence 03 Speed and Duration. Play the sequence to get a sense of normal playback speed.

2   Right-click the Eagle_Walk clip and choose Speed/Duration. You can also select the clip in the Timeline and choose Clip > Speed/Duration.

3   The Clip Speed/Duration dialog box gives you several options for controlling clip playback speed.

   • If you click the chain icon, you can toggle on and off keeping the clip duration and speed ganged together. If this is on, changing one updates the other.

   • Click the link icon so that it shows a broken link. Now, if you enter a new speed, the duration won't update, with one exception: If a new, higher speed reduces the duration so much that *all* the original clip media is used and the result is shorter than the Timeline clip, then the Timeline clip will shorten to fit. This way, you won't have blank video frames in your sequence.

- Once the settings are unganged, you can also change duration without changing speed. If there's another clip immediately after this one on the Timeline, shortening a clip will leave a gap. By default, if you make the clip longer than the space available, the speed change will have no effect. That's because the clip can't move the next clip to make room for the new duration when you change these settings. If you select the Ripple Edit, Shifting Trailing Clips option, you'll enable the clip to make space for itself.

- To play a clip backward, select the Reverse Speed option. You'll see a negative symbol next to the new speed displayed in the sequence.

- If you're changing the speed of a clip that has audio, consider selecting the Maintain Audio Pitch check box. This will keep the clip's original pitch at the new speed. With this option disabled, the pitch will naturally go up or down. This option is more effective for small speed changes; dramatic resampling can produce unnatural results—consider adjusting the audio in Adobe Audition if you need to make a more significant speed change.

4 Make sure Speed and Duration are linked (with the chain icon [🔗] on), change the speed to 50%, and click OK.

Play the clip in the Timeline. You may need to render the clip by pressing Enter (Windows) or Carriage Return (Mac OS) to see smooth playback. Notice that the clip is now 10 seconds long. That's because you slowed it to 50%: half the playback speed means twice the original length.

5 Choose Edit > Undo or press Control+Z (Windows) or Command+Z (Mac OS).

6 Select the clip on the Timeline and press Control+R (Windows) or Command+R (Mac OS) to open the Clip Speed/Duration dialog box.

7 Click the chain icon (🔗) to make sure the Speed and Duration settings are unlinked (shown here). Then change Speed to 50%.

8 Click OK; then play the clip.

The clip is now playing at 50% speed, so it should play for twice as long. But because you've turned off the link between playback speed and duration, the second half has been trimmed to maintain the 5-second duration in the sequence.

Now try reversing playback.

9 Open the Clip Speed / Duration dialog box again.

10 Leave Speed at 50%, but this time select Reverse Speed; then click OK.

11 Play the clip. Now it plays in reverse at 50% slow motion.

Changing the speed/duration with the Rate Stretch tool

Sometimes you'll have a clip that has perfect content to fill a gap in your sequence, but it is just a little too short or a little too long. This is where the Rate Stretch tool helps.

1 Open the sequence 04 Rate Stretch.

This sequence is synchronized to music, and the clips contain the desired content, but the first clip is too short. You can make a guess and try to make an exact Speed/Duration adjustment, but it's easier and faster to use the Rate Stretch tool to drag the end of the clip to fill the gap.

2 Select the Rate Stretch tool ( ) in the Tools panel.

3 Using this tool, drag the right edge of the first video clip until it meets the second video clip.

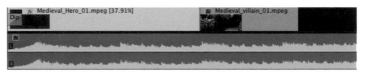

The speed of the clip changes to fill the gap. The contents haven't changed; the clip is playing more slowly.

4 Using the same tool, drag the right edge of the second clip until it meets the third clip.

5 Drag the right edge of the third clip until it matches the end of the audio.

6 Play the Timeline to view the result.

7 Press the V key or click the Selection tool to select it.

Changing the speed/duration with time remapping

Time remapping lets you vary the speed of a clip using keyframes. This means one portion of a clip could play in slow motion while another portion of the same clip plays in fast motion.

In addition to giving you flexibility, variable-speed time remapping allows you to smoothly transition from one speed to another, whether from fast to slow or from forward motion to reverse motion.

1 Open the sequence 05 Remapping.

This sequence has a single shot.

2 Adjust the height of the Video 1 track to make it taller. To do this, drag the horizontal divider between audio and video tracks down to make more room for the video tracks. Then, also on the header, drag the header between the Video 1 track and Video 2 track and drag up.

▶ **Tip:** You can also change track height by positioning the mouse cursor over the track header and scrolling.

Increasing track height makes adjusting Timeline clip keyframes easier.

3 Right-click the Fx badge on the clip and choose Time Remapping > Speed.

With this option selected, the thin white line across the clip represents the playback speed. The higher the line is set, the faster the clip will play.

4 Position the Timeline playhead to the point where the couple have met and are turning around (about 00:00:15:00).

5 Press and hold the Control (Windows) or Command (Mac OS) key as you hover your mouse over the white line.

The pointer turns to a small plus (+) symbol.

6 Click the white line around 15 seconds into the clip to create a keyframe, visible near the top of the clip.

You're not changing the speed yet; you're just adding keyframes.

▶ **Tip:** By default, Premiere Pro does not display video-clip keyframes. You can enable them by clicking the Timeline settings menu and choosing Show Video Keyframes.

7 Using the same technique, add another speed keyframe at about 00:00:24:00, just as the couple parts ways.

By adding those two speed keyframes, you've divided the clip into three "speed sections." Now you'll set different speeds between the keyframes.

8 Position the Selection tool over the white line between the first and second keyframes, and drag it up to approximately 300%. A tool tip will appear to show you the speed setting as you adjust it.

The clip shortens because of the faster playback.

9 Choose Sequence > Render Effects In to Out to render the clip for the smoothest playback. If you have the Timeline Work Area option enabled, this menu option changes to Sequence > Render Effects in Work Area.

10 Play the clip. The speed changes from 100% to 300% and back to 100%.

Variable-clip speed changes can be dramatic. So far, you have applied a speed change that switches from one speed to another instantly. That can be highly effective, but it's also possible to smoothly transition from one speed to another.

11 Speed keyframes are actually in two halves. You can drag to separate them. Try it now: Drag the right half of the first speed keyframe to the right to create a speed transition ramp.

The white line ramps up now, rather than making a sudden change from 100% to 300%.

12 Drag the left half of the second speed keyframe to the left to create a transition there as well.

Recognizing the downstream effects of changing time

If you change the speed of a clip at the beginning of the Timeline after assembling many clips in your sequence, it's important to understand the way this will affect the rest of the sequence "downstream." You might cause the following:

- Unwanted gaps caused by clips growing shorter because they are playing faster than they did originally.

- Unwanted duration changes to the overall sequence because of the Ripple Edit option.

- Potential audio problems created by changes in speed—including changing pitch.

- If you use Time Remapping, clip audio is not affected, which means you'll need to work on the audio timing separately.

When you're making speed or duration changes, be careful to view the overall impact on the sequence. You may want to change the zoom level of the Timeline to view the entire sequence or segment at once.

13 Right-click the clip and choose Time Interpolation > Optical Flow. This smooths playback when changing clip speed. It's a more advanced system for rendering motion changes and takes longer to render.

14 Render and play the sequence to see the effect.

Replacing clips and footage

During the editing process, it's common to swap one clip in a sequence for another as you try different versions of an edit.

This might mean making a global replacement, such as replacing one version of an animated logo with a newer file. You might also want to swap out one clip in your sequence for another that you have in a bin. Depending on the task at hand, you'll use different methods.

Dragging in a replacement clip

You can drag a new shot onto the existing sequence clip you'd like to replace.

Let's try it.

1 Open the 06 Replace Clip sequence.

2 Play back the Timeline.

Notice that the same clip is played twice as a picture-in-picture (PIP) for clips 2 and 3. The clip has some animated motion keyframes that cause it to spin onto the screen and then spin off. You'll learn how to create these kinds of effects in the next lesson.

Let's replace the first instance of the clip (SHOT4) in the V2 track with a new clip called Boat Replacement. However, you don't want to have to re-create the effects and animation. This is a perfect scenario for replacing a sequence clip.

3 From the Clips to Load bin, drag the Boat Replacement clip over the first instance of the SHOT4 clip on the Timeline, but don't release the mouse button yet.

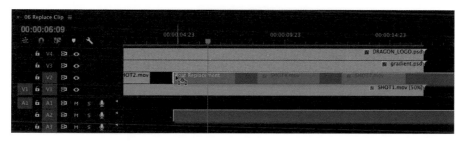

The clip is longer than the existing clip that you intend to replace.

> ● **Note:** To remove a time-remapping effect, select the clip and view the Effect Controls panel. Click the disclosure triangle next to the Time Remapping effect to open it. Click the toggle animation button (stopwatch) next to the word *Speed*. This sets it to the off position. A warning dialog box appears. Click OK to remove the effect.

4 Hold the Alt (Windows) or Option (Mac OS) key.

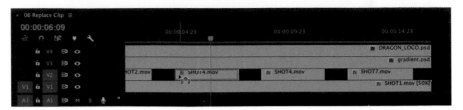

While you're holding this modifier key, the replacement clip snaps to fit the exact length of the clip it's replacing. Release the mouse button to replace the clip.

5 Play the Timeline. All the PIP clips have the same effect applied to different footage. The new clip inherits the settings and effects from the clip it replaced. This is a quick and easy way to try different shots in a sequence.

Making a replace edit

When you drag and drop to replace a sequence clip, Premiere Pro synchronizes the first frame (or In point) of the replacement clip with the first visible frame of the clip in the sequence. This is often fine, but what if you need to synchronize a particular moment in the action, such as hands clapping or a door closing?

If you'd like to have more control over a replace edit, you can use the Replace Edit command. This allows you to synchronize a particular frame of the replacement clip with a particular frame of the clip it's replacing.

1 Open the sequence 07 Replace Edit.

This is the same sequence you previously fixed, but this time you'll position the replacement clip precisely.

2 Position the playhead in the sequence at approximately 00:00:06:00. The playhead will be the sync point for the edit you are about to perform.

3 Click the first instance of the SHOT4 clip in the sequence to select it.

4 From the Clips to Load bin, open the clip Boat Replacement in the Source Monitor.

5 In the Source Monitor, position the playhead to choose a good piece of action for the replacement. There's a marker on the clip for guidance.

6 Make sure the Timeline is active, with the first instance of SHOT4.mov selected, and choose Clip > Replace With Clip > From Source Monitor, Match Frame.

The clip is replaced.

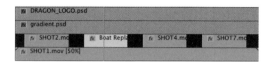

7 Play the newly edited sequence to check the edit.

The playhead position in the Source Monitor and Program Monitor was synchronized. The sequence clip duration, effects, and settings are all applied to the replacement clip. This technique can be a huge time-saver!

Using the Replace Footage feature

The Replace Footage feature replaces footage in the Project panel so that the clip links to a different media file. This can be of great benefit when you need to replace a clip that occurs several times in a sequence or in multiple sequences. You might use this to update an animated logo or a piece of music.

When you replace footage in the Project panel, all instances of the clip you replace are changed anywhere the clip was used.

1 Load the sequence 08 Replace Footage.

2 Play the sequence.

Let's replace the graphic with something more interesting.

3 In the Clips to Load bin, select the clip DRAGON_LOGO.psd in the Project panel.

Note: The Replace Footage command cannot be undone. To switch back to the original clip, choose Clip > Replace Footage again to navigate to and relink the original file.

4 Choose Clip > Replace Footage, or right-click the clip and choose Replace Footage.

5 Navigate to the Lessons/Assets/Graphics folder, and choose the DRAGON_LOGO_FIX.psd file. Double-click to select it.

6 Play the Timeline. The graphic has been updated throughout the sequence and project. Even the clip name in the Project panel has updated to match the new file.

Nesting sequences

A *nested* sequence is a sequence contained within another sequence. You can break up a long project into more manageable parts by creating separate sequences for each section. Then, you can drag each sequence—with all its clips, graphics, layers, multiple audio/video tracks, and effects—into another, "Master" sequence. Nested sequences look and behave like single audio/video clips, but you can edit their contents and see the changes update inside the master sequence.

Nested sequences have many potential uses.

- They simplify editing by allowing you to create complex sequences in separate parts. This can help you avoid running into conflicts or accidentally moving clips and ruining your edit.

- They allow you to apply an effect to a group of clips in a single step.

- They let you use sequences as a source in multiple other sequences. You can create one intro sequence for a multipart series and add it to each episode. If you need to change the intro sequence, you can do so once and see the results update everywhere it's nested.

- They allow you to organize your work in the same way you might create sub-folders in the Project panel.

- They allow you to apply transitions to a group of clips as a single item.

When editing one sequence into another, a button in the upper-left corner of the Timeline panel lets you choose between adding the contents of the sequence (![icon]) or nesting it (![icon]).

Adding a nested sequence

One reason to use a nest is to reuse an existing edited sequence. Let's add an edited opening title into a sequence now.

1 Open the sequence 09 Bike Race, and make sure the option is set to nest sequences (![icon]).

2 Set an In point at the start of the sequence.

3 Make sure that source track V1 is patched to the Video 1 track in the Timeline. You may need to open a clip in the Source Monitor to see the source track enable buttons.

4 In the Project panel, find the sequence 09A Race Open.

5 Drag the sequence 09A Race Open into the Program Monitor (rather than the Timeline), dropping the clip onto the Insert option.

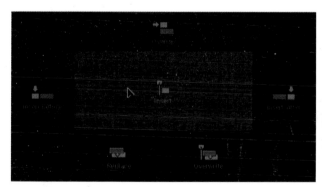

Tip: A quick way to create a nested sequence is to drag a sequence from the Project panel into the appropriate track or tracks of the currently active sequence. You can also drag a sequence into the Source Monitor, apply In and Out points, and perform insert and overwrite edits to add it to another sequence.

This performs an insert edit.

6 Play the 09 Bike Race sequence to see the result.

The 09A Race Open sequence is added as a single clip, even though it contains multiple video tracks and audio clips.

Tip: If you need to make a change to a nested sequence, double-click it and it will open in a new Timeline.

Performing regular trimming

You can adjust the part of a clip used in a sequence in several ways. This process is generally called *trimming*. When you trim, you can make the selected part of the original clip shorter or longer. Some trimming types affect a single clip, whereas others adjust the relationship between two adjacent clips.

Trimming in the Source Monitor

You can view a sequence clip (that is, the instance of a clip that's in a sequence) by double-clicking it. Once open in the Source Monitor, you can adjust its In and Out marks, and the clip will update in the sequence. There are two basic ways of changing existing In and Out points in the Source Monitor.

- **Mark new In and Out points:** Simply add new In or Out points. Double-click a clip on the Timeline to load it. With the clip loaded, position the playhead and press the I or O key for In or Out. Alternatively, you can use the Mark In and Mark Out buttons at the bottom of the Source Monitor. If the clip has another clip adjacent to it in the Timeline, you can only make the current clip shorter, leaving a gap on the side where you made the trim.

- **Drag In and Out points:** You can change the In and Out points by dragging them. Simply place your cursor over an In or Out point in the mini Timeline at the bottom of the Source Monitor. The cursor changes into a red-and-black icon, indicating that a trim can be performed.

You can drag left or right to change the In or Out point. Once again, if the clip has another clip adjacent to it on the Timeline, you can only make it shorter, and a gap will appear after making a trim.

Trimming in a sequence

Another, faster way to trim clips is directly on the Timeline. Making a single clip shorter or longer is called a *regular* trim, and it's fairly easy.

1 Open the sequence 10 Regular Trim.

2 Play the sequence.

   The last shot is cut off, and it needs to be extended to match the end of the music.

3 Choose the Selection tool (V).

4 Position the mouse cursor over the Out point of the last clip in the sequence.

Music: "Reverie (small theme)"
by _ghost (http://ccmixter.org/
files/_ghost/25389)

The pointer changes into the red Trim In tool (head side) or Trim Out tool (tail side) with directional arrows. Hovering the mouse over the edge of the clip changes it between trimming the Out point (open to the left) or In point (open to the right) of a clip.

5 Drag an edge to the right until it meets the end of the audio file.

A tool tip shows you how much you've trimmed.

6 Release the mouse button to apply the trim.

Performing advanced trimming

The trimming methods you've learned so far have their limitations. They can leave unwanted gaps in the Timeline caused by shortening a clip. They can also prevent you from lengthening a shot if there's an adjacent clip.

Fortunately, Premiere Pro offers several more ways of trimming.

Making ripple edits

You can avoid creating gaps when trimming by using the Ripple Edit tool ( ), one of the tools in the Tools panel.

You use the Ripple Edit tool to trim a clip in the same way you used the Selection tool. When you use the Ripple Edit tool to change the duration of a clip, the adjustment ripples through the sequence. That is, clips after the clip you adjust slide to the left to fill the gap, or they slide to the right to make room for the longer clip.

Let's try it.

1 Open the sequence 11 Ripple Edit.

2 Select the Ripple Edit tool (or press B on your keyboard).

Note: A regular trim is also referred to as a single-sided or overwrite trim.

Note: If you make a clip shorter, it will leave a gap between it and any adjacent clips. Later in this lesson you'll learn to use the Ripple Edit tool to automatically remove any gaps or push clips later to avoid overwriting them.

Note: When performing a ripple edit, you can knock items on other tracks out of sync. Use the sync locks with care when ripple trimming.

3 Hover the Ripple Edit tool over the inside-right edge of the seventh clip (SHOT7) until it turns into a yellow, left-facing bracket and arrow.

The shot is too short, so let's add some more footage from the clip.

4 Drag to the right until the timecode in the tool tip reads +00:00:01:10.

Notice that while you're using the Ripple Edit tool, the Program Monitor displays the last frame of the first clip on the left and the first frame of the second clip on the right. Watch the moving edit position on the left half of the Program Monitor.

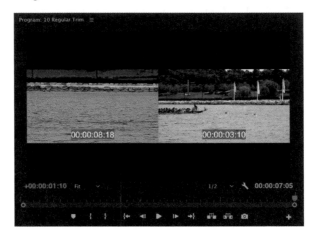

5 Release the mouse button to complete the edit.

The clip expands, and the clip to its right slides along with it. Play that portion of the sequence to see whether the edit works smoothly. The edit has exposed a slight on-camera shake that you'll work on next.

▶ **Tip:** You can temporarily use the Selection tool as a Ripple Edit tool by holding Control (Windows) or Command (Mac OS). Be sure to click to one side of the edit to avoid performing a rolling edit (described next).

Making rolling edits

When you used the Ripple Edit tool, it made changes to the overall length of the sequence. This is because one clip got longer or shorter while the rest of the sequence moved to close the gap (or move out of the way).

There's another way to change the timing of an edit: a rolling edit.

With a rolling edit, the overall length of the sequence does not change. Instead, a rolling edit shortens one clip and lengthens another at the same time, simultaneously adjusting them by the same number of frames.

For example, if you use the Rolling Edit tool to extend a clip by 2 seconds, you will also shorten the adjacent clip by 2 seconds.

Note: A rolling edit trim is sometimes referred to as a double-roller or dual-roller trim.

1 Continue working with the sequence 11 Ripple Edit.

   Several clips are already on the Timeline, with enough leftover handle frames to allow the edits you're about to perform.

2 Select the Rolling Edit tool (keyboard shortcut N) () in the Tools panel.

▶ **Tip:** Zoom in to the Timeline to make more accurate adjustments.

3 Drag the edit point between SHOT7 and SHOT8 (the last two clips on the Timeline). Use the Program Monitor split screen to find a better matching edit between the two shots. Drag the edit left to remove the camera shake.

   Try rolling the edit to the left to 00:17 (17 frames). You can use the Program Monitor timecode or the pop-up timecode in the Timeline to find that edit.

Note: When trimming, it's possible to trim a clip to a 0 (zero) duration (removing it from the Timeline).

Making sliding edits

The slide edit is a special kind of trim. It's not used often but can be a time-saver in some situations. The Slide tool works by leaving the duration of the clip you're sliding unchanged. Instead, the Out point of the clip to the left and the In point of the clip to the right are changed by equal amounts, in opposite directions. It's another form of dual-roller trim.

Because you're changing the other clip durations by an equal number of frames, the length of the sequence doesn't change.

1 Continue working with the sequence 11 Ripple Edit.

2 Select the Slide tool (U) ( ).

3 Position the Slide tool over the middle of the second clip in the sequence, SHOT2.

4 Drag the clip left or right.

5 Take a look at the Program Monitor as you perform the slide edit.

The Slide tool moves a clip over two adjacent clips, and the Program Monitor updates to show the new cut points.

SHOT2 In point (unchanged)

SHOT2 Out point (unchanged)

SHOT1 Out point (changed)

SHOT3 In point (changed)

The two top images are the In point and Out point of SHOT2—the clip you are dragging. They do not change because you are not changing the selected part of SHOT2.

The two larger images are the Out point and In point of the previous and next clips. These edit points change as you slide the selected clip over those adjacent clips.

Making slip edits

A slip trim changes both the In point and Out point of a sequence clip at the same time, by the same amount, rolling the visible contents in position. Because a slip trim changes the beginning and end by equal amounts, it doesn't change the duration of your sequence. In this way, it's the same as rolling trims and slide trims.

Slip trims change only the clip you select; adjacent clips before or after the clip you adjust are not affected. Using the Slip tool to adjust a clip is a little like moving a conveyor belt: The visible part of the original clip changes inside the Timeline clip segment without changing the length of the clip or the sequence.

1 Continue working with the sequence 11 Ripple Edit.

2 Select the Slip tool (Y) (![icon]).

3 Drag SHOT5 left and right.

4 Take a look at the Program Monitor while you perform the slip edit.

The Slip tool changes the contents of a clip in position.

SHOT4
Out point
(unchanged)

SHOT6
In point
(unchanged)

00:00:00:07

00:00:04:18

SHOT5 In point
(changed)

SHOT5 Out point
(changed)

The two top images are the Out point and In point of SHOT4 and SHOT6, before and after the clip you are adjusting; they don't change. The two larger images are the In point and Out point of SHOT5; these edit points do change.

The Slip Trim tool is well worth taking time to get to grips with. It can be the fastest tool for adjusting timing when cutting action.

Trimming in the Program Monitor

If you'd like to trim with more control, you can use the Program Monitor Trim mode. This allows you to see both the outgoing and incoming frames of the trim you're working on and has dedicated buttons for making precise adjustments.

When the Program Monitor is set to Trim mode, playback loops appear around the edit you have selected until you stop playback. This means you can continually adjust the timing of an edit and view the result immediately.

You can perform three types of trim using the Program Monitor Trim mode controls. You learned about each of these earlier in this lesson.

* **Regular trim:** This basic type of trim moves the edge of the selected clip. This method trims only one side of the edit point. It moves the selected edit point either forward or backward in the Timeline, but it doesn't shift any of the other clips.

* **Roll trim:** The roll trim moves the tail of one clip and the head of the adjacent clip. It lets you adjust an edit point (provided there are handles). No gap is created, and the sequence duration doesn't change.

* **Ripple trim:** This moves the selected edge of the edit either earlier or later. Clips after the edit shift to close a gap or make room for a longer clip.

Using Trim mode in the Program Monitor

When you're in Trim mode, some of the Program Monitor controls change to make it easier to focus on trimming. To use Trim mode, you need to activate it by selecting an edit point between two clips. There are three ways to do this.

● **Note:** You can use the Selection tool with the Control (Windows) or Command (Mac OS) key as a shortcut to the Ripple Edit tool or Rolling Edit tool.

- Double-click an edit point on the Timeline with a selection tool or trimming tool.

- With the correct Track selection button enabled, press the T key. The playhead will move to the nearest edit point, and Trim mode will open in the Program Monitor.

- Drag around one or more edits using the Ripple Edit tool or Rolling Edit tool to select them and open the Program Monitor to Trim mode.

When invoked, Trim mode shows two video clips. The box on the left shows the outgoing clip (also called *A side*). The box on the right shows the incoming clip (also called *B side*). Below the frames are five buttons and two indicators.

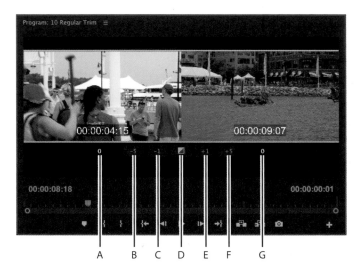

A Out Shift counter: This shows how many frames the Out point for the A side has changed.

B Trim Backward Many: When clicked, this performs the selected trim, adjusting by multiple frames earlier. The size of the adjustment depends on the Large Trim Offset option in the Trim Preferences tab of Preferences.

C Trim Backward: This performs the selected trim, adjusting by one frame at a time earlier.

D Apply Default Transitions to Selection: This applies the default transition (usually a dissolve) to video and audio tracks that have their edit points selected.

E Trim Forward: This is like Trim Backward except it adjusts the edit one frame later.

F Trim Forward Many: This is like Trim Backward Many except it adjusts the edit multiple frames later.

G In Shift counter: This shows how many frames the In point for the B side has changed.

Choosing a trimming method in the Program Monitor

You've already learned about the three types of trims you can perform (regular, roll, and ripple). You also tried each in the Timeline. Using Trim mode in the Program Monitor makes the process easier because it provides rich visual feedback. It also provides subtle control when dragging, regardless of the Timeline view scale: Even if the Timeline is zoomed a long way out, you'll be able to make frame-accurate trim adjustments in the Program Monitor Trim view.

1 Open the sequence 12 Trim View.

2 With the Selection tool (V), hold down Alt (Windows) or Option (Mac OS) and double-click the video edit between the first clip and the second clip in the sequence. Holding this modifier key selects just the video edits and leaves the audio tracks untouched.

3 In the Program Monitor, move the cursor slowly across the A and B clips.

As you move the cursor from left to right, you'll see the tool change from Trim Out (left side) to Roll (center) to Trim In (right).

4 Drag in between both clips in the Program Monitor to perform a rolling edit trim.

Adjust the timing until the time display on the lower-right side of the Program Monitor reads 01:26:59:01.

● **Note:** Clicking the A or B side will switch which side is being trimmed. Clicking in the center will switch to a rolling edit.

5 Press the Down Arrow key to jump between edits until you have selected the edit between the third and fourth clips.

The outgoing shot is too long and shows the actor sitting down twice.

6 Change your trimming method to a ripple edit for the outgoing clip (drag on the left in the Trim view).

You can also change the trimming method by pressing the shortcut Shift+T (Windows) or Control+T (Mac OS) to cycle Trim modes. There are five options to cycle through. Tap the key combo once to cycle to the next shortcut. The five choices loop. You've selected a ripple edit when the Trim tool shows a yellow trim arrow.

● **Note:** The type of trim that's used by default may seem random, but it's not. The initial setting is chosen by the type of tool that was used to select the edit point. If you click with the Selection tool, Premiere Pro chooses a regular Trim In or Trim Out. If you click with the Ripple Edit tool, then the Ripple In or Ripple Out trim is chosen. In both cases, cycling the roller will result in a rolling trim. If you use the keyboard shortcut T, you'll always select a rolling edit.

7 Drag to the left for the outgoing clip (on the left) to make the clip shorter.

Make sure the time display on the left reads 01:54:12:18.

The rest of the clips ripple to close the gap. The timing of the edit works now.

Modifier keys

You can use multiple modifier keys to refine a trim selection.

- Hold down Alt (Windows) or Option (Mac OS) when selecting clips to temporarily unlink audio and video. This makes it easier to select just the audio or video portion of a clip.

- Hold down the Shift key to select multiple edit points. You can trim multiple tracks or even multiple clips at the same time. Wherever you see a trim "handle," adjustments will be made when you apply a trim.

- Combine these two modifier keys to make advanced selections for trimming.

Performing dynamic trimming

Much of the trimming work you will perform will be to tune the rhythm of an edit. In many ways, achieving perfect timing for a cut is the point at which the craft of editing becomes the art.

The trim mode looping playback makes it easier to get a feel for the timing of an edit, but you can also update a trim using keyboard shortcuts or buttons while the sequence plays back in real time.

1   Continue working with the sequence 12 Trim View.

2   Press the Down Arrow key to move to the next video edit point, between the fourth and fifth video clips. Set the trim type to a rolling trim. You can use the shortcut Shift+T (Windows) or Control+T (Mac OS) to cycle Trim modes.

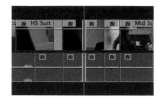

You can stay in Trim mode while switching between edit points.

3   Press the spacebar to loop playback.

You'll see a playback loop lasting a few seconds, with the shot before and after the cut playing back. This helps you get a feel for the content of the edit.

Note: To control the pre-roll and post-roll durations, go to Premiere Pro Preferences and select the Playback category. You can set the duration in seconds. Most editors find a duration of 2 to 5 seconds most useful.

4   Try adjusting the trim using the methods you've learned while the playback loops.

The Trim Forward and Trim Backward buttons at the bottom of Trim mode view work well and can adjust the edit while the clip plays back.

Now let's try using the keyboard for more dynamic control. The same J, K, and L keys you use to control playback can also be used to control trimming.

5   Click Stop or press the spacebar to stop the playback loop.

6   Press the L key to shuttle the trim to the right.

Pressing once trims in real time. You can tap the L key multiple times to trim faster.

7   Press the K key to stop trimming.

Let's refine and trim back a little earlier.

Note: The Timeline clip duration updates when you press K to stop trimming.

8   Hold down the K key and press the J key to shuttle left in slow motion.

9   Release both keys to stop the trim.

10 To exit Trim mode, click away from the edit on the Timeline to deselect the edit. You can also use the Deselect All keyboard shortcut, which is Control+Shift+A (Windows) or Command+Shift+A (Mac OS).

Trimming with the keyboard

Here are some of the most useful keyboard shortcuts to use when trimming.

Table 8.1 Trimming in the Timeline

MAC	WINDOWS
Trim Backward: Alt+Left Arrow	**Trim Backward:** Control+Left Arrow
Trim Backward Many: Alt+Shift+Left Arrow	**Trim Backward Many:** Control+Shift+Left Arrow
Trim Forward: Alt+Right Arrow	**Trim Forward:** Control+Right Arrow
Trim Forward Many: Alt+Shift+Right Arrow	**Trim Forward Many:** Control +Shift+Right Arrow
Slide Clip Selection Left Five Frames: Alt+Shift+, (comma)	**Slide Clip Selection Left Five Frames:** Alt+Shift+, (comma)
Slide Clip Selection Left One Frame: Alt+, (comma)	**Slide Clip Selection Left One Frame:** Alt+, (comma)
Slide Clip Selection Right Five Frames: Alt+Shift+. (period)	**Slide Clip Selection Right Five Frames:** Alt+Shift+. (period)
Slide Clip Selection Right One Frame: Alt+. (period)	**Slide Clip Selection Right One Frame:** Alt+. (period)
Slip Clip Selection Left Five Frames: Command+Alt+Shift+Left Arrow	**Slip Clip Selection Left Five Frames:** Control+Alt+Shift+Left Arrow
Slip Clip Selection Left One Frame: Command+Alt+Left Arrow	**Slip Clip Selection Left One Frame:** Control+Alt+Left Arrow
Slip Clip Selection Right Five Frames: Command+Alt+Shift+Right Arrow	**Slip Clip Selection Right Five Frames:** Control+Alt+Shift+Right Arrow
Slip Clip Selection Right One Frame: Command+Alt+Right Arrow	**Slip Clip Selection Right One Frame:** Control+Alt+Right Arrow

Review questions

1 If you change the playback speed of a clip to 50%, what effect will this have on the clip duration?

2 Which tool allows you to stretch a sequence clip to change its playback speed?

3 Can you make time-remapping changes directly on the Timeline?

4 How do you create a smooth ramp-up from slow motion to normal speed?

5 What's the difference between a slide edit and a slip edit?

6 What is the difference between replacing a clip and replacing footage?

Review answers

1 The clip will be twice as long. Reducing a clip's speed causes the clip to become longer, unless the Speed and Duration parameters are unlinked in the Clip Speed/Duration dialog box or the clip is bound by another clip.

2 The Rate Stretch tool allows you to adjust playback speed as if you were trimming. This is useful when you need to fill a small extra amount of time in a sequence.

3 Yes. In fact, time remapping is best performed on the Timeline, where you can easily see the results.

4 Add a speed keyframe and split it by dragging away half of the keyframe to create a transition between the two speeds.

5 You slide a clip over adjacent clips, retaining the selected clip's original In and Out points. You slip a clip under adjacent clips, changing the selected clip's In and Out points.

6 Replacing a clip replaces a single sequence clip on the Timeline with a new clip from the Project panel. Replacing footage replaces a clip in the Project panel with a new source clip. Any instance of the clip in any sequence in the project is replaced. In both cases, effects applied to the replaced clip are maintained.

9 PUTTING CLIPS IN MOTION

Lesson overview

In this lesson, you'll learn about the following:

- Adjusting the Motion effect for clips

- Changing clip size and adding rotation

- Adjusting the anchor point to refine rotation

- Working with keyframe interpolation

- Enhancing motion with shadows and beveled edges

 This lesson will take approximately 60 minutes.

The Motion effect controls can add movement to a clip. This can be useful for animating a graphic or for sizing and repositioning a video clip within the frame. You can animate an object's position using keyframes and enhance that animation by controlling their interpolation between values.

201

Getting started

Video projects are often motion graphics–oriented, and it's common to see multiple shots combined as complex compositions. These are often put into motion. Perhaps you'll see multiple video clips streaming past in floating boxes, or you'll see a video clip shrunk down and placed next to an on-camera host. You can create those effects (and more) in Adobe Premiere Pro CC by using the Motion settings or a number of clip-based effects that offer Motion settings.

The Motion effect controls allow you to position, rotate, or scale a clip within the frame. Some adjustments can be made directly in the Program Monitor. It's important to be clear that the adjustments you make in the Effect Controls panel relate exclusively to the clip you have selected and not to the sequence it is in. The sequence settings can be considered the output settings, and these are in the Sequence Settings, in the Sequence menu.

● **Note:** Bézier curve controls were originally used in automotive design but became popular in other design applications because of the fine control they offer for natural curves.

A *keyframe* is a special kind of marker that defines settings at a particular point in time. If you use two (or more) keyframes, Premiere Pro can automatically animate the settings between them. You can use advanced *Bézier* controls to make subtle adjustments to the timing or settings for an effect.

Adjusting the Motion effect

Every visual clip in a Premiere Pro sequence automatically has a number of effects applied as *fixed effects* (also sometimes called *intrinsic effects*). Motion is one of these effects.

To adjust the effect, select the clip in a sequence and look in the Effect Controls panel. Expand the Motion effect to adjust the settings.

▶ **Tip:** Unlike other effect controls, if you expand or collapse the settings for the Motion effect, the settings will remain expanded or collapsed for all clips.

The Motion effect allows you to adjust the position, scale, or rotation of a clip. Let's look at the way this effect has been used to reposition a clip in a sequence.

1 Open Lesson 09.prproj in the Lesson 09 folder.

2 Choose Effects in the Workspaces panel, or choose Window > Workspaces > Effects.

   This workspace was created to make it easier to work with transitions and effects. If you have been using Premiere Pro for a while, you may need to reset the workspace to the saved version by clicking the Effects menu in the Workspaces panel.

3 Open the sequence 01 Floating.

4 Make sure the Select Zoom Level menu in the Program Monitor is set to Fit. It's important to see the whole composition when setting up visual effects.

5 Play the sequence.

This clip's Position, Scale, and Rotation properties have been changed. Keyframes have been added, with different settings at different points in time, so the clip animates.

Understanding Motion settings

Though these controls are called Motion, there's no movement until you add it. By default, clips are displayed at 100% scale in the center of the Program Monitor.

Here are the options:

- **Position:** This places the clip along x- and y-axes. Coordinates are calculated based on the pixel position of an anchor point (covered later in this list) from the upper-left corner of the image. So, the default position for a 1280x720 clip would be 640, 360, that is, the exact center.

- **Scale (Scale Height, when Uniform Scale is deselected):** Clips are set to their full size by default (100%). To shrink a clip, reduce this number. You can scale up to 10,000%—though be warned, scaling up will make images pixelated and soft.

- **Scale Width:** Deselect Uniform Scale to make Scale Width available. This lets you change the clip width and height independently.

- **Rotation:** You can rotate an image along the z axis—a flat spin (as if viewing a spinning turntable or carousel from above). You can enter degrees or a number of rotations. For example, 450 is the same as 1 x 90 (the 1 counts as one full 360-degree turn). Positive numbers give clockwise rotation, and negative numbers give counterclockwise rotation.

- **Anchor Point:** Rotation and position adjustments are all based on the anchor point, which is at the center of a clip by default. This can be changed to any point, including one of the clip's corners or even a point outside the clip. For example, if you set the anchor point to the corner of the clip, when you adjust the Rotation setting, the clip will rotate around that corner rather than around the center of the image. If you change the anchor point in relation to the image, you may have to reposition the clip in the frame to compensate for the adjustment.

- **Anti-flicker Filter:** This feature is useful for interlaced video clips and for images that contain high detail, such as fine lines, hard edges, or parallel lines (that can cause moiré problems). These high-detail images can flicker during motion. To add some blurring and reduce flicker, use 1.00.

Let's look closer at the animated clip, continuing to work with the sequence 01 Floating.

1 Click the clip on the Timeline to make sure it is selected.

● **Note:** If the frame containing the Effect Controls panel is narrow, some of the controls will overlap, making it difficult to interact with them. If this is the case, make the frame wider before working with the Effect Controls panel.

2 Make sure the Effect Controls panel is visible. It should have appeared when you reset the Effects workspace, but if you can't find it, look for it in the Window menu.

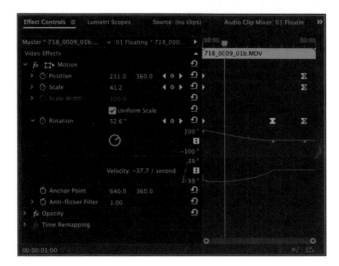

3 In the Effect Controls panel, expand the Motion effect controls by clicking the angled mark next to the Motion heading ( ).

4 At the upper right of the Effect Controls panel settings, to the right of the master clip name and sequence clip name (these can be different if you choose), a small triangle toggles the display of an integrated Timeline. Make sure the Effect Controls Timeline is visible.

If it isn't, click the triangle to show it. The Timeline in the Effect Controls panel displays keyframes.

5 Click the Go to Previous Keyframe or Go to Next Keyframe arrows to jump between existing keyframes. Each control has its own keyframes.

● **Note:** It can be difficult to line up the playhead with an existing keyframe. Using the Previous/Next Keyframe buttons helps you avoid adding unwanted keyframes.

Now that you know how to view an animation, let's reset the clip. You'll animate from scratch later in this lesson.

6 Click the Toggle animation stopwatch button for the Position property to turn off its keyframes.

7 Click OK when prompted that all keyframes will be deleted if you apply the action.

8 Turn off keyframes for the Scale and Rotation properties too.

9 Click the Reset button, to the right of the Motion effect heading in the Effect Controls panel.

Now the Motion settings are all set to their default settings.

Examining Motion properties

The Position, Scale, and Rotation properties are *spatial*. That means the changes you make are easy to see because the object will change in size and position. You can adjust these properties by entering numerical values, by using the scrubbable text, or by dragging the Transform controls.

1 Open the sequence 02 Motion.

2 In the Program Monitor, make sure the zoom level is set to 25% or 50% (or a zoom amount that allows you to see space around the active frame).

Setting the zoom very small makes it easy to position items outside the frame.

3 Drag the playhead anywhere in the clip so you can see the video in the Program Monitor.

4 Click the clip in the Timeline so it's selected, with its settings displayed in the Effect Controls panel.

If necessary, expand the Motion settings.

5 Click the Motion effect heading in the Effect Controls panel to select it.

When you select the motion effect, a bounding box with a crosshair and handles appears around the clip in the Program Monitor.

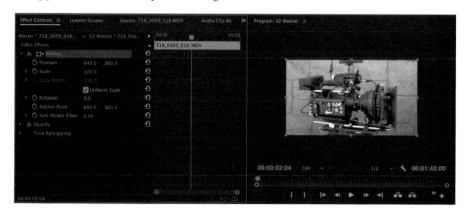

Note: Each control has its own Reset button. If you reset the whole effect, every control is returned to its default state.

Note: When the Toggle animation button is on, clicking the Reset button will not change any existing keyframes. Instead, a new keyframe is added with default settings. It's important to turn off animation before resetting the effect to avoid this.

Note: Several effects, like the Motion effect, have a Transform icon ( ) to indicate that you can use direct manipulation in the Program Monitor when you select the effect heading. Try this with Corner Pin, Crop, Mirror, Transform, and Twirl.

6 Click anywhere inside the clip bounding box in the Program Monitor and drag the clip around.

Position values in the Effect Controls panel update as you move the clip.

7 Position the clip so that it's centered on the upper-left corner of the screen. Use the circle and crosshair in the center (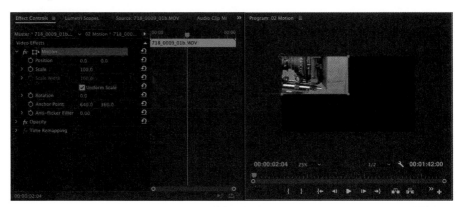) to line up the clip with the edge of the picture.

That crosshair is the anchor point, which is used for position and rotation controls. Be careful not to click the anchor point, or you'll move it in relation to the image.

You'll see that the Position settings in the Effect Controls panel are 0, 0 (or close to that, depending on where you placed the center of the clip).

This is a 720p sequence, so the lower-right corner of the screen is 1280, 720.

● **Note:** Premiere Pro uses a coordinate system that has the upper-left corner of the screen as 0, 0. All x and y values, respectively, to the left of and above that point are negative. All x and y values to the right of and below that point are positive.

8 Click the Reset button for the motion settings to restore the clip to its default position.

9 Drag the blue number for the Rotation setting in the Effect Controls panel. As you drag left or right, the clip rotates.

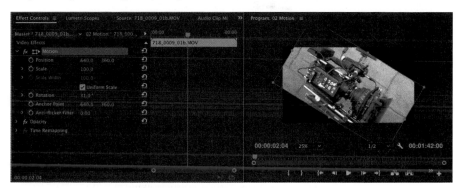

10 Click the Reset button for the Motion heading in the Effect Controls panel to restore the clip to its default position.

Changing clip position, size, and rotation

Sliding a clip around the screen only begins to exploit the possibilities of the Motion effect. What makes the Motion effect so useful is the ability to change the scale of the clip as well as rotate it. In this example, you'll build a simple intro segment for the behind-the-scenes features of a DVD.

Changing position

Let's begin by using keyframes to animate the position of a layer. For this exercise, the first thing you'll do is change the clip position. The picture will start off-screen and then move across the screen from right to left.

1 Open the sequence 03 Montage.

The sequence has several tracks, some of which are currently disabled. You'll use them later.

2 Move the playhead to the start of the sequence.

3 Set the Program Monitor zoom level to Fit.

4 Click once to select the first video clip on V3.

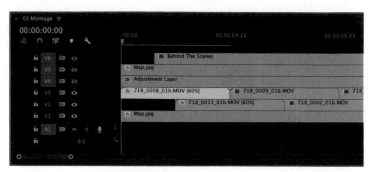

You might want to make the track taller to see it better.

The clip's controls appear in the Effect Controls panel.

5 In the Effect Controls panel, click the Toggle animation stopwatch button for Position. This turns on keyframing for that setting and automatically adds a keyframe at the playhead position.

From now on, when you change the setting, Premiere Pro will add (or update) a keyframe automatically.

6 The Position control has two numbers. The first is the x-axis, and the second is the y-axis. Enter a Position setting of **–640** into the x-axis (the first number) as a starting position.

Where there are two numbers for a control, they usually represent the x-axis and y-axis.

The clip moves off-screen to the left, revealing the clips on the V1 and V2 tracks.

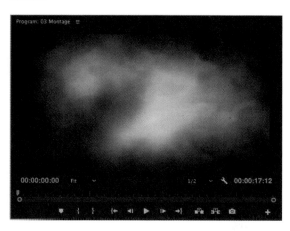

7 Drag the playhead to the last frame of the clip (00:00:4:23). You can do this in the Timeline panel or in the Effect Controls panel.

8 Enter a new setting for the position x-axis. If you enter **1920**, the clip will move off the right edge of the screen.

9 Play the sequence and you'll see the clip move from off-screen left to off-screen right.

The second clip on V3 pops up suddenly. You'll animate this clip and others next.

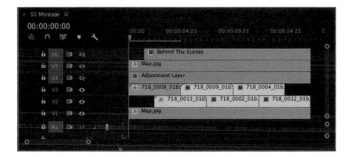

Reusing Motion settings

Now you've applied keyframes and effects to a clip, you can save time by reusing them on other clips. It's as easy as copying and pasting to apply effects from one clip to one or more other clips. In this example, you'll apply the same left-to-right floating animation to other clips in the project.

There are several methods for reusing effects. Let's try one now.

1 On the Timeline, select the clip you just animated. It's the first clip on V3.

2 Choose Edit > Copy.

The clip *and* its effects and settings are temporarily stored on your computer's clipboard.

3 With the Selection tool (V), drag from right to left to select the five other clips on the V2 and V3 tracks (you may need to zoom out a little to see all the clips). You could also hold the Shift key and select the first and last of the five clips.

4 Choose Edit > Paste Attributes.

Note: As an alternative to selecting a clip in the Timeline, you can always select one or more effect headings in the Effect Controls panel. Control-click (Windows) or Command-click (Mac OS) to select multiple noncontiguous effects. You can then select another clip (or clips) and choose Edit > Paste to paste the effects onto other clips.

5. The Paste Attributes dialog opens, letting you selectively apply effects and keyframes copied from another clip. Select only the Motion and Scale Attribute Times check boxes, and click OK.

6. Play the sequence to see the result.

Adding rotation and changing the anchor point

Moving clips around the screen can be effective, but you can really bring things to life using two more properties. Let's start with Rotation.

The Rotation property revolves a clip around its anchor point on the z-axis. By default, the anchor point is in the center of the image. However, you can change the relationship between the anchor point and the image for more interesting animation.

Let's add some rotation to a clip.

1. On the Timeline, click the Toggle Track Output button for V6 (⊗) to enable it. The clip on the layer is a title called Behind The Scenes.

2. Move the playhead to the start of the title (00:00:01:13). Try holding the Shift key while you drag the playhead to do this.

3. Select the title in the Timeline.

   The title's controls appear in the Effect Controls panel.

4. Select the Motion effect heading to see the anchor point and bounding box controls in the Program Monitor. Notice the position of the anchor point.

   Let's adjust the Rotation property and see the effect it has.

5. Enter a value of **90.0** into the Rotation field.

   The title rotates in the center of the screen.

6. Choose Edit > Undo.

7 Make sure Motion settings heading is still selected in the Effect Controls panel.

8 In the Program Monitor, drag the anchor point until the crosshair sits on the upper-left corner of the letter *B* in the first word.

The Position settings control the anchor point, and now that you have moved it in the image, the settings have updated automatically.

9 Your playhead should still be on the first frame of the clip. Click the Toggle animation stopwatch for Rotation to toggle on animation. This adds a keyframe automatically.

10 Set the rotation to **90.0**. This updates the keyframe you just added.

11 Move the playhead forward to 00:00:06:00, and set the clip rotation to **0.0** in the Effect Controls panel. This adds another keyframe automatically.

12 Play the sequence to see your animation.

Changing clip size

There are a few approaches to changing the size of items in a sequence. By default, items added to a sequence come in at 100% of their original size. However, you can choose to manually adjust the size or let Premiere Pro do it for you automatically.

You can choose from these methods:

- Use the Scale property of the Motion effect in the Effect Controls panel.

- If the clip has a different frame size to your sequence, right-click the clip on the Timeline and choose Set to Frame Size. This automatically adjusts the Scale property of the Motion effect to match the frame size of the clip with the size of the sequence.

- If the clip has a different frame size to your sequence, right-click the clip on the Timeline and choose Scale to Frame Size. This has a similar result to the Set to Frame Size option, but Premiere Pro resamples the image at the new (usually lower) resolution. If you scale back up now using the Motion > Scale setting, the image might look soft, even if the original clip was very high resolution.

- You can also select Scale To Frame Size by default in the preferences. Choose Edit > Preferences > General (Windows) or Premiere Pro > Preferences > General (Mac OS), select the "Default scale to frame size" option, and click OK. The setting is applied to assets as you import them.

For maximum flexibility, use the first or second method so you can scale as needed without sacrificing quality. Let's try this.

1 Open the sequence 04 Scale.

2 Scrub through the sequence to view the clips.

The second and third clips on the V1 track are much larger than the first two. In fact, your system may struggle to play those clips without dropping frames, and they are dramatically cropped by the edge of frame.

3 Right-click the last clip in the sequence, on the V1 track, and choose Scale to Frame Size.

This conveniently scales the image to fit the sequence resolution, though it re-samples the image, losing the original picture quality. However, there's an issue: The clip is full 4K, with a resolution of 4096x2160, and that is not a perfect 16:9 image. It doesn't fit the aspect ratio of the sequence, and black bars are introduced at the top and bottom of the image. These bars are often called *letterboxing*.

This is a common outcome when working with content that has a different aspect ratio than your sequence, and there is no easy way around it. You'll need to make a manual adjustment.

4 Right-click the clip again and select Scale to Frame Size again to deselect it. This is an option you can turn off and on at any time.

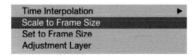

5 With the clip selected, open the Effect Controls panel.

6 Use the Scale setting to adjust the frame size until the clip image fits the sequence frame without showing letterboxing; a setting of roughly 34% should work. You can choose any framing and adjust the Position settings to reframe the shot if necessary.

When you scale an image to avoid letterboxing, you'll have to crop the sides. When aspect ratios don't match, you have to choose between letterboxing, cropping, or changing the aspect ratio of the image by unchecking the Uniform Scale option in the Effect Controls panel.

Animating clip size changes

In the previous example, the clip image has a different aspect ratio to the sequence.

Let's try a different example, with animation.

1   Position the Timeline playhead over the first frame of the second clip in the 04 Scale sequence, at 00:00:05:00.

This clip is 3840x2160-pixel ultra-high definition (UHD), which is the same image aspect ratio as the sequence, which is 1280x720. It's also the same aspect ratio as full HD, at 1920x1080. This makes shooting UHD content convenient if you intend to include it in an HD production.

2   Select the clip and open the Effect Controls panel. The scale is set to 100%.

3   Right-click the clip in the Timeline panel and choose Set to Frame Size.

● **Note:** The settings in the Effect Controls panel don't show if they are pixels, percentages, or degrees. This can take a little getting used to, but you'll find with experience the controls do make sense for each setting.

When you select Set to Frame Size, Premiere Pro resizes the clip using the Scale setting so that it fits inside the frame of the sequence. The amount of adjustment varies depending on the image size of the clip and the resolution of the sequence.

This clip scales down to 33.3% to fit the image. You now know you can scale this clip between 33.3% and 100% and maintain quality, while still filling the frame.

4 Turn on keyframing for Scale by clicking the Toggle animation stopwatch button for Scale in the Effect Controls panel.

5 Position the playhead over the last frame of the clip.

6 Click the reset button ( ) for the Scale setting in the Effect Controls panel.

7 Scrub through the clip to see the result.

This creates an animated zoom effect for the clip. Because the clip never scales to more than 100%, it maintains full quality.

8 Turn on the Track Output option for the V2 track.

This track has an adjustment layer clip on it. Adjustment layers apply effects to all footage on lower video tracks. Select the Adjustment Layer clip to display its values in the Effect Controls panel. You'll see that two more effects have been added: a Black and White effect, which removes color saturation, and a Luma Curve effect, which increases contrast. You'll learn more about adjustment layers in Lesson 13, "Adding Video Effects."

9 Play the sequence.

You may need to render the sequence to see smooth playback because some of the clips are high resolution and will take a lot of computer processing power to play. To render the sequence, go to the Sequence menu, and choose Render In to Out.

Working with keyframe interpolation

Throughout this lesson you've been using keyframes to define your animation. The term *keyframe* originates from traditional animation, where the lead artist would draw the key frames (or major poses) and then assistant animators would animate the frames in between. When animating in Premiere Pro, you're the master animator, and the computer does the rest of the work as it interpolates values in between the keyframes you set.

Using different keyframe interpolation methods

While you've already used keyframes to animate, you've only touched on their power. One of the most useful yet least utilized features of keyframes is their interpolation method. This is a fancy way of saying how to get from point A to point B. Think of it as describing the sharp ramp-up as a runner takes off from the starting line and the gradual slowdown after they cross the finish line.

Premiere Pro has five interpolation methods. Changing the method can create a very different animation. You can access the available interpolation methods by right-clicking a keyframe to see the options (some effects have both spatial and temporal options).

- (⬥) **Linear:** This is the default method of keyframe interpolation. This method gives a uniform rate of change between keyframes. Changes begin instantly at the first keyframe and continue to the next keyframe at a constant speed. At the second keyframe, the rate of change switches instantly to the rate between it and the third keyframe, and so on. This can be effective, but it can also look a little mechanical.

- (⬛) **Bezier:** This gives the most control over keyframe interpolation. Bezier keyframes (named after the French engineer Pierre Bézier) provide manual handles you can adjust to change the shape of the value graph or motion path on either side of the keyframe. By dragging the Bezier handles, you can create smooth curved adjustments or sharp angles. For example, you could have an object move smoothly to a position onscreen and then sharply take off in another direction.

- ( ) **Auto Bezier:** Auto Bezier keyframes create a smooth rate of change through the keyframe. They automatically update as you change settings. This is a good quick-fix version of Bezier keyframes.

- ( ) **Continuous Bezier:** This option is similar to the Auto Bezier option, but it provides some manual control. The motion or value path will always have smooth transitions, but you can adjust the shape of the Bezier curve on both sides of the keyframe with a control handle.

- ( ) **Hold:** This is available only for temporal (time-based) properties. Hold-style keyframes hold their value across time, without a gradual transition. This is useful if you want to create staccato-type movements or make an object suddenly disappear. When the Hold style is used, the value of the first keyframe will hold until the next hold keyframe is encountered, and then the value will change instantly.

Temporal vs. spatial interpolation

Some properties and effects offer a choice of temporal and spatial interpolation methods for transitioning between keyframes. You'll find that all properties have temporal controls (which relate to time). Some properties also offer spatial interpolation (which refers to space or movement).

Here's what you need to know about each method:

- **Temporal interpolation**: Temporal interpolation deals with changes in time. It's an effective way to determine the speed at which an object moves. For example, you can add acceleration and deceleration with special kinds of keyframes called Ease or Bezier.

- **Spatial interpolation**: The spatial method deals with changes in an object's position. It's an effective way to control the shape of the path an object takes across the screen. That path is called a *motion path*. For example, does an object create hard angular ricochets as it moves from one keyframe to the next, or does it have a more sloping movement with round corners?

Adding Ease to Motion

A quick way to add a feeling of inertia to clip motion is to use a keyframe preset. For example, you can create a ramp-up effect for speed by right-clicking a keyframe and choosing Ease In or Ease Out. Ease In is used for approaching a keyframe, and Ease Out is used when leaving a keyframe.

1 Continue working with the previous sequence.

2 Select the second video clip in the sequence.

3 In the Effect Controls panel, locate the Rotation and Scale properties.

4 Click the disclosure icon next to the Scale property to reveal the control handles and velocity graphs.

You might want to increase the height of the Effect Controls panel to make room for the extra controls.

Don't be overwhelmed by the next numbers and graphs. Once you understand one of these, you'll understand them all because they all use a common design.

The graph makes it easier to view the effects of keyframe interpolation. A straight line means essentially no change in speed or acceleration.

5 Right-click the first Scale keyframe, displayed in the Effect Controls panel mini timeline, and choose Ease Out.

6 Right-click the second Scale keyframe and choose Ease In.

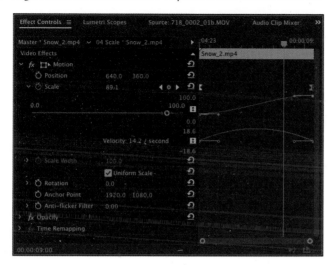

The graph now shows a curved line, which translates as a gradual acceleration and deceleration of the animation.

7 Play the sequence to see your animation.

8 Experiment by dragging the blue Bezier handles in the Effect Controls panel to see their effects on speed and ramping.

The steeper the curve you create, the more sharply the animation's movement or speed increases. After experimenting, you can choose Edit > Undo repeatedly if you don't like the changes.

► **Tip:** If you want to create inertia (such as a rocket lifting off), try using Ease. Right-click a keyframe and choose Ease In or Ease Out (for approaching and leaving a keyframe, respectively).

Using other motion-related effects

Premiere Pro offers a number of other effects to control motion. While the Motion effect is the most intuitive, you may find yourself wanting more.

The Transform and Basic 3D effects are also useful and give more control over an object (including 3D rotation).

Adding a drop shadow

A drop shadow creates perspective by adding a small shadow behind an object. This is often used to help create a sense of separation between foreground and background elements.

Try adding a drop shadow.

1 Open the sequence 05 Enhance.

2 Make sure the Program Monitor zoom level is set to Fit.

3 In the Effects panel, browse into Video Effects > Perspective. Drag the Drop Shadow effect onto the Journey to New York Title clip on the V3 track.

4 Experiment with the Drop Shadow settings in the Effect Controls panel. You may need to scroll down to see them all. When you have finished experimenting, choose the following settings:

- Set Distance to **15** so the shadow is further offset from the clip.

- Drag the Direction value to about 320° to see the shadow's angle change.

- Darken the shadow by changing Opacity to **85%**.

- Set Softness to **25** to soften the edges of the shadow. Generally, the greater the Distance setting, the more softness you should apply.

Note: To make shadows fall away from a light source, add or subtract 180° from a perceived light source direction to get the correct direction for the shadow to fall.

5 Play the sequence to watch your animation.

Adding a bevel

Another way to enhance the edges of a clip is to add a bevel. This type of effect is useful on a picture-in-picture effect or on text. There are two bevels to choose from. The Bevel Edges effect is useful when the object is simply a standard video clip. The Bevel Alpha effect works better for text or logos because it detects the complex transparent areas in the image before applying the beveled edge.

Note: The Bevel Edges effect produces slightly harder edges than the Bevel Alpha effect. Both effects work well on rectangular clips, but the Bevel Alpha effect is better suited to text or logos.

Let's enhance the title a little.

1 Continue working with the 05 Enhance sequence.

2 Select the Journey to New York Title clip on V3 to see its controls in the Effect Controls panel.

3 In the Effects panel, choose Video Effects > Perspective and drag the Bevel Alpha effect into the Effect Controls panel, under the Drop Shadow effect.

The edges of the text should appear slightly beveled.

4 In the Effect Controls panel, increase Bevel Alpha Edge Thickness to **10** to make the edge more pronounced. You might need to scroll down in the Effect Controls panel to see all the settings.

5 Increase Light Intensity to **0.80** to see a brighter edge effect.

> **Tip:** You can apply effects by dragging them onto clips, by dragging them into the Effect Controls panel, or by double-clicking them in the Effects panel.

The effect is looking pretty good, but it's currently applied to both the text and the drop shadow. This is because the effect is below the drop shadow in the Effect Controls panel (the stacking order matters).

6 In the Effect Controls panel, drag the Bevel Alpha effect heading up, until it's just above the Drop Shadow effect. You'll see a black line where the effect will be placed. This changes the rendering order.

> **Note:** If you're not getting the look you want when applying multiple effects to a clip, drag the order around and see whether that produces a better result.

7 Reduce the Edge Thickness amount to **8**.

8 Examine the subtle differences in the bevel.

● **Note:** You may need to render the sequence to see smooth playback because of the high-resolution clips and nonaccelerated effect.

9 Play the sequence to see your animation.

Adding motion with the Transform effect

An alternative to the Motion effect settings is the Transform effect. These two effects offer similar controls, but there are three key differences.

- The Transform effect processes changes to a clip's Anchor Point, Position, Scale, and Opacity settings in the stack with other effects, unlike the Motion settings. This means effects such as drop shadows and bevels can behave differently.

- The Transform effect includes Skew, Skew Axis, and Shuttle Angle settings to allow a visual angular transformation to clips.

- The Transform effect is not Mercury Playback Engine GPU–accelerated, so it may take longer to process and doesn't offer as much real-time performance.

Let's compare the two effects using a prebuilt sequence.

1 Open the sequence 06 Motion and Transform.

2 Play the sequence to familiarize yourself with it.

There are two sections in the sequence. Each has a picture-in-picture (PIP), rotating twice over a background clip, while moving from left to right. Look carefully at the position of the shadow on each pair of clips.

- In the first example, the shadow follows the bottom edge of the PIP and appears on all four sides of the clip as it rotates, which obviously isn't realistic because the light source producing the shadow wouldn't be moving.

- In the second example, the shadow stays on the lower right of the PIP, which is more realistic.

3 Click the first clip on the V2 track, and view the effects applied in the Effect Controls panel: the Motion effect and the Drop Shadow effect.

4 Now click the second clip on the V2 track. The Transform effect is producing the motion this time, with the Drop Shadow effect again producing the shadow.

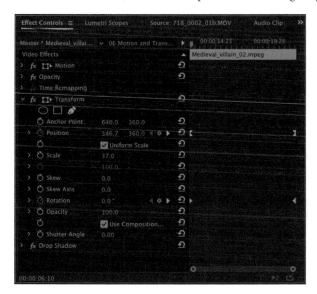

The Transform effect has many of the same options as the Motion effect, with the addition of Skew, Skew Axis, and Shutter Angle. As you can see, the Transform effect also works more realistically with the Drop Shadow effect than the Motion effect because of the order in which the effects are applied; the Motion effect is always applied after other effects.

Manipulating clips in 3D space with Basic 3D

Another option for creating movement is the Basic 3D effect, which can manipulate a clip in 3D space. It allows you to rotate the image around horizontal and vertical axes as well as move it toward or away from you. You'll also find an option to enable a specular highlight, which creates the appearance of light reflecting off the rotating surface.

Let's explore the effect using a prebuilt sequence.

1 Open the sequence 07 Basic 3D.

2 Drag the playhead over the sequence Timeline (scrub) to view the contents.

The light that follows the motion comes from above, behind, and to the left of the viewer. Since the light comes from above, you won't see the effect until the image is tilted backward to catch the reflection. Specular highlights of this kind can be used to enhance the realism of a 3D effect.

The following are four major properties of the Basic 3D effect:

- **Swivel:** This controls the rotation around the vertical y-axis. If you rotate past 90°, you'll see the back of the image, which is a mirror of the front.

- **Tilt:** This controls the rotation around a horizontal x-axis. If you rotate beyond 90°, the back will also be visible.

- **Distance to Image:** This moves the image along the z-axis to simulate depth. As the distance value gets larger, the image moves farther away.

- **Specular Highlight:** This adds a glint of light that reflects off the surface of the rotated image, as though an overhead light were shining on the surface. This option is either on or off.

3 Experiment with the Basic 3D options.

Review questions

1 Which fixed effect will move a clip in the frame?

2 You want a clip to appear full-screen for a few seconds and then spin away. How do you make the Motion effect's Rotation feature start within a clip rather than at the beginning?

3 How can you start an object rotating gradually and have it stop rotating slowly?

4 If you want to add a drop shadow to a clip, why might you choose to use a different motion-related effect from the Motion fixed effect?

Review answers

1 The Motion effect lets you set a new position for a clip. If keyframes are used, the effect can be animated.

2 Position the playhead where you want the rotation to begin, and click the Add/Remove Keyframe button or the stopwatch icon. Then move to where you want the spinning to end and change the Rotation parameter; another keyframe will appear.

3 Use the Ease Out and Ease In options to change the keyframe interpolation to be gradual rather than sudden.

4 The Motion effect is the last effect applied to a clip. Motion takes whatever effects you apply before it (including Drop Shadow) and spins the entire assemblage as a single unit. To create a realistic drop shadow on a spinning object, use Transform or Basic 3D and then place a Drop Shadow below that in the Effect Controls panel.

10 MULTICAMERA EDITING

Lesson overview

In this lesson, you'll learn about the following:

- Synchronizing clips based on audio
- Adding clips to a sequence
- Creating a multicamera target sequence
- Switching between multiple cameras
- Recording a multicamera edit
- Finalizing a multicamera editing project

 This lesson will take approximately 45 minutes.

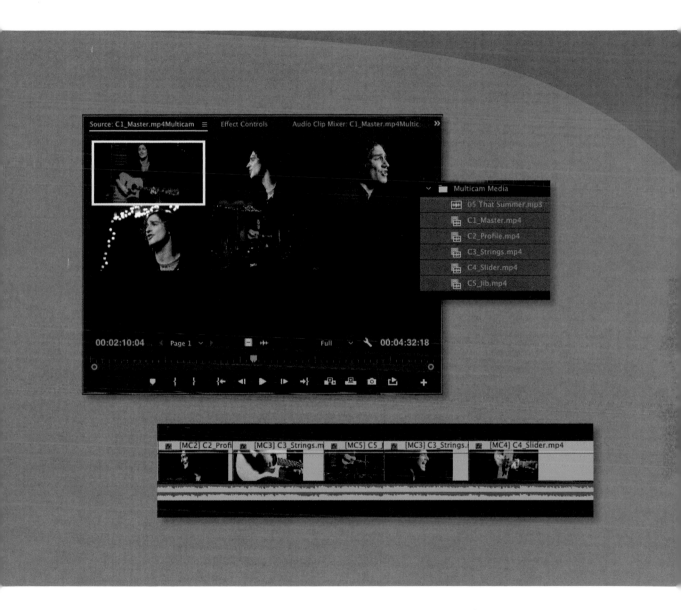

The process of multicamera editing begins with synchronizing multiple camera angles. You can do this using timecode or a common sync point (such as the closing of a clapboard or a common audio track). Once your clips are synced, you can seamlessly cut between multiple angles in Adobe Premiere Pro CC.

Getting started

In this lesson, you'll learn how to quickly edit multiple angles of footage that were shot simultaneously. Because the clips were shot at the same time, Adobe Premiere Pro CC makes it possible to cut seamlessly from one angle to another.

The Premiere Pro multicamera editing feature is a tremendous time-saver when you're editing footage from a shoot or event captured with multiple cameras.

1   Open the project Lesson 10.prproj.

    This project has five camera angles of a musical performance and a synchronized audio track.

2   In the Workspaces panel, click Editing. Then click the menu adjacent to the Editing option, and choose Reset to Saved Layout.

Following the multicamera process

The multicamera editing process has a standardized workflow. Once you know how to do it, it's straightforward.

There are six stages.

1   Import your footage. Ideally, the cameras will be closely matched in frame rate and frame size, but you can mix and match if needed.

2   Determine your sync points. The goal is to keep the multiple angles running in sync with each other so you can seamlessly switch between them. You'll need to identify a point in time that exists in all angles to synchronize or use matching timecode. Alternatively, you can automatically sync if all the clips have the same audio.

3   Create a multicamera source sequence. The clips are added to a specialized sequence type called a *multicamera source sequence*. This is essentially a nested sequence clip that contains multiple video angles stacked on different video tracks.

4   Nest the multicamera sequence in another sequence for editing (edit the multicamera sequence into another sequence). This new sequence is the multicamera master sequence in which you will perform edits. Your original multicamera sequence is now effectively a multilayered source clip.

5   Record multicamera edits. A special view in the Program Monitor (the Multi-Camera view) lets you switch between camera angles during playback.

6   Adjust and refine edits. Once the edit is roughed out, you can refine the sequence with standard editing and trimming commands.

Who uses multicamera editing?

The popularity of multicamera editing has grown immensely as prices for high-quality cameras have fallen. There are many potential uses for a multicamera shoot and edit, ranging from simple fiction dialogue to large-scale reality TV series.

- **Visual and special effects**: Because of the expense associated with many special-effects shots, it's common practice to cover the shot with multiple angles. This means less cost associated with the staging of the shot and allows for greater flexibility during editing.

- **Action scenes**: For scenes that involve a lot of action, producers often use multiple cameras. Doing so can reduce the number of times that stunts or dangerous action needs to be performed.

- **Once-in-a-lifetime events**: Events such as weddings and sporting competitions rely heavily on multiple angles of coverage to ensure that the shooters capture all the critical elements of the event.

- **Musical and theatrical performances**: If you've watched a concert film, you're used to multiple camera angles being used to show the performance. Multi-camera editing can improve the pacing of theatrical performances as well.

- **Talk-show formats**: Interview-driven segments often cut between the interviewer and subject, as well as to a wide shot to show both subjects at the same time. Not only does this maintain visual interest, but it makes it easier to edit an interview to a shorter run time.

Creating a multicamera sequence

You can play multiple camera angles at the same time; the only limiting factor is the computing power required to play back your clips. If your computer and storage drives are fast enough, you should be able to play back several streams in real time.

Determining the sync points

Decide how you want to synchronize the multiple angles of footage when creating the multicamera sequence. You can select from five options for the sync references. The method you choose will be partly a matter of personal choice and partly how the footage was shot.

- **In points:** If you have a common starting point, you can set an In point on all clips you want to use. This method is effective as long as all cameras are rolling before the critical action starts.

- **Out points:** This method is similar to syncing with an In point but instead uses a common Out point. Out-point syncing is ideal when all cameras capture the ending of critical action (such as crossing the finish line) but were started at different times.

- **Timecode:** Many professional cameras allow timecode to be synchronized across multiple cameras. You can sync cameras by connecting them to a common sync source. In some cases, the Hours number is offset to identify the camera number. For example, camera 1 would start at 1:00:00:00, and camera 2 would start at 2:00:00:00. For this reason, you can choose to ignore the Hours number when syncing with timecode.

▶ **Tip:** If you don't have a good visual clue in the video to sync multiple clips to, look for a clap or loud noise in the audio track. It's often easier to sync clips by looking for a common spike in the audio waveform. Add a marker at each point and then use the markers to sync.

- **Clip marker:** In and Out points can be accidentally removed from a clip. If you'd like to mark a clip in a more robust fashion, you can use a marker to identify a common sync point. Markers are more difficult to accidentally remove from a clip. They can also be based on any part of the action, perhaps an event partway through the recording that all cameras captured. If you don't have sync timecode or audio, a marker is probably the most efficient way to work.

- **Audio:** If every camera recorded audio (even if it's just poor-quality reference audio from a camera-mounted shotgun or even an integrated microphone), Premiere Pro may be able to synchronize the clips automatically. The results with this method depend on your audio being reasonably clean.

Syncing with markers

Consider a scenario where you have four clips that recorded the same bike race from four different camera angles but the four cameras started recording at different times. Your first task is to find the same point in time for all four clips so they will be in sync.

This could be accomplished by using a common event (such as the firing of a starter's pistol or a camera flash). Simply load each clip into the Source Monitor and add a marker (M) for each instance of the event. You can then use these markers to synchronize the clips.

When recording multicamera media, it's a good idea to avoid stopping and starting recording. Each time a camera begins to record again, a new clip is created, and you will need to re-create sync in Premiere Pro.

Adding clips to a multicamera source sequence

Once you've identified the clips you want to use (as well as a common sync point), you can create a multicamera source sequence, the specialized type of sequence for multicamera editing. Let's try this:

1   Select all the clips in the Multicam Media bin.

    The order in which you select the clips is the order in which they will be added to the sequence—and by extension, this sets the camera angle number. By holding Control (Windows) or Command (Mac OS), you can select one clip after another to define them as specific camera angles. For example, if you click to select clips 1, then 2, then 3, they'll become Camera Angle 1, then 2, then 3.

If you select clips 1, then 3, then 2, they'll become Camera Angle 1, then 2, then 3. You can easily change this later, of course.

For this example, click the clips in their number order, selecting the audio-only clip last.

2   Right-click one of the selected clips and choose Create Multi-Camera Source Sequence. You can also choose Clip > Create Multi-Camera Source Sequence.

A new dialog box opens, asking how you want to create the multicamera source sequence.

3   Under Synchronize Point, choose the Audio method, and leave the Track Channel set to 1.

4   Leave the Sequence Preset menu set to Automatic. The newly created sequence will match the media files you are using. All available sequence presets are listed here, so you can choose a particular option if you prefer.

5   Leave the Audio > Sequence Settings menu set to Camera 1. In fact, because one of the clips is audio-only, it will automatically be used as the audio for the newly created multicamera sequence. If you didn't have that audio-only clip, Premiere Pro would use the first selected shot.

> **Tip:** The clip you click first in the bin when selecting angles will become the audio track that is used for the multicamera source sequence (even when changing angles), unless you include an audio-only clip (which Premiere Pro will presume you want to use).

Another approach is to place a dedicated audio recording on another track and sync it. A third option, Audio Follows Video, can be chosen from the Multi-Camera Monitor view (upper-right corner of the panel) to sync the audio changes to the video.

6   The clips have useful names that you can use as Camera Angle names. Under Camera Names, choose Use Clip Names, and click OK.

Premiere Pro analyzes the clips and adds a new multicamera source sequence to the bin.

7 Double-click the new multicamera source sequence to view it in the Source Monitor.

● **Note:** Premiere Pro automatically adjusts the multicamera grid to accommodate the number of angles in use. For example, if you have up to four clips, you would see a 2x2 grid. If you used between five and nine clips, you'd see a 3x3 grid; if you used 16 angles, the grid would be 4x4; and so on.

8 Drag the Source Monitor playhead through the clip to view the multiple angles.

The clips are displayed in a grid to show you all the angles at once. Some angles start in black because the cameras began recording at different times.

In this workflow, you're using an automated option in the Project panel to create a multicamera sequence. You could also manually create a multicamera sequence, giving you more control but taking more time. Explore the Adobe Online Help for more information about multicamera editing.

Creating the multicamera target sequence

Once you've made the multicamera source sequence, you need to place it in another sequence, nesting it. The nested sequence will behave like any other clip in your master sequence. However, this clip has multiple angles of footage to choose from as you edit.

1 Locate the multicamera source sequence you just created. It should be named something like C1_Master.mp4Multicam.

2 Right-click the multicamera source sequence and choose New Sequence From Clip, or drag the clip onto the New Item menu at the bottom of the Project panel.

You now have a ready-to-use multicamera target sequence.

3 Right-click the nested multicamera sequence on the Timeline, and look at the Multi-Camera options.

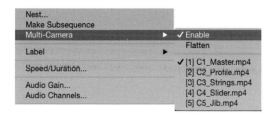

For a multicamera sequence clip to work, the Multi-Camera option must be enabled.

Multi-Camera mode is automatically enabled for this clip because of the way you created it. You can turn this option off or on at any time.

4 A camera angle is already selected. Try choosing another angle and see the Program Monitor update. The clip name updates in the sequence too.

When you choose a different angle, the clip name updates in the sequence.

> **Tip:** To view the contents of a multi-camera sequence, hold Control (Windows) or Command (Mac OS) and double-click it. You can edit the contents of the sequence as you would any other. Changes you make will update in the target sequence.

Switching multiple cameras

Once you've built the multicamera source sequence and added it to a multicamera target sequence, you're ready to edit. You'll do this in real time using the Multi-Camera view in the Program Monitor. You can switch between the different angles by clicking in the Program Monitor or using a keyboard shortcut.

Performing a multicamera edit

Multicamera editing works by selecting camera angles for the current clip on the Timeline using a special Multi-Camera mode in the Program Monitor.

If playback is stopped, you can click an angle on the left of the Program Monitor and the current clip in the sequence will update to match.

During playback, when you click an angle in the Program Monitor, the sequence clip updates accordingly. However, this time an edit is also applied to the clip, separating the camera angle selected just before you clicked from the newly selected angle. You won't see edits that are added until after playback stops.

Let's try it now:

1   Click the Settings menu on the Program Monitor, and choose Multi-Camera.

2   Play the sequence to get familiar with it.

3   Hover your mouse over the Program Monitor and press the ` (grave) key to maximize the panel. If your keyboard doesn't have a ` (grave) key, click the panel menu, and choose Panel Group Settings > Maximize Panel Group.

4   Set the playhead at the start of the sequence, and press the spacebar to start playback.

    The first few seconds are silent until the click track begins. You will hear a series of short beeps followed by the professionally recorded track.

● **Note:** On an English-language keyboard, the first nine camera angles are assigned to keys 1–9 along the top of your keyboard (not the numerical keypad) by default. For example, press the 1 key to select Camera 1, press the 2 key to select Camera 2, and so on.

Featured track, used with permission: "That Summer," by Jason Masi (www.jasonmasi.com)

5   Click the images on the left to switch between the multiple camera angles during playback. You can also use the keyboard shortcuts, 1–5, that correspond to the camera angle you want to select.

    When the sequence finishes playback, it will have multiple edits. Each separated clip's label starts with a number that represents the camera angle used for that clip.

6   Press the ` (grave) key, or click the panel menu and choose Panel Group Settings > Maximize Panel Group, to restore the Program Monitor panel to normal size.

7 Play the sequence and review your edit.

Imagine the director on this production decides the audio is too loud for the planned distribution medium.

8 Right-click the audio track and choose Audio Gain.

A new dialog box opens.

9 In the Adjust Gain By field, enter **−8** and click OK to lower the audio.

Re-recording multicamera edits

The first time you record a multicamera edit, it's possible you will miss a few edits. Perhaps you cut too late (or too early) to an angle. You also may decide that you like one angle better than another. This is easy to correct.

1 Move the playhead to the start of the Timeline panel.

2 Press the Play button in the Multi-Camera view to start playback.

The angles in the Multi-Camera view switch to match the existing edits in your Timeline.

3 When the playhead reaches the spot you want to change, switch the active camera.

If your keyboard has the keys, you can press one of the shortcuts (in this case, 1–5), or you can click your preferred angle in the Multi-Camera view of the Program Monitor.

4 When you finish editing, stop playback by pressing the spacebar.

5 Click the Program Monitor Settings menu and choose Composite Video to return to a regular viewing mode.

● **Note:** If you have effects applied to your clips, these are displayed as usual in the Program Monitor. This is helpful if you have applied color adjustments to match different angles.

● **Note:** After making your edits, you can always change them in the Multi-Camera view of the Program Monitor or on the Timeline. You can even trim parts of the multicamera sequence as you would any other clip.

Finalizing multicamera editing

Once you've performed a multicamera edit in the Multi-Camera view, you can refine and then finalize it. The resulting sequence is like any other sequence you've built, so you can use any of the editing or trimming techniques you've learned so far. There are some additional options available, however.

Switching an angle

If you're happy with the timing of an edit but not the angle you chose, you can always swap the angle for another. There are a few ways to do this.

- Right-click a clip, choose Multi-Camera, and specify an angle.
- Use the Multi-Camera view of the Program Monitor (as you did earlier in the lesson).
- If the correct track is enabled or a nested multicamera sequence clip is selected and your keyboard has the keys, use the keyboard shortcuts 1–9.

Flattening a multicamera edit

● **Note:** If you flatten your multicamera sequence, audio adjustments are lost. Leave audio work until later.

You can flatten a multicamera edit to reduce the amount of processing power needed for playback and to simplify the sequence. When you flatten the edit, the nested multicamera sequence clips are replaced with the original selected camera angle clips.

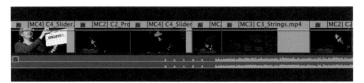

The process is simple.

1 Select all the multicamera clips you'd like to flatten.

2 Right-click any clip and choose Multi-Camera > Flatten.

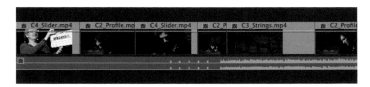

Once the clips are flattened, the process cannot be reversed, other than by choosing Edit > Undo.

Review questions

1 Describe five kinds of sync points for multicamera clips.

2 Identify two ways to have the multicamera source and multicamera target sequences match settings.

3 Name two ways to switch between angles in the Multi-Camera view.

4 How can you choose a different angle after closing the Multi-Camera view?

Review answers

1 The five ways are In points, Out points, timecode, audio, and markers.

2 You can either right-click the multicamera source sequence and choose New Sequence From Clip or drag the multicamera source sequence into an empty sequence and let it autoconform the settings.

3 To switch angles, you can either click the preview angle in the Program Monitor or, if your keyboard has the keys, use the corresponding shortcut key (1–9) for each angle.

4 You can use any of the standard trimming tools in the Timeline to adjust the edit points for an angle. If you want to swap the camera angle, right-click it in the Timeline, choose Multi-Camera from the context menu, and choose the camera angle you want to use, or press the corresponding keyboard shortcut, 1–9.

11 EDITING AND MIXING AUDIO

Lesson overview

In this lesson, you'll learn about the following:

- Working in the Audio workspace
- Understanding audio characteristics
- Adjusting clip audio volume
- Adjusting audio levels in a sequence
- Using the Audio Clip Mixer

 This lesson will take approximately 60 minutes. In this lesson, you'll learn some audio-mixing fundamentals using the powerful tools provided by Adobe Premiere Pro CC. Believe it or not, good sound will often make the pictures look better.

Until now, our focus has been primarily on working with visuals. No doubt about it, the pictures count, but professional editors generally agree that sound is at least as important as the images on the screen—sometimes more important!

Getting started

It's rare to have audio recorded on-camera that is perfect for your final output. There are several things you might want to do with sound in Premiere Pro.

- Set Premiere Pro to interpret recorded audio channels differently from the way they were recorded in-camera. For example, audio recorded as stereo can be interpreted as separate mono tracks.

- Clean up background sound. Whether it's system hum or the sound of an air-conditioning unit, Premiere Pro has tools for adjusting and tuning your audio.

- Adjust the volume of different frequencies in your clips (different tones) using EQ effects.

- Adjust the volume level on clips in the bin and on clip segments in your sequence. The adjustments you make on the Timeline can vary over time, creating a complete sound mix.

- Add music and mix levels between music clips.

- Add audio spot effects, such as explosions, door slams, or atmospheric environmental sound.

Consider the difference it makes if you turn the sound off when watching a horror movie. Without an ominous soundtrack, scenes that were scary a moment ago can seem like comedy.

Music works around many of our critical faculties and directly influences our emotions. In fact, your body reacts to sound whether you want it to or not. For example, it's normal for your heart rate to be influenced by the beat of the music you're listening to. Fast music tends to raise your heart rate, and slow music tends to lower your heart rate. Powerful stuff!

In this lesson, you'll begin by learning how to use the audio tools in Premiere Pro and then make adjustments to clips and a sequence. You'll also use the Audio Mixer to make changes to your volume "on the fly" while your sequence plays.

Setting up the interface to work with audio

Let's begin by switching to the Audio workspace.

1 Open Lesson 11.prproj.

2 In the Workspaces panel, click Audio. Then click the menu adjacent to the Audio option, and choose Reset to Saved Layout.

Working in the Audio workspace

You'll recognize most of the components of the Audio workspace from the video-editing workspaces you've used. One obvious difference is that the Audio Clip Mixer is displayed in place of the Source Monitor. The Source Monitor is still in the frame; it's just hidden, grouped with the Audio Clip Mixer.

You'll notice that the audio meters have disappeared too. This is because the Audio Mixers have their own audio meters.

You can modify the appearance of the Timeline track headers to include an audio meter for each track, along with track-based level and pan controls.

To add audio meters to your tracks, follow these steps:

1 Click the Timeline Settings menu (), and choose Customize Audio Header.

The Audio Header Button Editor appears.

2 Drag the Track Meter button (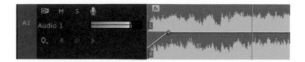) onto an audio header, and click OK.

You may need to resize an audio header vertically and horizontally to see the new meter.

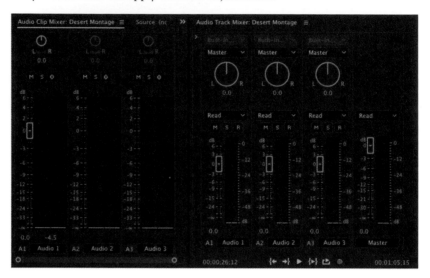

It's important to understand the key differences between the Audio Clip Mixer and the Audio Track Mixer.

They look similar but apply different adjustments.

- **Audio Clip Mixer:** Provides controls to adjust the audio level and pan of clips. As you play your sequence, you can make adjustments, and Premiere Pro will add keyframes to clips.

- **Audio Track Mixer:** Works in a similar way, but adjusts audio level and pan on tracks. Clip adjustments and track adjustments are combined for final output. So, if you reduce the clip audio level by –3 dB and then also reduce the track audio level by –3 dB, you'll have a total drop of –6 dB. The more advanced Audio Track Mixer also offers track-based audio effects and submixes, which allow you to combine the outputs from multiple tracks.

You can apply clip-based audio effects and modify their settings in the Effect Controls panel. Audio adjustments applied using clip-based effects and Audio Track Mixer effects are combined, but clip-based effects are applied first.

Defining master track output

When you create a new sequence, you define the number of audio channels it outputs by choosing an audio master setting. It's easiest to think of your sequence as a media file. It will have a frame rate, frame size, audio sample rate, and channel configuration.

The audio master setting is the number of audio channels the sequence would have if it were a file.

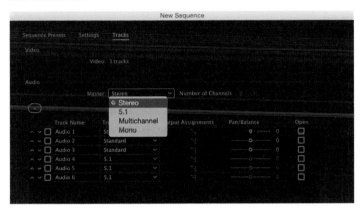

- Stereo has two audio channels: Left and Right.

- 5.1 has six audio channels: Middle, Front-Left, Front-Right, Rear-Left, Rear-Right, and Low Frequency Effects (LFE)—that's the subwoofer.

- Multichannel has between 1 and 32 audio channels—you can choose.

- Mono has one audio channel.

What is an audio channel?

You could be forgiven for thinking that Left and Right audio channels were in some way identifiably different. In fact, they are both simply mono audio channels designated as Left or Right. When recording sound, it's the standard configuration to have Audio Channel 1 as Left and Audio Channel 2 as Right.

What makes Audio Channel 1 Left is simply the following:

- It's recorded from a microphone pointing left.

- It's interpreted as Left in Premiere Pro.

- It's output to a speaker positioned on the left.

None of these factors changes the fact that it is still a single mono channel. They are nothing more than conventions.

If you perform the same recording from a microphone pointing right (but with Audio Channel 2), then you have stereo audio. They are, in fact, two mono audio channels.

You can change most sequence settings later, but not the audio master setting. This means that, with the exception of multichannel sequences, you cannot change the number of channels that your sequence will output.

You can add or remove audio tracks at any time, but the audio master setting is fixed. If you need to change your audio master setting, you can easily copy and paste clips from a sequence with one setting to a new sequence with a different setting.

Using the audio meters

The primary function of the audio meters is to give you an overall mix output volume for your sequence. As your sequence plays, you'll see the level meter dynamically change to reflect the volume.

To see the audio meters, follow these steps:

1 Choose Window > Audio Meters.

In the default Audio workspace, the audio meters are quite small. You'll want to make them bigger so you can work with them.

2 Drag the left edge of the panel a little to make the meters wider so you can see the buttons at the bottom of the panel. Keep them onscreen while going through this lesson.

If you right-click the audio meters, you can choose a different display scale. The default is a range from 0 dB to −60 dB, which clearly shows the main level information you'll want to see.

You can also choose between static and dynamic peaks. When you get a loud "spike" in audio levels that makes you glance at the meters, the sound is gone by the time you look. With static peaks, the highest peak is marked and maintained in the meters so you can see what the loudest level was during playback up to that point.

You can click the audio meters to reset the peak. With dynamic peaks, the peak level will continually update; keep watching to check the levels.

Viewing samples

In this exercise, you'll look at an audio sample.

1 In the Project panel, open the Music bin, and double-click the clip Cooking Montage.mp3 to open it in the Source Monitor.

Because this clip has no video, Premiere Pro displays the waveforms for the two audio channels.

At the bottom of the Source Monitor and Program Monitor, a time ruler represents the total duration of the clip.

About audio level

The scale displayed on the audio meters is decibels, denoted by dB. The decibel scale is a little unusual in that the highest volume is designated as 0 dB. Lower volumes become larger and larger negative numbers until they reach negative infinity.

If a recorded sound is too quiet, it might get lost in the background noise. Background noise might be environmental, such as an air-conditioning system making a hum. It also might be system noise, such as the quiet hiss you hear from your speakers when no sound is playing.

When you increase the overall volume of your audio, background noise gets louder too. When you decrease the overall volume, background noise gets quieter. This means it's often better to record audio at a higher level than you need (while avoiding over-driving), and then reduce the volume later to remove (or at least reduce) the background noise.

Depending on your audio hardware, you may have a bigger or smaller signal-to-noise ratio; that's the difference between the sound you want to hear (the signal) and the sound you don't want to hear (the background noise). Signal-to-noise ratio is often shown as SNR, also measured in dB.

2 Click the Source Monitor Settings menu, and choose Time Ruler Numbers to enable the time rulers.

The time ruler now shows timecode indicators on the time ruler. Try zooming in to the time ruler using the navigator. The maximum zoom shows you an individual frame.

3 Click the Source Monitor Settings menu again, and choose Show Audio Time Units.

This time, you'll see individual audio samples counted on the time ruler. Try zooming in a little more. Now you can zoom in to an individual audio sample—in this case, one 48,000th of a second.

4 The Timeline has the same option to view audio samples in the panel menu. For now, switch off the Time Ruler Numbers option and the Show Audio Time Units option in the Source Monitor using the Settings menu.

Note: The audio sample rate is the number of times per second the recorded sound source is sampled. It's common for professional camera audio to take a sample 48,000 times per second.

Showing audio waveforms

When you open a clip in the Source Monitor that has only audio (no video), Premiere Pro automatically shows the audio waveforms.

When you use the waveform display option in the Source Monitor or Program Monitor, you'll see an extra navigator zoom control for each channel. These controls work in a way that's similar to the navigator zoom control at the bottom of the panel. You can resize the vertical navigator to see the waveforms larger or smaller, which is useful if your audio is quiet.

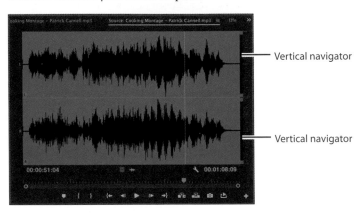

Vertical navigator

Vertical navigator

● **Note:** This option is great if you are trying to locate some specific dialogue and you are not so concerned about the visuals.

You can choose to display audio waveforms for any clip that has audio by selecting Audio Waveform in the Source Monitor and Program Monitor Settings menus.

If a clip has video as well as audio, the video will be displayed in the Source Monitor by default. You can switch to viewing the audio waveform by clicking the Drag Audio Only button (⊬⊬).

1 Open the clip HS John from the Theft Unexpected bin.

2 Click the Source Monitor Settings menu, and choose Audio Waveform.

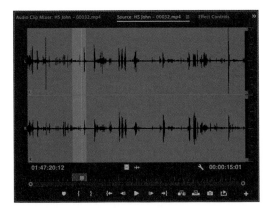

You can easily see where the dialogue begins and ends.

3 Switch back to viewing the Composite Video using the Source Monitor Settings menu.

You can also turn off and on the display of waveforms for clip segments on the Timeline.

4 Open the Theft Unexpected sequence in the Master Sequences bin.

5 Click the Timeline Settings menu, and make sure Show Audio Waveform is enabled.

6 Resize the Audio 1 track until the waveform is visible. Notice that two audio channels are displayed on one audio track in this sequence: The clips have stereo audio.

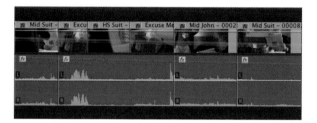

The audio waveform on these clips looks a little different from the waveforms in the Source Monitor. That's because it's a Rectified audio waveform, which makes it easier to see lower volume audio, like the dialogue in this scene. You can switch between Rectified and regular audio waveforms:

7 Go to the Timeline panel menu, and choose Rectified Audio Waveforms to deselect it.

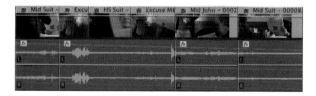

The regular waveform display works well for louder audio, but notice the quieter parts of the speech; it's much harder to follow the level changes.

8 Go to the Timeline panel menu, and restore the Rectified Audio Waveforms.

Working with standard audio tracks

The standard audio track type can accommodate both mono audio clips and stereo audio clips. The controls in the Effect Controls panel, the Audio Clip Mixer, and the Audio Track Mixer work with both kinds of media.

If you're working with a combination of mono and stereo clips, you'll find it more convenient to use the standard track type than the traditional separate mono or stereo tracks.

This standard audio track has a mix of stereo and mono clips.

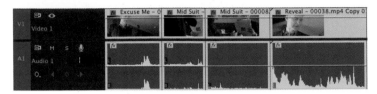

Monitoring audio

You can choose which sequence audio channels you hear when monitoring.

Let's try this with a sequence.

1   Open the Desert Montage sequence.

2   Play the sequence, and while you do, try clicking each of the Solo buttons at the bottom of the audio meters.

Each Solo button allows you to hear only the channel you select. You can solo multiple channels to hear a specific combination—though in this example it wouldn't help much as you have only two channels to choose between. When working with multichannel sequences, you'll solo output channels more often.

Soloing is particularly useful if you're working with audio where the sound from different microphones is recorded onto different tracks. This is common with professionally recorded location sound.

The number of channels and associated Solo buttons you'll see depends on your current sequence audio master setting.

You can also use the track header Mute button (M) or Solo button (S) for individual audio tracks. This gives you precise control over what's included or excluded in your mix.

Solo

Examining audio characteristics

When you open a clip in the Source Monitor and view the waveform, you're seeing each channel displayed. The taller the waveform is, the louder the audio for that channel will be.

Three factors affect the way audio sounds to your ears. Consider them in terms of a television speaker.

*   **Frequency:** This refers to how fast the surface of the speaker moves. The number of times the surface of the speaker beats the air per second is measured as Hertz (Hz). Human hearing ranges from approximately 20 Hz to 20,000 Hz.

Many factors, including age, affect the frequency range you can hear. The higher the frequency, the higher the perceived tone.

- **Amplitude:** This is how far the speaker moves. The bigger the movement, the louder the sound will be because it produces a higher air pressure wave, which carries more energy to your ears.

- **Phase:** This is the precise timing with which the surface of the speaker moves out and in. If two speakers push out air and pull in air in sync, they are considered "in phase." If they move out of sync, they become "out of phase," and this can produce problems with sound reproduction. One speaker can reduce the air pressure at exactly the moment the other speaker is attempting to increase it. The result is that you may not hear parts of the sound.

The movement of the surface of a speaker as it emits sound provides a simple example of the way sound is generated, but, of course, the same rules apply to all sound sources.

What are audio characteristics?

Imagine the surface of a speaker moving as it beats the air. As it moves, it creates a high- and low-pressure wave that moves through the air until it arrives at your ear in much the way that surface ripples move across a pond.

As the pressure wave hits your ear, it makes a tiny part of it move, and that movement is converted into electrical energy that is passed to your brain and interpreted as sound. This happens with extraordinary precision, and since you have two ears, your brain does an impressive job of balancing the two sets of sound information to produce an overall sense of what you can hear.

Much of the way you hear is active, not passive. That is, your brain is constantly filtering out sounds it decides are irrelevant and identifying patterns so you can focus your attention on things that matter. For example, you have probably had the experience of being at a party where the general hubbub of conversation sounds like a wall of noise until someone across the room mentions your name. You perhaps didn't realize your brain was listening to the conversation the whole time because you were concentrating on listening to the person standing next to you.

There's a body of research on this subject that broadly falls under the title *psychoacoustics*. For these exercises, we'll be focusing on the mechanics of sound more than on the psychology, though it's a fascinating subject worthy of further study.

Recording equipment makes no such subtle discrimination, which is part of the reason why it's so important to listen to location sound with headphones and to take care to get the best possible recorded sound. It's usual practice to try to record location sound with no background noise at all. The background noise is added in post-production at precisely the right level to add atmosphere to the scene but not drown out the dialogue.

Creating a voice-over "scratch track"

If you have a microphone set up, you can record audio directly to the Timeline using the Audio Track Mixer or a special Voice-over Record button on an audio track header. To record audio in this way, check that your Audio Hardware preferences are set up to allow input. You can check your audio hardware settings by choosing Edit > Preferences > Audio Hardware (Windows) or Premiere Pro > Preferences > Audio Hardware (Mac OS).

Try the Voice-over Record button by following these steps:

1 Open the Voice-over sequence in the Master Sequences bin. This is a simple sequence with visuals only, you'll add the VO.

2 Take a look at header for the A1 track. Increase the height of the track to see all the controls available. If you don't see the Voice-over Record button (🎤), click the Timeline Settings menu, and choose Customize Audio Header.

3 If necessary, drag the Voice-over Record button onto the Audio 1 track header, and close the Button Editor. You may need to resize the header to make enough space for the button.

4 Mute your speakers or wear headphones while recording voice-over to avoid getting microphone feedback.

5 Position the playhead at the beginning of the sequence, and click the Voice-over Record button. The Program Monitor gives a short countdown, and you can begin. Describe the shots that come up to create an accompanying voice-over.

As you record, the Program Monitor shows you're recording, and the Audio Meter shows the input level.

6 When you're finished recording, press the spacebar, or click the Voice-over Record button to stop.

The new audio appears on the Timeline, and an associated clip appears in the Project panel. Premiere Pro will create a new audio file in the location specified in the Scratch Disks settings in the project settings. By default, this is the same location as your project file.

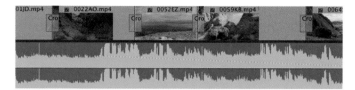

You can use this technique to record professional-quality audio using a studio microphone and soundbooth. Or you can use it with the built-in microphone on a laptop to record guide-track voice-over while on your way back from a shoot. That voice-over can form the basis for an outline edit, saving significant time later.

Adjusting audio volume

There are several ways to adjust the volume of clips with Premiere Pro, and they are all nondestructive. Changes you make don't affect your original media files, so you can experiment freely.

Adjusting audio in the Effect Controls panel

Earlier, you used the Effect Controls panel to make adjustments to the scale and position of clips in a sequence. You can also use the Effect Controls panel to adjust volume.

1 Open the Excuse Me sequence from the Master Sequences bin.

This is a simple sequence with two clips in it. In fact, it's the same clip added to the sequence twice. One version has been interpreted as stereo, and the other has been interpreted as mono channels.

2 Click the first clip to select it, and go to the Effect Controls panel.

3 In the Effect Controls panel, expand the Volume, Channel Volume, and Panner controls.

Each control gives the right options for the type of audio you have selected.

- **Volume** adjusts the combined volume of all the audio channels in the selected clip.

- **Channel Volume** allows you to adjust the audio level for individual channels in the selected clip.

- **Panner** gives you overall stereo left/right output balance control for the selected clip.

  Notice that the keyframe toggle stopwatch icon is automatically enabled for all the controls. This means every change you make will add a keyframe.

  However, if you add only one keyframe and use it to set the audio level, the adjustment will apply to the whole clip.

4 Position the Timeline playhead over the clip where you would like to add a keyframe (it doesn't make too much difference if you intend to make only one adjustment).

5 Click the Timeline panel Settings menu, and make sure Show Audio Keyframes is selected.

6 Increase the height of the Audio 1 track so you can see the waveform and special thin white line for adding keyframes, often referred to as a rubber band.

7 In the Effect Controls panel, drag left on the blue number that sets the volume level.

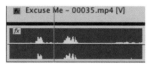

Note: The rubber band uses the entire height of the audio clip to adjust the volume.

Premiere Pro adds a keyframe, and the rubber band moves down to show the reduced volume. The difference is subtle, but as you become more familiar with the Premiere Pro interface, it'll stand out more and more clearly.

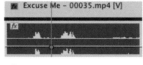

Before.   After.

8 Now select the second version of the Excuse Me clip in the sequence.

  You'll notice you have similar controls available in the Effect Controls panel, but now there is no Channel Volume option. This is because each channel is its own clip segment, so the Volume control for each channel is already an individual one.

9 Experiment with adjusting the volume for these two independent clips.

Adjusting audio gain

Most music is created with the loudest possible signal to maximize the difference between the signal and the background noise. This is too loud to use in most video sequences. To address this issue, you need to adjust the clip's audio gain.

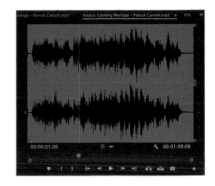

1 Open the clip Cooking Montage.mp3 from the Music bin. Notice the size of the waveform.

   ● **Note:** You may need to adjust the zoom level on the Source Monitor to see the waveform.

2 Right-click the clip in the bin and choose Audio Gain.

   There are two options in the Audio Gain panel that you should pay attention to for now

   • **Set Gain to:** Use this option to specify a particular adjustment for your clip.

   • **Adjust Gain by:** Use this option to specify an incremental adjustment for your clip. For example, if you apply –3 dB, this will adjust the "Set Gain to" amount to –3 dB. If you go into this menu a second time and apply another –3 dB adjustment, the "Set Gain to" amount will change to –6 dB, and so on.

3 Set the gain to **–12** dB, and click OK.

   Right away, you'll see the waveform change in the Source Monitor.

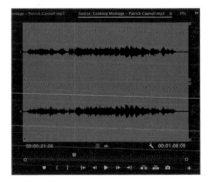

   ● **Note:** None of the changes you make to the volume of your clips will change the original media files. You can make a change to the overall gain here, in the bin, or on the Timeline, in addition to any changes you make using the Effect Controls panel, and your original media files will remain unmodified.

   Changes like this, where you are adjusting the audio gain in the bin, will not update clips already edited into a sequence. However, you can right-click one or more clips in a sequence, choose Audio Gain, and make the same kind of adjustment there.

Normalizing audio

Normalizing audio is similar to adjusting gain. In fact, normalization results in an adjustment to the clip gain. The difference is that normalization is based on automated analysis rather than on your subjective judgment.

When you normalize a clip, Premiere Pro analyzes the audio to identify the single highest peak, the loudest part of the audio. The gain for the clip is then adjusted automatically so that the highest peak matches a level you specify.

You can have Premiere Pro adjust the volume for multiple clips so that they match any perceived volume you like.

Imagine working with multiple clips of a voice-over, recorded over several days. Perhaps because of different recording setups or working with different microphones, several clips might have different volumes. You can select all the clips and, in a single step, have Premiere Pro automatically set their volumes to match. This saves significant time you would have spent manually going through each clip, one by one, to make adjustments.

Try normalizing some clips by following these steps:

1 Open the Journey to New York sequence.

2 Play the sequence, and watch the level on the audio meters.

   The voice level varies quite a lot, particularly in the third and fourth clips.

3 Select all the voice-over clips in the sequence. To do so, you can lasso them or make an item-by-item selection.

4 Right-click any of the selected clips and choose Audio Gain, or press the G key.

5 Enter −8 for Normalize All Peaks To, and click OK. Listen again.

Note: You may need to adjust the track size to see the audio waveforms. Do this by dragging the divider on the Track Header.

Tip: You can apply normalization in the bin too. Just select all the clips you want to automatically adjust, go to the Clip menu and choose Audio Options > Audio Gain, or press the G key.

Every selected clip is adjusted so that the loudest peaks are at −8 dB.

Notice the way the waveforms for the clips level out. If you choose Normalize Max Peak To, rather than Normalize All Peaks To, Premiere Pro will make an adjustment based on the loudest moment of all the clips combined, as if they were one clip.

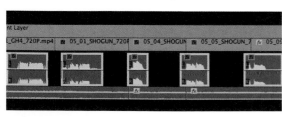

Before

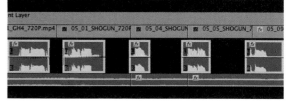

After

Sending audio to Adobe Audition CC

While Premiere Pro has advanced tools to help you achieve most audio-editing tasks, it can't compete with Adobe Audition, which is a dedicated audio post-production application.

Audition is a component of Adobe Creative Cloud. It integrates neatly into your workflow when editing with Premiere Pro.

You can send your current sequence to Adobe Audition automatically, bringing all your clips and a video file based on your sequence, to produce an audio mix that follows along with the pictures.

To send your sequence to Adobe Audition, follow these steps:

1 Open the sequence you want to send to Adobe Audition.

2 Choose Edit > Edit in Adobe Audition > Sequence.

3 You'll be creating new files to work with in Adobe Audition to keep your original media unchanged, so choose a name and browse for a location, then choose the remaining options as you prefer, and finally click OK.

4 In the Video menu, you can choose Send Through Dynamic Link to view the view part of your Premiere Pro sequence live in Audition.

Adobe Audition has fantastic tools for working with sound. It has a special spectral display that helps you identify and remove unwanted noises, a high-performance multitrack editor, and advanced audio effects and controls.

It's also easy to send an individual clip to Audition to benefit from its superior audio cleanup, editing, and adjustment features. To send a clip to Audition, right-click the clip in your Premiere Pro sequence and choose Edit Clip in Adobe Audition.

Premiere Pro duplicates the audio clip, replaces the current sequence clip with the duplicate, and opens the duplicate in Audition, ready to work on it.

From now on, every time you save changes you have made to the clip in Audition, they'll automatically update in Premiere Pro.

For more information about Adobe Audition, go to www.adobe.com/products/audition.html.

Creating a split edit

A split edit is a simple, classic editing technique that offsets the cut point for audio and video. The audio from one clip is played with the visuals from another, carrying the feeling of one scene into another.

Adding a J-cut

The J-cut gets its name from the shape of the edit. Picture the letter J over an edit. The lower part (the audio cut) is to the left of the upper part (the video cut).

1 Open the Theft Unexpected sequence.

2 Play the last cut in the sequence. The join in the audio between the last two clips is rather abrupt. You may need to turn up your speaker volume to hear the join. You'll improve things by adjusting the timing of the audio cut.

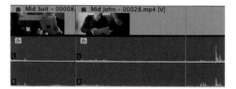

3 Select the Rolling Edit tool (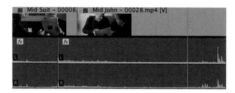).

▶ **Tip:** You can apply a rolling edit using the Selection tool if you hold Control (Windows) or Command (Mac OS).

4 While holding the Alt key, click the audio segment edit (not the video), and drag a little to the left. Congratulations! You've created a J-cut!

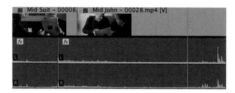

5 Play through the edit.

You might want to experiment with the timing to make the cut seem more natural, but for practical purposes the J-cut works. You can smooth it over and improve it further with an audio crossfade later.

Remember to switch back to the Selection tool (V).

Adding an L-cut

An L-cut works in the same way as a J-cut but in reverse. Repeat the steps in the previous exercise, but try holding Alt (Windows) or Option (Mac OS) as you drag the audio segment edit a little to the right. Play through the edit and see what you think.

Adjusting audio levels for a clip

As well as adjusting clip gain, you can use the rubber-band to change the volume of clips in a sequence. You can also change the volume for tracks, and the two volume adjustments will combine to produce an overall output level.

If anything, using rubber bands to adjust volume is more convenient than adjusting gain because you can make incremental adjustments at any time, with immediate visual feedback.

The result of adjusting the rubber bands on a clip is the same as adjusting the volume using the Effect Controls panel. In fact, one control will automatically update the other.

Adjusting overall clip levels

To adjust overall clip levels, do the following:

1 Open the Desert Montage sequence in the Master Sequences bin.

The music already fades up and down at the beginning and end. Let's adjust the volume between those fades.

2 Use the Selection tool to drag down at the bottom of the A1 track header, or hover the mouse cursor over the track header and scroll to make the track taller. This will make it easier to apply fine adjustments to the volume.

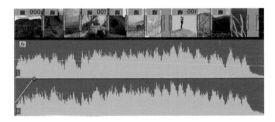

3 The music is a little too loud. Click the middle part of the rubber band on the music clip in the sequence, and drag down a little.

As you drag, a tool tip appears, displaying the amount of adjustment you are making.

Because you're dragging a segment of the rubber band rather than a keyframe, you're adjusting the overall level for the segment between the two existing keyframes. If the clip did not have existing keyframes, you'd be adjusting the overall level for the entire length of the clip.

Tip: You can find these, and many more available keyboard shortcuts, by choosing Edit > Keyboard Shortcuts (Windows) or Premiere Pro > Keyboard Shortcuts (Mac OS).

Changing clip volume with keyboard shortcuts

If the Timeline playhead is over a clip, you can also raise and lower clip volume using keyboard shortcuts. The result is the same, although you won't see a tool tip informing you about the amount of adjustment. These are particularly convenient shortcuts for quick, precise audio level adjustments:

- Use the [key to decrease clip volume by 1 dB.
- Use the] key to increase clip volume by 1 dB.
- Use Shift + [to decrease clip volume by 6 dB.
- Use Shift +] Increase clip volume by 6 dB.

Keyframing volume changes

If you use the Selection tool to drag an existing keyframe, you'll adjust it. This is the same as making adjustments to visual effects using keyframes.

The Pen tool ( ) adds keyframes to rubber bands. You can also use it to adjust existing keyframes or to lasso lots of keyframes to adjust them together.

You don't need to use the Pen tool, though. If you want to add a keyframe where there is none, you can hold Control (Windows) or Command (Mac OS) when you click the rubber band.

The result of adding and adjusting the position of keyframes up or down on audio clip segments is that the rubber band is reshaped. Just as before, the higher the rubber band, the louder the sound.

Tip: If you adjust the clip audio gain, Premiere Pro combines the effect with the keyframe adjustments dynamically. You can change either at any time.

Add a few keyframes to the music now and listen to the results.

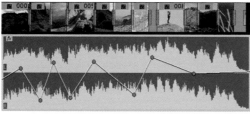

Smoothing volume between keyframes

The adjustments you made in the previous exercise are probably pretty dramatic. You might want to smooth the adjustments over time, and this is easy to do.

To do so, right-click any of your keyframes. You'll see a range of standard options, including Ease In, Ease Out, and Delete. If you use the Pen tool, you can lasso multiple keyframes, and then right-click any one of them to apply a change to them all.

The best way to learn about the different kinds of keyframes is to select each kind, make some adjustments, and see the results.

Using clip vs. track keyframes

Until now, you've made all your keyframe adjustments to sequence clip segments. Premiere Pro has similar controls available for the audio tracks those clips are placed onto. Track-based keyframes work in the same way as the clip-based ones. The difference is that they don't move with the clips.

● **Note:** Adjustments you make to your clips are applied before adjustments you make to your tracks.

This means you can set up keyframes for your audio level using track controls and then try different music clips. Each time you put new music into your sequence, you'll hear it via the adjustments you have made to your track.

As you develop your editing skills with Premiere Pro and create more complex audio mixes, explore the flexibility offered by combining clip and track keyframe adjustments.

Working with the Audio Clip Mixer

The Audio Clip Mixer provides intuitive controls to adjust clip volume and pan keyframes over time.

Each sequence audio track is represented by a set of controls. You can mute or solo a track, and you can enable the option to write keyframes to clips during playback by dragging a fader.

Faders are industry-standard controls based on real-world audio-mixing desks. You move the fader up to increase the volume and move it down to decrease the volume. You can also use the volume faders to add keyframes to your clip audio rubber band while you play the sequence.

Try this for yourself.

1 Continue working with the Desert Montage sequence. Make sure the Audio 1 track is set to show audio keyframes.

2 Open the Audio Clip Mixer, and play the sequence.

   Because you already added keyframes to this clip, the Audio Clip Mixer fader moves up and down during playback.

3 Position the Timeline playhead at the beginning of the sequence.

4 In the Audio Clip Mixer, enable the Write Keyframes button (⬛) for Audio 1.

Note: You won't see new keyframes until you stop playback.

Tip: You can adjust pan in the same way as you would adjust volume using the Audio Clip Mixer. Simply play your sequence, and make adjustments using the Audio Mixer's Pan control.

5 Play the sequence, and while it plays, make some adjustments to the Audio 1 fader. When you stop playback, you'll see the new keyframes that you added.

6 If you repeat the process, you'll notice that the fader follows existing keyframes until you make a manual adjustment.

You can adjust keyframes you have created this way just as you would adjust keyframes that were created using the Selection tool or the Pen tool.

You have now discovered several ways to add and adjust keyframes in Premiere Pro. There's no right or wrong way to work with keyframes; it's entirely a matter of personal preference.

Review questions

1 How can you isolate an individual sequence audio channel to hear only that channel?

2 What is the difference between mono and stereo audio?

3 How can you view the waveforms for any clip that has audio in the Source Monitor?

4 What is the difference between normalization and gain?

5 What is the difference between a J-cut and an L-cut?

6 Which option in the Audio Clip Mixer must be enabled before you can add keyframes to sequence clips during playback?

Review answers

1 Use the Solo buttons at the bottom of the audio meters to selectively hear an audio channel.

2 Stereo audio has two audio channels, and mono audio has one. It is the universal standard to record audio from a Left microphone as Channel 1 and audio from a Right microphone as Channel 2 when recording stereo sound.

3 Use the Settings menu on the Source Monitor to choose Audio Waveform. You can do the same with the Program Monitor, but you probably won't need to; clips can display waveforms on the Timeline. You can also click the Drag Audio Only button at the bottom of the Source Monitor.

4 Normalization automatically adjusts the Gain setting for a clip based on the original peak amplitude. You use the Gain setting to make manual adjustments.

5 The sound for the next clip begins before the visuals when using a J-cut (sometimes described as "audio leads video"). With L-cuts, the sound from the previous clip remains until after the visuals begin (sometimes described as "video leads audio").

6 Enable the Write Keyframes option for each track you would like to add keyframes to.

12 SWEETENING SOUND

Lesson overview

In this lesson, you'll learn about the following:

- Sweetening sound with audio effects

- Adjusting equalization (EQ)

- Cleaning up noisy audio

 This lesson will take approximately 60 minutes.

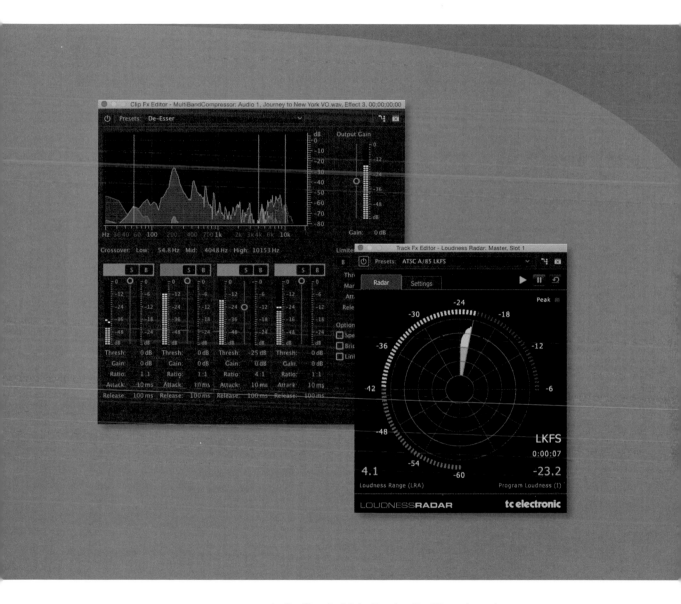

Audio effects in Adobe Premiere Pro CC can dramatically change the feel of your project. To take your sound to a higher level, leverage the integration and power of Adobe Audition CC.

Getting started

You'll find many audio effects in Adobe Premiere Pro CC. These effects can be used to change pitch, create an echo, add reverb, and remove tape hiss. You can set keyframes for effects and adjust their settings over time.

1 Open the project Lesson 12.prproj.

2 In the Workspaces panel, click Audio. Then click the menu adjacent to the Audio option and choose Reset to Saved Layout.

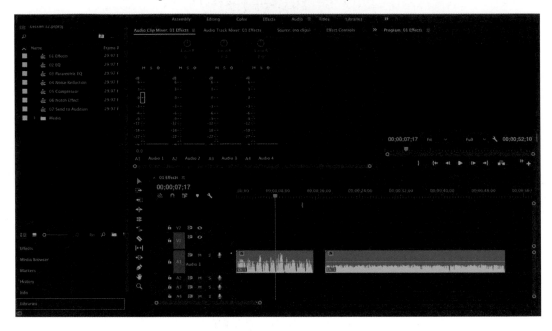

Sweetening sound with audio effects

Note: Expand your knowledge about audio effects in Premiere Pro by experimenting. These effects are nondestructive, which means they do not change your original audio files. You can add any number of effects to a clip, change settings, and then delete them and start again.

Ideally, your audio would come in perfectly. Unfortunately, video production is rarely an ideal process. At some point, you'll need to turn to audio effects to fix problems. In this lesson, you'll try a few of the most useful effects in Premiere Pro.

Not all audio hardware plays all audio frequencies evenly. For example, listening to deep bass notes on a laptop is never the same as listening on larger speakers.

It's important to listen to your audio using high-quality headphones or studio monitor speakers to avoid accidentally compensating for a flaw in your playback hardware as you adjust the sound. Professional audio-monitoring hardware is carefully calibrated to ensure that all frequencies play evenly, giving you confidence you'll produce a consistent sound for your listeners.

Premiere Pro offers a variety of helpful effects, including the following:

- **EQ:** This effect allows you to make subtle and precise adjustments to the audio level at different frequencies.

- **Reverb:** This can increase the "presence" in the recording with reverb. Use it to simulate the sound of a larger room.

- **Delay:** This effect can add a slight (or pronounced) echo to your audio track.

- **Bass:** This effect can amplify the low-end frequencies of a clip. It works well on narration clips, particularly for male voices.

- **Treble:** This effect adjusts the higher-range frequencies in an audio clip.

Adjusting bass

Adjusting the amplitude of the lower frequencies can improve the overall sound of a male voice. In this example, let's try this with an announcer's voice.

1 Open the 01 Effects sequence.

2 Play the first clip in the sequence, Ad Cliches Mono.wav, to get familiar with the sound. It sounds OK but would benefit from a little more low-frequency power.

   If clip names aren't visible, click the Timeline Settings menu (![icon]), and make sure that Show Audio Names is selected.

3 Browse the Audio Effects folder in the Effects panel, and look for the Bass effect.

4 Drag the Bass effect onto the Ad Cliches Mono.wav clip on the Timeline. Note that the Fx icon on the clip changes color to indicate that an effect has been applied.

5 Open the Effect Controls panel.

6 Increase the Boost property to add more bass.

Experiment using different values to increase or decrease the presence of bass until you hear a sound you like. Be sure to pay attention to your overall audio levels because an adjustment of this kind can change the volume of the clip. You may need to use the Audio Clip Mixer panel to maintain proper levels.

Adding a delay

A delay is a stylized effect. It can be used on an announcer's voice to add drama, or it can be used to create a feeling of space using stylized echoes.

1 In the Audio Effects folder in the Effects panel, locate the Delay effect. Apply this effect to the Ad Cliches Mono clip.

2 In the Timeline panel, set an In mark at the start of the Ad Cliches clip, and set an Out mark at the end. You can do this quickly by selecting the clip and pressing the (forward slash) / key.

3 At the bottom right of the Effect Controls panel, there's a button to play the audio for the clip and a Loop Play button (). With the Loop Play option on, playback will loop between your In and Out marks. Turn on the Loop Play option and click the Effect Controls panel play button to hear the Delay effect. By default, there's an echo that's offset by a second. You can leave the clip playing this way while you experiment.

4 Try adjusting these parameters:

   • **Delay:** The time before the echo plays

   • **Feedback:** The percentage of echo added to the original audio to create echoes of echoes

   • **Mix:** The relative loudness of the echoes

5 Press the spacebar to stop the playback.

   When selectively playing audio, using the button at the bottom of the Effect Controls panel, any audio adjustments you make will automatically create key-frames. This handy shortcut can speed up working on audio, but you don't need the keyframes you just created for now.

6 Click the Stopwatch icons for the Delay, Feedback, and Mix controls in the Effect Controls panel to remove the unwanted keyframes.

7 Set up the effect as follows to get a classic stadium announcer effect:

   • Delay: 0.**250** seconds

   • Feedback: **20%**

   • Mix: **10%**

8 Play the clip, and move the sliders to experiment further.

Lower values are a bit more palatable, even with this over-the-top audio clip. A subtle effect is usually more pleasant for listeners. Remember, your audience is likely to be much less tolerant of bad audio than of bad images.

9 Remove the Delay effect by selecting it in the Effect Controls panel and pressing Backspace (Windows) or Delete (Mac OS).

Adjusting pitch

Another adjustment you can make is pitch. This is a useful way to change the overall tone of a sound. By altering the pitch, you can change the energy level, apparent age, or even gender of a speaker.

1 In the Effects panel, locate the Pitch Shifter effect—be sure to use Pitch Shifter, rather than Pitch Shifter (Obsolete). This new version of the effect was originally available only in Adobe Audition.

2 Drag the Pitch Shifter effect onto the Ad Cliches Mono.wav clip.

3 In the Effect Controls panel, click the Edit button next to the Custom Setup properties to show the parameters for the effect.

> **Tip:** Quite a few audio effects have additional interface elements accessible by clicking the appropriate setup button.

A floating panel opens.

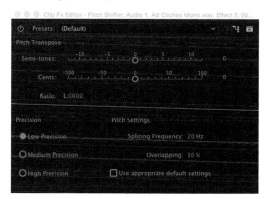

4 Adjust a few settings and listen to the results. Try wildly different pitch settings, from −12 to +12 semi-tone steps. Close the panel.

5 Back in the Effect Controls panel, there's a button to the right of the effect name that looks a little like a Reset button, but it's actually a menu with a list of presets for this effect (). Click the button to see the options.

6 You don't need to close the floating panel to use the presets. Try some now, and notice the changes they make to the floating panel settings. When you're finished, close the floating panel.

Adjusting treble

Earlier you applied and adjusted the Bass effect to modify the lower frequencies of an audio clip. To modify the high frequencies, use the Treble effect.

Treble is not simply the Bass effect in reverse. Treble increases or decreases higher frequencies (4000 Hz and greater), whereas the Bass effect changes low frequencies (200 Hz and less).

1 Drag the sequence playhead so it's over the second clip in the Timeline panel (Music Mono).

2 Play the clip to get familiar with its sound.

3 In the Audio Effects folder in the Effects panel, find the Treble effect.

4 Drag the Treble effect onto the Music Mono clip.

5 Increase the Boost property to add more treble.

Increasing the treble can give your audio more clarity. Experiment until you get a sound you like.

Adding reverb

Reverb is similar to the Delay effect but is usually more subtle and can simulate the way a sound would be perceived in different types of environments—like different-sized rooms.

It works particularly well for pieces that feature a strong single instrument or voice but can be used on just about any clip. It's a powerful effect that can give life to audio recorded in an acoustically flat room, which is common in a recording studio with minimal reflective surfaces.

1 In the Effects panel, locate the Studio Reverb effect.

2 Drag the Studio Reverb effect onto the Music Mono clip.

3 In the Effect Controls panel, click the Edit button for the Reverb effect.

There are a lot of controls here you may not be familiar with. Don't worry; the presets will help you learn about the options, and in many case you'll be able to start with a preset and make adjustments to it.

4 Try a few of the presets, and notice the effect they have on the settings.

5 Experiment with the settings. Here's an overview of what they do:

- **Room Size:** Lets you specify the size of the virtual room your audio will play in.

- **Decay:** Controls how quickly reflected sounds lose volume. The shorter the decay, the quicker the reverb will disappear.

- **Early Reflections:** Sets how much reflected sound is heard right away. The higher this setting, the more apparent the reverb will be, but if it's set too high, the result can sound artificial. Aim for approximately half the room size for natural results.

- **High Frequency Cut:** High-frequency sounds have a higher tone. This control allows you to set a highest frequency for the reflected sounds created by the effect.

- **Low Frequency Cut:** Low-frequency sounds have a lower tone. This control allows you to set a lowest frequency for the reflected sounds created by the effect.

- **Damping:** Sets the percentage of higher frequency sounds that are reduced over time. A higher percentage leads to a warmer sound.

- **Diffusion:** Simulates softer surfaces that absorb more sound—imagine carpeted floors with a high Diffusion setting and tiles with a low setting.

- **Output Level:** Allows you to set the mix of original sound (Dry) and the resulting affected sound (Wet). If the Wet level is set to 0%, you'll hear only the original sound.

6 When you have finished experimenting, close the panel.

Adjusting EQ

If you have a good amplifier or car stereo, it probably features a graphic equalizer (EQ) of some kind. The EQ controls go beyond simple Bass and Treble and add multiple controls for specific frequencies (often called *bands*) for greater control over the sound. There are several audio equalization effects in Premiere Pro. You'll take a look at two that will give you a good overall understanding of the options.

● **Note:** In the next exercise, use the suggested numbers for guidance, but feel free to experiment with different settings. Your taste and speakers may vary.

Simple Parametric EQ

If you want precise control over the volume of a clip at particular frequencies, the Simple Parametric EQ effect may meet your needs. You can select only one frequency range with the Simple Parametric EQ, but you can apply the effect multiple times and select a different frequency each time. This lets you build as complex an equalizer as you need in the Effect Controls panel.

Let's check this out:

1 Open the sequence 02 Simple Parametric EQ.

2 Play the clip to get familiar with its sound. Then select the clip in the sequence and look in the Effect Controls panel.

There are seven Simple Parametric EQ effects applied to the clip, but they all have the Bypass option enabled, meaning the effect is not applied. The effects are arranged from low frequencies (at the top of the list) to high frequencies (at the bottom of the list).

3 Deselect the first Bypass check box for the first Parametric EQ effect.

4 Play the sequence to listen to the change.

5 Continue deselecting the Parametric EQ Bypass check boxes one at a time, and listen to the changes in the audio track after each one.

The overall audio level is likely to become too loud as you add more and more of these Parametric EQ adjustments. Enable the Bypass check boxes for effects you have already listened to, which prevents the effects from being applied.

▶ **Tip:** Another way to use the Parametric EQ effect is to target a specific frequency and either boost it or cut it. You can use this effect to cut a particular frequency, like a high-frequency noise or a low hum.

Parametric EQ

The Parametric Equalizer effect offers a more nuanced and intuitive interface for precise audio-level adjustment than the Simple Parametric EQ effect.

It includes a graphic interface you can use to drag level adjustments that are linked together.

The bottom edge of the graph display shows frequency, while the vertical edge on the right shows amplitude. The blue line across the middle of the graph represents any adjustments you have made, and you can reshape the line directly. Wherever the blue line is higher, or lower in the display, adjustments are made to audio level at those frequencies.

You can drag any of the five control points directly, as well as the Low Pass and High Pass controls at the ends.

On the left is an overall Master Gain level adjustment, which offers a quick fix if the changes you make result in audio that is too loud or too quiet overall.

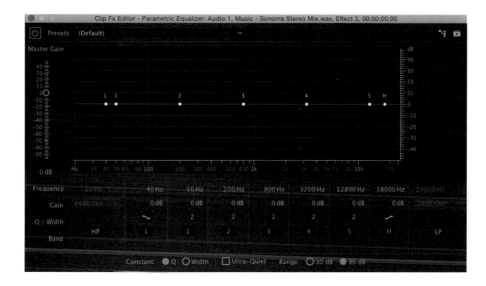

Let's try this effect:

1 Open the sequence 03 Full Parametric EQ. This sequence has one musical clip.

2 Locate the Parametric Equalizer effect in the Effects panel (try using the Find box at the top of the window), and drag it onto the clip.

3 In the Effect Controls panel, click the Edit button to access the Custom Setup controls for the Parametric Equalizer effect.

4 Play the clip to get familiar with its sound.

5 Drag Control Point 1 quite a long way down in the graph to reduce the audio level at low frequencies. Listen to the music again.

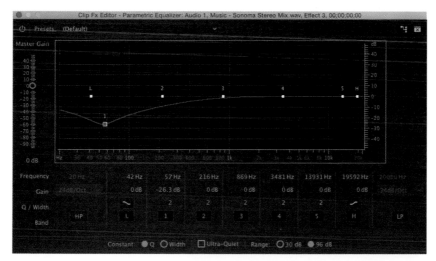

What's special about this interface is that changes you make to one area of the blue line impact surrounding frequencies, resulting in a more natural sound.

The control points you drag have a range of influence that is defined by their Q setting.

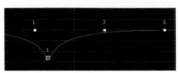

In the previous example, Control Point 1 has been set to 57 Hz (which is very low frequency), with a gain adjustment of -26.3 dB (which is a big gain reduction) and a Q of 2 (which is quite wide).

6 Change the Q factor for Control Point 1 from 2 to 7. You can click the 2 and type in a new setting directly.

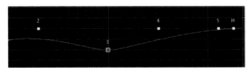

The line has a much sharper curve, so the adjustment you have made now applies to fewer frequencies.

7 Play the sequence to hear the changes.

Let's refine the vocals.

8 Drag Control Point 3 down to about -20 dB, and set the Q factor to 1 for a very broad adjustment.

9 Play the sequence to hear the changes—the vocals are much quieter.

10 Drag Control Point 4 to around 1500 Hz, with a gain of +6.0 dB. Adjust the Q factor to 3 for more precise adjustment on the EQ adjustment.

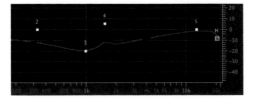

11 Play the sequence to hear the changes.

12 Drag the High frequency filter (the H control), and set its gain to around −8.0 dB to make the highest frequencies quieter.

13 Use the Master Gain control to adjust the overall level. You may need to see your audio meters to find out whether your mix is right.

▶ **Tip:** If your audio meters are not displayed, you can access them by choosing Window > Audio Meters.

14 Play the sequence to hear the changes.

These are dramatic changes intended to illustrate a technique. In general use, you'll usually make subtler adjustments.

● **Note:** Avoid setting the volume too high (the Peak meter line will turn red, and the peak monitors will light up). This can lead to distortion.

Audio Plug-in Manager

It's easy to install third-party plug-ins. Choose Edit > Preferences > Audio (Windows) or Premiere Pro > Preferences > Audio (Mac OS). Then click the button for the Audio Plug-in Manager.

1 Click the Add button to add any additional directories that contain AU or VST plug-ins. AU plug-ins are Mac only.

2 If needed, click the Scan for Plug-ins button to find all available plug-ins.

3 Use the Enable All button or the individual enable check boxes to activate a plug-in.

4 Click OK to commit your changes.

● **Note:** Listing all the attributes of all the audio effects in Premiere Pro is beyond the scope of this book. To learn more about audio effects, search Premiere Pro Help.

Cleaning up noisy audio

While it's always best to record perfect audio at the source, sometimes you can't control the origin of the audio, and it might be impossible to re-record it. You may find you need to repair a bad audio clip. Premiere Pro has versatile tools for fixing common audio problems.

Highpass and Lowpass effects

The Highpass and Lowpass effects often work to improve a clip, used together or independently. The Highpass effect is used to remove all frequencies that fall below a certain frequency (think of it as letting all audio frequencies pass through if they are higher than the threshold you set). The Lowpass filter is the direct opposite. It only allows frequencies below the specified Cutoff frequency.

1 Open the sequence 04 Noise Reduction.

2 Play the sequence to get familiar with the sound quality.

There's a clear hiss and a low hum that sounds like electrical interference.

3 In the Effects panel, locate the Highpass effect and drag it onto the clip. This effect allows audio over a particular frequency to pass through—and be audible.

4 Play the sequence.

The sound is probably thin because the Highpass threshold is set too high. Too many frequencies are removed.

5 Make sure the clip is selected and, in the Effect Controls panel, adjust the Cutoff slider for the Highpass effect to a lower value.

You can make adjustments while the clip plays to hear the result in real time. Play with the value to minimize some of the lower-frequency noise in the background. A setting around 160.0 Hz works well.

6 In the Effects panel, locate the Lowpass effect, and drag it onto the clip.

7 Play with the Cutoff slider for the Lowpass effect. A setting around 5000.0 Hz works well.

Experiment with different settings to familiarize yourself with the way these two effects interact. It's possible to remove the audio completely by setting the two effects to overlap frequencies. Pull down some of the higher frequencies that are making the recording sound "tinny."

MultiBandCompressor effect

The MultiBandCompressor effect offers independent control over four different frequency bands. Each band typically contains unique audio content, making this a useful tool for audio mastering. Additionally, you can refine crossover frequencies between bands. These will let you adjust each band independently.

1 Open the sequence 05 Compressor.

2 Play the sequence to hear the audio. It sounds fine but has quite a lot of sibilance—high frequency sounds produced when speakers pronounce strong s's and f's.

3 In the Effects panel, locate the MultiBandCompressor effect, and drag it onto the clip.

4 In the Effect Controls panel, click the Edit button to view the MultiBandCompressor custom setup controls.

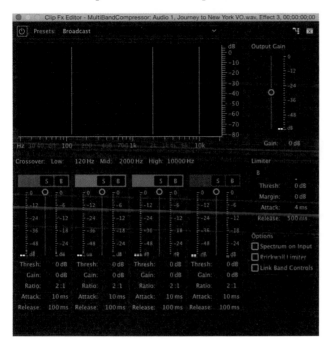

The effect has a number of presets.

5 Experiment with the Presets list at the top of window to get a sense of the impact this effect has.

6 From the Presets list, choose De-Esser. This automatically pulls down some of the higher frequencies.

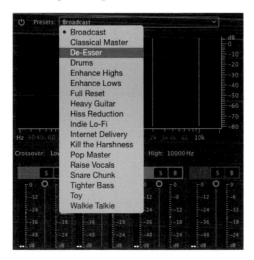

7 Listen to the audio to hear the results.

It's better, but it could have a little more punch.

8 Click the Solo button for Band 2 (the orange one).

9 Start audio playback so you can hear results.

10 While the audio plays, drag the white vertical audio crossover markers to refine the mid-frequency band, that is, the range of frequencies controlled by the second band.

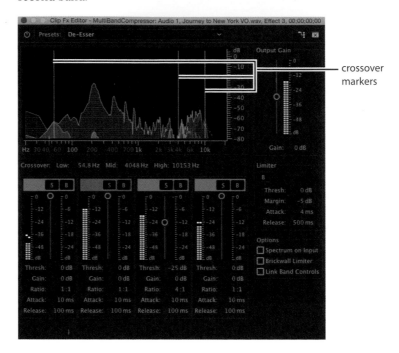

crossover markers

11 At the bottom of Band 2 there are a series of numerical controls. You can click and drag these, just as you would click and drag the blue numbers you see in the rest of the Premiere Pro interface. Experiment by reducing the threshold and increasing the gain settings to give the vocal more consistent intensity.

12 Switch off the Solo switch on Band 2.

13 Experiment with the crossover markers, threshold, and gain controls. Close the panel when you're finished.

The MultiBandCompressor effect can add power to audio without raising the peak level. This makes it easier on your audience's ears without losing impact.

Notch effect

The Notch effect removes frequencies near a specified value. The effect targets a frequency range and eliminates those sounds. The effect works well for removing power-line hum and other electrical interference. In this clip, you can hear the sounds of fluorescent light bulbs buzzing overhead.

1 Open the sequence 06 Notch Effect.

2 Play the sequence, and listen for the electrical hum. You may need to turn up your speakers.

3 In the Effects panel, locate the Notch effect and apply it to your clip.

4 Adjust the Center setting to target the frequency to be removed. If you expand the Center controls by clicking the disclosure triangle, you can use a slider.

Power-line hum tends to be at either 50 Hz or 60 Hz. In this case, it's 60 Hz, so choose that.

5 The Q adjustment allows for extra frequencies to be selected, around the chosen frequency. The higher the Q setting, the more precise the selection. In this case, you can set the Q setting to the maximum, 10.

6 Play the sequence to hear the result.

It's common for power hum to occur at harmonic frequencies. This means you may have interferences at 50 Hz, 100 Hz, 150 Hz, and so on, or at 60 Hz, 120 Hz, 180 Hz, and so on. It sounds like there's at least one harmonic frequency in this example.

7 Repeat the process, adding the Notch effect to the clip, and configuring it. This time, set the Center setting to 120 Hz.

8 Listen to the sequence again.

Even though the interference was at precise frequencies, this made it difficult to take in the vocals. Now it's removed, and everything sounds much clearer.

● **Note:** A 60 Hz or 50 Hz hum can be caused by many electrical problems, cable problems, or equipment noise. The frequency varies because of the different electrical systems used around the world.

Removing background noise with Adobe Audition

Adobe Audition offers advanced mixing and effects to improve your overall sound. If you have Audition installed, you can try the following:

1   In Premiere Pro, open the sequence 07 Send to Audition from the Project panel.

2   Right-click the Noisy Audio.aif clip in the Timeline and choose Edit Clip in Adobe Audition. A new copy of the audio clip is created and added to your project.

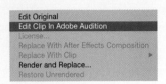

Audition opens, along with the new clip.

3   Switch to Audition.

4   The stereo clip should be visible in the Editor panel.

Audition shows a large waveform for the clip. To use Audition's advanced noise reduction tools, you need to identify a part of the clip that's just the noise so Audition knows what to remove.

5   If you don't see the Spectral Frequency Display under the waveform, choose View > Show Spectral Frequency Display. Play the clip. The beginning contains a few seconds of just noise, which is perfect for making a selection.

6   Using the Time Selection tool (the I-bar tool in the toolbar), drag to highlight the section of noise you just identified.

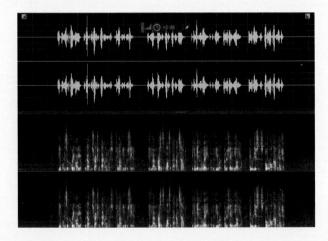
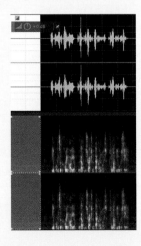

7 With the selection active, choose Effects > Noise Reduction/Restoration > Capture Noise Print. You can also press Shift+P.

If a dialog appears informing you that the noise print will be captured, click OK to confirm.

8 Choose Edit > Select > Select All to select the entire clip.

9 Choose Effects > Noise Reduction/Restoration > Noise Reduction (process). You can also press Shift+Control+P (Windows) or Shift+Command+P (Mac OS). A new panel opens so you can process the noise.

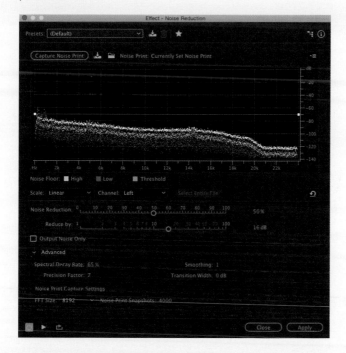

10 Select the Output Noise Only check box. This option allows you to hear only the noise you're removing, which helps you make an accurate selection so you don't accidentally remove too much of the audio you want to keep.

11 Click the Play button at the bottom of the window, and adjust the Noise Reduction and Reduce By sliders to remove noise from the clip. Try not to pull down much or any of the voice.

12 Deselect the Output Noise Only check box and listen to your cleaned-up audio.

13 Sometimes noise reduction results in distortion in vocals. In the Advanced section, there are a number of controls for refining the noise reduction. Experiment with the following:

- Reduce the Spectral Decay Rate option (this will shorten the delay between reducing noise and allowing it to be heard).

- Increase Precision Factor (this will take longer to process but improve results).

- Increase Smoothing (this will soften the adjustment from no noise reduction to full noise reduction based on an automatic selection of specific frequencies).

- Increase Transition Width, which allows some variation in level without applying full noise reduction.

14 When you're happy with the results, click the Apply button to apply the cleanup.

15 Choose File > Close, and save your changes.

16 Saving in Audition automatically updates the clip in Premiere Pro. Switch back to Premiere Pro, where you can listen to the cleaned-up audio clip.

Loudness Radar effect

If you are producing content for broadcast, it's likely you will be supplying media files according to strict delivery requirements.

One of those requirements will relate to the maximum volume for the audio—and there is more than one approach to this.

A popular modern way of measuring the audio level for broadcast is called the Loudness scale, and there's a way to measure your sequence audio using this scale.

You can measure the loudness for clips, for tracks, or for whole sequences. The precise settings you'll require for your audio should be given to you as part of your delivery specifications.

To measure the loudness for a whole sequence, follow these steps:

1 Switch to the Audio Track Mixer panel (rather than the Audio Clip Mixer). You may need to resize the frame to see all the controls in the Audio Track Mixer.

The Audio Track Mixer allows you to add effects to tracks, rather than clips, and the Master output track is no exception. Unlike the Audio Clip Mixer, the Audio Track Mixer includes the Master track, and this is the part of the interface you want.

2 The controls in the Audio Track Mixer are arranged in columns, one column per track plus the Master track at the right. At the top of the Master control, click the tiny triangle to open the Effect Selection menu and choose Special > Loudness Radar.

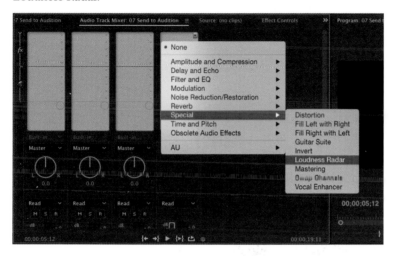

3 The effect appears at the top of the stack, with controls at the bottom.

4 Right-click the Loudness Radar effect in the Audio Track Mixer and choose Post-Fader.

The Fader controls on the Audio Track Mixer adjust the audio level for the track. It's important that the Loudness Radar analyzes the audio level after any Fader adjustments because otherwise adjustments made with the fader are ignored.

5 Double-click the name of the effect at the top of the interface to get access to full controls.

6 Press the spacebar to play, or click Play on the Program Monitor. During play-back, the Loudness Radar monitors loudness and displays it as a range of values illustrated in blue, green, and yellow (there's also a peak indicator).

The goal is to keep loudness generally within the green band on the Loudness Radar, though what that level will be depends on the standard you are working to, and this will be defined by your broadcast specifications.

You can change the levels indicated by the various bands in the Loudness Radar by clicking Settings. You can also use a preset, based on widely used standards, by choosing the Presets menu.

For more information about the Loudness Rader, see Premiere Pro Help.

Review questions

1   To change the tone of an audio clip without changing its duration, which effect would you use?

2   What's the difference between the Delay and Reverb effects?

3   Name three ways to remove background noise from a clip.

4   How can you send a clip to Adobe Audition directly from the Premiere Pro timeline?

Review answers

1   The Pitch Shifter effect can modify the apparent pitch or energy level for a clip while still maintaining sync with a video clip.

2   Delay creates a distinct, single echo that can repeat and gradually fade. Reverb is a more complex effect that creates a mix of echoes to simulate a room. It has multiple parameters that take the hard edge off the echo you hear in the Delay effect.

3   You can use a Highpass, Lowpass, MultiBandCompressor, and Notch effects within Premiere Pro, or you can send the clip to Adobe Audition to use its advanced noise reduction controls.

4   It's easy to send a clip to Audition. Right-click the clip and choose Edit Clip In Adobe Audition.

13 ADDING VIDEO EFFECTS

Lesson overview

In this lesson, you'll learn about the following:

- Working with fixed effects
- Browsing effects with the Effects panel
- Applying and removing effects
- Using effect presets
- Masking and tracking visual effects
- Using keyframing effects
- Exploring frequently used effects
- Rendering effects

 This lesson will take approximately 120 minutes.

Adobe Premiere Pro CC features more than 100 video effects. Most effects come with an array of parameters, all of which you can animate (have them change over time) by using precise keyframe controls.

Getting started

You might use video effects for many reasons. They can solve problems with image quality, such as exposure or color balance. They can create complex visual effects through compositing with techniques such as chromakey. They can also help solve a number of production problems, such as camera shake and rolling shutter.

Effects can also serve stylistic purposes. You can alter the color or distort footage, and you can animate the size and position of a clip within the frame. The challenge is to know when to use effects and when to keep it simple.

Standard effects can be constrained to elliptical or polygon masks, and these masks can automatically track your footage. For example, you might blur someone's face to hide their identity and have the blur follow them as they move through the shot.

Working with effects

Adobe Premiere Pro makes working with effects easy. You can drag a visual effect onto a clip, as you have already done with audio effects, or you can select the clip and double-click the effect in the Effects panel. In fact, you already know how to apply effects and change their settings. You can combine as many effects as you want on a single clip, which can produce surprising results. Moreover, you can use an adjustment layer to add the same effects to a collection of clips.

When it comes to deciding which video effects to use, the number of choices in Premiere Pro can be a bit overwhelming. Many additional effects are also available from third-party manufacturers for sale or free download.

While the range of effects and their controls can be complex, applying, adjusting, and removing effects are always straightforward.

Fixed effects

If you add a clip to a sequence, it will automatically have a few effects applied. These effects are called *fixed* effects, or intrinsic effects, and you can think of them as controls for the usual geometric, opacity, speed, and audio properties that every clip should have. You can modify all fixed effects using the Effect Controls panel.

1 Open Lesson 13.prproj.

2 Open the sequence 01 Fixed Effects.

3 Click to select the first clip in the Timeline.

4 Switch to the Effects workspace by clicking Effects on the Workspaces panel or by choosing Window > Workspaces > Effects.

5 Then reset the workspace by clicking the Effects menu on the Workspace panel and choosing Reset to Saved Layout or by choosing Window > Workspaces > Reset to Saved Layout.

6 In the Effect Controls panel, look at the fixed effects applied to this clip.

   Fixed effects are automatically applied to every clip in a sequence, but they don't change anything until you modify the settings.

7 Click the disclosure triangle next to each control to show its properties.

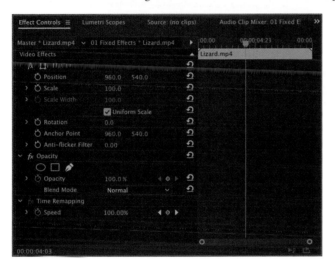

- **Motion:** The Motion effect allows you to animate, rotate, and scale a clip. You can also use the Anti-flicker Filter control to decrease shimmering edges for an animated object. This comes in handy when you scale a high-resolution source and Premiere Pro must resample the image.

- **Opacity:** The Opacity effect lets you control how opaque or transparent a clip is. You can also access special blend modes to create visual effects from multiple layers of video. You'll explore this more in Lesson 15, "Exploring Compositing Techniques."

- **Time Remapping:** This effect lets you slow down, speed up, or reverse playback, and it even lets you freeze a frame. You learned about time remapping in Lesson 8, "Performing Advanced Editing Techniques."

- **Audio Effects:** If a clip has audio, Premiere Pro displays its Volume, Channel Volume, and Panner controls. You learned about these in Lesson 11, "Editing and Mixing Audio."

8 Click to select the second clip in the Timeline, and look at the Effect Controls panel.

These effects have keyframes, meaning that their settings change over time. In this case, a small Scale and Pan were applied to the clip to create a digital zoom that didn't exist before and to recompose the shot.

You'll explore keyframes later in this lesson.

9 Press Play to watch the current sequence and compare the two shots.

The Effects panel

In addition to the fixed video effects, Premiere Pro has standard effects, which change a clip's appearance. Because there are so many to choose from, effects are organized into 16 categories. If you install third-party effects, you may have more choices.

There's an additional category of Obsolete effects. These effects have been replaced with newer, better designed versions, but they have been kept in Premiere Pro to ensure compatibility with older project files.

Effects are grouped into functions, including Distort, Keying, and Time, to make it easier to navigate them.

Each category has its own bin in the Effects panel.

1 Open the sequence 02 Browse.

2 Click to select the clip on the Timeline.

3 Open the Effects panel. You can use the keyboard shortcut Shift+7 to select it.

4 In the Effects panel, expand Video Effects.

5 Click the New Custom Bin button () at the bottom of the panel.

> ● **Note:** With so many Video Effect subfolders, it's sometimes tricky to locate the effect you want. If you know part or all of an effect's name, start typing it in the Find box at the top of the Effects panel. Premiere Pro will display all effects and transitions that contain that letter combination, narrowing the search as you type.

The new custom bin appears in the Effects panel at the bottom of the list (you may need to scroll down to see it). Let's rename it.

6 Click once to select the bin.

7 Click once more, directly on the bin's name (Custom Bin 01), to highlight it and change it.

8 Change its name to something like **Favorite Effects**.

9 Open any Video Effects folder, and drag a few effects to copy them into your custom bin. You may need to resize the panel to make it easier to drag and drop effects. Choose any effects that sound interesting to you. You can add or remove effects from a custom bin whenever you like.

As you browse the video effects, you'll notice icons next to many of the effect names. Understanding these icons might influence your choices when working with effects.

> ● **Note:** When you add effects to a custom bin in the Effects panel, you're making a copy. Effects also remain in their original folder. You can use custom bins to create effect categories to suit your work style.

32-bit color

Accelerated   YUV
effects   effects

Accelerated effects

The Accelerated effect icon ( ) indicates that the effect can be accelerated by your graphics processing unit (GPU). The GPU (often called the *video card* or *graphics card*) can greatly enhance the Premiere Pro's performance. The range of cards supported by the Mercury Playback Engine is broad, and with the right card installed, these effects often offer accelerated or even real-time performance and need rendering only on final export. You'll find a list of recommended cards on the Premiere Pro product page.

32-bit color (high-bit-depth) effects

Effects with the 32-bit color support icon ( ) can process in a 32-bits-per-channel mode, which is also called *high-bit-depth* or *float* processing.

You should use high-bit-depth effects in the following situations:

- When you're working with video shot with 10- or 12-bits-per-channel codecs, such as RED, ARRIRAW, or AVC-Intra 100, or 10-bit DNxHD, ProRes, or GoPro CineForm

- When you want to maintain greater image fidelity after applying multiple effects to any footage

Also, 16-bit photos or Adobe After Effects files rendered in 16- or 32-bits-per-channel color space can take advantage of high-bit-depth effects.

If you are editing without GPU acceleration, in Software mode, take advantage of high-bit-depth effects by making sure your sequence settings have the Maximum Bit Depth video-rendering option selected. You'll also find this choice on the Video tab of the Export Settings dialog.

YUV effects

Note: When using any 32-bit effects on a clip, try to use only combinations of 32-bit effects for maximum quality. If you mix and match effects, the non-32-bit effects switch processing back to 8-bit space.

Effects with the YUV icon (▦) process color in YUV. This is important if you're adjusting clip color. Effects without the YUV icon process in the computer's native RGB space, which can make adjusting exposure and color less accurate.

● **Note:** To learn more about YUV effects, be sure to read the article at http://bit.ly/yuvexplained.

YUV effects break down the video into a Y (or luminance) channel and two channels for color information, which is how most video footage is structured natively. These filters make it easy to adjust contrast and exposure without shifting color.

Applying effects

Virtually all the video effect settings are accessible in the Effect Controls panel. You can add keyframes to nearly every setting, making it easy to apply changes over time (just look for settings with a stopwatch icon). In addition, you can use Bézier curves to adjust the velocity and acceleration of those changes.

1   Open the sequence 02 Browse.

2   Type **white** into the Effects panel Find box to narrow the results. Locate the Black & White video effect.

▶ **Tip:** If you type **black** instead of **white** into the Effects panel Find box, you'll see a fantastic list of presets for lens distortion removal. As you grow more familiar with Premiere Pro, you'll discover the most efficient way to search for effects.

3   Drag the Black & White video effect onto the JG_2 clip in the Timeline.

This effect immediately converts your full-color footage to black and white or, more accurately, *grayscale*.

▶ **Tip:** You can select any of the three effect type icons at the top of the Effects panel to only display effects with those features.

4   Make sure the JG_2 clip is selected in the Timeline panel, and open the Effect Controls panel.

5   Toggle the Black & White effect off and on by clicking the "fx" button (𝑓𝑥) next to the effect name in the Effect Controls panel. Be sure the sequence playhead is over this footage clip to view the effect.

Toggling an effect on and off is a good way to see how it works with other effects.

On

Off

6 Make sure the clip is selected so its settings are displayed in the Effect Controls panel. Click the Black & White effect heading to select it, and press the Delete key.

This removes the effect.

7 Type **direction** into the Effects panel search box to locate the Directional Blur video effect.

8 In the Effects panel, double-click the Directional Blur effect to apply it to the selected clip.

● **Note:** Remember, if you have a clip selected, you can apply effects by double-clicking them in the Effects panel or by dragging them into the Effect Controls panel directly.

9 In the Effect Controls panel, expand the Directional Blur effect's controls. This effect has these settings: Direction, Blur Length, and a stopwatch next to each option (the stopwatch icon activates keyframing).

10 Set Direction to **90.0** degrees and Blur Length to **45**.

Visual effects can look overdramatic unless they're used in moderation. One way to limit an effect is to use keyframes to control when, and how much, an effect is applied (see "Keyframing effects" later in this lesson)

11 Click the disclosure triangle to expand the Blur Length control, and move the slider.

As you change the setting, the result is displayed in the Program Monitor. The slider limit may be smaller than the number you can enter by typing.

12 Click the panel menu for the Effect Controls panel, and choose Remove Effects.

● **Note:** You won't always use visual effects to create dramatic results. Sometimes effects are intended to look like in-camera results.

13 Click OK in the dialog that pops up asking which effects you want to remove; you want to remove them all.

This is an easy way to start fresh.

▶ **Tip:** Fixed effects in Premiere Pro are processed in a particular order, which can lead to unwanted scaling or resizing. You can't reorder fixed effects, but you can bypass them and use other, similar effects. For example, you can use the Transform effect instead of the Motion fixed effect, or you can use the Alpha Adjust effect instead of the Opacity fixed effect. These effects are not identical, but they're a close match, they behave similarly, and they can be placed in any order you choose.

Other ways to apply effects

To make working with effects more flexible, there are three ways to reuse an effect you have already configured.

- You can select an effect from the Effect Controls panel, choose Edit > Copy, select a destination clip (or several clips), and choose Edit > Paste.

- You can copy all the effects from one clip so you can paste them onto another clip, select the clip in the Timeline and choose Edit > Copy, select the destination clip (or clips), and choose Edit > Paste Attributes.

- You can create an effect preset to store a particular effect (or multiple effects) with settings for reuse later. You'll learn about this technique later in this lesson.

Using adjustment layers

Sometimes you'll want to apply an effect to multiple clips. One easy way to do this is to use an *adjustment layer*. The concept is simple: Create an adjustment layer clip that can hold effects, and position it above other clips on the Timeline. Everything beneath the adjustment layer clip is viewed through it, receiving any effects it has.

You can easily adjust the duration and opacity of an adjustment layer clip, as you would adjust any graphics clip, making it easy to control which other clips are seen through it. Adjustment layers make it faster to work with effects because you can change the settings on it (a single item) to influence the appearance of several other clips.

Let's add an adjustment layer to a sequence that's already been edited.

1 Open the sequence 03 Multiple Effects.

2 At the bottom of the Project panel, click the New Item menu, and choose Adjustment Layer.

The Adjustment Layer dialog allows you to specify settings for the new item you're creating. By default, the settings will be based on your current sequence.

3 You have the correct sequence open for the new item, so click OK.

Premiere Pro adds a new adjustment layer to the Project panel.

4 Drag the adjustment layer to the beginning of the Video 2 track in the current Timeline.

5 Drag to trim the right edge of the adjustment layer so it extends to the end of the sequence.

The adjustment layer should look like this:

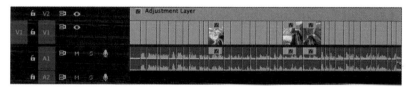

Let's create a more nuanced look by using effects and then modifying the opacity of the adjustment layer.

6 In the Effects panel, search for and locate the Gaussian Blur effect.

7 Drag the effect onto the adjustment layer.

8 Move the playhead position to 27:00 to have a good close-up shot to use when designing the effect.

9 In the Effect Controls panel, set Blurriness to a heavy value, like **25.0** pixels. Select the Repeat Edge Pixels option to apply the effect evenly.

Let's blend the adjustment layer with the clips beneath it using a blend mode to create the film look. *Blend modes* let you mix two layers together based on their brightness and color values. You'll learn more about them in Lesson 15.

10 With the adjustment layer still selected in the sequence, click the disclosure triangle next to the Opacity control in the Effect Controls panel.

11 Change the blend mode to Soft Light to create a gentle blend with the footage.

12 Set Opacity to **75%** to reduce the effect.

You can enable and disable the visibility icon for the Video 2 track ( ) in the Timeline panel to see the before and after states of the effect.

Sending a clip to Adobe After Effects

If you're working with a computer that also has Adobe After Effects installed, you can easily send clips back and forth between Premiere Pro and After Effects. Thanks to the close relationship between Premiere Pro and After Effects, you can seamlessly integrate the two applications more easily than with any other editing platform. This is a useful way to significantly extend the effects capabilities of your editing workflow.

The process you use to share clips is called Dynamic Link. With Dynamic Link you can seamlessly exchange clips with no unnecessary rendering.

Let's try this.

1 Open the sequence 04 Dynamic Link.

2 Right-click the clip in the sequence and choose Replace With After Effects Composition.

3 If it's not running already, After Effects launches. If the After Effects Save As dialog appears, enter a name and location for the After Effects project. Name the project **Lesson 13-01.aep** and save it to a new folder inside the Lessons folder.

After Effects creates a new composition, which inherits the sequence settings from Premiere Pro. The new composition is named based on the Premiere Pro project name, followed by "Linked Comp."

After Effects compositions are analogous to Premiere Pro sequences.

4 If the composition isn't already open, look for it in the After Effects project panel, and double-click to load it. It should be called Lesson 13 Linked Comp 01 (the number may be higher if you have tried this workflow before).

Clips become layers in After Effects compositions to make it easier to work with advanced controls on the Timeline.

There are lots of ways to apply effects with After Effects. To keep things simple, let's work with animation presets. For more on effects workflows, see *Adobe After Effects CC Classroom in a Book*.

5 Locate the Effects & Presets panel (you can find this in the Window menu if it's not onscreen already). Click the disclosure triangle to expand the *Animation Presets category.

The animation presets in After Effects use standard built-in effects to achieve impressive results. They are an excellent shortcut to producing a professional finish for your work.

6 Expand the Image – Creative folder. You may need to resize the panel a little to read the full preset names.

7 Double-click the "Contrast – Saturation" preset to apply it to the selected layer.

8 Click to select the clip on the Timeline, and press the E key to view any applied effects. You can click the disclosure triangles for each effect to see the controls, right inside the Timeline panel.

The Contrast – Saturation preset actually uses an effect with a different name, Calculations, to make changes to the appearance of the clip.

9 Now look at the Effect Controls panel. The same effect is displayed here.

10 Press the spacebar to play the clip.

After Effects displays the clip, with the effect applied, as fast as possible (depending on the power of your editing system). The green line at the top of the Timeline panel indicates a temporary preview has been created. Playback of the highlighted section of the timeline will be smooth.

The effect is subtle but gives richer color saturation and stronger contrast to a shot that would otherwise be a little flat.

11 Choose File > Save to capture your changes.

12 Switch back to Premiere Pro and play the sequence to view the results.

13 Quit After Effects.

The original clip on the Timeline in Premiere Pro has been replaced with the dynamically linked After Effects composition.

The frames are processed in the background and handed off from After Effects to Premiere Pro. You can also select the clip in the Timeline and choose Sequence > Render Effects In To Out to improve playback performance.

Master clip effects

While all the effects work you have performed so far has been applied to clips on the Timeline, Premiere Pro also allows you to apply effects to master clips in the Project panel. You use the same visual effects and work with them in the same way. With master clips, any instance of a clip you add to a sequence will inherit the effects you have applied.

For example, you could add a color adjustment to a clip in the Project panel so that it matches other camera angles in a scene. Each time you use that clip or part of that clip in a sequence, the adjustment will already be applied.

To add, adjust, and remove a master clip effect, do the following:

1 Continue working with the 04 Dynamic Link sequence.

2 Locate the clip Laura_03.mp4 in the Project panel. Edit this clip into the sequence, after the existing clip. Position the Timeline playhead over the clip so you can see it in the Program Monitor.

3 In the Project panel, double-click the Laura_03.mp4 clip to view it in the Source Monitor. Don't double-click the clip in the sequence because this will open the wrong instance for master clip effects.

● **Note:** If you want to open the Project panel instance of a clip you are viewing on the Timeline, position the playhead over the clip, select it, and press the F key. This is the keyboard shortcut for Match Frame, which opens the original master clip in the Source Monitor at the same frame as that displayed in the Program Monitor.

You now have the same clip open in the Source Monitor and displayed in the Program Monitor, so you can see the changes as you apply them in both monitors.

4 In the Effects panel, locate the Fast Color Corrector effect.

5 Drag the Fast Color Corrector effect into the Source Monitor, adding it to the master clip. Click the Source Monitor to make sure it's the active panel.

▶ **Tip:** You can also apply an effect to a master clip by dragging the effect onto the clip directly in the Project panel.

6 Go to the Effect Controls panel to see the Fast Color Corrector controls.

Because you applied the effect to the clip in the Source Monitor and then selected the Source Monitor to make it active, the Effect Controls panel shows the effect applied to the master clip, rather than the Timeline instance of the clip.

The Timeline instance of the clip (the sequence clip) does not have the effect applied to it, but it will inherit any changes you make.

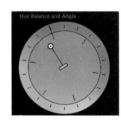

7 Drag the Fast Color Corrector color wheel puck from the center toward the red edge.

You can see the results of the effect in the Program Monitor.

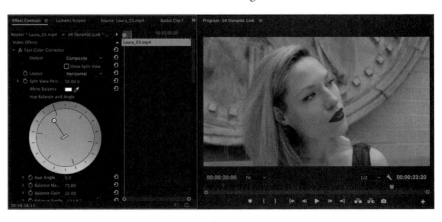

From now on, anytime you use this clip, or part of it, in a sequence, Premiere Pro will include the same effect.

To understand this workflow, it helps to be clear that there's a distinction between clips on the Timeline and clips in the Project panel.

8 Click once on the sequence instance of the clip on the Timeline to select it, and look in the Effect Controls panel—no Fast Color Corrector effect. However, the Fixed effects *are* present.

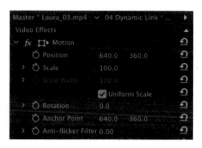

You can often tell if you're looking at Source effect settings or sequence clip effect settings by looking to see whether the Fixed effect controls are displayed.

At the top of the Effect Controls panel there are two tabs. The tab on the left shows the name of the master clip. The tab on the right shows the name of the sequence followed by the name of the clip.

Because you selected the clip in the sequence, the tab on the right is highlighted in blue, showing that you're working on that instance of the clip.

There's no Fast Color Corrector effect displayed because you haven't applied the effect to the Timeline instance of the clip.

9 In the Effect Controls panel, click the tab at the top that shows the clip name.

You'll see the effect again.

10 Select the name of the Fast Color Corrector effect in the Effect Controls panel and press the Delete key. The effect is removed, and the Program Monitor updates to reflect this change.

Working with master clips is a powerful way to manage effects in Premiere Pro. You may need to experiment a little to make the most of them. You use the same visual effects as you would use on the Timeline, so the techniques you're learning in this book will work the same way, but the planning is a little different. You can tell a master clip effect is applied to a clip because the "fx" badge has a red underline (▦).

Masking and tracking visual effects

All standard visual effects can be constrained to elliptical, polygon, or custom masks, which you can manually animate using keyframes. Premiere Pro can also motion-track your shots to animate the position of the masks you create, following the action with the constrained special effect.

Masking and tracking effects are great ways to hide a detail like a face or logo behind a blur. You can also use the technique to apply subtle creative effects or modify the lighting in a shot.

Let's try this out in the 04 Dynamic Link sequence.

▶ Tip: You can quickly locate the JG_1.mp4 clip by clicking into the Find box at the top of the Project panel and typing **jg**.

1   In the Project panel, locate the clip JG_1.mp4.

2   Drag the clip into the sequence, just after the Laura 03 clip.

This clip shows actors Andrea Sweeney and Matt Torrance. It looks good, but it would benefit from a natural-looking highlight on Matt as the daylight is clearly behind him. The clip is also higher resolution than the sequence—the edges are cropped.

3   Right-click the JG_1 clip in the sequence, and choose Set To Frame Size. This fixes the framing problem.

4   Search the Effects panel for the Fast Color Corrector effect. Apply this effect to the clip.

5   In the Effect Controls panel, scroll down to the Input Levels controls. Choose the following settings:

- Input Black Level 10.
- Input Gray Level 1.5.
- Input White Level 230.

You can set these levels by clicking the blue numbers above the slider, by using the slider controls, or by clicking the named blue numbers under the slider control.

6 Set Saturation to 120.

● **Note:** This example uses a vivid adjustment to illustrate a technique. You will usually make subtler adjustments.

This effect changes the entire picture. You're going to constrain the effect to just one area of the shot.

Just under the name of the Fast Color Corrector effect in the Effect Controls panel, you'll see three buttons that allow you to add a mask to the effect.

7 Click the first button to add an elliptical mask.

Immediately, the effect is constrained to the mask you just created. You can add multiple masks to an effect. If you select a mask in the Effect Controls panel, you can click and modify the shape in the Program Monitor.

8 Position the playhead at the start of the clip, and use the mask handles to reposition the mask so it covers Matt's face on the left, overlapping the railings and leaves in the background.

9 Feathering softens the edge of the mask. Set Mask Feather to about 240.

If you deselect the mask in the Effect Controls panel, you'll see that you have lifted the area around the Matt's face, with a natural return to regular lighting in the rest of the picture. Now you just need to track the picture.

10 Make sure the playhead is still on the first frame of the clip. Click the Track Selected Mask Forward button (▶) in the Effect Controls panel, just under the mask name, Mask (1).

The movement is quite subtle, so it should be easy for Premiere Pro to follow the action. If the mask stops following the clip, click Stop, reposition the mask, and begin again.

11 Play the sequence to view the result.

Premiere Pro can also track backward, so you can select an item partway through a clip and then track in both directions to create a natural path for the mask to follow.

Keyframing effects

When you add keyframes to an effect, you're setting particular values at that moment in time. One keyframe will keep information for one setting. If, for example, you were intending to keyframe Position, Scale, and Rotation, you would need three separate keyframes.

Set keyframes at precise moments where you need a particular setting and let Premiere Pro work out how to animate the controls between them.

Adding keyframes

You can change almost all parameters for all video effects over time using keyframes. For example, you can have a clip gradually change out of focus, change color, or lengthen its shadow.

1 Open the sequence 05 Keyframes.

2 View the sequence to get familiar with the footage and then position the Timeline playhead over the first frame of the clip.

3 In the Effects panel, locate the Lens Flare effect and apply it to the video layer in the sequence.

4 View the sequence to get familiar with the footage.

5 In the Effect Controls panel, select the Lens Flare effect heading. With the effect selected, the Program Monitor displays a small control handle. Use the handle to reposition the lens flare to match the following figure, so the center of the effect is at the top of the waterfall.

6 Make sure the Effect Controls panel Timeline is visible. If it isn't, click the Show/Hide Timeline View button (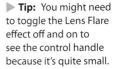) at the top right of the panel to toggle the display.

7 Click the stopwatch icons to toggle animation for the Flare Center and Flare Brightness properties.

Clicking the Stopwatch icon enables keyframing and adds a keyframe at the current location with the current settings.

Note: Be sure to move the playhead over the clip you're working with when applying effects so you can view your changes as you work. Selecting the clip alone will not make it visible in the Program Monitor.

Tip: You might need to toggle the Lens Flare effect off and on to see the control handle because it's quite small.

8 Move the playhead to the end of the clip.

You can drag the playhead directly in the Effect Controls panel. Make sure you see the last frame of video and not black.

9 Adjust Flare Center and Flare Brightness settings so the flare drifts across the screen with the camera pan and gets brighter. Use the following figure for guidance.

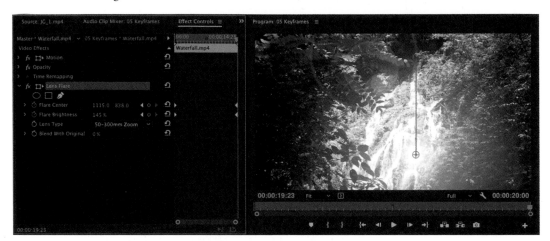

10 Play the sequence to watch the effect animate over time.

▶ **Tip:** Be sure to use the Next Keyframe and Previous Keyframe buttons to move between keyframes efficiently. This will keep you from adding unwanted keyframes.

Adding keyframe interpolation and velocity

Keyframe interpolation changes the behavior of an effect setting as it moves between keyframes with different settings. The default behavior you've seen so far is linear; in other words, you have a constant change between keyframes. What generally works better is something that mirrors your experience or exaggerates it, such as a gradual acceleration or deceleration.

Premiere Pro offers a way to control those changes: keyframe interpolation and the Velocity graph. Keyframe interpolation is easy (two clicks), whereas tweaking the Velocity graph can be challenging. Getting a handle on this feature will take some time and practice.

1 Open the sequence 06 Interpolation.

2 Position the playhead at the beginning of the clip, and select the clip.

A Lens Flare effect has already been applied to this clip and is currently animated. However, the movement begins before the camera, which isn't very natural-looking.

3 Toggle the Lens Flare effect off and on by clicking the "fx" button () next to the effect name in the Effect Controls panel so you can see the result.

4 In the Timeline view of the Effect Controls panel, right-click the first keyframe for the Flare Center property.

5 Choose the Temporal Interpolation > Ease Out method to create a gentle transition into the move from the keyframe.

6 Right-click the second keyframe for the Flare Center property and choose Temporal Interpolation > Ease In. This creates a gentle transition from the stationary position of the last keyframe.

Let's modify the Flare Brightness property.

7 Click the first keyframe for Flare Brightness and then hold down the Shift key and click the second keyframe so both are active.

8 Right-click either Flare Brightness keyframe and choose Auto Bézier to create a gentle animation between the two properties.

● **Note:** When working with position-related parameters, the context menu for a keyframe will offer two types of interpolation: spatial (related to location) and temporal (related to time). You can make spatial adjustments in the Program Monitor as well as in the Effect Controls panel if you select the effect. You can make temporal adjustments on the clip in the Timeline and in the Effect Controls panel. These motion-related topics are covered in Lesson 9, "Putting Clips in Motion."

9 Play back the animation to watch the changes you've made.

Let's further refine the keyframes with the Velocity graph.

10 Hover the mouse cursor over the Effect Controls panel and then, if your keyboard has the key, press ` (grave) to maximize the panel full-screen; or, click the panel menu and choose Panel Group Settings > Maximize Panel Group. This will give you a clearer view of the keyframe controls.

11 If necessary, click the disclosure triangles next to the Flare Center and Flare Brightness properties to show the adjustable properties.

The Velocity graph shows the velocity between keyframes. The sudden drops or jumps represent sudden changes in acceleration—*jerks*, in physics parlance. The farther the point or line is from the center, the greater the velocity.

12 Select a different keyframe and then adjust its handle to change the steepness of the velocity curve.

13 Press the ` (grave) key, or use the panel menu to restore the Effect Controls panel.

14 Play back your sequence to see the impact of your changes. Experiment some more until you have the hang of keyframes and interpolation.

Effect presets

To save time on repeated tasks, Premiere Pro supports effect presets. You'll find that there are several presets included for specific tasks already, but their true power lies in creating your own presets to solve repetitive tasks. When you create an effect preset, it can store more than one effect and can even include keyframes for animation.

Understanding interpolation methods

Here's a rundown of the keyframe interpolation methods available in Premiere Pro:

- **Linear:** This is the default behavior and creates a uniform rate of change between keyframes.

- **Bézier:** This lets you manually adjust the shape of the graph on either side of a keyframe. Béziers allow for sudden or smooth acceleration into or out of a keyframe.

- **Continuous Bézier:** This method creates a smooth rate of change through a keyframe. Unlike Béziers keyframes, if you adjust one handle of a Continuous Bézier keyframe, the handle on the other side moves equally, to maintain a smooth transition through the keyframe.

- **Auto Bézier:** This method creates a smooth rate of change through a keyframe even if you change the keyframe value. If you choose to manually adjust the keyframe's handles, it changes to a Continuous Bézier point, retaining the smooth transition through the keyframe. The Auto Bézier option can occasionally produce unwanted motion, so try one of the other options first.

- **Hold:** This method changes a property value without a gradual transition (a sudden effect change). The graph following a keyframe with the Hold interpolation applied appears as a horizontal straight line.

- **Ease In:** This method slows down the value changes entering a keyframe and converts it to a Bézier keyframe.

- **Ease Out:** This method gradually accelerates the value changes leaving a keyframe, converting it to a Bézier keyframe.

Using built-in presets

The effect presets provided with Premiere Pro are useful for tasks such as beveling, picture-in-picture effects, and stylized transitions.

1   Open the sequence 07 Presets.

    This sequence has a slow start—the emphasis is on the texture of the background. Let's use a preset to animate the opening of the shot.

2   In the Effects panel, browse inside the Presets > Solarizes category to find the Solarize In preset.

3   Drag the Solarize In preset onto the clip in the sequence.

4 Play back the sequence to watch the Solarize effect transform the opening.

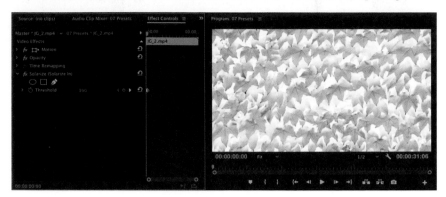

5 Click the clip, and view its controls in the Effect Controls panel.

6 Experiment with adjusting the position of the second keyframe in the Effect Controls panel to customize the effect. If you extend the timing of the effect, it creates a more pleasing start to the shot.

Saving effect presets

Although there are several built-in effect presets to choose from, creating your own is also easy. You can also import and export presets to share them between editing systems.

1 Open the sequence 08 Creating Presets.

This Timeline has two clips, each with an adjustment layer, and two instances of an opening title.

2 Play the sequence to watch the initial animation.

3 Select the first instance of the "Laura in the snow" clip on V3.

4 Click in the Effect Controls panel to make it active, and choose Edit > Select All to select all the effects applied to the clip.

You can also select individual effects if you want to include only some of them in the preset.

5 Right-click any of the selected effects in the Effect Controls panel, and choose Save Preset.

6 In the Save Preset dialog, name the effect **Logo Animation**.

7 Choose one of the following preset types to specify how Premiere Pro should handle keyframes in a preset:

- **Scale:** Proportionally scales the source keyframes to the length of the target clip. Any existing keyframes on the original clip are deleted.

- **Anchor to In Point:** Preserves the position of the first keyframe as well as the relationship of other keyframes in a clip. Other keyframes are added to the clip relative to its In point. Use this option for this exercise.

- **Anchor to Out Point:** Preserves the position of the last keyframe as well as the relationship of other keyframes in a clip. Other keyframes are added to the clip relative to its Out point.

8 Click OK to store the effects and keyframes as a new preset.

9 In the Effects panel, locate the Presets category.

10 Locate the newly created Logo Animation preset.

11 Drag the Logo Animation preset onto the second instance of the "Laura in the snow" clip in the Timeline.

12 Watch the sequence play back to see the newly applied title animation.

Using multiple GPUs

If you'd like to speed up the rendering of effects or export of clips, consider adding an additional GPU card. If you're using a tower or workstation, you may have an additional slot that can support a second graphics card. Premiere Pro takes full advantage of computers with multiple GPU cards to significantly accelerate export times. You can find additional details about supported cards on the Adobe website.

Frequently used effects

Throughout this lesson you've explored several effects. Although it's beyond the scope of this book to explore all the options, here are a few additional effects that are useful in many editing situations. By looking at the possibilities, you'll have a better appreciation for the options that lie ahead.

Image stabilization and rolling shutter reduction

The Warp Stabilizer effect can remove jitter caused by camera movement (which is more and more common with today's lightweight cameras). The effect is useful because it can remove unstable parallax-type movements (where images appear to shift on planes).

Let's explore the effect.

1   Open the sequence 09 Warp Stabilizer.

2   Play the first clip in the sequence to see the wobbly shot.

3   In the Effects panel, locate the Warp Stabilizer effect and apply it to the shot.

    The clip is analyzed.

The analysis is in two stages. A banner across the footage lets you know you'll need to wait before working with the effect. There's also a detailed progress indicator in the Effect Controls panel. The analysis takes place in the background, so you can carry on working on your sequence while waiting for it to complete.

4   Once the analysis has completed, you can adjust settings in the Effect Controls panel to improve results by choosing options that better suit the shot.

    • **Result:** You can choose Smooth Motion to retain the general camera movement (albeit stabilized), or you can choose No Motion to attempt to remove all camera movement. For this exercise, choose Smooth Motion.

- **Method:** You can use the four methods available. The two most powerful, because they warp and process the image more heavily, are Perspective and Subspace Warp. If either method creates too much distortion, you can try switching to Position, Scale, Rotation or just to Position.

- **Smoothness:** This option specifies how much of the original camera movement should be retained for Smooth Motion. Use a higher value to smooth out the shot the most. Experiment with this shot until you're happy with its stability.

5 Play back the clip.

The impact is pretty dramatic.

▶ **Tip:** If you notice that some of the details in the shot appear to wobble, you may be able to improve the overall effect. In the Advanced section, choose Detailed Analysis. This makes the Analysis phase do extra work to find elements to track. You can also use the Enhanced Reduction option from the Rolling Shutter Ripple option under the Advanced category. These options are slower to calculate but produce superior results.

6 Repeat the process for the second clip in the sequence. This time, set the Warp Stabilizer Result menu to No Motion.

This is a common example of a shot that was intended to be static but, being handheld, has a little wobble. The Warp Stabilizer is effective at locking these kinds of shots in position.

Timecode and Clip Name

If you need to send a review copy of a sequence to a client or colleague, the Timecode and Clip Name effects are useful. You can apply the Timecode effect to an adjustment layer and have it generate a visible timecode for the entire sequence. You can enable a similar Timecode overlay when exporting media, but the effect has more options.

This is helpful because it allows others to make specific feedback based on a unique point in time. You can control the display of position, size, opacity, the timecode itself, and its format and source. The Clip Name effect needs to be applied to each clip.

1 Open the sequence 10 Timecode Burn-In.

2 At the bottom of the Project panel, click the New Item menu, and choose Adjustment Layer. Click OK.

A new adjustment layer is added to the Project panel, with settings that match your current sequence.

3 Drag the adjustment layer to the beginning of track V2 in the current sequence.

● **Note:** If you work with multiple sequences with different settings in a single project, it's worth naming adjustment layers to make it easier to identify their resolution.

4 Drag the right edge of the new adjustment layer to the right to trim it to the end of the sequence. The adjustment layer should cover all three clips.

5 In the Effects panel, locate the Timecode effect. Drag it onto the adjustment layer to apply it.

6 In the Effect Controls panel, set Time Display to 24 to match the frame rate of the sequence.

7 Choose a timecode source. In this case, use the Generate option, set the Starting Timecode option to 01:00:00:00 to match the sequence, and deselect the Field Symbol option (this footage is progressive, so it does not have fields).

8 Adjust the Position and Size options for the effect.

It's a good idea to move the timecode window so it's not blocking critical action in the scene or obscuring any graphics. If you plan to post the video to the web for review, be sure to size the timecode burn-in so it's easy to read.

Now let's apply an effect that will display the name of each clip in the exported movie. This will make it easier to get specific feedback from a client or collaborator.

9 The first two clips in the sequence already have the Clip Name effect applied. Select the last clip in the sequence on track V1.

10 In the Effects panel, search for the Clip Name effect.

11 Double-click the Clip Name effect to apply it to the selected clip. You can use this workflow to apply an effect or preset to multiple selected clips in a single step.

12 Adjust the effect properties to taste to ensure that both the Timecode and Clip Name effects are readable.

The last clip in the sequence, with a timecode overlay

13 Clear the Effects panel search box.

Shadow/Highlight

The Shadow/Highlight effect is useful for quickly adjusting the contrast issues in a clip. It can brighten a subject in dark shadows. It can also darken areas that are slightly overexposed. The effect makes relatively isolated adjustments based on surrounding pixels. The default settings are for fixing images with backlighting problems, but you can modify the settings as needed.

Let's try the effect.

1 Open the sequence 11 Shadow/Highlight.

2 Play the sequence to evaluate the shot. It's a little dark.

3 Select the clip in the Timeline panel.

4 In the Effects panel, locate the Shadow/Highlight effect. Apply it to the shot.

5 Play the sequence to see the results of the effect.

By default, the effect uses Auto Amounts mode. This option deactivates most of the controls but often gives usable results quickly.

6 Deselect the Auto Amounts check box in the Effect Controls panel.

7 Use the disclosure triangle to expand the controls for More Options to refine the effect.

Let's adjust the definition of what's a shadow and what's a highlight and then refine the exposure of each.

8 Adjust the following properties to taste (or use the figure for guidance):

- **Shadow Amount:** Use this adjustment to control how much shadows are lightened.

- **Highlight Amount:** Use this control to darken the highlights in the image.

- **Shadow Tonal Width and Highlight Tonal Width:** Use the range to define what is considered a highlight or shadow. Use a higher value to expand the range and a narrower value to limit it. These controls are useful for isolating regions that you need to adjust.

- **Shadow Radius and Highlight Radius:** Adjust the radius controls to blend the selected and unselected pixels. This can create a smoother blend of the effect. Avoid values that are too high or an unwanted glow may appear.

- **Color Correction:** As you adjust exposure, the color in an image may become washed out. Use this slider to restore a natural look to the adjusted areas of the footage.

- **Midtone Contrast:** Use this control to add more contrast to the midtone areas. This can be useful if you need the middle of the image to better match the adjusted shadow and highlight regions.

Lens distortion removal

Action and point-of-view (POV) cameras such as the GoPro and DJI Phantom are increasingly popular, especially with the advent of affordable aerial camera mounts. While the results can be amazing, the popular wide-angle lenses can introduce a lot of unwanted distortion.

The Lens Distortion effect can be used to introduce the appearance of lens distortion as a creative look. It can also be used to correct lens distortion. In fact, Premiere Pro has a number of built-in presets intended to correct distortion from popular cameras. You'll find the presets in the Effects panel, under Lens Distortion Removal.

Remember, you can make a preset from any effect, so if you are working with a camera that has no existing preset, you can always create your own.

Render all sequences

If you have several sequences with effects you want to render, you can render them all as a batch, without opening each sequence to render it individually.

Simply select the sequences you would like to render in the Project panel and choose Sequence > Render Effects In to Out.

All effects that need to render in the selected sequences will be rendered.

Render and replace

If you are working on a low-powered system and your media is high resolution, you may find media tends not to play back without dropping frames. You may also see dropped frames when working with dynamically linked After Effects compositions or complex third-party visual effects that don't support GPU acceleration.

If all of your media is high resolution, you may decide to use the Proxy workflow. However, if just one or two clips are difficult to play back, Premiere Pro can render the clips as a new media file and replace the original item in a sequence quickly and easily.

To replace a sequence clip segment with a version that's easier to play back, right-click the clip and choose Render and Replace.

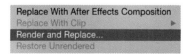

The Render and Replace dialog has similar options to the Proxy workflow. Here are the main settings:

- **Source:** Create a new media file that matches the frame rate and frame size of the sequence or of the original medial, or use a preset.

- **Format:** Specify your preferred file type. Different formats give access to different encoders.

- **Preset:** While you can use a custom preset created with Adobe Media Encoder, several are included by default—choose one here.

Once you have chosen a preset and a location for the new file, click OK and the sequence clip is replaced.

A rendered and replaced clip is no longer directly linked to the original media. This means changes made to a dynamically linked After Effect composition will not update in Premiere Pro. To restore the link to the original item, right-click the clip and choose Restore Unrendered.

Review questions

1 What are two ways to apply an effect to a clip?

2 List three ways to add a keyframe.

3 Dragging an effect onto a clip turns on its parameters in the Effect Controls panel, but you don't see the effect in the Program Monitor. Why not?

4 Describe how you can apply one effect to a range of clips.

5 Describe how to save multiple effects to a custom preset.

Review answers

1 Drag the effect to the clip, or select the clip and double-click the effect in the Effects panel.

2 Move the playhead in the Effect Controls panel to where you want a keyframe and activate keyframing by clicking the "Toggle animation" button; move the playhead and click the Add/Remove Keyframe button; and with keyframing activated, move the playhead to a position and change a parameter.

3 You need to move the Timeline playhead to the selected clip to see it in the Program Monitor. Selecting a clip does not move the playhead to that clip.

4 Select the clips you would like to apply the effect to and then drag the effect onto the group. You can also add an adjustment layer above the clips you want to affect. You can then apply an effect that will modify all the clips below the layer.

5 You can click the Effect Controls panel and choose Edit > Select All. You can also Control-click (Windows) or Command-click (Mac OS) multiple effects in the Effect Controls panel. Once the effects are selected, choose the Save Preset command from the Effect Controls panel menu.

14 IMPROVING CLIPS WITH COLOR CORRECTION AND GRADING

Lesson overview

In this lesson, you'll learn about the following:

- Working in the Color workspace

- Using the Lumetri Color panel

- Using vectorscopes and waveforms

- Using color correction effects

- Fixing exposure and color balance problems

- Working with special effects

- Creating a look

This lesson will take approximately 90 minutes.

In this lesson, you'll learn some key techniques for improving the look of your clips. Industry professionals use these techniques every day to give television programs and films the "pop" and atmosphere that set them apart. This chapter is not a "deep dive" into color theory but should get you up and running with some of these powerful tools in Adobe Premiere Pro CC.

Editing your clips together is just the first part of the
creative process. Now it's time to work with color.

Getting started

Until now you've been organizing your clips, building sequences, and applying special effects. All of these skills come together when working with color correction.

Consider the way your eyes register color and light, the way cameras record it, and the way your computer screen, a television screen, a video projector, or a cinema screen displays it. There are a great many factors when considering the final look of your production.

Premiere Pro has multiple color correction tools and makes it easy to create your own presets. In this lesson, you'll begin by learning some fundamental color correction skills and then meet some of the most popular color correction special effects, before using them to deal with some common color correction challenges.

1   Open Lesson 14.prproj in the Lesson 14 folder.

2   Choose Color in the Workspaces panel, or choose Window > Workspaces > Color. Reset the workspace.

   This changes the workspace to the preset that was created to make it easier to work with color correction effects and, in particular, the Lumetri Color panel and Lumetri Scopes panel. If you have been using Premiere Pro for a while, you may need to reset the workspace to the saved version by clicking the Color menu in the Workspaces panel.

The subject of color science requires ongoing learning and development, but you can get by with a rudimentary understanding of key concepts.

About 8-bit video

It's worth knowing that regular 8-bit video works on a scale from 0 to 255. That means each pixel has red, green, and blue (RGB) values somewhere on that scale, which combine to produce a particular color. You can think of 0 as 0% and 255 as 100%. A pixel that has a red value of 127 is equivalent to having a red value of 50%.

Without going into the deeper details of the technology behind this number range, you can be reassured that the numbers 0 and 255 will come up a lot when working with video. It's *the* most commonly used range to measure video image pixel values.

However, we're talking about RGB images, and broadcast video uses a similar but different range, with a color system called YUV.

If you compare YUV video with RGB video, mapping one scale against the other, you'll find that YUV pixel values range from 16 to 235, on the RGB 0 to 255 scale. TVs usually use YUV color, not RGB. However, your computer screen will almost certainly be RGB. If you are producing broadcast video, this can create issues because you are looking at your video footage on a different kind of screen than the kind it will ultimately be viewed on. There is only one sure way of overcoming the uncertainty this creates: Connect a TV to your editing system and view your footage on that screen.

The difference is a little like comparing a photograph you view onscreen with a printed version. The printer and your computer screen use different color systems, and it's an imperfect translation from one to the other.

When working with the Lumetri Scopes panel, you can check your media to make sure it fits within one color system or another. In particular, look out for 16 to 235 ranges in the waveform display, and look for the smaller inner boxes in the vector-scope that indicate the YUV color range or the larger outer boxes that indicate RGB.

Any value less than 16 or greater than 235 is effectively chopped off and displayed as 0% or 100% when shown on a regular TV screen.

This means sometimes you will view footage with visible detail on an RGB screen like your computer display that disappears when viewed on a TV screen. You'll need to color correct to bring those details into the TV screen range.

Some TVs give you the option to display color as RGB, using a range of names such as Game Mode or Photo Color Space. If your screen is set up this way, you may see the full 0 to 255 range.

Following a color-oriented workflow

Now that you've switched to a new workspace, it's a good time to switch to a different kind of thinking. With your clips in place, it's time to look at them less in terms of the action and more in terms of whether they fit together and have the right look.

There are two main phases to working with color.

- Make sure clips in each scene have matching colors, brightness, and contrast so they look like they were shot at the same time, in the same place, and with the same camera.

- Give everything a "look," in other words, a particular tonality or color tint.

You'll use the same tools to achieve both of these goals, but it's common to approach them in this order, separately. If two clips from the same scene don't have matching colors, it creates a jarring continuity problem.

Color correction and color grading

You've probably heard of both color correction and color grading. There is often confusion about the difference. In fact, both types of color work use the same tools, but there's a difference of approach.

Color correction is usually aimed at standardizing the shots to make sure they fit together and to improve the appearance in general to give brighter highlights and stronger shadows or to correct a color bias captured in-camera. This is more craft than art.

Color grading is aimed at achieving a look that conveys the atmosphere of the story more completely. This is more art than craft.

There is, of course, a debate about where one ends and the other begins.

The Color workspace

The Color workspace displays the Lumetri Color panel, which has a number of sections offering color adjustment controls, and places the Lumetri Scopes panel behind the Source Monitor. The Lumetri Scopes are a set of image analysis tools.

The remaining screen area is devoted to the Program Monitor, Timeline, and Project panel. The Timeline shrinks to accommodate the Lumetri Color panel.

Remember, you can open and close any panel at any time, but this workspace focuses on finishing work, rather than organizing or editing your project.

By default, clips on the Timeline are selected automatically as the playhead moves over them. Only clips on tracks that have the track selection button on will be selected. This feature is important because adjustments made with the Lumetri Color panel are applied to the selected clip. You can apply an adjustment and move the playhead along the Timeline to select the next clip and work on it.

You can enable or disable automatic clip selection by choosing Sequence > Selection Follows Playhead.

The Lumetri Color panel

The Lumetri Color panel is divided into six sections. You can browse color adjustment controls selectively or work from the top downward, working with increasingly advanced tools.

● **Note:** You can expand or collapse a section in the Lumetri Color panel by clicking its heading.

Each section provides a group of controls with different approaches to color adjustment. Let's take a look at each section.

Basic Correction

This section provides you with simple controls to apply quick fixes to your clips.

You can apply a preset adjustment to your media in the form of an Input LUT file, which makes standard adjustments to media that might otherwise look quite flat.

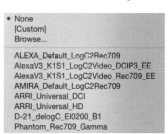

If you're familiar with Adobe Lightroom, you'll recognize the list of simple controls in the Basic section. You can work your way down the list making adjustments to improve the look of your footage, or you can click the Auto button to let Premiere Pro work it out for you.

Creative

As the name suggests, the Creative section allows you to go a little further into developing a look for your media.

A number of creative looks are included, with a preview based on your current clip.

You can make subtle adjustments to the color intensity, and there are color wheels configured to adjust the color for the shadow (darker) pixels or highlight (lighter) pixels in the image.

Curves

Curves allow quick but precise adjustments to visuals, and make it easier to achieve more natural-looking results with just a few clicks.

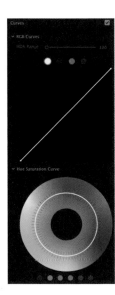

▶ **Tip:** You can reset most controls in the Lumetri Color panel by double-clicking a blank area of the control.

These are some of the more advanced controls, providing nuanced adjustments to the luminance, red, green, and blue pixels.

The Hue Saturation Curve control gives precise control over color saturation based on hue range.

 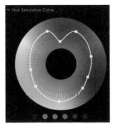

Color Wheels

This section provides precise control over the shadow, midtone, and high-light pixels in the image. Simply drag the control puck from the center of a wheel toward the edge to apply an adjustment.

Each color wheel also has a luminance control slider, which allows you to make simple adjustments to the brightness and, by appropriate adjustment, the contrast of your footage.

HSL Secondary

An HSL Secondary is a color adjustment made to specific areas of an image, selected using Hue, Saturation, and Luminance ranges.

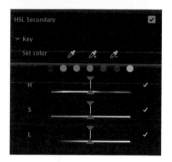

This is the section of the Lumetri Color panel you would use to make a blue sky even more blue, or make a field of grass a deeper green, without affecting other areas of the picture.

Vignette

It's surprising how much difference a simple vignette effect can make to a picture.

A vignette was originally caused by camera lenses darkening the edge of frame, but modern lenses rarely have this issue.

Instead, a vignette is commonly used to create focus in the center of an image, and it can be highly effective, even when the adjustment is subtle.

The Lumetri Color panel in action

When you make adjustments using the Lumetri Color panel, they are added collectively as a regular Premiere Pro effect applied to the selected clip. You can enable and disable the effect in the Effect Controls panel, or you can create an effect preset. The controls are repeated in the Effect Controls panel too.

Let's try some prebuilt looks.

1 Open the sequence Jolie's Garden in the Sequences bin.

This is a simple sequence with a series of clips that have a good range of color and contrast.

2 Position the Timeline playhead over the first clip in the sequence. The clip should highlight automatically.

3 Click the Creative section heading in the Lumetri Color panel to reveal its controls.

4 Browse through several prebuilt looks by clicking the arrow on the right side of the preview display. When you see a look you like, click the preview to apply it.

5 Try adjusting the Intensity slider to vary the amount of adjustment.

This is a good time to experiment with the other controls in the Lumetri Color panel. Some controls will make sense immediately, while others will take time to master. Use the clips in this sequence as a testing ground to learn about the Lumetri Color panel through experimentation; just drag all the controls from one extreme to the other to see the result. You'll learn about many of these controls in detail later in this lesson.

Lumetri Scopes essentials

You might have wondered why the Premiere Pro interface is so gray. There's a good reason: Vision is highly subjective. In fact, it's also highly relative.

If you see two colors next to each other, the way you see one is changed by the presence of the other. To prevent the Premiere Pro interface from influencing the way you perceive colors in your sequence, Adobe has made the interface almost entirely gray. If you've ever seen a professional color-grading suite, where artists provide the finishing touches to films and television programs, you've probably noticed that most of the room is gray. Colorists sometimes have a large gray piece of card, or a section of a wall, that they can look at for a few moments to "reset" their vision before checking a shot.

The combination of your subjective vision and the variation that can occur in the way computer monitors and television monitors display color and brightness creates a need for an objective measurement.

Video scopes provide just that. And they're used throughout the media industry; learn them once, and you'll be able to use them everywhere.

1   Open the sequence Lady Walking.

2   Position the Timeline playhead so that it's over the clip in the sequence.

3   The Lumetri Scopes panel should be sharing the frame with the Source Monitor. Click to select the panel and make it active, or select it in the Window menu.

4   Click the Settings menu ( ) in the Lumetri Scopes panel and choose Presets > Premiere 4 Scope YUV (float, no clamp).

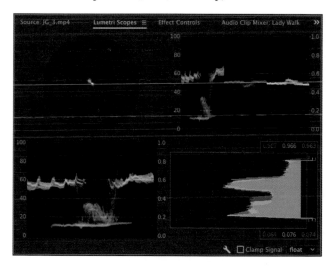

You should see the lady walking in the street in your Program Monitor, along with a second, synchronized display of the same clip in the Lumetri Scopes panel.

The Lumetri Scopes panel

The Lumetri Scopes panel displays an array of industry-standard meters to get an objective view of your media.

The full complement of displays can be a little overwhelming at first, plus you'll have smaller graphs. You can turn individual items off and on by clicking on the Settings menu and choosing items on the list.

You can also specify whether you are working to an ITU Rec. 2020 (UHD), ITU Rec. 709 (HD), or ITU Rec. 601 (SD) color space. If you're producing content for broadcast television, you will almost certainly be working to one of these standards. If not or if you're not sure, you will probably be happy with Rec. 709. Check with your ingest department for confirmation.

You can choose the color space in the Settings menu.

You can also choose to display 8 Bit, the default float (which is 32-bit floating-point color), or even HDR. HDR refers to High Dynamic Range, which has a much higher range between the darkest and brightest parts of the picture. Though HDR is beyond the scope of these lessons, it's an important new technology and one that will be increasingly important as new cameras and displays support it.

Let's simplify the view. You can access the Settings menu by right-clicking anywhere in the Lumetri Scopes panel. Do so now by clicking each of the selected items to deselect them and remove them from the display. Right-click in the panel and choose Presets > Waveform RGB.

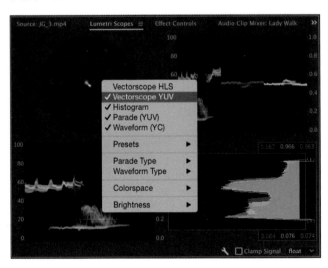

Let's take a look at two of the main components in the Lumetri Scopes panel.

Waveform

If you're new to waveforms, they can look a little strange, but they're actually simple. They show you the brightness and color saturation of your images.

Every pixel in the current frame is displayed in the waveform. The brighter the pixel, the higher it appears. The pixels have their correct horizontal position (that is, a pixel halfway across the screen will be displayed halfway across the waveform), but the vertical position is not based on the image.

Instead, the vertical position indicates brightness or color intensity; the brightness and color intensity waveforms are displayed together, using different colors.

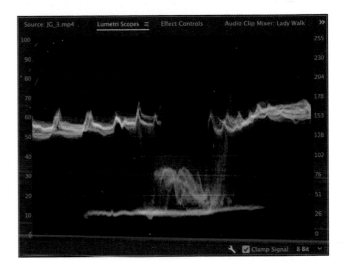

- 0, at the bottom of the scale, represents no luminance at all and/or no color intensity.

- 100, at the top of the scale, represents a pixel that is fully bright. On the RGB scale, this value would be 255 (you can see this scale on the right side of the waveform display).

This all might sound rather technical, but in practice it's straightforward. There's a visible baseline that represents "no brightness" and a top level that represents "fully bright." The numbers on the edge of the graph might change, but the use is essentially the same.

You can view the waveform in several ways. To access each type, click the Lumetri Scopes Settings menu, and choose Waveform Type, followed by one of these options:

- **RGB:** Shows the Red, Green, and Blue pixels in their own colors.

- **Luma:** Shows the IRE value of pixels, from 0 to 100, against a scale of −20 to 120. This allows for precise analysis of bright spots and contrast ratio.

- **YC:** Shows the image luminance (brightness) in green, and chrominance (color intensity) in blue.

- **YC no Chroma:** Shows the luminance with no chrominance.

Why YC?

The letter *C*, for chrominance, makes simple sense, but the letter *Y*, for luminance, takes a little explaining. It comes from a way of measuring color information that uses x-, y-, and z-axes, where *y* represents the luminance. The idea was originally to create a simple system for recording color, and the use of *y* to represent brightness, or luminance, stuck.

Let's test this display a little.

1   Continue using the Lady Walking sequence. Set the Timeline playhead to 00:00:07:00 so you can see the lady against the smoky background.

2   Set the waveform display to YC no Chroma.

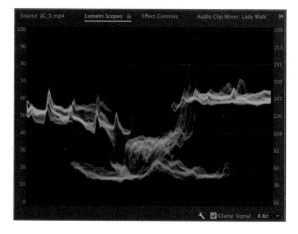

The smoky parts of the image have little contrast and are displayed as a relatively flat line in the waveform display. The lady's head and shoulders are darker than the smoky background. They're around the middle of the image, and they are clearly visible in the middle area of the waveform display.

3 Expand the Basic Correction section of the Lumetri Color panel.

4 Experiment with the Exposure, Contrast, Highlights, Shadows, Whites, and Blacks controls. As you adjust the controls, watch the waveform display to see the result.

▶ **Tip:** You can double-click any part of a slider control in the Lumetri Color panel to reset it.

If you make an adjustment to the image and then wait a few seconds, your eyes will adjust to the new appearance, and it will seem normal. Make another adjustment, and a few seconds later the new appearance seems normal too. Which is correct?

Ultimately, the answer is based on perceived quality. If you like what you see, it's right. However, the waveform display will give you objective information about how dark or bright pixels are or how much color is in the shot, which is useful when attempting to meet standards.

You should be able to see the parts of the picture where the smoky background of the image is displayed, toward the left and right (with some ridges where there is a pattern in the background). You should also be able to see a darker section, in the middle, where the lady is. If you scrub through the sequence or play the sequence, you'll see the waveform display update live.

▶ **Tip:** It can sometimes seem as if the waveform display is showing an image. Remember, the vertical position of the pixels in your images is not used in a waveform display.

The waveform display is useful for showing how much contrast you have in your images and for checking whether you are working on video that has "legal" levels (that is, the minimum and maximum brightness or color saturation permitted by a broadcaster). Broadcasters adopt their own standards for legal levels, so you will need to find out for each case where your work will be broadcast.

You can see right away that you do not have great contrast in this shot. There are some strong shadows but few *highlights* in the upper part of the waveform display.

YUV Vectorscope

Whereas the YC waveform shows luminance in terms of the vertical position of pixels displayed, with brighter pixels displayed at the top and darker pixels displayed at the bottom, the vectorscope shows only color.

1 Open the sequence Skyline.

2 Click the Lumetri Scopes Settings menu () and select Vectorscope YUV; then go to the Settings menu again and select Waveform (YC no Chroma) to deselect it.

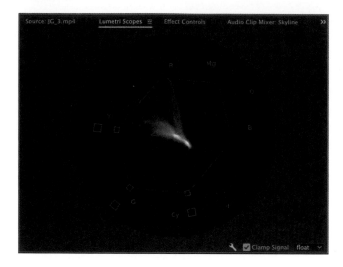

Pixels in the image are displayed in the vectorscope. If a pixel appears in the center of the circle, it has no color saturation. The closer to the edge of the circle, the more color a pixel has.

If you look closely at the vectorscope, you'll see a series of targets indicating primary colors.

- R = Red
- G = Green
- B = Blue

There are two boxes for each target. The smaller, inner box is the YUV color limit, while the larger, outer box is the RGB color limit. RGB color extends to a greater level of saturation than YUV. The thin line between the inner boxes shows the YUV color gamut (the range of YUV colors).

You'll also see a series of targets indicating secondary colors.

- YL = Yellow
- CY = Cyan
- MG = Magenta

The closer a pixel is to one of these targets, the more of that color it has. While the waveform display indicates where a pixel is in the picture, thanks to the horizontal position, there is no position information in the vectorscope.

About primary and secondary colors

Red, green, and blue are primary colors. It's common for display systems, including television screens and your computer monitor, to combine these three colors in varying relative amounts to produce all the colors you see.

There's a beautiful symmetry to the way a standard color wheel works, and a color wheel is essentially what the vectorscope displays.

Any two primary colors will combine to produce a secondary color. Secondary colors are the opposite of the remaining primary color.

For example, red and green combine to produce yellow, which is the opposite of blue.

It's clear enough to see what's happening in this shot of Seattle. There's a lot of darker blue, and there are a few spots of red and yellow. The small amount of red is indicated by the streak of peaks reaching out toward the R marking in the vectorscope.

The vectorscope is helpful because it gives you objective information about the colors in your sequence. If there's a color cast, perhaps because the camera was not calibrated properly, it's often obvious in the vectorscope display. You can simply use one of the Lumetri Color panel controls to reduce the amount of the unwanted color or add more of the opposite color.

Some of the controls for color correction effects, such as Fast Color Corrector, have the same color wheel design as the vectorscope, making it easy to see what you need to do.

Let's make an adjustment and observe the result in the vectorscope display.

1 Continue working with the Skyline sequence. Position the Timeline playhead at 00:00:01:00, where the colors are more vivid.

2 In the Lumetri Color panel, expand the Basic Correction section.

3 While watching the result in the vectorscope display, drag the Temperature slider from one extreme to the other.

The pixels displayed in the vectorscope move between the orange and blue areas of the display.

4 Reset the Temperature slider by double-clicking the slider control.

5 In the Lumetri Color panel, drag the Tint slider from one extreme to the other.

The pixels displayed in the vectorscope move between the green and magenta areas of the display.

6 Reset the Tint slider by double-clicking the slider control.

By making adjustments while checking the vectorscope, you can get an objective indication of the change you're making.

Additive and subtractive color

Computer screens and televisions use additive color, which means the colors are created by generating light in different colors and combining them to produce a precise mix. You produce white by combining equal amounts of red, green, and blue.

When you draw with color on paper, it is usually white paper, which reflects a full spectrum of colors. You subtract from the white of the paper by adding pigment. The pigment prevents parts of the light from reflecting. This is called *subtractive color*.

Additive color uses primary colors; subtractive color uses secondary colors. In a sense, they're flip sides of the same color theory.

RGB parade

Click the Lumetri Scopes Settings menu, and choose Preset > Parade RGB.

The RGB parade provides another form of waveform-style display. The difference is that the red, green, and blue levels are displayed separately. To fit all three colors in, each image is squeezed horizontally to one-third of the width of the display.

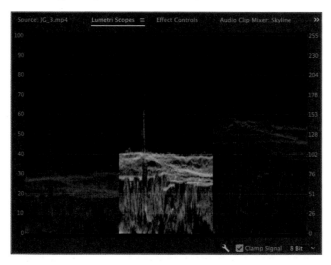

You can choose which kind of parade you see by clicking the Lumetri Scopes Settings menu or by right-clicking in the Lumetri Scopes panel and choosing Parade Type.

The three parts of the parade have similar patterns in them, particularly where there are white or gray pixels, because these parts will have equal amounts of red, green, and blue. The RGB parade is one of the most frequently used tools in color correction because it clearly shows the relationship between the primary color channels.

To see the impact color adjustments can have on the parade, go to the Basic Correction section of the Lumetri Color panel and try adjusting the Color Balance Temperature and Tint controls. Be sure to reset them when you finish by double-clicking each control.

An overview of color-oriented effects

As well as adjusting color using the Lumetri Color panel, there are a number of color-oriented effects worth familiarizing yourself with. You add, modify, and remove color correction effects in the same way that you manage the other effects in Premiere Pro. Just as with the other effects, you can use keyframes to modify color correction effect settings over time.

As you build familiarity with Premiere Pro, you may find yourself wondering which effect is best for a particular purpose; this is normal! There are often several ways of achieving the same outcome in Premiere Pro, and sometimes the choice comes down to which interface you prefer.

Here are a few effects you may want to try first. If you want to look at these effects and experiment with the controls now, you may want to use the Effects workspace, rather than the Color workspace.

Tip: You can always find an effect using the search box at the top of the Effects panel. Often, the best way to learn how to use an effect is to apply it to a clip with a good range of colors, highlights, and shadows and then adjust all the settings to see the result.

Coloring effects

Premiere Pro features several effects for adjusting existing colors. The following two are for creating a black-and-white image and applying a tint and for simply turning a color clip into a black-and-white one.

Tint

Use the eyedroppers or color pickers to reduce any image to just two colors. Whatever you map to black-and-white replaces any other colors in the image.

Black & White

Convert any image to simple black-and-white. This is useful when combined with other effects that can add color.

Black-and-white images can often withstand much stronger contrast. Consider combining effects for the best results.

Color removal or replacement

These effects allow you to make changes to colors selectively, rather than modifying the entire image. You'll be working with some of these effects later.

Leave Color

You can use the advanced HSL Secondary section of the Lumetri Color panel to achieve a similar result, but this filter is often faster.

Use the eyedropper or color pickers to select a color you want to keep. Adjust the Amount to Decolor setting to turn down the saturation on every other color.

Use the Tolerance and Edge Software controls to produce a subtler effect.

Change to Color

Use the eyedroppers or color pickers to select a color you want to change and the color you'd like it to become.

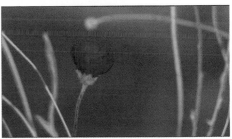

Use the Change menu to select the method you'd like the effect to use to apply the adjustment.

Change Color

Similar to the Change to Color effect, this effect gives subtle controls to adjust one color to another.

Rather than matching another color, you change the hue and finesse the selection using the Matching Tolerance and Matching Softness controls.

Color correction

These effects include a range of controls to adjust the overall look of your video or to make precise selections to adjust individual colors or color ranges. You may find yourself using the Lumetri Color panel for some kinds of adjustments and using some of the effects covered in the following sections for others.

Fast Color Corrector

As the name suggests, Fast Color Corrector is a quick and easy-to-use effect for adjusting the overall color and luminance levels in your clips.

You used the Fast Color Corrector effect earlier to make simple adjustments to clips.

Three-Way Color Corrector

Similar to Fast Color Corrector, this effect has separate controls for adjusting color for the shadows, midtones, and highlights of your clips.

The Lumetri Color panel has similar controls. However, this effect allows you to specify which pixels are affected by each color wheel based on luminance levels.

RGB Curves

The RGB Curves effect is a graph control that gives natural-looking, subtle results. The horizontal axis of each graph represents the original clip, with shadows on the left and highlights on the right. The vertical axis represents the output from the effect, with shadows at the bottom and highlights at the top.

A straight line from the lower-left corner to the upper-right corner means no change. Drag the line to reshape it, changing the relationship between the original clip levels and the resulting output levels. These controls are available as a separate effect or as part of the Lumetri color panel. However, the Lumetri color panel version provides a switchable control for each color channel. This effect gives access to all color channels at the same time in separate controls, which is a little easier to navigate.

Video Limiter

In addition to creative effects, Premiere Pro's color correction repertoire includes effects used for professional video production.

When video is broadcast, there are specific limits that are permitted for maximum luminance, minimum luminance, and color saturation. Although it's possible to confine your video levels to the limits permitted using manual controls, it's easy to mix parts of your sequence that need adjustment.

The Video Limiter effect automatically limits the levels of clips to ensure they meet the standards you set.

Tip: While it's common to apply the Video Limiter effect to individual clips, you might also choose to apply it to the whole sequence by using it on an adjustment layer.

You'll need to check the limits applied by your broadcaster before setting the Signal Min and Signal Max controls with this effect. Then it's simply a question of choosing the Reduction Axis option. Do you want to just limit the luminance, the chrominance, or both, or do you want to set an overall "smart" limit?

The Reduction Method menu allows you to choose the parts of your video signal you would like to adjust. You'll usually choose Compress All.

Fixing exposure problems

Let's look at some clips that have exposure issues and use some of the Lumetri Color panel controls to address them.

1   Make sure you are in the Color workspace, and reset it to the saved version if necessary.

2   Open the sequence Color Work.

3   In the Lumetri Scopes panel, right-click or click the Settings menu to select the Waveform.

4   Again, in the Lumetri Scopes panel, right-click or click the Settings menu to choose Waveform Type > YC no Chroma.

5   Position the Timeline playhead over the first clip in the sequence. It's the shot of the lady walking. You're going to add some contrast.

The environment is smoky; 100 IRE (displayed on the left on the waveform) means fully exposed, and 0 IRE means not exposed at all. No part of the image comes close to these levels. Your eye quickly adjusts to the image, and it'll soon appear fine. Let's see whether you can bring it to life a little.

6   In the Lumetri Color panel, click to display the Basic Correction controls.

7   Use the Exposure and Contrast controls to make adjustments to the shot, while checking the waveform display to make sure the image doesn't become too dark or too light.

You'll get the best perceived results if you have a frame from a later part of the clip onscreen. Around 00:00:07:09 there's a section of sharp focus.

Try an Exposure setting of 0.6 and a Contrast setting of 60.

8   Your eye is likely to adjust quickly to the new image. Use the check box to toggle the Basic Correction adjustment off and on to compare the image before and after.

The subtle adjustment you made adds more depth to the image, giving it stronger highlights and shadows. As you toggle the effect off and on, you'll see the Waveform changing in the Lumetri Scopes panel. You still don't have bright highlights in the image, but that's fine because the natural colors are mainly midtones.

Underexposed images

Now let's work with an underexposed image.

1 Switch to the Effects workspace.

2 Position the Timeline playhead over the second clip in the Color Work sequence. When you first look at this clip, it might look OK. The highlights don't look strong, but there's a reasonable amount of detail throughout the image. The face, especially, is sharp and detailed.

▶ **Tip:** Remember, you can open any panel by selecting it in the Window menu. The Lumetri Scopes panel isn't limited to the Color workspace.

3 Open the Lumetri Scopes panel so you can view this clip in the waveform. At the bottom of the waveform there are quite a few dark pixels, with some touching the 0 line.

In this instance, it looks like the missing detail is in the right shoulder of the suit. The problem with such dark pixels is that increasing the brightness will simply change the strong shadows into gray, and no detail will emerge.

4 In the Effects panel, locate the Brightness & Contrast effect. Apply the effect to the clip.

5 Position the panels so you can see the Lumetri Scopes panel, Effect Controls panel, and Program Monitor.

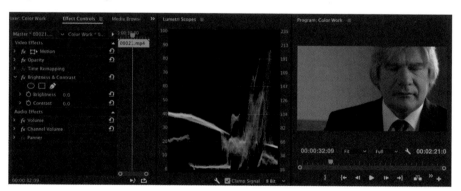

6 Use the Brightness control in the Effect Controls panel to increase the brightness. Rather than clicking the number and typing a new number, drag to the right so you can see the change happening incrementally.

As you drag, notice that the whole waveform moves up. This is fine for bringing out the highlights in the image, but the shadows remain a flat line. You're simply changing the black shadows to gray. If you drag the Brightness control all the way to 100, you'll see just how flat the image still is.

▶ **Tip:** The Brightness & Contrast effect offers a quick, easy fix, but it's easy to accidentally clip the black (dark) or white (bright) pixels, losing detail. The Curves control keeps adjustments inside the 0 to 255 scale unless you drag the end control points.

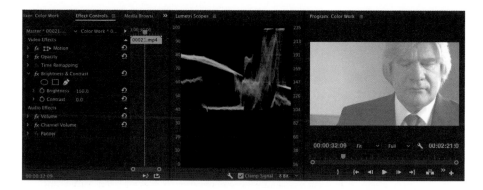

7 Remove the Brightness & Contrast effect.

8 Switch back to the Color workspace. Try to make an adjustment using the RGB Curves control in the Lumetri Color panel. Here's an example of an RGB Curves adjustment that would improve the image.

Experiment with the third clip in the sequence. This clip demonstrates that there are limits to what can be "fixed in post" (post-production)!

Overexposed images

The next clip you'll work with is overexposed.

1 Move the Timeline playhead to the fourth clip in the sequence. Notice that a lot of the pixels are burned out. Just as with the flat shadows in the second clip in the sequence, there's no detail in burned-out highlights. This means that lowering the brightness will simply make the character's skin and hair gray; no detail will emerge.

2 Notice that the shadows in this shot don't reach the bottom of the Waveform Monitor. The lack of properly dark shadows has a flattening effect on the image.

▶ **Tip:** You can reset Lumetri Color controls by double-clicking on them.

3 Try using the RGB Curves control in the Lumetri Color panel to improve the contrast range. This approach might work, although the clip definitely ends up looking processed.

When is color correction right?

Making adjustments to images is highly subjective. Though there are precise limits for image formats and broadcast technologies, whether an image should be light, dark, blue-tinted, or green is ultimately a subjective choice. The reference tools that Premiere Pro provides, such as the Lumetri Scopes panel, are a helpful guide, but only you can decide when the picture looks right.

If you're producing video for display on televisions, it's vital that you have a television screen connected to your Premiere Pro editing system to view your content. Television screens usually display color differently from computer monitors, and consumer screens sometimes have special color modes that change the appearance of video. For professional broadcast television, editors will usually have a carefully calibrated monitor that displays YUV color.

The difference is comparable to the difference between looking at colors in photos on your computer monitor and then seeing the colors as they are produced by your printer.

The same rule applies if you are producing content for digital cinema projection, Ultra High Definition TV, or High Dynamic Range TV. The only way to know exactly how the picture will look is to view it using the destination medium. This means if your ultimate destination is a computer screen, perhaps as web video or part of a software interface, you are already looking at the perfect test monitor.

Fixing color balance

Your eyes adjust to compensate for changes in the color of light around you automatically. It's an extraordinary ability that allows you to see white as white, even if objectively it's orange, for example, because it's lit by tungsten light.

Cameras can automatically adjust their white balance to compensate for different lighting in the way that your eyes do. With the right calibration, white objects look white, whether you are recording indoors (under more orange tungsten light) or outdoors (in more blue daylight).

Sometimes, automatic settings are hit or miss, so professional shooters often prefer to adjust white balance manually. If the white balance is set wrong, you can end up with some interesting results. The most common reason for a color balance problem in a clip is that the camera was not calibrated properly.

Basic white balance (Fast Color Corrector)

Let's look at a clip in this sequence where the color calibration is pretty awful.

1   Switch to the Color workspace.

2   Move the Timeline playhead to the fifth clip in the sequence.

On first inspection, this clip looks reasonably well balanced, but the background wall was originally white, and now it has a warm color cast.

3   Expand the Basic Correction section of the Lumetri Color panel.

4   Select the White Balance eyedropper (🖊).

5   In the Program Monitor, click the wall just under the subject's chin. Be careful to avoid her skin and the paper lower down.

The eyedropper tells the Lumetri Color panel what should be white and adjusts the Temperature and Tint controls accordingly.

> **Tip:** When using the eyedropper, you might find it helpful to change the zoom setting for the Program Monitor to 100%, making it easier to click the pixels you want.

> **Tip:** You may need to try a few times to find the perfect spot to click with the eyedropper. Try holding Control (Windows) or Command (Mac OS) to get a 5×5 pixel average selection.

Temperature ──○── -48.1
Tint ──────○── 11.4

In this example, you selected a tan color, which is the result of the lighting on the scene. The Lumetri Color panel adjusted all colors in the scene toward blue.

Let's try this with a more challenging shot.

1   Position the Timeline playhead over the last clip in the sequence. This shot has a severe blue tint, caused by a badly calibrated camera.

2   Select the eyedropper in the Basic Correction section of the Lumetri Color panel.

3   Click the same part of the wall in the background of the image.

> **Tip:** The difference made with the Lumetri Color panel can be quite subtle. Toggle the effect off and on to see a "before" and "after" comparison.

The effect does a good job of automatically correcting the color cast, though perhaps you could do better with manual adjustments—it may look a little too orange. Try this now, using the Temperature and Tint controls in the Lumetri Color panel.

> **Tip:** Make an extreme adjustment first to see a more dramatic result in the Lumetri Scopes. This can make the type of adjustment clearer.

Try using the Lumetri Scopes vectorscope (YUV) to observe the results of your adjustments. When you have finished, look in the Effect Controls panel to see the Lumetri Color effect. Every time you make adjustments to a clip using the Lumetri Color panel, a Lumetri Color effect is added, or updated, in the Effect Controls panel.

Remove the effect by selecting it and pressing the Delete key.

Primary color correction

The words *primary* and *secondary* have multiple meanings. Historically, the place where "color timing" was applied was during processing. A *primary correction* involved adjusting the relationship between the primary colors (red, green, and blue). A *secondary correction* involved focusing on certain color ranges within an image, often through adding adjustments of secondary colors. So, while *primary* and *secondary* define types of colors on a color wheel, you can also use these terms to describe stages in the color correction workflow.

Broadly speaking, primary color correction still involves overall color correction adjustments to the whole image. These days, you can also employ adjustments through secondary colors and still consider it "primary" because the entire image is affected *and* it's typically most effective to make these adjustments first.

Because secondary color correction (so called because it's typically performed second) usually involves subtler fine-tuning, the name has come to mean applying adjustments to selected ranges of pixels within an image.

Let's look at primary color correction. The Three-Way Color Corrector effect works in a similar way to the Fast Color Corrector effect, but with more advanced controls. It's a powerful color correction tool that, combined with the Lumetri Scopes panel, adjustment layers, master clip effects, and effect masks, helps you achieve professional color correction results.

Many of the same controls are available in the Lumetri Color panel, but the Three-Way Color Corrector offers more automatic adjustment options.

Let's run through the main controls.

- **Output:** Use this menu to view your clip in color (choose Video) or black-and-white (choose Luma). Viewing in black-and-white is useful for identifying contrast.

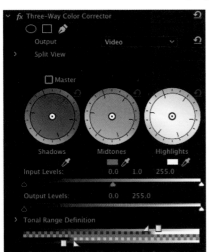

- **Show Split View:** Turn on Show Split View to see a "before" and "after" version of your clip, with one half changed by the effect and the other half unaffected. You can choose a horizontal or vertical layout and change the percentage of the split.

- **Shadows Balance, Midtones Balance, Highlights Balance:** Each color wheel allows you to make subtle adjustments to the colors in your clip. If you select the Master check box, Premiere Pro will apply the adjustments you make to all three controls at once. Note that the adjustments you make with the Master mode enabled are independent of adjustments you make to the individual parts of the clip; you can apply both.

- **Input Levels:** Use the slider controls to change the Shadows, Midtones, and Highlights levels for this clip.

- **Output Levels:** Use the slider controls to adjust the minimum brightness and maximum brightness for the clip. The Input Levels settings relate directly to this control, so, for example, if you set your Input Shadow level to 20 and your Output Shadow level to 0, anything in your clip that has a pixel brightness of 20 or less will be lowered to 0.

About levels controls

Eight-bit video, which describes all digital standard-definition broadcast video, is measured on a brightness scale from 0 to 255. When you adjust Input Levels or Output Levels settings, you change the relationship between the displayed levels and the original clip levels.

For example, if you set the Output white level to 255, Premiere Pro will use the maximum brightness range for the video. If you set the Input white level to 200, Premiere Pro will stretch the original clip brightness so that 200 becomes 255. The result is that your highlights will get brighter, and pixel values originally greater than 200 will clip, or become flat white, losing any detail.

The Input Levels settings have three controls: Shadows, Midtones, and Highlights. By changing these levels, you change the relationship between the original clip levels and the way those levels are displayed during playback.

- **Tonal Range Definition:** Use the sliders to define the range of pixels affected by the Shadows, Midtones, and Highlights color wheel controls. For example, if you drag the highlight slider left, you'll increase the number of pixels adjusted when using Highlights controls. The triangle-shaped slider allows you to define the extent of the softening between the levels you're adjusting.

  Click the Tonal Range Definition disclosure triangle to get access to individual controls and to the Show Tonal Range check box. If you select the check box, Premiere Pro displays your image in just three gray tones so you can identify which parts of your picture will be affected when you make adjustments. Black pixels are shadows, gray pixels are midtones, and white pixels are highlights.

- **Saturation:** Use this to adjust the amount of color in the clip. You have a Master control that will adjust the overall clip and separate controls for Shadows, Midtones, and Highlights.

- **Secondary Color Correction:** This advanced color correction feature allows you to define specific pixels you would like to adjust, based on their hue, saturation, or luminance range. The Show Mask option shows you which pixels you have selected to apply the color correction adjustment to. Using this feature, you could, for example, selectively adjust pixels with a particular shade of green.

- **Auto Levels:** Use this feature to automatically adjust the Input Levels controls. You can click the Auto buttons or use the eyedroppers. To use the eyedroppers, select one (Black, Gray, or White) and then click a correlating part of the picture. For example, select the White Level eyedropper and then click the brightest part of the picture. Premiere Pro updates the Levels controls based on the selections you make.

- **Shadows, Midtones, Highlights, Master:** These controls allow you to make the same adjustments as the Shadows, Midtones, Highlights, and Master color balance controls but with more precision. When you change one, the other updates automatically.

- **Master Levels:** These controls allow you to make the same adjustments as the Input Levels and Output Levels graphic controls but with more precision. When you change one, the other updates automatically.

Apply the Three-Way Color corrector effect to the last clip in the Color Work sequence, and try using the controls to obtain a nuanced result.

Balancing Lumetri color wheels

It's up to you which tools you use to work on color. As you gain familiarity with the options, you will tend to use one set of tools for one kind of task and a different set for another.

Let's try using the Lumetri Color panel color wheels to adjust the last shot in the sequence.

The Fast Color Corrector effect helped, and perhaps you obtained even better results using the Three-Way Color Corrector. Perhaps you can do even better using the new Lumetri Color panel.

1 Switch to the Color workspace, and reset it if necessary.

2 Right-click the last clip in the Color Work sequence and choose Remove Attributes. Click OK in the confirmation dialog.

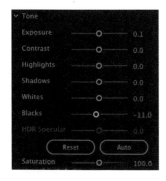

3 In the Lumetri Color panel, expand the Basic Correction section, and click the Auto button to automatically adjust the levels.

The Tone controls change to reflect the new levels.

Premiere Pro has identified the darkest pixels and the brightest pixels and has balanced automatically.

The adjustment is tiny! Clearly, the problem is not with the range of contrast in the shot.

4 Set the Lumetri Scopes panel to display the YUV Vectorscope.

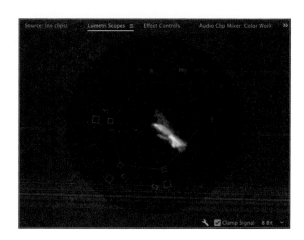

It's clear there's a reasonable range of colors in the shot, but there's a strong bias toward the blue. In fact, this scene has mixed lighting, with more blue daylight coming from the window and warmer tungsten light coming from the interior of the room.

5 In the Basic section of the Lumetri Color panel, use the Temperature slider to push the colors toward the orange. You'll need to push the adjustment all the way to 100 to see a reasonable result because the color shift is so strong in the clip.

The result is pretty good, but perhaps it could be better.

The darker pixels in this shot are generally lit by the interior, warmer room light, while the lighter pixels are generally lit by the bluer daylight. This means different color wheels will interact with different areas of the picture in convincing and natural ways.

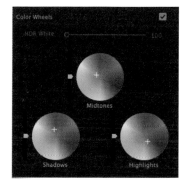

6 Expand the Color Wheels section of the Lumetri Color panel. Try using the Shadows color wheel to pull the color toward the red, while using the Highlights color wheel to pull the color toward orange.

7 Adjust the color wheels to warm up the shadows and cool down the highlights. Experiment with the midtones to obtain the most natural result possible. Use the image as a guide.

Experiment with the other controls in the Lumetri Color panel to see whether you can improve the result further.

Using special color effects

Several special effects give you great creative control over the colors in your clips. Here are a few effects of note.

Gaussian Blur

While not technically a color adjustment effect, adding a tiny amount of blurring can soften the results of your adjustments, making an image look more natural. Premiere Pro has a number of blur effects. The most popular is Gaussian Blur, which has a natural-looking, smoothing effect on an image.

Stylize

The Stylize category of effects includes some dramatic options, some of which, like the Mosaic effect, you'll use for more functional applications in combination with an effect mask, such as hiding someone's face.

The Solarize effect gives vivid color adjustments that can be used to create stylized back plates for graphics or intro sequences.

Lumetri looks

The Lumetri Color panel includes a list of built-in looks you experimented with earlier. There are also a number of Lumetri looks available as presets in the Effects panel.

These effects all make use of the Lumetri effect.

The Lumetri effect allows you to browse to an existing .look or .lut file to apply nuanced, subtle color adjustments to your footage. If you're just starting out with color adjustments, you may want a quicker fix.

The Lumetri looks available in the Effects panel are a set of Lumetri effects that already have .look files associated with them. When you select a look, a Looks browser appears in the Effects panel, making it easy to select the look you want.

Lumetri looks are an excellent way of achieving a more filmic look with almost no work because they already have more nuanced color adjustments than you're likely to achieve using regular color correction.

Creating a look

Once you've spent a little time with the color correction effects available in Premiere Pro, you should have a feel for the kinds of changes you can make and the impact those changes have on the overall look and feel of your footage.

You can use effect presets to create a look for your clips. You can also apply an effect to an adjustment layer to give your sequence, or part of a sequence, an overall look. Changes made using the Lumetri Color panel apply just as well when applied to an adjustment layer.

In the most common color correction scenario, you would do the following:

- Adjust each shot so that it matches the other shots in the same scene. That way, there is color continuity.

- Next, apply an overall look to your production.

Try using an adjustment layer.

1 Open the Theft Unexpected sequence.

2 In the Project panel, click the New Item menu and choose Adjustment Layer. The settings automatically match the sequence, so click OK.

3 Drag and drop the new adjustment layer onto the V2 track in the sequence.

The default duration for adjustment layers is the same as the duration of still images. It's too short for this sequence.

4 Trim the adjustment layer until it stretches from the beginning to the end of the sequence.

5 In the Effects panel, browse to Lumetri Presets > SpeedLooks > Universal. Drag one of these SpeedLooks onto the adjustment layer. The look will apply to every clip in the sequence.

You can apply any standard visual effect this way and use multiple adjustment layers to apply different looks to different scenes.

This is just a brief introduction to color adjustment, and there's an enormous amount more to explore. It's worth investing the time to familiarize yourself with the advanced controls in the Lumetri Color panel. There are a great many visual effects that can add nuance or a striking look to your footage. Experimentation and practice are key to developing your understanding in this important aspect of post-production.

Review questions

1 How do you change the display in the Lumetri Scopes panel?

2 How do you access the Lumetri Scopes panel when not viewing the Color workspace?

3 Why should you use the vectorscope rather than depending on your eyes?

4 How can you apply a look to a sequence?

5 Why might you need to limit your luminance or color levels?

Review answers

1 Right click in the panel or click the Settings menu and choose the display type you would like.

2 Access the Lumetri Scopes panel, like all panels, in the Windows menu.

3 The way you perceive color is highly subjective and relative. Depending on the colors you have just seen, you will see new colors differently. The vectorscope display gives you an objective reference.

4 You can use effect presets to apply the same color correction adjustments to multiple clips, or you can add an adjustment layer and apply the effects to that. Any clips on lower tracks covered by the adjustment layer will be affected.

5 If your sequence is intended for broadcast television, you'll need to ensure you meet the stringent requirements for maximum and minimum levels. The broadcaster you're working with will be able to tell you their required levels.

15 EXPLORING COMPOSITING TECHNIQUES

Lesson overview

In this lesson, you'll learn about the following:

- Using the alpha channel

- Using compositing techniques

- Working with opacity

- Working with a greenscreen

- Using mattes

 This lesson will take approximately 50 minutes.

Premiere Pro has powerful tools that enable you to combine layers of video in your sequences.

In this lesson, you'll learn about the key technologies that make compositing work and about approaches to preparing for compositing, adjusting the opacity of clips, and keying greenscreen shots with chromakey and mattes.

Compositing comprises blending, combining, layering, keying, masking, and cropping, in any combination. Anything that combines two images is compositing.

Getting started

Until now, you have been mainly working with single, whole-frame images. You have created edits where you have transitioned between one image and another or edited clips onto upper video tracks to have them appear in front of clips on lower video tracks.

In this lesson, you'll learn about ways to combine those layers of video. You'll still use clips on upper and lower tracks, but now they will become foreground and background elements in one blended composition.

This title…

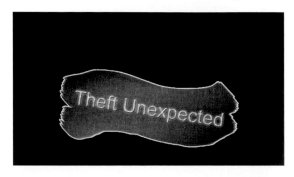

…combines with this video…

…to produce this composite image.

The blend might come from cropping part of the foreground image or from *keying*—selecting a specific color to become transparent—but whatever the method, the way you edit clips onto a sequence is the same as ever.

Let's begin by learning about the important concept of *alpha*, which explains the way pixels are displayed, and then try several techniques.

1 Open Lesson 15.prproj in the Lesson 15 folder.

2 Switch to the Effects workspace by clicking Effects in the Workspaces panel or by choosing Window > Workspaces > Effects.

3 Reset the workspace by clicking the Effects menu in the Workspace panel and choosing Reset to Saved Layout or by choosing Window > Workspaces > Reset to Saved Layout.

What is an alpha channel?

Everything begins with cameras selectively recording the red, green, and blue parts of the light spectrum as separate color channels. Because each channel is monochrome (just one of the three colors), they are commonly described as *grayscale*.

Adobe Premiere Pro CC uses these three monochromatic (single color) channels to produce the corresponding primary color channels. They are combined using what's called *additive color* to create a complete RGB image. You see the three channels combined as full-color video.

Finally, there is a fourth monochromatic channel: alpha.

The fourth channel defines no colors at all. Instead, it defines *opacity*—how visible the pixel is. Several different words are used in the world of post-production to describe this fourth channel, including visibility, transparency, mixer, and opacity. The name is not particularly important. What matters is that you can adjust the opacity of each pixel independently of its color.

Just as you might use color correction to adjust the amount of red in a clip, you can use Opacity controls to adjust the amount of alpha.

By default, the alpha channel, or opacity, of a typical camera footage clip is at 100%, or fully visible. On the 8-bit video scale of 0 to 255, this means it will be at 255. Clips that are animations or text or logo graphics will often have alpha channels that control which parts of an image are opaque or transparent.

You can set the Source Monitor and Program Monitor to display transparent pixels as a checkerboard, just as in Adobe Photoshop.

1 Open the file Theft_Unexpected.png in the Source Monitor.

It looks as if the graphic has a black background, but those black pixels are actually displayed in place of transparency. Think of them as the background of the Source Monitor.

2   Click the Source Monitor Settings menu (![icon]) and choose Transparency Grid.

Now you can clearly see which pixels are transparent. However, for some kinds of media, the transparency grid is an imperfect solution. In this case, for example, it can be a little difficult to see the edges of the text against the grid.

3   Click the Source Monitor Settings menu button, and select Transparency Grid again to deselect it.

Making compositing part of your projects

The use of compositing effects and controls can take your post-production work to a whole new level. Compositing means creating new image compositions from existing ones. Once you begin working with the compositing effects available in Premiere Pro, you'll find yourself discovering new ways of filming and new ways of structuring your edit to make it easier to blend images together.

It's the combination of pre-production planning, filming techniques, and dedicated effects that produces the most powerful results when compositing. You can combine still images of environments with complex, interesting patterns to produce extraordinary textured moods. Or, you can cut out parts of an image that don't fit and replace them with something else.

Compositing is one of the most creative parts of nonlinear editing with Premiere Pro.

Shooting videos with compositing in mind

Much of the most effective compositing work begins when you are planning your production. Right at the start, you can think about how you can help Premiere Pro identify the parts of the image you'd like to be transparent. Premiere Pro has a limited number of ways of identifying which pixels you'd like to make transparent. Consider chromakey, for example, a standard special effect used by major feature film productions to allow action to take place in environments that would otherwise be too dangerous—like the inside of a volcano!

The actors are actually standing in front of a screen that is solid green. Special-effects technology uses the green color to identify which pixels should be transparent. The video image of the actors is used as the foreground of a composition, with some visible pixels (the actors) and some transparent pixels (the green background).

Next, it's just a question of putting the foreground video image in front of another background image. In an epic action feature film, it's the prebuilt set, a real-world location, or a composite created by visual effects artists; it could be anything.

Planning ahead makes a big difference to the quality of your compositing. For that greenscreen to work well, it needs to be a consistent color. It also needs to be a color that does not appear anywhere on your subject. Green-colored jewelry, for example, might turn transparent when the key effect is applied.

If you're shooting greenscreen footage, the way you film can make a big difference to the finished result. Capture the background with soft light and try to avoid *spill*, where light reflected from the greenscreen bounces onto your subject. If this happens, you'll be in danger of *keying out*, or making transparent, parts of your subject.

This…

…combined with this…

…becomes this.

Essential terminology

In this lesson, you'll encounter some terms that might be new to you. Let's run through the important ones.

- **Alpha/alpha channel:** The fourth channel of information for each pixel. An alpha channel defines transparency for a pixel. It's a separate grayscale (monochromatic) channel, and it can be created entirely independently of the content of the image.

- **Key/keying:** The process of selectively making pixels transparent based on their color or brightness. The Chromakey effect uses color to generate transparency (that is, to change the alpha channel), and the LumaKey effect uses brightness.

- **Opacity:** The word used to describe the overall alpha channel value for clips in a sequence in Premiere Pro. You can adjust the opacity for a clip over time using keyframes.

- **Blend mode:** A technology originally seen in Adobe Photoshop. Rather than simply placing foreground images in front of background images, you can select one of several different blend modes that cause the foreground to interact with the background. You might, for example, choose to view only pixels that are brighter than the background or to apply only the color information from the foreground clip to the background. Experimentation is often the best way to learn about blend modes.

- **Greenscreen:** The common term that describes the overall process of filming a subject in front of a screen that is solid green and then using a special effect to selectively turn green pixels transparent by creating an alpha matte based on the color background. The clip is then composited over a background image. An old-style weather report is a good example of greenscreen.

- **Matte:** An image, shape, or video clip used to identify a region of your image that should be transparent or semitransparent. Premiere Pro allows multiple types of mattes, and you'll work with them in this lesson.

Working with the Opacity effect

You can adjust the overall opacity of a clip using keyframes on the Timeline or in the Effect Controls panel.

1 Open the sequence Desert Jacket. This sequence has a foreground image of a man in a jacket, with a background image of a desert.

2 Increase the height of the Video 2 track a little by hovering the mouse cursor over the track header and scrolling or by dragging the top of the track header upward.

3 Click the Timeline Settings menu and make sure the option to Show Video Keyframes is enabled.

4 Now you can use the clip rubber band to adjust the settings and keyframe any effect you apply to a clip. Since the fixed effects include Opacity, this option is automatically available. In fact, it's the default option, which means that the rubber band already represents clip opacity. Try dragging the rubber band up and down using the Selection tool on the clip on Video 2.

In this example, the foreground is set to 63% opacity.

▶ **Tip:** When adjusting the rubber band, after you begin dragging, you can hold Control (Windows) or Command (Mac OS) for fine control. Be careful not to hold the modifier key before clicking or you'll add a keyframe.

When you use the Selection tool in this way, the rubber band is moved without additional keyframes being added.

Keyframing opacity

Keyframing opacity on the Timeline is almost the same as keyframing volume. You use the same tools and keyboard shortcuts, and the results are likely to be exactly what you expect: The higher the rubber band, the more visible a clip will be.

1 Open the Theft Unexpected sequence in the Sequences bin.

This sequence has a title in the foreground, on track Video 2. It's common to fade titles up and down at different times and with different durations. You can do so using a transition effect, just as you would add a transition to a video clip; or, for more control, you can use keyframes to adjust the opacity.

2 Make sure track Video 2 is expanded so you can see the rubber band for the foreground title, Theft_Unexpected.png.

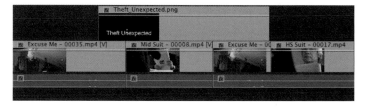

3 Control-click (Windows) or Command-click (Mac OS) the rubber band for the title graphic to add four keyframes—two near the beginning and two near the end.

▶ **Tip:** It's often easier to add the keyframe markers to the rubber band first and then drag them to adjust them.

4 Adjust the keyframes so they represent a fade-up and a fade-down in the same way that you would adjust audio keyframes to adjust volume. Play the sequence, and watch the results of your keyframing.

You can also use the Effect Controls panel to add keyframes to the opacity for a clip. Like the audio volume keyframes controls, the Opacity setting has keyframing turned on by default in the Effect Controls panel.

Combining tracks based on a blend mode

Blend modes are special ways for foreground pixels to combine with background pixels. Each blend mode applies a different calculation to combine the foreground red, green, blue, and alpha (RGBA) values with those of the background. Each pixel is calculated in combination with the pixel directly behind it.

The default blend mode is called Normal. In this mode, the foreground image has a uniform alpha channel value across the entire image. The more opacity the foreground image has, the more strongly you will see those pixels in front of the pixels in the background.

The best way to find out how blend modes work is to try them.

1 Replace the current title in the Theft Unexpected sequence with the more complex title Theft_Unexpected_Layered.psd in the Graphics bin.

You can replace the existing title by dragging and dropping the new item onto it while holding Alt (Windows) or Option (Mac OS). Replacing a clip this way retains the Timeline clip's keyframes.

2 Select the new title on the Timeline, and take a look at the Effect Controls panel.

3 In the Effect Controls panel, expand the Opacity controls, and browse through the Blend Mode options.

4 Right now, the blend mode is set to Normal. Try a few different options to see the results. Each blend mode calculates the relationship between the foreground layer pixels and the background pixels differently. See Premiere Pro Help for a description of the blend modes. Choose the Normal blend mode when you have finished experimenting.

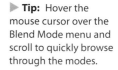 **Tip:** Hover the mouse cursor over the Blend Mode menu and scroll to quickly browse through the modes.

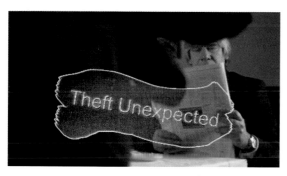

In this example, the graphic has the Lighten blend mode.

Working with alpha-channel transparencies

Many types of media will already have varying alpha channel levels for pixels. A title graphic is an obvious example: Where text exists, pixels have 100% opacity, and where there is no text, pixels usually have 0% opacity. Elements such as drop shadows behind text typically have a value somewhere in between. Keeping some transparency in a drop shadow helps it look a bit more realistic.

Premiere Pro sees pixels with higher values in the alpha channel as being more visible. This is the most common way to interpret alpha channels, but occasionally you might come across media that is configured in the opposite way. You will immediately recognize the problem because you'll see a cutout in an otherwise black image. This is easy to address because, just as Premiere Pro can interpret the audio channels on a clip, it's also possible to choose a different interpretation of an alpha channel.

You can see the results using a title in the Theft Unexpected sequence.

1 Locate Theft_Unexpected_Layered.psd in your project.

2 Right-click the clip and choose Modify > Interpret Footage. In the lower half of the Modify Clip dialog, you'll find the Alpha Channel interpretation options.

The Alpha Channel Premultiplication options relate to the way semitransparent areas are interpreted. If you find that soft semitransparent image areas are blocky or poorly rendered, try selecting Premultiplied Alpha and view the results.

3   Try selecting Ignore Alpha Channel; then try selecting Invert Alpha Channel. Observe the results in the Program Monitor (you will need to click OK before the display will update.)

- **Ignore Alpha Channel:** Treats all pixels as having 100% alpha. This can be useful if you don't intend to use a background clip in your sequence and would prefer black pixels.

- **Invert Alpha Channel:** Reverses the alpha channel for every pixel in the clip. This means that pixels that were fully opaque will become fully transparent, and pixels that were transparent will become opaque.

It's easy to spot when there's an issue with the alpha channel.

Color keying a greenscreen shot

When you change the opacity level of a clip using the rubber band or the Effect Controls panel, you adjust the alpha for every pixel in the image by the same amount. There are also ways to selectively adjust the alpha for pixels, based on their position on the screen, their brightness, or their color.

Chromakey effects adjust the opacity for a range of pixels based on their specific luminance, hue, and saturation values. The principle is quite simple: You select a color or range of colors, and the more similar a pixel is to the selection, the more transparent it becomes. The more closely a pixel matches the selection, the more its alpha channel value is lowered, until it becomes fully transparent.

Let's make a chromakey composition.

1   Drag the clip Timekeeping.mov, in the Greenscreen bin, onto the New Item button menu in the Project panel. This creates a sequence that matches the media perfectly, with the clip on Video 1.

2 In the sequence, drag the Timekeeping.mov clip up to Video 2—this will be the foreground.

3 Drag the clip Seattle_Skyline_Still.tga from the Shots bin to track Video 1, under the Timekeeping.mov clip on the Timeline.

Because this is a single-frame graphic, its default duration is too short.

4 Trim the Seattle_Skyline_Still.tga clip so that it's long enough to be a background for the full duration of the foreground clip on Video 2.

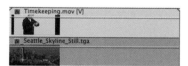

5 In the Project panel, your sequence is still called after Timekeeping.mov, and it's stored in the same Greenscreen bin. Rename the sequence **Seattle Skyline**, and drag it into the Sequences bin.

You now have foreground and background clips. All that remains is to make the green pixels transparent.

● **Note:** There's no special secret to creating multilayered compositions in Premiere Pro. Place clips on multiple tracks, knowing that clips on upper tracks will appear in front of clips on lower tracks.

Preprocessing the footage

In a perfect world, every greenscreen clip you work with would have a flawless green background and nice, clean edges on your foreground elements. In reality, there are lots of reasons why you might be faced with less than perfect material.

Of course, there are always potential problems caused by poor lighting when the video is created. However, there's a further problem caused by the way many video cameras store image information.

Because your eyes do not register color as accurately as they do brightness information, it's common for cameras to reduce the amount of color information stored.

Camera systems achieve reductions in file size using this system of reduced color capture, and the approach varies from system to system. Sometimes color information is stored for every other pixel; other times it might be recorded for every other pixel on every second line. Whatever the system, it's going to make keying more difficult because there simply isn't as much color detail as you'd like.

If you find that your footage is not keying well, try the following:

- Consider applying a light blur effect before keying. This blends pixel detail, softening the edges and often giving a smoother-looking result. If the amount of blur is light, it should not dramatically reduce the quality of your image. You can simply apply a blur effect to the clip, adjust the settings, and then apply a chromakey effect on top. The chromakey effect will be affected by the blur because it appears next on the list in the Effect Controls panel, so it's applied after it.

- Consider color correcting your shot before you key it. If your shot lacks good contrast between your foreground and background, you can sometimes help the key by adjusting the picture first with an effect like the Three-Way Color Corrector or the Fast Color Corrector.

Using the Ultra Key effect

Premiere Pro has a powerful, fast, and intuitive chromakey effect called Ultra Key. The workflow is simple: Choose a color you want to become transparent and then adjust settings to suit. The Ultra Key effect, like every greenscreen keyer, dynamically generates a matte (defining which pixels should be transparent) based on the color selection. The matte is adjustable using the detailed settings of the Ultra Key effect.

1 Apply the Ultra Key effect to the Timekeeping.mov clip in the new Seattle Skyline sequence. You can find the effect easily by typing **Ultra** in the Effects panel search box.

The Key Color can be set by clicking the color swatch and using the color picker or by clicking in the picture using the eyedropper.

2 In the Effect Controls panel, select the Key Color eyedropper.

Use the eyedropper to click a green area in the Program Monitor. This clip has a consistent green background, so it's not too important where you click. With other footage, you may need to experiment to find the right spot.

The Ultra Key effect identifies all pixels that have the green you selected and sets their alpha to 0%.

► **Tip:** If you hold Control (Windows) or Command (Mac OS) when you click with the eyedropper, Premiere Pro takes a 5×5 pixel sample average, rather than a single-pixel selection. This often captures a better color for keying.

3   In the Effect Controls panel, change the Output setting for the Ultra Key effect to Alpha Channel. In this mode, the Ultra Key effect displays the alpha channel as a grayscale image, where dark pixels will be transparent and light pixels will be opaque.

It's a pretty good key, but there are a few areas of gray where the pixels will be partially transparent, which you don't want. The right and left sides don't have any green, so none of those pixels can be keyed. You'll fix that later.

4   In the Effect Controls panel, change the Setting menu for the Ultra Key effect to Aggressive. This cleans up the selection a little. Scrub through the shot to see whether it has clean black areas and white areas. If you see gray pixels in this view where there should not be, the result will be partially transparent parts in the picture.

5 Switch the Output setting back to Composite to see the result.

The Aggressive mode works better for this clip. The Default, Relaxed, and Aggressive modes modify the Matte Generation, Matte Cleanup, and Spill Suppression settings. You can also modify manually to get a better key with more challenging footage.

Here's an overview of the settings:

- **Matte Generation:** Once you've chosen your key color, the Matte Generation category of controls change the way it's interpreted. You'll often get positive results with more challenging footage just by adjusting these settings.

- **Matte Cleanup:** Once your matte is defined, you can use these controls to adjust it. Choke shrinks the matte, which is helpful if your key selection misses some edges. Be careful not to choke the matte too much because you'll begin to lose edge detail in the foreground image, often supplying a "digital haircut" in the vernacular of the visual-effects industry. The Soften setting applies a blur to the matte, which often improves the apparent "blending" of the foreground and background images for a more convincing composite. Contrast increases the contrast of the alpha channel, making that black-and-white image a stronger black-and-white version and more clearly defining the key. You will often get cleaner keys by increasing the contrast.

● **Note:** In this example, you're using footage with a green background. It is also possible you'll have footage with a blue background for keying. The workflow is the same.

- **Spill Suppression:** Spill suppression compensates for color that bounces from the green background onto the subject. When this happens, the combination of the green background and the subject's own colors are usually different enough that it does not cause parts of the subject to be keyed transparent. However, it does not look good when the edges of your subject are green. Spill suppression automatically compensates by adding color to the foreground element edges that are positioned opposite, on a color wheel, to the key color. For example, magenta is added when greenscreen keying, or yellow is added when blue-screen keying. This neutralizes the color "spill" in the same way that you'd fix a color cast.

For more information about each of these controls, see Premiere Pro Help.

The built-in Color Correction controls give you a quick and easy way to adjust the appearance of your foreground video to help it blend in with your background.

Often, these three controls are enough to make a more natural match. Note that these adjustments are applied after the key, so you won't cause problems for your key by adjusting the colors with these controls. You can use any color adjustment tools in Premiere Pro, including the Lumetri Color panel.

Masking clips

The Ultra Key effect generates a matte dynamically, based on the colors in your shot. You can also create your own custom matte or use another clip as the basis for a matte.

When you create your own matte, you'll use the mask feature applied to the Opacity settings for your clip. Let's create a matte to remove the edges from the Timekeeping.mov clip.

1   Return to the Seattle Skyline sequence.

    As you discovered earlier, the foreground clip has an actor standing in front of a greenscreen, but the screen does not reach the edge of the picture. It's common to shoot greenscreen footage this way, particularly when filming on location where full studio facilities may not be available.

2   Disable the Ultra Key effect, without removing it, by clicking the Toggle Effect button ( ) in the Effect Controls panel. This allows you to clearly see the green areas of the picture again.

3   Still in the Effect Controls panel, expand the Opacity controls and click the Create 4-point Polygon Mask button ( ) just under that heading.

    A mask is applied to the clip, making most of the image transparent.

Tip: If you deselect the mask, the control points displayed in the Program Monitor will disappear. Select the mask in the Effect Controls panel to reactivate them.

4 Resize the mask so that it reveals the central area of the shot but hides the black edges. You will almost certainly need to reduce the Program Monitor zoom to 25% to see beyond the edges of the image. You can click directly in the Program Monitor to reposition the corner control points for the mask.

This mask extends beyond the edge of the image. This is fine—the main goal is to choose what you will exclude. In this case, the curtain is successfully excluded.

5 Set the Program Monitor zoom option to Fit.

Tip: A rough mask of this kind, used to remove unwanted image elements, is often referred to as a *garbage matte*.

6 Toggle the Ultra Key effect back on in the Effect Controls panel, and deselect the clip to remove the visible mask handles.

The result is a clean key.

Using mattes that use graphics or other clips

Adding a mask to the Opacity settings in the Effect Controls panel sets user-defined regions that should be visible or transparent. Premiere Pro can also use another clip as a reference for a matte.

The Track Matte Key effect uses the luminance information or alpha channel information from any clips on a track to define a transparency matte for a selected clip on another track. With a little planning and preparation, this simple effect can produce powerful results because you can use any clips as a reference and even apply effects to them, changing the resulting matte.

Using the Track Matte Key effect

Let's use the Track Matte Key effect to add a layered title to the Seattle Skyline sequence.

1 Edit the clip Laura_06.mp4, from the Shots bin, onto the V3 track, at the beginning of the sequence.

2 Drag the title clip SEATTLE from the Graphics bin onto the Timeline V4 track, directly above the Laura_06.mp4 clip.

● **Note:** There's no Video 4 track at the moment, but that doesn't matter. You can drag the clip from the Project panel onto the black space in the Timeline above the Video 3 track and Premiere Pro will automatically create a new Video track for the clip.

3 Trim the SEATTLE graphic clip to match the duration of the Laura_06.mp4 clip.

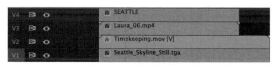

4 Find the Track Matte Key effect in the Effects panel, and apply it to the Laura_06.mp4 clip on the V3 track.

5 In the Effect Controls panel, set the Track Matte Key Matte menu to Video 4.

Scrub through the sequence to see the result. The top clip is no longer visible. It's being used as a guide to define the visible and transparent regions of the clip on V3.

The Track Matte Key effect is an unusual effect because most other effects exclusively change the clip they are applied to. The Track Matte Key effect changes both the clip it's applied to *and* the clip used as a reference.

The colors in the Laura_06.mp4 clip work well against the blue in the background clip, but they could be more vivid. Experiment with color correction tools to make the red stronger and brighter so it's a more compelling composition.

You might also want to try adding a blur effect and changing the playback speed to create a softer, slower-moving texture.

▶ **Tip:** In this example, you're using a still image as a reference for the Track Matte Key effect. You can use any clip, though, including other video clips.

Review questions

1 What is the difference between the RGB channels and the alpha channel?

2 How do you apply a blend mode to a clip?

3 How do you keyframe clip opacity?

4 How do you change the way a media file's alpha channel is interpreted?

5 What does it mean to key a clip?

6 Are there any limits to the kinds of clips you can use as a reference for the Track Matte Key effect?

Review answers

1 The difference is that the RGB channels describe color information, whereas the alpha channel describes opacity.

2 Blend modes are under the Opacity category in the Effect Controls panel.

3 You adjust clip opacity in the same way you adjust clip volume, on the Timeline or in the Effect Controls panel. To make an adjustment on the Timeline, make sure you're viewing the rubber band for the clip you want to adjust and then drag with the Selection tool. If you hold Control (Windows) or Command (Mac OS) while clicking, you'll add keyframes. You can work with keyframes using the Pen tool.

4 Right-click the file and choose Modify > Interpret Footage. The Alpha Channel options are at the bottom of the panel.

5 A key is usually a special effect where the color or brightness of pixels is used to define which part of the image should be transparent and which part should be visible.

6 You can use just about anything to create your key with the Track Matte Key effect. In fact, you can even apply special effects to the reference clip, and the results of those effects will be reflected in the matte. You can even use multiple clips, because the setting is based on the track, rather than a particular clip.

16 CREATING TITLES

Lesson overview

In this lesson, you'll learn about the following:

- Using the Titler
- Working with video typography
- Creating titles
- Stylizing text
- Working with shapes and logos
- Making text roll and crawl
- Working with templates

This lesson will take approximately 90 minutes.

While you will rely upon audio and video sources as the primary ingredients for building a sequence, you will often need to incorporate text into your project. The Adobe Premiere Pro CC Titler is a powerful tool set for text and shape creation.

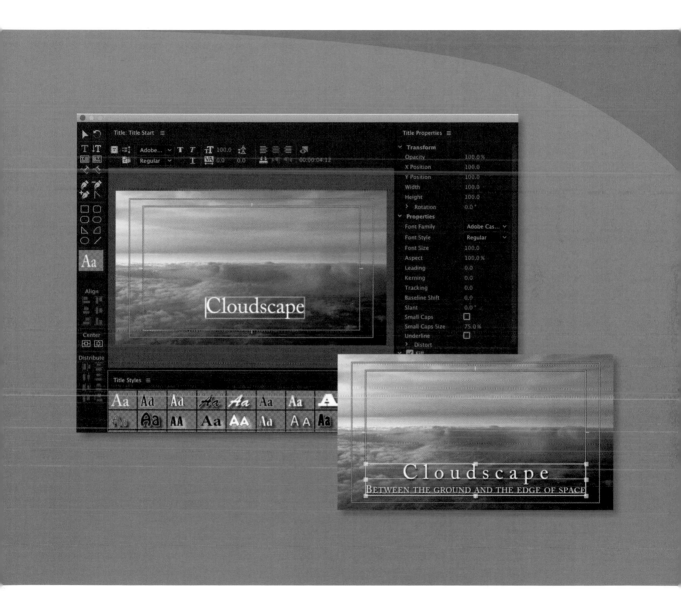

You can use the Titler in Premiere Pro to create text and shapes. You can place these objects above video or use them as stand-alone clips to convey information to an audience.

Getting started

Text is effective when you need to convey information quickly to your audience. For example, you can identify a speaker in your video by superimposing their name and title during the interview (often called a *lower-third*). You can also use text to identify sections of a longer video (often called *bumpers*) or to acknowledge the cast and crew (with credits).

Text, properly used, is clearer than a narrator and allows for information to be presented in the middle of dialogue. Text can be used to reinforce key information.

Premiere Pro has a versatile Titler. It offers you a range of text-editing and shape-creation tools that you can use to design effective titles. You can use the fonts loaded on your computer (and those available via Adobe Typekit as part of your Creative Cloud membership).

You can also control opacity and color and insert graphic elements or logos created using other Adobe applications, such as Adobe Photoshop or Adobe Illustrator. The Titler is a customizable and powerful tool.

1 Switch to the Effects workspace by clicking Effects on the Workspaces panel or by choosing Window > Workspaces > Effects.

2 Reset the workspace by clicking the Effects menu on the Workspace panel and choosing Reset to Saved Layout or by choosing Window > Workspaces > Reset to Saved Layout.

An overview of the Titler window

Let's start with some preformatted text and modify it. This is a good way to get an overview of the powerful features of the Premiere Pro Titler. Later in this lesson, you'll build titles from scratch.

1 Open the project Lesson 16.prproj.

The sequence 01 Clouds should already be open. If not, open it now.

2 Double-click the clip Title Start in the Project panel.

This is a Premiere Pro title, so it opens in the Titler, with the title displayed over the current frame in the Program Monitor. The text object should be selected by default; if not, find the Selection tool ( ) at the top left, and click once to choose it.

Here's a quick rundown of the Titler's panels:

- **Designer:** This is where you build and view text and graphics.
- **Tools:** These tools select objects, set text position, define text boundaries, set text paths, and select geometric shapes.

- **Properties:** Here you'll find text and graphic options, including font characteristics and effects.

- **Actions:** You'll use these to align, center, or distribute text and groups of objects.

- **Styles:** Here you'll find preset text styles.

3 Click a few thumbnails in the Title Styles panel to acquaint yourself with the default styles available.

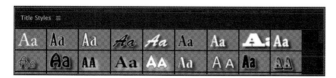

Each time you click a style, Premiere Pro changes the selected object to that style. Some of the styles are so large that some of the text disappears off-screen; you'll adjust these settings shortly. When you're finished looking at styles, choose the style Adobe Garamond White 90, the seventh from the left (shown here).

4 Click the Font Browser menu at the top of the Titler. This is a duplicate of the Font Browser menu in the Properties panel.

5 Scroll through the fonts. Each time you choose a new font, the text updates. If you click into the menu without using the drop-down option, you can use the Up Arrow and Down Arrow keys on your keyboard to choose different fonts.

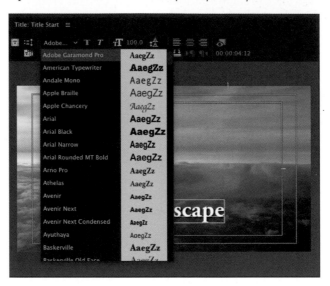

The specific fonts loaded on each system will vary, and your Adobe Creative Cloud membership includes access to many more fonts than you will have available to begin with.

To add more fonts, go to the Title menu and choose Add Fonts from Typekit to visit the Adobe Typekit website and access thousands of fonts.

6 Click the Font Family menu in the Title Properties panel, on the right side of the Titler. This is another way to change fonts in the Titler. Experiment with changing the font through this panel. You can also experiment with the Font Style menu.

7 When you've finished experimenting, choose the Caslon Pro font family.

8 Change the font size to 140 by typing **140** in the Font Size field or by dragging the Size number until it reaches 140.

> ▶ **Tip:** You may need to manually resize the text box container to see the text properly when you increase the font size.

 9 In case the text has moved when selecting it, click the Center button to center the text.

10 In the Title Properties panel, change Tracking to **25.0**. Tracking changes the spacing between the characters.

Let's add a drop shadow.

Note: You may have to expand the window or scroll to see all the Title Properties options.

11 In the Title Properties panel, enable the Shadow option. Change Shadow Distance to **10**, Shadow Size to **15**, and Shadow Spread to **45**. You can enter numbers into each field or drag the numbers to scrub their values.

Note: With all the clicking and testing, it's easy to accidentally deselect the text. If there's no bounding box with handles around the text, select it using the Selection tool (in the upper-left corner of the Titler) by clicking anywhere in the text.

12 In the Title Actions panel, click the Horizontal Center and Vertical Center buttons to align the text object to the absolute center of the screen.

The finished title stands out better against the mixed background.

Note: Using the Selection tool, click away from items in the Designer panel to hide the control handles and see the result more clearly.

13 Close the Titler by clicking the *x* in the upper-right corner (Windows) or the Close button in the upper-left corner (Mac OS).

14 Drag the Title Start clip from the Project panel to the V2 track on the Timeline, trim it so it fits above the video clip, and drag the playhead through it to see how it looks over the video clip.

Note: Premiere Pro automatically saves your updated title in the project file. It does not show up as a separate file on your hard drive.

Mastering video typography essentials

▶ **Tip:** If you'd like to learn more about typography, consider the book *Stop Stealing Sheep & Find Out How Type Works, Third Edition* (Adobe Press, 2013), by Erik Spiekermann.

When you design text for video, it's essential that you follow typography conventions. If text is composited over a moving video background with multiple colors, it can take some work to create a clear design.

Find a balance between legibility and style, making sure enough information is on the screen without crowding it. If there's too much text, it will quickly become hard to read, frustrating the viewer.

Font choice

Your computer probably has many fonts, which can make choosing a good font for video work difficult. To simplify the selection process, try using a triage mentality and consider these factors:

- **Readability:** Is the font easy to read at the size you're using? Are all the characters readable? If you look at it quickly and then close your eyes, what do you remember about the text block?

- **Style:** Using adjectives only, how would you describe the font you've chosen? Does the font convey the right emotion? Type is like a wardrobe or a haircut; picking the right font is essential to the overall success of the design.

- **Flexibility:** Does the font mix well with others? Does it come in various weights (such as bold, italic, and semibold) that make it easier to convey significance? Can you create a hierarchy of information that conveys different kinds of information, such as a name and title for a speaker's lower-third name graphic?

The answers to these guiding principles should help steer you toward better-designed titles. You may need to experiment to find the best font. Fortunately, you can easily modify an existing title or duplicate it and change the copy for a side-by-side comparison.

Color choice

Although you can create a nearly infinite number of possible color combinations, choosing the right colors to use in a design can be surprisingly tricky. This is because only a few colors work well for text while remaining clear for the viewer. This task becomes even more difficult if you're editing your video for broadcast or if your design must match the style and branding of a series or product. The text may also need to work when placed over a busy moving background.

White text has good readability over a dark background.

● **Note:** When creating text for use in a video, you will often find yourself placing it over a background that has many colors present. This will make it difficult to achieve proper contrast (which is essential to preserving legibility). To help in this case, you may need to add an edge stroke or shadow to get a contrasting edge.

This blue text is more difficult to read because it's a similar color and tone to parts of the sky.

While it may feel a little conservative, the most common color for text in video is white. Not surprisingly, the second most popular color is black. If colors are used, they tend to be very light or very dark shades. The color you choose must provide suitable contrast from the background that the text is being placed over. This is why it's so helpful to have the current video frame displayed in the background of the Title Designer.

Kerning

It's common to adjust the spacing between the letters in a title to improve the appearance of text and help match it to the design of the background. This process is called *kerning*. Taking the time to manually adjust text becomes more important the larger the font gets (because it makes improper kerning that much more visible). The goal is to improve the appearance and readability of your text while creating optical flow.

▶ **Tip:** A common place to start kerning is to adjust between an initial capital letter and the succeeding lowercase letters, particularly in the case of a letter with very little "base," such as T, which creates the illusion of excessive space along the baseline.

You can learn a lot about kerning by studying professionally designed materials such as posters and magazines.

Kerning is applied per letter, allowing for creative use of spacing.

Kerning is easy to adjust.

1 Double-click a text box in the Title Designer to edit the contents, or click the text box with the Type tool. Once inside the text box, you can move the blinking I-bar using the arrow keys.

2 When the I-bar is between the two letters you want to kern, hold down Alt (Windows) or Option (Mac OS).

3 Press the Left Arrow key to pull the letters closer or the Right Arrow key to push them farther apart. You can also use the Kerning control in the Properties panel.

4 Move to the next letter pair and adjust as needed.

Tracking

Another important text property is *tracking* (which is similar to kerning). This is the overall control of spacing between all the letters in a line of text. Tracking can be used to globally condense or expand a line of text.

It's often employed in the following scenarios:

- **Tighter tracking:** If a line of text is too long (such as a lengthy title for a speaker's lower-third), you may tighten it slightly to fit. This will keep the font size the same but fit more text into the available space.

- **Looser tracking:** A looser track can be useful when using all uppercase letters or if you need to apply an outside stroke to the text. It's used often for large titles or when text is used as a design or motion graphics element.

You can adjust tracking in the Title Properties panel of the Premiere Pro Titler.

Tracking is combined with the use of the Small Caps option to create a stylized title that is still easy to read.

Leading

Kerning and tracking control the horizontal space between characters. *Leading* (pronounced "led-ing") controls the vertical space between lines of text. The name comes from the time when strips of lead were used on a printing press to create space between lines of text.

You adjust the leading in the Title Properties panel.

The original leading causes the two lines of text to become difficult to read. Notice the way the *P* in the first line is touching the text on the second line.

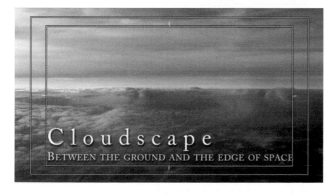

Increasing the leading adds space between lines and improves readability.

In most cases, you'll find the default setting of Auto works well for leading. Adjusting leading can have a big impact on your title. Don't set the leading too tight; otherwise, descenders from the top line (such as the downward lines on *j*, *p*, *q*, and *z*) will cross ascenders from the lower line (like the upward lines on *b*, *d*, *k*, and *l*). This collision will likely make the text more difficult to read.

Alignment

While you may be used to seeing text left-justified for things like a newspaper, there are no hard-and-fast rules for aligning video text. Generally, text used for a lower-third title is left- or right-justified.

● **Note:** When setting text, you can click and type (called *point text*), or you can drag using the Type tool to define a text box first. This is called *area type* and offers greater control over alignment and layout, though you need to remember to resize the box if your text gets too big.

On the other hand, you'll often center text used in a title sequence or segment bumper. In the Titler, you'll find buttons to align your text left, right, or centered.

● **Note:** You can turn off the title-safe margins or action-safe margins by opening the Titler panel menu (or choosing Title > View) and then choosing Safe Title Margin or Safe Action Margin.

Safe title margin

When you're designing in the Titler, you'll see a series of two nested boxes. The first box shows you 90 percent of the viewable area, which is considered the *action-safe margin*. Things that fall outside this box may get cut off when the video signal is viewed on a television monitor. Be sure to place all critical elements that are meant to be seen (like a logo) in this region.

The second box, which is 80 percent of the viewable area, is called the *title-safe zone*. Just as this book you're reading has margins to keep the text from getting too close to the edge, it's a good idea to keep text inside the innermost, or title-safe, zone. This will make it easier for your audience to read the information.

This image is too close to the edge (and outside the title-safe margin).

This image shows the text properly positioned inside the title-safe margin, which makes it more readable and visible even on a badly calibrated screen.

Creating titles

When you create a title, you'll need to make some choices about how the text is displayed. The Titler panel offers three approaches to creating text, each offering both horizontal and vertical text direction options.

- **Point text:** This approach builds a text bounding box as you type. The text runs on one line until you press Enter (Windows) or Return (Mac OS) or until you choose Title > Word Wrap. Changing the shape and size of the box changes the shape and size of the text.

- **Paragraph (area) text:** You set the size and shape of the text box before entering text. Changing the box size later displays more or less text but does not change the shape or size of the text.

- **Text on a path:** You build a path for the text to follow by clicking points in the text screen to create curves and then adjusting the shape and direction of those curves using the handles.

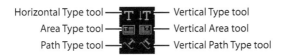

In the Title Tools panel, you can select a tool from the left or right column. This determines whether the text will appear horizontally or vertically.

Adding point text

Now that you have a basic understanding of how to modify and design a title, let's build one from scratch, working with a new sequence.

You'll create a new title to help promote a tourist destination.

1 If the Title panel is open, close it and then open the sequence 02 Cliff.

2 Open the New Title dialog by choosing File > New > Title or by pressing Control+T (Windows) or Command+T (Mac OS).

3 Type **The Dead Sea** in the Name box and click OK.

4 Try changing the background video frame by dragging the timecode next to the Show Background Video button. You can also move the Timeline playhead to change the background image in the Titler, but it may be hidden by the Titler frame.

5 Click the Show Background Video button to hide the video clip.

The background now shows a grayscale checkerboard, which represents transparency. If you reduce the opacity of text or graphics, you'll see some of the background show through.

6 Let's import an existing title and modify it. Go to the Title menu and choose Templates, or press Control+J (Windows) or Command+J (Mac OS).

7 In the Templates dialog, click the panel menu at the top right and choose Import File as Template.

8 Browse to the lesson files and into Assets / Video and Audio Files / Titles, and open The Dead Sea.prtl.

9 Click the Selection tool ( ) in the upper-left corner of the Title Tools panel. Handles appear on the text bounding box.

You won't be able to use a keyboard shortcut for the Selection tool because you're typing into a text bounding box.

▶ **Tip:** If you type a long title, you'll notice that point text does not wrap automatically, so your text will run off the screen. To make text wrap when it reaches the title-safe margin, choose Title > Word Wrap. If you want to force a new line to start, press Enter (Windows) or Return (Mac OS).

10 Drag the corners and edges of the text bounding box. Notice that the settings for Font Size, Width, and Height change as you do. Hold the Shift key to constrain the text so it scales uniformly.

11 Hover the pointer just outside a corner of the text box until a curved pointer appears. This allows you to rotate the text box. Drag to rotate the bounding box off its horizontal orientation.

12 With the Selection tool still active, click anywhere in the bounding box and drag the text and its bounding box somewhere else in the Title Designer.

Try to approximately match this look. Adjust the size, rotation, and position of the text using the techniques you've learned so far.

> **Tip:** Dragging the timecode with the background video displayed is a useful way to position text relative to the video contents. You can also use it to evaluate how the text looks over your video and make adjustments to improve readability. The video frame displayed behind the title is not saved with the title. It's there only as a reference for positioning and styling your title.

> **Tip:** Instead of dragging bounding box handles, you can change the Transform settings in the Title Properties panel. Your changes will show up immediately in the bounding box (as long as it is selected).

Adding paragraph text

While point text is flexible, you can take better control over layout with paragraph text. This option will automatically wrap the text as it reaches the edge of the paragraph text box.

Continue working with the same title.

1   Click the Area Type tool () in the Title Tools panel.

2   Drag in the Title Designer to create a text box that fills the lower-left corner of the title-safe area.

3   Start typing. Start entering names of participants who will be attending the tour. Use the names here or add your own.

Type enough characters to go beyond the end of the text box. You'll need to reduce the font size so you can see a few lines of text at once. Unlike point text, area text remains within the confines of the bounding box you defined, and it wraps at the edges of the box.

This name is too large to fit on one line, so it wraps to the next.

▶ **Tip:** A good way to avoid spelling mistakes is to copy and paste text from an approved script or email that has already been reviewed by your client or producer.

4   Press Enter (Windows) or Return (Mac OS) to go down a line.

5 Click the Selection tool and change the size and shape of the bounding box to fit around the text a little better.

As you resize the text box, the text stays the same size, adjusting its position in the text box. If you make the box too small to fit all your text, the extra text scrolls below the bottom edge of the text box, and a small plus sign (+) appears near the lower-right corner outside the box.

6 Close the title.

Because Premiere Pro automatically saves text to the project file, you can switch to a new or different title without losing your work.

Stylizing text

Earlier, you experimented with title styles. Title styles are fast and easy, but they're just the beginning. You can use the Title Properties panel to take precise control over the appearance of your text.

Changing a title's appearance

In the Title Properties panel, you'll find lots of options for modifying the appearance of text. You can improve the readability of your type and its overall appearance. It's easy to overdo it and add too many effects, which might produce amateurish results and affect readability. Now is the perfect time to turn everything on and make the most garish text you can (professionally, you might not get it signed off).

Here are some of the most useful tools for modern typographic design. You'll find them in the Title Properties panel.

- **Fill Type:** There are several choices of fill type. The most popular ones are Solid and Linear Gradient, but you will also find gradient, bevel, and ghosting options.

▶ **Tip:** Instead of using the Color Picker to change the Color Stop color, you can use the Eyedropper tool (located next to the color swatch) to select a color from your video. Click the Show Video button at the top of the Titler panel, move to a frame you want to use by scrubbing the timecode numbers left or right, and use the Eyedropper tool to select a color that suits your needs.

- **Color:** Set the color for your text. You can click the swatch or enter numerical values in the Color Picker, or you can use the Eyedropper tool to sample color from anywhere on your computer screen. If you start with a sample from your video and then adjust the color using the Color Picker, you can create titles that are clear to read and match the mood of the background.

  ● **Note:** If you see an exclamation point next to the color you've chosen, Premiere Pro is warning you that a color is not broadcast-safe. This means it can cause problems when the video signal is put into a broadcast environment (and can be problematic when burned to a DVD or Blu-ray Disc). Click the exclamation point to automatically choose the closest color that is still broadcast-safe.

- **Sheen:** A gentle highlight can add depth to your title. Be sure to adjust the size and opacity so the effect is subtle.

- **Stroke:** You can click to add inner and outer strokes. Strokes can be solid or gradient and add a thin edge to the outside of the text. Adjust the opacity of a gradient to create a gentle glow or soft edge. A stroke is commonly used to help keep text legible over moving video or a complex background.

- **Shadow:** A drop shadow is a common addition to video text because it makes the text easier to read. Be sure to adjust the softness of the shadow. Also, be sure to keep the angle of shadows identical for all titles in a project for consistency.

1 In the Project panel, double-click the title The Dead Sea to open it in the Titler.

2 Click the Show Background Video button to see the title over the video source.

3 Experiment with the options in the Title Properties panel to make the text more readable, and add more color to the composition.

4 Continue designing until you have a look that is visually pleasing to you.

Saving custom styles

If you create a look you like, you can save time by storing it as a style. A style describes the color and font characteristics for text. You can use a style to change the appearance of text with a single click; all the properties of the text update to match the preset.

Let's create a style from the text you modified in the previous exercise.

1 Continuing to work on the same title, use the Selection tool to select a text object that has the properties you want to save.

2 In the Title Styles panel menu (Title Styles ≡), choose New Style.

3 Enter a name and click OK. The style is added to the Title Styles panel.

4 To view styles more easily, you can click the Title Styles panel menu and choose to view the presets as Text Only, Small Thumbnails, or Large Thumbnails.

5 To manage a style, right-click its thumbnail. You can choose to duplicate a style to modify a copy, rename a style so it's easier to find, or delete a style if you want to remove it.

6 Close the title to store its changes.

Creating an Adobe Photoshop graphic or title

You can create titles or graphics for Premiere Pro in Adobe Photoshop. While Photoshop is known as the premier tool for modifying photos, it also has many capabilities for creating elegant titles or logo treatments. Photoshop offers several advanced options, including anti-aliasing (for smoother text), advanced formatting (such as scientific notation), flexible layer styles, and even a spell checker.

Try creating a new Photoshop document from inside Premiere Pro.

1 Choose File > New > Photoshop File.

2 The New Photoshop File dialog appears, with settings based on your current sequence.

3 Click OK.

4 Choose a location to store your new PSD file, name it, and click Save.

Tip: If you have
disabled guides in
Photoshop View
options, you can enable
them by going to
View > Show > Guides.

5   Photoshop opens, ready for you to edit the file.

Photoshop automatically displays safe action and safe title zones in the form of
guides. These guides won't appear in the finished image.

6   Select the Text tool by pressing T.

7   Draw a text block, and by dragging, draw from the upper-left corner of the title-
safe area to the lower-right corner. This creates a paragraph text box to hold the
text. As in Premiere Pro, using a paragraph text box in Photoshop allows you to
precisely control the layout of text.

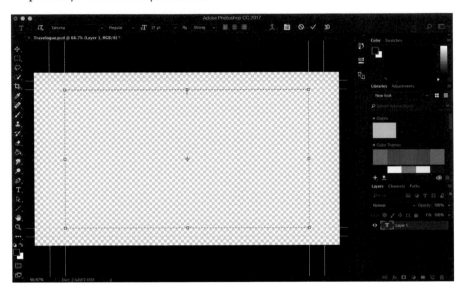

8   Enter some text you'd like to use.

9   Adjust the font, color, and point size to taste using the controls in the Options
bar across the top of the screen.

10 Click the Commit button (✓) in the Options bar to commit the text layer.

11 Add a drop shadow by choosing Layer > Layer Style > Drop Shadow. Adjust
to taste.

When you're finished in Photoshop, you can save and close the file. It will already
be in your Project panel in the Premiere Pro project.

If you'd like to edit the title in Photoshop, select it in the Project panel or Timeline
and choose Edit > Edit in Adobe Photoshop. When you save changes in Photoshop,
the title updates automatically in Premiere Pro.

Working with shapes and logos

When building titles for your program, you'll likely need more than just words to build a complete graphic. Fortunately, Premiere Pro also offers the ability to create vector shapes that can be filled and stylized to create graphic elements. Many of the title properties you worked with for text also apply to shapes. You can also import completed graphics (like a logo) to enhance your Premiere Pro title.

Creating shapes

If you've created shapes in graphics-editing software such as Photoshop or Adobe Illustrator, you'll find creating geometric objects in Premiere Pro similar.

Select from the various shapes in the Title Tools panel, drag and draw the outline, and release the mouse button.

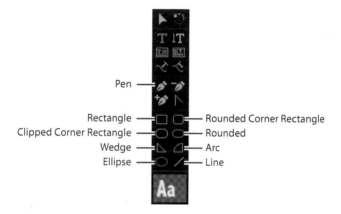

Follow these steps to draw shapes in Premiere Pro. (This exercise is just for practice.)

1 Open the sequence 03 Shapes.

2 Press Control+T (Windows) or Command+T (Mac OS) to open a new title.

3 Type **Shapes** in the Name box in the New Title dialog, and click OK.

4 Select the Rectangle tool (R), and drag in the Titler panel to create a rectangle.

5 Try a few title styles while the rectangle is still selected.

Title styles affect shapes as well as text.

6 Hold the Shift key as you drag in another location to create a square. The Shift key locks the aspect ratio of shapes.

7 Select the Rounded Corner Rectangle tool and Alt-drag (Windows) or Option-drag (Mac OS) to draw from the center of the shape.

The center remains in the spot where you first clicked, and the figure changes shape and size around that point as you drag.

8 Select the Clipped Corner Rectangle tool and Shift-Alt-drag (Windows) or Shift-Option-drag (Mac OS) to constrain the aspect ratio and draw from the center.

9 Press Control+A (Windows) or Command+A (Mac OS) and then press Backspace or Delete to make another clean slate.

10 Select the Line tool (L) and drag to create a single line.

11 Select the Pen tool and click in a blank area of the Title Designer to create an anchor point (don't drag to create handles).

12 Click somewhere else in the Title Designer to create a path. This creates another anchor point.

13 Keep clicking with the Pen tool to create additional straight segments. The last anchor point you add appears as a large square to show it's selected.

14 Complete the path by doing one of the following:

- Close the path by moving the Pen tool to the first anchor point. When you hover the cursor over the first anchor point, a little circle appears underneath the Pen pointer. Click to close the path.

- To leave the path open, Control-click (Windows) or Command-click (Mac OS) anywhere away from all objects. Alternatively, select a different tool in the Title Tools panel.

15 Experiment with the different shape options. Try overlapping them and using different styles. The possibilities are endless.

16 Close the current title.

Adding a graphic

You can add image files to your title designs using common file formats, including vectors (.ai, .eps) and still images (.psd, .png, .jpeg).

1 In the Project panel, double-click the file Lower-Third Start clip to open the title in the Titler Designer.

2 Choose Title > Graphic > Insert Graphic.

3 Select the file logo.ai from the Lessons/Assets/Graphics folder, and click Open.

4 With the Selection tool, drag the logo to position it where you want it in the title. Then adjust the size, opacity, rotation, or scale of the logo. Hold down the Shift key to constrain proportions when you scale to prevent unwanted distortion.

● **Note:** To restore a graphic to its original size, select it and choose Title > Graphic > Restore Graphic Size. If you accidentally distorted the logo, select the logo and choose Title > Graphic > Restore Graphic Aspect Ratio.

● **Note:** If you place a vector graphic into a title, Premiere Pro converts it into a bitmap graphic at its original size. You can scale the graphic smaller, but if you make it larger, the image may become pixelated.

5 When finished, close the title.

Aligning shapes and logos

As you design titles, you'll often want to keep the design uniform and neat. The Premiere Pro Titler can align and distribute elements in a title. The options in the Align panel set the position for multiple objects to match, such as the bottom edges or centers of two or more items. You can also take three or more objects and space them evenly in relation to one another.

1 In the Project panel, double-click the file Align Start to open the title in the Titler.

This title contains three shapes that are randomly positioned on the screen.

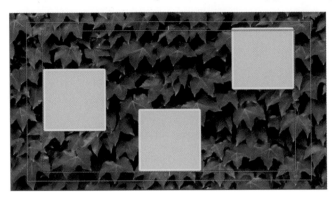

2 Use the Selection tool to lasso across all three squares, selecting them all.

When more than one object is selected, the Align tools become available.

3 Click the Align Vertical Bottom button ( ) to align the bottom edges of the three objects.

The three objects are now aligned, based on the lowest edge of the lowest object in the composition.

4 Click the Horizontal Center Distribute button ( ) to space the three objects equally from one another.

The objects are now evenly spaced and aligned with one another. Now, let's space them in relation to the canvas.

5 Click both the Horizontal Center and Vertical Center buttons.

You should have three perfectly aligned squares centered in the title area.

6 Close the title.

Making text roll and crawl

You can easily make rolling text for opening and closing credits and crawling text for items such as headline bulletins.

1 Choose Title > New Title > Default Roll.

2 Name your title **Rolling Credits**, and click OK.

> ▶ **Tip:** You can create a new title in several ways, but only the Title menu gives you direct access to the Roll and Crawl options.

3 Select the Type tool and then type some text with the Adobe Caslon Pro font set to a font size of around 100.

Create placeholder credits as shown here, pressing Enter (Windows) or Return (Mac OS) after each line. Type enough text to more than fill the screen vertically. Use the Title Properties panel to format your text as desired.

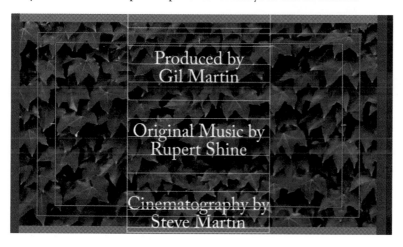

► **Tip:** Remember, you can view the title styles as a list by choosing the option in the Styles panel menu.

► **Tip:** It's often easier to write your credits in a word-processing application or text document. You can then copy and paste rather than type them into a title.

When text runs off the screen, a scroll bar appears automatically.

4 Click the Roll/Crawl Options button ( ).

You have the following options:

- **Still:** This sets the title as a still.

- **Roll (scroll text vertically):** This sets the title to scroll vertically.

- **Crawl Left, Crawl Right:** These set the title to scroll horizontally left or right.

- **Start Off Screen:** This sets whether the credit begins off-screen and rolls on or whether it begins where you placed it in the Title Designer.

- **End Off Screen:** This indicates whether the credits roll completely off the screen or end onscreen.

- **Preroll:** This sets the number of frames to delay before the first words appear onscreen.

- **Ease-In:** This specifies the number of frames at the beginning to gradually increase the speed of the roll or crawl from zero to full speed.

- **Ease-Out:** This specifies the number of frames to slow down the speed of the roll or crawl at the end.

- **Postroll:** This specifies the number of frames that play after the roll or crawl ends.

5 Select Start Off Screen and End Off Screen, and click OK.

6 Close the Titler.

7 Drag your newly created Rolling Credits title onto the Video 2 track of the Timeline above the video clip (if you have another title there, drag this one on top of it to perform an overlay edit).

8 Trim the duration of the new Rolling Credits title clip to the same length as the clip on the Video 1 track.

The length of a rolling or crawling title on the Timeline defines the playback speed. A shorter title will roll or crawl faster than a long one.

9 With the sequence selected, press the spacebar to view your rolling credits.

Introducing captions

There are two kinds of captions you might encounter when producing video for television broadcast and beyond: Closed and Open.

Closed captions are embedded in the video stream and can be enabled or disabled by the viewer. Open captions are always onscreen.

Premiere Pro allows you to work with either kind of caption in the same way—in fact, you can even convert one kind of caption file to another. However, there is one limitation; closed caption files have a more limited range of colors and design features than open captions. This is because they are actually displayed by the viewer's TV, set-top box, or online viewing software, so controls are in place before you begin.

The following workflow describes working with closed captions, but open captions work the same way—just right-click the imported caption file and choose Modify to access the option to change the file to an open caption, or create a new open caption item from the start.

Using closed captions

Video content can be enjoyed by more people when it is accessible. An increasingly used practice is to add closed-captioning information that can be decoded by television sets. Visible captions are inserted into a video file and travel through supported formats to specific playback devices.

Adding closed-captioning information is relatively easy as long as you have captions that have been properly prepared. Caption files are often generated with software tools such as MacCaption, CaptionMaker, and MovieCaptioner.

Here's how to add captions to an existing sequence:

1 Close the current project, and open Lesson 16_02.prproj.

2 Open the sequence NFCC_PSA.

3 Choose File > Import and navigate to a caption file (.scc and .mcc formats are supported). You'll find a sample file in the Lessons/Assets/Closed Captions folder.

   The caption file is added to the bin as if it were a video clip, with a frame rate and duration.

● **Note:** This public service announcement was produced by RHED Pixel and is provided courtesy of the National Foundation for Credit Counseling.

4 Edit the closed captions clip to a track above all the clips in your sequence.

5 Click the Settings menu button in the Program Monitor (🔧), and choose Closed Captions Display > Enable.

6 Play the sequence to see the captions. If your captions don't display properly, click the Settings menu button in the Program Monitor and choose Closed Captioning Display > Settings. Make sure the settings match the file type you're using. In this case, choose the CEA-608 option

7 You can adjust the captions using the Captions panel (Window > Captions). You can adjust the content, timing, and formatting of captions using the panel's controls.

You can also change the timing by dragging the handles for each caption on the Timeline.

You can create your own closed captions right within Premiere Pro.

1 Choose File > New > Captions. The New Captions dialog opens.

2 The default settings are based on your current sequence. These are fine, so click OK.

3 Another dialog opens, asking for advanced settings for broadcast workflows.

CEA-608 (also known as Line 21) is the most commonly used standard in countries that use the NTSC broadcast standard. The TeleText option (Line 16) is used in PAL countries. Open captions are always visible and give the maximum flexibility for appearance. This clip is NTSC, so for this clip choose CEA-608.

4 Choose CC1 from the Stream menu to set this as the first stream of closed captions (up to four streams can be added). Click OK. The Closed Captions clip is added to the Project panel.

5 Remove the existing closed caption clip on the Video 2 track. By selecting it and pressing Backspace (Windows) or Delete (Mac OS).

6 Edit the new closed caption clip onto the Video 2 track. It will be too short for the sequence (by default it is 3 seconds long). Drag the end of the caption to trim it to the duration you need. Select the closed caption clip on the Timeline and go to the Captions panel (Window > Captions).

7 Enter text that matches the dialogue and/or narration being spoken and then click the (plus button) + at the bottom of the panel to add another caption.

8 Adjust the In and Out durations for each caption in the Captions panel or directly on the Timeline.

Note: Using the Button Editor, you can customize the Program Monitor by adding a Closed Captions Display button for easy access to toggling viewable captions.

9 Use the formatting controls at the top of the Captions panel to adjust the appearance of each caption.

As the total length of captions gets longer, the sequence caption clip contents will get longer. You may need to trim the clip in the sequence to see the new contents.

Review questions

1 What are the differences between point text and paragraph (or area) text?

2 Why display the title-safe zone?

3 Why might the Align tools be dimmed?

4 How do you use the Rectangle tool to make a perfect square?

5 How do you apply a stroke or drop shadow?

Review answers

1 You create point text with the Type tool. Its text box expands as you type. Changing the text box shape changes the text size and shape accordingly. When you use the Area Type tool, you define a bounding box, and the characters remain within its confines. Changing the box's shape displays more or fewer characters.

2 Some TV sets cut off the edges of the picture. The amount lost varies from set to set. Keeping your text within the title-safe margin ensures that viewers will see all your title. This is less of a problem with newer flat-screen TVs and isn't important for online video, but it's still a good idea to use the title-safe zone to frame your titles.

3 The Align tools are active only if more than one object is selected in the Titler. The Distribute tools also become active when more than two objects are selected.

4 To create a perfect square, hold down the Shift key as you draw using the Rectangle tool.

5 To apply a stroke or drop shadow, select the text or object to edit, and use the Stroke (Outer or Inner) or Shadow properties to add a stroke or a drop shadow.

17 MANAGING YOUR PROJECTS

Lesson overview

In this lesson, you'll learn about the following:

- Working in the Project Manager

- Importing and exporting projects

- Managing collaboration

- Managing your hard drives

 This lesson will take approximately 40 minutes.

In this lesson, you'll learn how to stay organized when working with multiple Adobe Premiere Pro CC projects. The best kind of organizational system is the one you already have when you find that you need it. This lesson will help you be more creative with a little bit of planning.

Stay on top of your media and projects with a few
simple steps.

Getting started

When you start creating projects with Premiere Pro, you may not feel the need to invest time in staying organized. Perhaps you're working on your first project now, and if that's the case, it's going to be nice and easy to find it on your storage drive.

Once you start working on multiple projects, staying organized gets a little more complicated. You might use multiple media assets taken from multiple storage locations. You'll have multiple sequences, each with its own particular structure, and you'll be generating multiple titles. You may also have multiple effect presets and title templates. All in all, you'll need quite a filing system to keep all these project elements organized.

The solution is to create an organizational system for your projects and to have a plan in place for archiving those projects that you might want to work on again.

The thing about systems for organization is that they're usually easier to use if they exist before you need them. Look at this idea from the other direction: If you don't have an organizational system in the moment you need it—when you have a new video clip to put somewhere, for example—you might be too busy to think about things such as names and file locations. Consequently, it's common for projects to end up with similar names, stored in similar locations, with a mix of files that don't go together.

The solution is simple: Make your organizational system in advance. Map it out with pen and paper if it helps, and work out the journey you'll take, starting with acquiring your source media files, moving through your edit, and finishing with output, archiving, and beyond.

In this lesson, you'll begin by learning about features that help you stay in control, without losing focus on what matters most—your creative work.

Then you'll learn about some positive approaches to collaboration.

1 Open Lesson 17.prproj in the Lesson 17 folder.

2 In the Workspace panel, click Editing. Then click the menu adjacent to the Editing option, and choose Reset to Saved Layout.

Using the File menu

Though you can perform most of your creative work using buttons in the interface or using keyboard shortcuts, some important options are available only in the menus. The File menu gives you access to your project settings and to the Project Manager, a tool that automates the process of streamlining your project.

Using the File menu commands

The following are important File menu options for project management:

Batch Capture: This allows you to capture multiple clips from tape; see Lesson 3, "Importing Media." This option is available only if you select one or more "offline" clips with no associated media in the Project panel.

Link Media: If you have clips that have become unlinked, use this option to open the Link Media dialog and relink the media (see the next section).

Make Offline: You can deliberately break the connection between clips you select in the Project panel and their media files (see the next section).

▶ **Tip:** The options Link Media and Make Offline are also available in the Project panel when you right-click selected clips.

Project Settings: These are the settings you chose when you created your project; see Lesson 2, "Setting Up a Project."

Project Manager: This automates the process of backing up your project and associated media files and discarding unused media files (described later in this lesson).

Making a clip offline

The words *offline* and *online* have different meanings in different post-production workflows, depending on the context. In the language of Premiere Pro, they refer to the relationship between clips and the media files they link to.

* **Online:** The clip is linked to a media file.

* **Offline:** The clip is not linked to a media file.

When a clip is offline, you can still edit it into a sequence, and even apply effects to it, but you won't be able to see any video. Instead, you'll see the Media Offline warning.

In almost all operations, Premiere Pro is nondestructive. This means that no matter what you do with the clips in your project, nothing will happen to the original media files. Making a clip offline gives you a rare exception to this rule.

If you right-click a clip in the Project panel or go to the File menu and choose Make Offline, you'll have two options.

- **Media Files Remain on Disk:** This unlinks the clip from the media file and leaves the media file untouched.

- **Media Files Are Deleted:** This deletes the media file. The effect of deleting the media file is that the clip goes offline because there is no media file to link to anymore.

The benefit of making clips offline is that they can be reconnected with new media. If you've been working with low-resolution media, this means you can recapture tape-based media, or reimport file-based media, at a higher quality.

Working with low-resolution media is sometimes desirable if you have limited disk storage or a large number of clips. When your editing work is complete and you're ready for fine finishing, you can replace your low-resolution, small file-size media with selected high-resolution, large file-size media.

▶ **Tip:** You can make multiple clips offline in a single step. Just select any clips you want to make offline before you choose the menu option.

The Proxy editing workflow handles this process well (see Chapter 3), but there will be occasions when you want to set one or more particular clips to be offline to link to new media files.

Be careful with the Make Offline option, though! Once your media file is deleted, it's gone. Be cautious when using the option that deletes the actual media file.

Using the Project Manager

Let's take a look at the Project Manager. You can access it by choosing File > Project Manager.

The Project Manager provides several options that automate the process of *consolidating* your project, or gathering together any media files you've used in your project.

It's useful if you intend to archive your project or if you want to share your work. By using the Project Manager to gather all your media files, you can be confident nothing will be missing—or offline—when you hand the project over to colleagues.

The result of using the Project Manager is a new, separate project file. Because the new project file is independent of your current project, you should use the Project Manager and then double-check that the new project is as you want it before you delete anything.

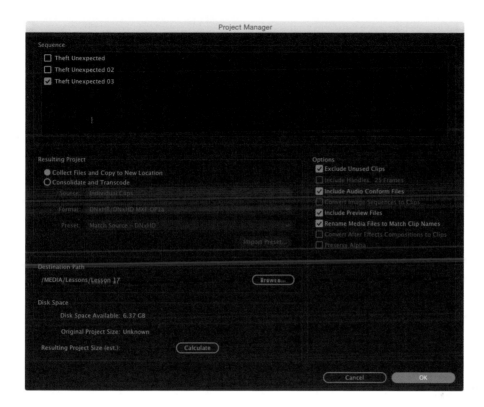

Here's an overview of the options:

- **Sequence:** Select one or all the sequences in your project. The Project Manager works with clips and media files based on the sequences you select.

- **Resulting Project:** Create a new project that has full copies of the clips included in your sequences, or create a new project with new media files based on only the trimmed parts of clips included in your sequences. You can choose a range of formats and codecs for the newly created media files when transcoding (that is, converting the media files to a new format and codec).

- **Exclude Unused Clips:** With this option selected, the new project will include only clips that are used in your selected sequences.

- **Include Handles:** If you're creating a trimmed project, using the Consolidate and Transcode option, this adds the number of frames you specify to the newly trimmed versions of the clips in your sequences. The extra content gives you the flexibility to trim and adjust the timing of your edits later.

- **Include Audio Conform Files:** This includes the audio conform files with your project, so Premiere Pro won't need to conduct analysis of your audio again. You don't need these, as Premiere Pro will create them automatically as required, but it can save time.

Note: Not all media formats can be trimmed. If you create a trimmed project that has media of this kind, the Project Manager creates copies of the full original clips.

- **Convert Images Sequences to Clip:** If you have imported one or more animated image sequences, or stop-motion photography sequences, as clips, this option converts them into regular video files. This is often a useful option because it will save space and simplify file management. It might also improve playback performance.

- **Include Preview Files:** If you've already rendered your effects, you can include the preview files with your new project so you won't need to render them again. These files aren't necessary but can save a considerable amount of time.

- **Rename Media Files to Match Clip Names:** As the name implies, this option renames your media files to match the clip names in your project. Consider carefully if you want to use this option because it can make it difficult to identify the original source media for your clips.

- **Convert After Effects Compositions to Clips:** Choose this option to exclude dynamically linked After Effects compositions, replacing them with a rendered video file. This can be valuable because the Project Manager is unable to collect dynamically linked After Effects compositions or the media files associated with them. This is a good reason to stay extra organized when working with After Effects and Premiere Pro together.

- **Preserve Alpha:** If you are transcoding your footage, you can choose to keep alpha channel information so transparent areas will stay transparent. This will lead to larger files but may mean you retain valuable picture information.

- **Destination Path:** Choose a location for your new project.

- **Disk Space:** Click Calculate to see an estimate of the total space needed for your new project.

Collecting files and copying them to a new location

Perhaps your media files are in too many locations in your storage system. Or perhaps you're sharing your work with another editor. Perhaps you're taking an edit on the road. You may not need every clip incorporated into your newly created project. This option lets you create perfect copies of your original, complete media files in a new single location, but selectively (using the Exclude Unused Clips option).

To collect all the files used in your selected sequences to a new, single location, follow these steps:

1 Go to the File menu and choose Project Manager.

2 Select the sequences you want to be included in your new project.

3 Select Collect Files and Copy to New Location.

4 Choose Exclude Unused Clips.

If you want to include every clip in your bins, regardless of whether they are used in a sequence, deselect this option. Deselect this option if you are creating a new project to organize your media files a little better—perhaps because you imported them from lots of different locations. When the new project is created, every media file linked to the project will be copied to the new project location.

5 Decide if you want to include existing preview files to save you from having to rerender your effects in the new project.

6 Decide if you want to include Audio Conform Files to save Premiere Pro from having to analyze the audio files again.

7 Decide whether you want to rename your media files. Generally, it's better to leave your media files with their original names. However, if you're producing a project to share with another editor, it might be helpful for them to identify the media files if they are renamed.

8 Click Browse and choose a location for your new project file.

9 Click Calculate to have Premiere Pro estimate the total new size of your project, based on your selections. Then click OK.

Premiere Pro will make copies of the original files in a single location. If you intend to create an archive of your entire original project, this is the way to do it.

Consolidating and transcoding

Premiere Pro can transcode all the media in your project to a new format and codec in a single step using this option in the Project Manager.

This is useful if you plan to use a so-called mezzanine codec (sometimes called a *house codec*), which all media is converted to before being stored on a media server or edited. These codecs are usually easier for editing systems to play back than in-camera codecs, as well as being high quality, often with a higher bit depth (and therefore more color acuity) than the original media. This doesn't add quality, but it helps maintain it.

To create copies of *all* your media, deselect Exclude Unused Clips. Otherwise, the options are similar to those you'd choose when creating a trimmed project.

Creating a trimmed project

To create a new trimmed project file with new media files, including only the parts of the clips you have used in your selected sequences, do the following:

1 Go to the File menu and choose Project Manager.

2 Select the sequences you want to be included in your new project.

3 Select Consolidate and Transcode.

4 Choose Exclude Unused Clips.

5 Use the Source menu to choose from the following options:

- **Sequence:** If clips in the selected sequence (or sequences) match the sequence settings (frame size, frame rate, and so on), the newly created clips will be formatted to match the sequence they are used in. If they don't match, the media files are copies instead.

- **Individual Clips:** The newly created clips will match their original frame size and format (though it is possible you will be changing the codec). It's likely you will generally choose this option.

- **Preset:** This allows you to specify a new format using the Preset menu; many options are available.

6 Use the Format menu to choose from the following options:

- **DNxHR/DNxHD MXF OP1a:** This selects an MXF file type with DNxHR/DNxHD preselected as the codec. DNxHR and DNxHD are the preferred codecs for Avid Media Composer.

- **MXF OP1a:** This selects an MXF file type with a range of codec options in the Preset menu.

- **QuickTime:** This selects a QuickTime MOV file type, giving access to the GoPro CineForm codec and Apple ProRes codec in the Preset menu.

7 Choose the codec you prefer, or click to import a preset. You can create a transcoding preset in Adobe Media Encoder.

The GoPro CineForm codec

While you may already be familiar with the idea of different file types (.mov, .avi, for example), you may not be as familiar with codecs. With each type of file you use, you can think of the file as a container. What's contained in the file is the encoded video and encoded audio. The word *codec* is a shortening of the words *compressor* and *decompressor*. It's the way the picture and sound information is stored.

As complex as codec technology might be, the decisions you make about choosing a codec are often quite simple. You'll probably choose based on the following:

- A requirement as part of an in-house workflow

- The desire to match the original media codec

- A personal preference for one codec over another (based on your personal research)

The GoPro CineForm codec is efficient, is well-suited to post-production, supports very high resolution video, and can store an alpha channel. This is important if you are working with media that has transparent pixels (such as animated titles).

8 Add some handles. The default is 1 second on each end of the clips used in your sequences. Consider adding more if you'd like to have more flexibility to trim and adjust your edits in the new project.

▶ **Tip:** Choosing to add 5 or 10 seconds of media at each end of the clip will do no harm; it will just mean your media files are a little larger.

9 Decide whether you want to rename your media files. Generally, it's better to leave your media files with the original names. However, if you're producing a trimmed project to share with another editor, it might be helpful for that editor to identify the media files if they are renamed.

10 Click Browse and choose a location for your new project file.

11 Click Calculate to have Premiere Pro estimate the new total size of your project, based on your selections. Then click OK.

The benefit of creating a newly transcoded, trimmed project is that you no longer have unwanted media files cluttering up your hard drive. It's a convenient way of transferring your project to a new location using the minimum storage space, and it's great for archiving.

● **Note:** If your media has a nonstandard frame size or you choose to preserve alpha but select a codec that does not support alpha, the media will be copied, instead of transcoded, and a warning message will inform you of this.

The danger with this option is that once your unused media files are deleted, they're gone! Be sure that you have a backup of your unused media or that you definitely do not want to use the media before you create a trimmed project.

When you create your trimmed project, Premiere Pro will not delete your original files. Just in case you selected the wrong items, you can always go back and check before manually deleting the files on your hard drive.

Rendering and replacing

Earlier, while working with visual effects, you explored the option to render and replace clips in sequences. There may be occasions that you will have a particular clip in a sequence that is hard for your system to play back without dropping frames. For example, if you have high-resolution raw media files, stop-motion photography, or a complex dynamically linked Adobe After Effects composition, you may find it necessary to render for playback at the full frame rate.

There is another way: If you right-click a clip segment in a sequence, you can choose Render and Replace.

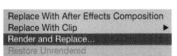

This will lead to the Render and Replace dialog.

The key benefit of this option, compared with simply rendering that section of the sequence, is that you can work with the rendered and replaced clip as you would any other. You can move it to a different location, combine it in a composition with other clips, and add visual effects. You'll probably experience markedly improved real-time performance.

You'll notice the options in the Render and Replace dialog are similar to those in the Project Manager.

When you render and replace a clip, the newly created media file is linked to a clip in the Project panel, which is used to replace the original sequence clip.

Remember, if you have replaced a clip using Render and Replace, you can restore the link to the original item (including a Dynamically Linked After Effects composition) by right-clicking the clip and choosing Restore Unrendered.

This allows you to make changes to the original item and have it update in Premiere Pro.

Using the Link Media panel and the Locate command

The Link Media panel gives you simple options to reconnect the clips in your bin with the media files on your storage drive.

The panel appears automatically if you open a project with clips that are not linked to media files.

● **Note:** Link Media is different from Replace Footage. Use Replace Footage to link a single clip to an alternative media file. The result is the same, but the automated search options are bypassed, allowing you to link a clip to a different file.

The default options work well, but if you're relinking to different file types or using a more complex system to organize your media files, you may want to enable or disable some of the options for file matching.

At the bottom of the panel, you'll find a series of buttons.

- **Offline All:** Premiere Pro will keep the clips in the project but won't automatically prompt you to relink them.

- **Offline:** Premiere Pro will keep the selected clip (highlighted in the list) in the project but won't automatically prompt you to relink it. The next clip on the list will be highlighted for you to make a selection.

- **Cancel:** This closes this dialog.

- **Locate:** If you would like to relink clips, choose options to define the search settings, including File Name or File Extension (or both), and click Locate. The Locate panel appears, and you can search for your missing media.

● **Note:** Premiere Pro also has an option for preserving your interpret footage settings. If you've modified the way Premiere Pro interprets media, select the "Preserve interpret footage settings" check box to apply the same settings to the newly linked media files.

The Locate File panel gives you a quick, easy way to locate your missing media. The simplest way to find a file is as follows:

1 Review the Last Path information as a guide to locating the file. Often the storage drive will have changed, but the path within the drive will be the same. You can use this information to manually search for a containing folder.

2 In the folder browser on the left, select a folder that you think contains the media, perhaps as a subfolder. Don't worry about choosing the particular subfolder that contains the media.

3 Click Search. Premiere Pro will locate a file that matches the selected missing clip. The file is highlighted.

4 Select the option Display Only Exact Name Matches. Premiere Pro will hide media files that do not match, making it easy to identify which file to select.

5 Double-click the correct file, or select it and click OK.

When you click OK, Premiere Pro will automatically search for other missing media files in the same location. This automation can dramatically speed up the process of relinking missing media files.

Performing the final project management steps

If your goal is to give yourself maximum flexibility to reedit your sequences based on the new project, consider going to the Edit menu and choosing the Remove Unused option before you use the Project Manager.

Remove Unused will leave you with only those clips currently used in sequences. Any clips that are not used will be removed (this can result in empty bins because they are not affected).

You can then continue to work on your project with less clutter.

Importing projects or sequences

As well as importing many kinds of media files, Premiere Pro can import sequences from existing projects, along with all the clips used to create them.

You can import other Premiere Pro project files as if they were a media file, giving limited access to project contents, or by browsing in the project file using the Media Browser. Let's look at both options.

1   Use any method you prefer to import a new media file. If you double-click a blank area in the Project panel, the Import dialog will appear.

2   Select the file Desert Sequence.prproj in the Lesson 17 folder, and click Import.

The Import Project dialog appears.

- **Import Entire Project:** This imports every sequence in the project you're importing and every clip already imported into a bin.

- **Import Selected Sequences:** This allows you to select the specific sequence you'd like to import. Only clips used in that sequence will be imported.

    ● **Note:** If you import a Premiere Pro project file and choose to import selected sequences, the Import Premiere Pro Sequence dialog appears. Using this dialog, you can selectively import specific sequences, bringing associated clips into your project automatically.

- **Create folder for imported items:** This creates a bin in the Project panel for the items you import rather than adding them to the main Project panel, potentially mixing them up with existing items.

- **Allow importing duplicate media:** If you import clips that link to media files you have already imported, by default Premiere Pro will consolidate the two clips into one. If you would prefer to have two copies of the clip, select this option.

3 For now, click Cancel. You'll use another method.

You can also import whole projects or individual clips and sequences using the Media Browser. Simply browse to a project and open it as if it were a folder.

Using the Media Browser to access the contents of project files this way gives you access to the entire contents of the project. You can browse inside bins, select clips to import, and even view the contents of sequences.

When you want to import an item (including a sequence), drag it into your current project file, or right-click it and choose Import.

Let's try this.

1 Save the current project.

2 Open the project Lesson 17 Desert Sequence.prproj in the Lesson 17 folder to make sure the media files are correctly relinked.

This is a montage sequence, showing images of a desert. Let's take clips from this project.

3 Save the project. This updates the project with links to the media you copied into your local storage.

4 Go to the File menu, choose Open Recent, and select Lesson 17.prproj in whichever location you chose for it, or browse to the Lesson 17 folder, and open Lesson 17.prproj.

5 In the Media Browser, browse to the Lesson 17 folder, and then double-click Lesson 17 Desert Sequence.prproj to browse inside the project.

6 Double-click the Desert Montage sequence.

The sequence opens in the Source Monitor, just as you would expect a clip to. The sequence also opens in a read-only Timeline panel.

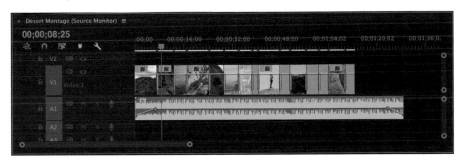

The sequence name includes the phrase (Source Monitor) to remind you that this is not a current project sequence.

You can easily import a whole sequence from the Media Browser by right-clicking it and choosing Import. However, you can also drag a clip or clips from this Source Monitor Timeline panel directly to your Project panel.

If you position the read-only Timeline panel next to your current sequence Timeline panel, you can drag clips directly from one to the other.

Managing collaboration

The option to import other projects presents novel workflows and opportunities for collaboration. You could, for example, share work on different parts of a program between different editors, all using the same media assets. Then, one editor could import all the other projects to combine them into a completed sequence.

Project files are small—often small enough to email. This allows editors to email each other updated project files, open them and compare, or import them to do a side-by-side comparison in the project, provided that each editor has a copy of the same media files. You can use local-folder file-sharing services to update a shared project file that links to duplicated copies of local media files. You can also share files using Creative Cloud.

You can add markers with comments to a Timeline. When updating a sequence, consider adding a marker to highlight changes for your collaborators.

▶ **Tip:** Although it is beyond the scope of this book, check out Adobe Creative Cloud for Teams for more advanced collaborative project-sharing workflows.

Be warned: Premiere Pro does not lock project files when they are in use. This means two people can access the same project file at the same time. This could be creatively dangerous! As one person saves the project file, it updates. As the next person saves the file, it updates again. Whoever saves last defines the file, replacing changes made by the last editor. If you intend to collaborate, work on separate project files and import sequences for comparison, or manage access to the project file carefully.

There are several dedicated media servers made by third parties that help you to collaborate using shared media files. These allow you to store and manage your media in a way that is accessible by multiple editors at the same time.

Keep these questions in mind:

- Who has the latest version of the edited sequence?

- Where are the media files stored?

As long as you have simple answers to these questions, you should be able to collaborate and share creative work using Premiere Pro.

Premiere Pro allows you to export a selection of clips and sequences as a new Premiere Pro project. This streamlined project file makes collaboration easier because it allows you to focus on precisely the content that matters.

To export a selection as a Premiere Pro project, select items in the Project panel, and choose File > Export > Selection as Premiere Project. Choose a name and location for the new project file, and click Save.

The new project file will link to your existing media files.

Using the Libraries panel

The Libraries panel gives you direct access to stock assets, graphics, and LUTS created elsewhere and shared via Creative Cloud, inside Premiere Pro.

You can also place media files in your Creative Cloud Files folder, which will automatically populate Creative Cloud Files folders on other computers if you are logged in to your Creative Cloud account on those systems.

It's easy to share folders with other users too, so the Creative Cloud Files folder is a useful way to share project files.

Managing your hard drives

Once you've used the Project Manager to create a new copy of your project or you have completed your project and finished with its media, you'll want to clean up your drives. Video files are *big*. Even with large storage drives, you'll quickly need to think about which files you want to keep and which ones you want to discard. You might also want to move your project media to slower, larger archive storage to keep as much fast media storage available as possible for current projects.

To make it easier to remove unwanted media when you've finished a project, consider importing all media files via your project folder or via a specific location on your media drive for your project. This means putting copies of your media into a single location before importing because when you import media, Premiere Pro creates a link to it wherever it is on your computer.

By organizing media files before you import them, you'll find it much easier to remove unwanted content at the end of the creative workflow because everything is conveniently located in one place.

Remember that deleting clips in a project, or even deleting the project file itself, will not delete any media files.

Remember to account for proxy files if you have used them. It's possible your proxy files will be stored in a different location to your full-resolution original media.

Additional files

The media cache uses storage space as you import new media files to your projects. Also, each time you render effects, Premiere Pro creates preview files.

To remove these files and reclaim extra space on your hard drive, there are several options:

- Choose Edit > Preferences > Media (Windows) or Premiere Pro > Preferences > Media (Mac OS), and click Clean in the Media Cache Database section. This will remove cache files that are no longer referenced by a project.

- Delete render files associated with your current project by choosing Sequence > Delete Render Files.

- Locate your Preview Files folder by checking under File > Project Settings > Scratch Disks. Then delete the folder and its contents using Windows Explorer (Windows) or Finder (Mac OS). This will remove *all* cache files.

Consider carefully when choosing the location of the media cache and your project preview files. The total size of these files can be significant, and the speed of the drive will impact playback performance in Premiere Pro.

Media management with Dynamic Link

Dynamic Link allows Premiere Pro to use After Effects compositions as imported media while they are still editable in After Effects. Text Template After Effects compositions also allow text contents to be edited in Premiere Pro. For Dynamic Link to work, Premiere Pro must have access to the After Effects project file that contains the composition, and After Effects must have access to the media files.

While working on a single computer with both applications installed and your media assets located on internal storage, this is achieved automatically.

If you use the Project Manager to collect files for a new Premiere Pro project, it will not bring copies of Dynamic Link files or duplicated audio files created when sending clips to Adobe Audition. Instead, you will need to make copies of the files yourself, in Windows Explorer (Windows) or Finder (Mac OS). This is easy to do: just copy the folder and include it with the assets already collected, or in After Effects, choose File > Dependencies > Collect Files.

Review questions

1 Why would you choose to make a clip offline?

2 Why would you choose to include handles when creating a trimmed project with the Project Manager?

3 Why would you choose the Project Manager option called Collect Files and Copy to a New Location?

4 What does the Remove Unused option in the Edit menu achieve?

5 How can you import a sequence from another Premiere Pro project?

6 Will the Project Manager collect Dynamic Link assets, such as After Effects compositions, when creating a new project?

Review answers

1 If you're working with low-resolution copies of your media files, you'll want to make your clips offline so you can recapture them or reimport them at full resolution.

2 Trimmed projects include only the parts of your clips used in sequences. To give yourself the flexibility to adjust your edit points later, you'd add handles; 24 frame handles would actually add 48 frames to the total duration of each clip because one handle is added at the beginning and end of each clip.

3 If you have imported media files from lots of different locations on your computer, it can be difficult to find everything and stay organized. By using the Project Manager to collect all the media files into one location, you'll make it easier to manage your project media files.

4 When you choose Remove Unused, Premiere Pro removes any clips from your project that are not used in a sequence. Remember, no media files are deleted.

5 To import a sequence from another Premiere Pro project, import the project file as you would import any media file. Premiere Pro will invite you to import the entire project or selected sequences. You can also browse inside project files with the Media Browser.

6 The Project Manager does not collect Dynamic Link assets when creating a new project. For this reason, it's a good idea to create any new Dynamic Link projects in the same location as your project folder or in a dedicated folder for your project. That way, it's easier to locate and copy the assets for the new project.

18 EXPORTING FRAMES, CLIPS, AND SEQUENCES

Lesson overview

In this lesson, you'll learn about the following:

- Choosing the right export options

- Exporting single frames

- Creating movie, image sequence, and audio files

- Using Adobe Media Encoder

- Uploading to social media

- Exporting to Final Cut Pro

- Exporting to Avid Media Composer

- Working with edit decision lists

This lesson will take approximately 90 minutes.

One of the best things about editing video is the feeling you have when you can finally share it with your audience. Adobe Premiere Pro CC offers a wide range of export options to record your projects to tape or convert them to additional digital files.

Exporting your project is the final step in the video production process. Adobe Media Encoder offers multiple high-level output formats. Within those formats you have dozens of options and can also export in batches.

Getting started

● **Note:** Premiere Pro can export clips selected in the Project panel, as well as sequences or ranges within sequences or the Source panel. The content that's selected when you choose File > Export is what Premiere Pro will export.

Nowadays, the primary form of media distribution is digital files. To create these files, you can use Adobe Media Encoder. Adobe Media Encoder is a stand-alone application that handles file exports in batches, so you can export in several formats simultaneously and process in the background while you work in other applications, including Premiere Pro and Adobe After Effects.

Overview of export options

Whether you've completed a project or you just want to share an in-progress review, you have a number of export options.

- You can export to a file to post online or create a DCP (Digital Cinema Package) file for theatrical distribution.

- You can export a single frame or a series of frames.

- You can choose audio-only, video-only, or full audio/video output.

- Exported clips or stills can be reimported into the project automatically for easy reuse.

- You can play directly to videotape.

Beyond choosing an export format, you can set several other parameters.

- You can choose to create files in a similar format and at the same visual quality and data rate as your original media, or you can compress them to a smaller size for distribution on disc or the Internet.

- You can transcode your media from one format to another to make it easier to exchange with other people involved in the post-production process.

- You can customize the frame size, frame rate, data rate, or audio and video compression choices if a particular preset doesn't fit your needs.

- You can apply a color lookup table (LUT) to assign a look; set overlay timecode and other clip text information; add an image overlay; or upload a file directly to social media accounts, an FTP server, or Adobe Creative Cloud.

- You can make an undetectable last-minute adjustment to the duration of your new media file by automatically shortening or extending periods of low activity.

Exporting single frames

While an edit is in progress, you may want to export a still frame to send to a team member or client for review. You might also want to export an image to use as the thumbnail of your video file when you post it to the Internet.

Premiere Pro makes exporting a still frame fast and easy.

When you export a frame from the Source Monitor, Premiere Pro creates a still image that matches the resolution of the source video file.

When you export a frame from the Program Monitor, Premiere Pro creates a still image that matches the resolution of the sequence.

Let's give it a try.

1 Open Lesson 18_01.prproj from the Lessons/Lesson 18 folder.

2 Open the sequence Review Copy. Position the Timeline playhead on a frame you want to export.

3 In the Program Monitor, click the Export Frame button (📷) on the lower right.

If you don't see the button, it may be because you've customized the Program Monitor buttons. You might also need to resize the panel. You can also select the Program Monitor and press Shift+Control+E (Windows) or Shift+E (Mac OS) to export a frame.

4 In the Export Frame dialog, enter a filename.

5 Use the Format menu to choose a still-image format.

- JPEG, PNG, GIF, and BMP work well for compressed graphic workflows (such as Internet delivery).

- TIFF, Targa, and PNG are suitable for print and animation workflows.

- DPX is often used for digital cinema or color-grading workflows.

- OpenEXR is used to store high dynamic range picture information.

  ● **Note:** In Windows, you can export to the BMP, DPX, GIF, JPEG, OpenEXR, PNG, TGA, and TIFF formats. On the Mac, you can export to the DPX, JPEG, OpenEXR, PNG, TGA, and TIFF formats.

6 Click the Browse button to choose a location to save the new still image. Create a folder named Exports on the desktop and select it.

7 Select the Import into Project option to add the new still image into your current project, and click OK.

● **Note:** The music in this project is titled "Tell Somebody," by Alex featuring AdmiralBob. Licensed under Creative Commons Attribution 3.0.

Exporting a master copy

Creating a master copy allows you to make a pristine digital copy of your edited project that can be archived for future use. A master copy is a self-contained, fully rendered digital file output of your sequence at the highest resolution and best quality possible. Once it's created, you can use a file of this kind as a separate source to produce other compressed output formats without opening the original project in Premiere Pro.

Matching sequence settings

Ideally, the frame size, frame rate, and codec of a master file will closely match the sequence it's based on. Premiere Pro makes this easy by offering a Match Sequence Settings option when you export.

1 Continue working with the Review Copy sequence in Lesson 18_01.prproj.

2 With the sequence selected (in either the Project panel or the Timeline panel), choose File > Export > Media.

The Export Settings dialog opens.

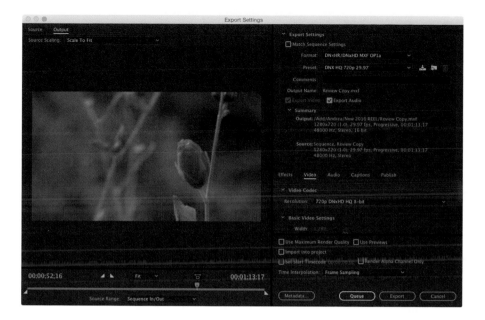

3   You'll learn more about this dialog later. For now, select the Match Sequence
    Settings check box.

4   The blue text showing the output name is actually a button that opens the
    Save As dialog. You'll find the same type of text-as-a-button in Adobe Media
    Encoder. Click the output name now.

    Output Name: Review Copy.mxf

5   Choose a target location (such as the Exports folder you created earlier), name
    the sequence **Review Copy 01.mxf**, and click Save.

6   Review the Summary information to check that the output format matches the
    sequence settings. In this case, you should be using DNxHD media (as MXF
    files) at 29.97fps. The Summary information is a quick, easy reference that
    helps you avoid minor errors that can have big consequences. If the Source and
    Output Summary settings match, it minimizes conversion, which helps main-
    tain the quality of the final output.

    ⌄ Summary
      Output: /Add/Andrea/New 2016 REEL/Review Copy.mxf
              1280x720 (1.0), 29.97 fps, Progressive, 00:01:13:17
              48000 Hz, Stereo, 16 bit

      Source: Sequence, Review Copy
              1280x720 (1.0), 29.97 fps, Progressive, 00:01:13:17
              48000 Hz, Stereo

    When exporting a sequence,
    the sequence itself is the
    source in this dialog—not
    the clips, which will have
    been conformed to the
    sequence settings.

● **Note:** In some cases,
the Match Sequence
Settings option cannot
write an exact match
of the original camera
media. For example,
XDCAM EX will write to
a high-quality MPEG2
file. In most cases, the
file written will have
an identical format
and closely match the
data rate of the original
sources.

7 Click the Export button to create a media file based on the sequence.

Choosing another codec

When you export to a new media file, you can choose the codec that's used. Some camera formats (such as DSLR) are already heavily compressed. Using a higher-quality mastering codec can help to preserve quality.

1 With the same sequence selected, choose File > Export > Media or press Control+M (Windows) or Command+M (Mac OS).

2 In the Export Settings dialog, click the Format pop-up menu and choose QuickTime.

3 Click the output name (the blue text) and give the file a new name, **Review Copy 02.mov**. Save it to the same destination you used in the previous exercise.

4 Click the Video tab near the bottom of the window.

5 Choose a video codec that you have installed.

One option that should be installed on your system is the GoPro CineForm codec. This produces a high-quality (but reasonably sized) file. Make sure the frame size and frame rate match your source settings. You might need to scroll down or resize the panel to see all the settings. Use the settings shown here.

6 In the Basic Audio Settings section, choose 48000 Hz as the sample rate, and set the Sample Size to 16 bit. Set Audio Channel Configuration to output Stereo.

Note: GoPo CineForm is a professional codec that is supported natively by Adobe Creative Cloud applications. This codec will not play back in media applications that do not support it.

About GoPro CineForm Codec options

The GoPro CineForm codec comes in three configurations, which can be selected using the Preset menu at the top of the Export Settings dialog.

- **GoPro CineForm RGB 12-bit with Alpha at Maximum Bit Depth:** This produces a high-quality file, storing picture information with 12-bit color (rather than the more common 8-bit) and using the full RGB color gamut, with effects calculated in 32-bit floating point and with an alpha channel. It'll take a little lon ger to produce the file, and it'll be a little larger, but the quality will be excellent.

- **GoPro CineForm RGB 12-bit with Alpha:** This produces the same high-quality file as the first option, but the encoding is performed using the standard color bit depth. It's still a high-quality result, and the encoding will take place faster.

- **GoPro CineForm YUV 10-bit:** This produces a high-quality video file using YUV color, the most common color mode for camera media and televisions. There is no alpha channel, but it's rare that you will need It. While this file is created with 10-bit color rather than 12-bit, remember most video is produced in just 8 bit.

7 Click the Export button at the bottom of the dialog to export the sequence and transcode it to a new media file.

Working with Adobe Media Encoder

Adobe Media Encoder is a stand-alone application that can be run independently or launched from Premiere Pro. One advantage of using Media Encoder is that you can send an encoding job directly from Premiere Pro and then continue working on your edit as the encoding is processed. If your client asks to see your work before you finish editing, Media Encoder can produce the file without interrupting your flow.

Media Encoder pauses when you play video in Premiere Pro to maximize playback performance.

Choosing a file format for export

It can be a challenge to know how to deliver your finished work. Ultimately, choosing delivery formats is a process of planning backward; find out how the file will be presented, and it's usually straightforward to identify the best file type for the purpose.

Often clients will have a delivery specification you must follow, making it easy to select the right options for encoding.

▶ **Tip:** HEVC/H.265 is a new compression system formulated by the same Motion Picture Experts Group that brought us H.264. It's more efficient, but fewer players support it. You may be asked to supply media using this codec when producing UHD content.

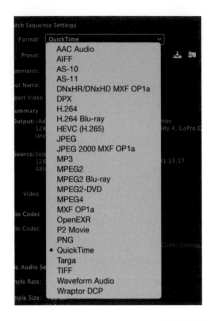

Premiere Pro and Adobe Media Encoder can export to many formats; let's run through them quickly to identify when you should use them.

- **AAC Audio:** The Advanced Audio Coding format is the audio-only format that is most often used with H.264 encoding. It's more efficient than the commonly known MP3 codec.

- **AIFF:** The Audio Interchange File Format is an uncompressed audio-only file format.

- **AS-10:** This format is based on MXF (covered later in the list), with precise configuration for broadcast television delivery. If you're producing content for TV, you might be asked to deliver in this format.

- **AS-11:** Like AS-10, this format is based on MXF (covered later in the list), with precise configuration for broadcast television delivery. If you're producing content for TV, you might be asked to deliver in this format.

- **DNxHR / DNxHD MXF OP1a:** Native support for these codecs provides compatibility with Avid editing systems. They are high-quality, cross-platform file formats for professional editing. DNxHR supports ultra-high-definition resolutions, while the DNxHD supports high-definition resolutions.

- **DPX:** Digital Picture Exchange is a high-end image sequence format for digital intermediate and special-effects work.

- **H.264:** This is the most flexible and widely used format today, with many presets for devices such as smartphones and set-top boxes and for online services such as YouTube and Vimeo. H.264 files can be played on smartphones or used as high-quality, high-bit-rate intermediate files for work in other video editors.

- **H.264 Blu-ray:** This option produces H.264 files configured specifically for Blu-ray Discs.

- **JPEG:** This setting creates a sequential series of still images.

- **JPEG 2000 MXF OP1a:** This creates a video file with similar compression to MPEG2 but with each frame compressed individually, giving more consistent quality and a more robust file.

- **MP3:** This compressed audio format is popular because it produces a relatively small file that still sounds good to the ear.

- **MPEG2:** This file format is primarily used for DVDs and Blu-ray Discs. Presets in this group allow you to produce files that can be distributed for playback on your own or other computers. Many broadcasters use MPEG2 as a format for digital delivery.

- **MPEG2 Blu-ray:** This creates a Blu-ray-compliant MPEG2 video and audio file for HD discs.

- **MPEG2-DVD:** This creates a DVD-compliant MPEG2 video and audio file for standard-definition discs.

- **MPEG4:** This produces lower-quality H.263 3GP files for playback on older cell phones.

- **MXF OP1a:** These MXF presets let you create files compatible with several video-editing systems and media servers, including AVC-INTRA, DV, IMX, and XDCAM.

- **P2 Movie:** This produces standard Panasonic P2 media.

- **PNG:** This is a lossless but efficient still-image format for Internet use or for image sequences that contain transparency. Unlike many still image formats, PNG files can include an alpha channel.

- **QuickTime:** This container format can store media using one of several codecs. QuickTime files use the .mov extension, regardless of the codec.

- **Targa:** This is a rarely used uncompressed still-image file format. Like PNG files, Targa files can include an alpha channel.

- **TIFF:** This popular high-quality still-image format offers both lossy and lossless compression options.

- **Waveform Audio:** This is an uncompressed audio file format.

- **Wraptor DCP:** If you're supplying content for digital cinema projection, the settings can be complex. This option produces a standard DCP file you can be confident will be accepted, with few settings to choose between.

The following formats are available only on Windows:

- **AVI:** Like QuickTime files, this "container format" can store files using one of several *codecs*. While not officially supported by Microsoft for a number of years, AVI files are still in widespread use.

- **BMP:** This is an uncompressed, rarely used still-image format.

- **Animated GIF and GIF:** These compressed still-image and animated formats are used primarily on the Internet. They're available only on the Windows version of Premiere Pro.

- **Uncompressed Microsoft AVI:** This is a high-bit-rate intermediate format that is not widely used and is available only on the Windows version of Premiere Pro.

- **Windows Media:** This produces WMV files, ideal for Microsoft Silverlight applications (Windows only).

Note: If working with a professional mastering format (such as MXF OP1a, DNxHD MXF OP1a, or QuickTime), you can export up to 32 channels of audio where the format allows. The original sequence must use a multichannel master track with the corresponding number of tracks.

Configuring the export

To export from Premiere Pro to Adobe Media Encoder, you'll need to queue the export. The first step is to use the Export Settings dialog to make choices about the file you're going to export.

1   Make sure the sequence you want to export is selected in the Project panel, or is open in the Timeline panel, with the Timeline panel active.

2   Choose File > Export > Media, or press Control+M (Windows) or Command+M (Mac OS).

It's best to work through the Export Settings dialog from the top down. Choose your format and presets first, then pick the output, and finally decide whether you'd like to export audio, video, or both.

3   Choose H.264 from the Format menu. This is a popular choice for files you'll upload to online video websites.

4   In the Preset menu, choose Vimeo 720p HD.

These settings match the frame size and frame rate of the sequence. The codec and data rate match the requirements for the Vimeo.com website.

5   Click the output name (the blue text) and give the file a new name, **Review Copy 03.mp4**. Save it to the same destination you selected in the previous exercise.

6   Examine the Summary information text to check your choices.

Here's an overview of the various tabs displayed under Summary:

Note: The settings tabs displayed in the Export Settings dialog change depending on the format you choose. Most of the critical options are contained on the Format, Video, and Audio tabs.

- **Effects:** You can add a number of useful effects and overlays as you output your media (see a list of these options in the next section).

- **Video:** The Video tab allows you to adjust the frame size, frame rate, field order, and profile. The default settings are based on the preset you chose, but you can change them to anything you like.

- **Audio:** The Audio tab allows you to adjust the bit rate of the audio and, for some formats, the codec. The default settings are based on the preset you chose, but you can change them to anything you like.

- **Multiplexer:** These controls let you determine whether the encoding method is optimized for compatibility with a specific device. This can also control whether the video and audio are combined or delivered as separate files.

- **Captions:** If your sequence has captions, you can specify whether they are ignored, embedded in the output file, "burned in" (added to the visuals permanently), or exported as an additional file.

- **Publish:** This tab lets you enter the details of several social media services for your file to be delivered to. More on this later in this lesson.

Export effects

As you export your media file, you can apply several effects, add information overlays, and make automated adjustments to the output. Here's a brief overview of each option:

- **Lumetri Look/LUT:** Choose from a list of built-in Lumetri looks or browse to your own, allowing you to quickly apply a nuanced adjustment to the appearance of your output file.

- **SDR Conform:** If your sequence is high dynamic range, you can produce a standard dynamic range version.

- **Image Overlay:** Add a graphic, like a company logo or network "bug," and position it onscreen. The graphic will be incorporated into the image.

- **Name Overlay:** Add a text overlay to the image. This is particularly useful as a simple watermark to protect your content or as a way of marking different versions.

- **Timecode Overlay:** Display timecode for your finished video file, making it easy for viewers without specialized editing software to note reference times for commenting purposes.

- **Time Tuner:** Specify a new duration or playback speed, up to + /−10%, achieved by applying subtle adjustments to periods of low action. Results vary depending on the media you are working with, so test different speeds to compare the end result.

- **Video Limiter:** While it's usually best to get your video levels right in the sequence, you can apply a limiter here too, just in case.

- **Loudness Normalization:** Use the Loudness scale to normalize audio levels in your output file. Like video levels, it's best to get this right in the sequence, but it can be a helpful extra security to know your levels will be limited during export.

Using the Source and Output panels

Moving to the left side of the Export Settings dialog, there's a Source Range drop-down menu. Use this menu to choose to export the entire sequence, a range you set by placing an In mark and an Out mark, a range set by the Timeline Work Area bar, or a custom region selected now using the small triangular handles and navigator directly above the menu. By default, In and Out marks are used if they exist in your sequence or clip when exporting.

In the upper-left corner of the Export Settings dialog are the Output and Source tabs. The Output tab shows a preview of the video to be encoded. It's useful to view the video on the Output tab to spot errors such as unwanted letterboxing or distortion caused by the irregularly shaped pixels used in some video formats.

The Source tab gives access to basic cropping controls. Be sure to check the Output tab after making changes on the Source tab.

Queuing the export

When you're ready to create your media file, you have a few more options to consider.

- **Use Maximum Render Quality:** Consider enabling this setting when scaling from larger image sizes to smaller image sizes. This option requires more RAM, which can dramatically slow down the output. This option is usually not needed except when working without GPU acceleration, scaling the image down, and seeking the highest possible quality.

- **Use Previews:** When you render special effects, preview files are produced that look like your original footage combined with the effects. If you enable this option, the preview files will be used as the source for the new export. This can save a significant amount of time that would otherwise be spent rendering the effects again. The result might be lower quality, depending on the sequence preview files format (see Lesson 2, "Setting Up a Project").

- **Import into project:** This option automatically imports the newly created media file into your current project.

- **Set Start Timecode:** This allows you to specify a new file start timecode. This is particularly useful if you are working in a broadcast environment where a specific timecode start may be a delivery requirement.

- **Render Alpha Channel Only:** Some post-production workflows require a separate grayscale file representing the Alpha channel (the channel that defines opacity). This option produces just that file.

- **Time Interpolation:** If your exported file will have a different frame rate to your sequence, this menu lets you specify the way the frame rate change is rendered. The options are the same as those that apply when changing clip playback speed in a sequence.

Using the formats

Adobe Media Encoder supports many formats. Knowing which setting to use can seem a little overwhelming. Let's take a look at some common scenarios and review which formats are typically used. There are few absolutes, but these should get you close to the correct output. It's a good idea to test your output on a short section of your video before producing a full-length finished file.

- **Encoding for uploading to user-generated video sites:** The H.264 format includes presets for YouTube and Vimeo in widescreen, SD, HD, and 4K. Use these presets as a starting point for your service, being careful to observe resolution and file size.

- **Encoding for devices:** Use the H.264 format for current devices (Apple iPod/iPhone, Apple TV, Kindle, Nook, Android, and TiVo), as well as for some generic 3GPP presets; use MPEG4 for older MPEG4-based devices. Be sure to check the manufacturer's specifications on its website.

- **Encoding for DVD/Blu-ray:** Generally, you'll use MPEG2 for shorter video projects—namely, the MPEG2-DVD preset for DVD and MPEG2 Blu-ray preset for Blu-ray Discs. The visual quality of MPEG2 is indistinguishable from H.264 in these high-bit-rate applications and encodes faster. However, the H.264 codec is more efficient, letting you fit more content into a smaller storage space.

In general, the Premiere Pro presets are proven and will work for your intended purpose. Avoid adjusting settings when using presets designed for devices or optical discs because changes that seem subtle might make the files unplayable; hardware players have stringent media requirements.

Most Premiere Pro presets are conservative and will deliver good results with the default settings, so you probably won't improve the quality by tinkering.

- **Metadata:** Click this button to open the Metadata Export panel. You can specify a wide range of settings, including information about copyright, creator, and rights management. You can even embed useful information such as markers, script, and speech transcription for advanced delivery options. In some cases, you may prefer to set the Metadata Export Options setting to None, removing all metadata from the newly created file.

- **Queue:** Click the Queue button to send the file to Adobe Media Encoder, which will open automatically, allowing you to continue working in Premiere Pro while the export takes place.

● **Note:** On the Video tab, you'll also find the option Render at Maximum Depth. When working without GPU acceleration, this can improve the visual quality of your output by using greater precision to generate colors. However, this option can add to the render time.

- **Export:** Select this option to export directly from the Export Settings dialog rather than sending the file to the Adobe Media Encoder queue. This is a simpler workflow and usually a faster export, but you won't be able to edit in Premiere Pro until the export is complete.

Click the Queue button to send the file to Adobe Media Encoder, which starts up automatically.

Additional options in Adobe Media Encoder

Using Adobe Media Encoder brings a number of benefits. Although it involves a few extra steps beyond simply clicking the Export button in the Export Settings panel of Premiere Pro, the extra options are worth it.

Here are some of the most useful features you'll find in Adobe Media Encoder:

- **Add files for encoding:** You can add files to Adobe Media Encoder by choosing File > Add Source. You can even drag and drop files into it from Windows Explorer (Windows) or Finder (Mac OS).

- **Import Premiere Pro sequences directly:** You can choose File > Add Premiere Pro Sequence to select a Premiere Pro project file and choose sequences to encode (without ever launching Premiere Pro).

- **Render After Effects compositions directly:** You can import and encode compositions from Adobe After Effects by choosing File > Add After Effects Composition. Once again, you don't need to open Adobe After Effects.

- **Use a watch folder:** If you'd like to automate some encoding tasks, you can create watch folders by choosing File > Add Watch Folder and then assigning a preset to that watch folder. Media files placed into the folder are automatically encoded to the format specified in the preset.

- **Modify a queue:** You can add, duplicate, or remove any encoding tasks using buttons at the top of the list.

- **Starting encoding:** If you haven't set the queue to start automatically, click the Start Queue button (▶) to start encoding. Files in the queue are encoded one after another. You can add files to the queue after encoding has begun. You can even add files to the queue directly from Premiere Pro while encoding is taking place.

- **Modify settings:** Once the encoding tasks are loaded into the queue, changing settings is easy; click the item's Format or Preset, and the Export Settings dialog appears.

> **Note:** Adobe Media Encoder does not have to be used from Premiere Pro. You can launch Adobe Media Encoder on its own.

∨ H.264	∨ Vimeo 1080p HD

Uploading to social media

Export settings include the option to publish exported videos to your Creative Cloud Files folder, Adobe Behance, Facebook, an FTP server (FTP is a standard way to transmit files to a remote file server), Twitter, Vimeo, and YouTube when the encoding is complete.

Social media platforms are increasingly important media distribution outlets, and Adobe is closely involved in developing new technologies and workflows to make it easier to share your creative work and maximize audience engagement. Watch this space for new developments in this area.

Exchanging with other editing applications

Collaboration is often essential in video post-production. Premiere Pro can both read and write project files that are compatible with many of the top editing and color-grading tools on the market. This makes it straightforward to share creative work, even if you and your collaborators are using different editing systems.

Exporting a Final Cut Pro XML file

Using Final Cut Pro XML allows you to exchange a Premiere Pro project with many applications. You can bring your project directly into Final Cut Pro 7 or convert it to Final Cut Pro X XML using SendToX from Assisted Editing. You can also export your project to applications such as DaVinci Resolve and Grass Valley EDIUS.

Some of your special effects and keyframes will not be supported by the Final Cut Pro 7 XML standard, so you should test this workflow to find out how much of your creative work can be shared using this system.

Exporting from Premiere Pro to Final Cut Pro—and importing the XML file into Final Cut Pro—is simple.

1 In Premiere Pro, choose File > Export > Final Cut Pro XML.

2 In the Save As dialog, name the file, choose a location, and click Save. Premiere Pro will let you know if there were any issues exporting the XML file.

   This file can now be imported into another application. You may need to batch import or batch capture the media into the other application and relink it.

Exporting to OMF

● **Note:** If you're working on a multicamera edit, flatten the edit before exporting the OMF file because nested sequence clips are not included properly.

Open Media Framework (OMF) has become a standard way of exchanging audio information between systems (typically for audio mixing). When you export an OMF file, the typical method is to create a single file with all your audio tracks inside. When the OMF file is opened by a compatible application, it will show all the tracks.

Here's how to create an OMF file:

1 With a sequence selected, choose File > Export > OMF.

2. In the OMF Export Settings dialog, enter a name for the file in the OMF Title field.

3. Check that the Sample Rate and Bits per Sample settings match your footage; 48000 Hz and 16 bits are the most common settings.

4. From the Files menu, choose one of the following:

   - **Embed Audio:** This option exports an OMF file that contains the project metadata and all the audio files for the selected sequence.

   - **Separate Audio:** This option exports separate mono audio files into an omfiMediaFiles folder.

5. If you're using the Separate Audio option, choose between the AIFF and Broadcast Wave formats. Both are high quality, but check with the system you need to exchange with. AIFF files tend to be the most compatible.

6. Using the Render menu, choose either Copy Complete Audio Files or Trim Audio Files (to reduce the file size). You can specify that handles (extra frames) be added to give you some flexibility when modifying the clips.

7. Click OK to generate the OMF file.

8. Choose a destination, and click Save. You can target your lesson folder for now.

> **Note:** All OMF files have 2GB file limit—if you're working on a long sequence, you may need to separate it into two sections and export them separately.

Exporting to AAF

Another way to exchange files is by using the Advanced Authoring Format (AAF) standard. This method is typically used to exchange both project information and source media with other NLE software, including Avid Media Composer or with Avid ProTools for audio finishing.

Some of your special effects and keyframes will not be supported by the AAF standard, so you should test this workflow to find out how much of your creative work can be shared using this system.

1. Choose File > Export > AAF.

2. Choose if you'd like to create a Mixdown video, which is a flattened video of your sequence that will be displayed if the AAF file is opened in ProTools.

3. Choose if you'd like to break audio clips out to mono, which can be useful when sending an AAF file to Avid Media Composer. If you do, choose the settings you'd like for the newly encoded audio.

4. Click OK, and choose a location to save the AAF file.

Final practice

Congratulations! You have now learned enough about Adobe Premiere Pro to import media, organize projects, create sequences, add, modify, and remove effects, mix audio, work with graphics and titles, and output to share your work with the world.

Now that you have completed this book, you may want to practice a little. To make this easier, the media files for a few productions have been combined in a single project file so you can explore the techniques you have learned.

These media files can be used only for personal practice and are not licensed for any form of distribution, including YouTube or any other online distribution, so please do not upload any of the clips or the results of any editing work you do with them. They are not for sharing with the public, just for you to practice with.

The Final Practice.prproj project file, in the Lessons folder, contains original clips for a few productions:

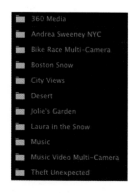

- **360 Media:** A short excerpt from an introduction to a 360 feature film. Use this media to experiment with the VR Video playback controls.

- **Andrea Sweeney NYC:** This is a short road-movie diary piece. Use the voice-over as a guide and practice combining 4K and HD footage in a single timeline. Experiment with panning and scanning inside the 4K footage if you choose to use HD sequence settings.

- **Bike Race Multi-Camera:** This is simple multicamera footage. Experiment with live editing on a multicamera project.

- **Boston Snow:** A mixture of shots of Boston Common filmed in three resolutions. Use this media to experiment with the Scale to Frame Size, Set to Frame Size, and keyframe controls to scale shots. Try using the Warp Stabilizer effect to lock one of the high-resolution clips and then scale up the clip and create a pan from one side to the other.

- **City Views:** A series of shots from the air and on land. Use these to experiment with image stabilization, color adjustment, and visual effects.

- **Desert:** Use the diverse colors to try color correction tools and combine the footage with music to produce a montage.

- **Jolie's Garden:** Atmospheric tableaux shot at 96fps, set to play back at 24fps, filmed for a new feature film social media marketing campaign. Use these to experiment with the Lumetri Color panel looks and speed change effects.

- **Laura in the Snow:** This is a spec commercial shot at 96fps, set to play back at 24fps. Use this footage to practice color correction and grading adjustments. Experiment with ramping slow motion and masking both the video and the effects you apply.

- **Music:** Use these music clips to practice creating an audio mix and editing visuals to music.

- **Music Video Multi-Camera:** A music video shoot. Practice multicamera editing skills with this media.

- **Theft Unexpected:** This is an award-winning short film directed and edited by Maxim Jago. Use this footage to experiment with trimming and practice adjusting timing in simple dialogue.

Review questions

1 What's an easy way to export digital video if you want to create a self-contained file that closely matches the original quality of your sequence preview settings?

2 What Internet-ready export options are available in Adobe Media Encoder?

3 What encoding format should you use when exporting to most mobile devices?

4 Must you wait for Adobe Media Encoder to finish processing its queue before working on a new Premiere Pro project?

Review answers

1 Use the Match Sequence Settings option in the Export dialog.

2 This varies by platform. Both operating systems include H.264 and QuickTime, and the Windows version includes Windows Media as well.

3 H.264 is the encoding format used when exporting to most mobile devices.

4 No. Adobe Media Encoder is a stand-alone application. You can work in other applications or even start a new Premiere Pro project while the render queue is processed.

INDEX

Contributors

Maxim Jago is a filmmaker, screenwriter, futurist, Adobe Master Trainer, and the author of over 30 books and video training courses on Premiere Pro, After Effects, Photoshop, Audition, Muse, Prelude, Bridge, and Story.

In addition to training clients around the world, Maxim speaks regularly on futurism, creativity, and media technology at conferences and film festivals, including BVE, NAB, IBC, Adobe MAX, Cannes, and Sundance. Maxim also teaches a master class on presentation skills using ESP, a custom teaching and communication system that he developed to help clients deliver exceptional presentations. www.maximjago.com

Production Notes

The *Adobe Premiere Pro Classroom in a Book (2017 release)* was created electronically using Adobe InDesign CC 2015. Art was produced using Adobe InDesign CC, Adobe Illustrator CC, Adobe Premiere Pro, and Adobe Photoshop CC.

References to company names, websites, or addresses in the lessons are for demonstration purposes only and are not intended to refer to any actual organization or person.

Images

Photographic images and illustrations are intended for use with the tutorials.

Typefaces used

Adobe Myriad Pro and Adobe Warnock Pro are used throughout this book. For more information about OpenType and Adobe fonts, visit www.adobe.com/type/opentype/.

Media credits

Thanks to Patrick Cannell for the music "Ambient Heavens," Copyright © by 2015 Patrick Cannell

Thanks to Patrick Cannell for the music "Cooking Montage," Copyright © 2015 by Patrick Cannell

Footage from *Andrea Sweeney NYC*, Copyright © 2015 by Maxim Jago

Footage from *Laura in the Snow*, Copyright © 2015 by Maxim Jago

Footage from *Theft Unexpected*, Copyright © 2014 by Maxim Jago

Footage from *Jolie's Garden*, Copyright © 2016 by Maxim Jago

Footage from *Boston Snow*, Copyright © 2016 by Maxim Jago

Lesson project credits

The following individuals contributed artwork for the lesson files for this edition of the Adobe Premiere Pro CC Classroom in a Book (2017 release):

Patrick Cannell (www.patrickcannell.com.): Musical compositions.

Danielle Fritz (www.behance.net/danielle_fritz): The hand lettering for "A Quick Tour of Adobe Illustrator CC (2017 release)."

Dan Stiles (www.danstiles.com): Lesson 4, "Editing and Combining Shapes and Paths."